Alice in Kyoto Forest

2

Art by Haruki Niwa
Story by Mai Mochizuki

Contents

Chapter 7 003

Chapter 8 031

Chapter 9 059

Chapter 10 077

Chapter 11 099

Chapter 12 127

Chapter 13 158

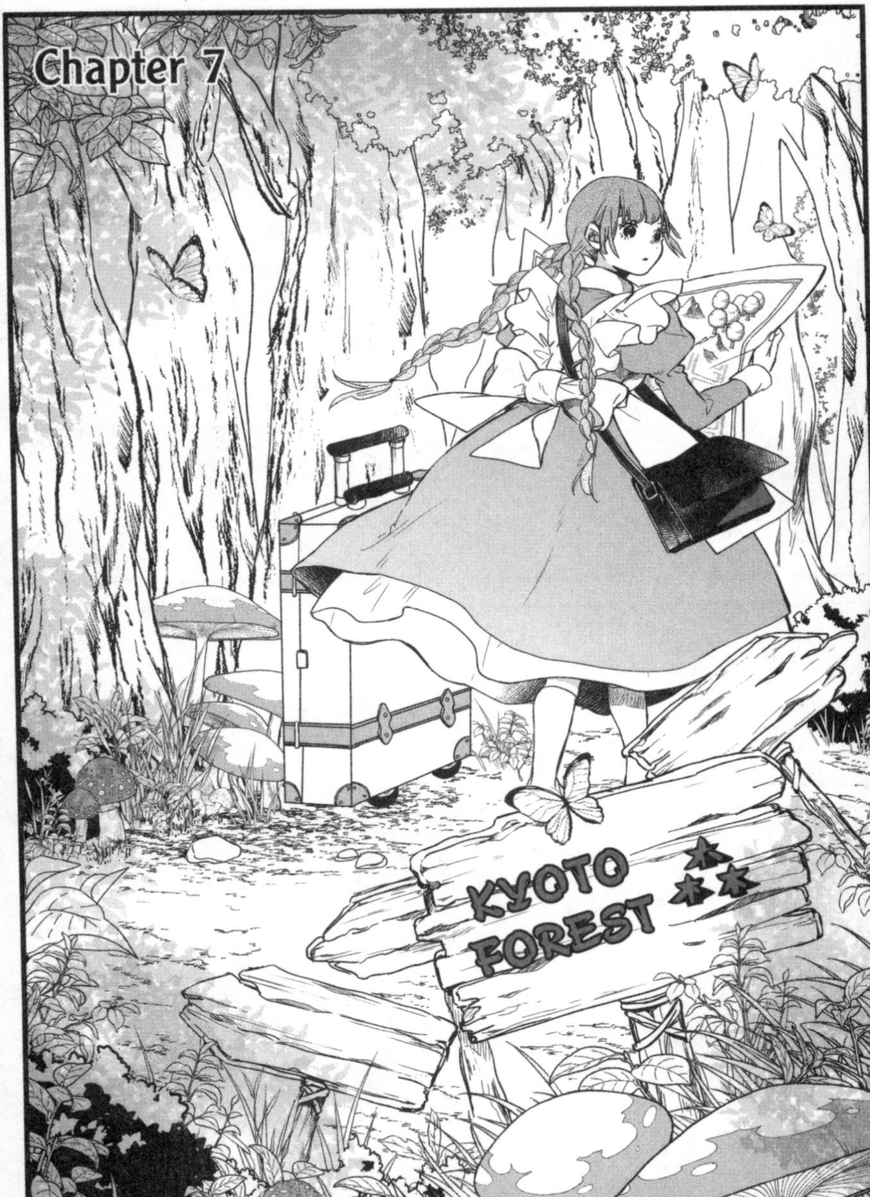
Chapter 7
KYOTO FOREST

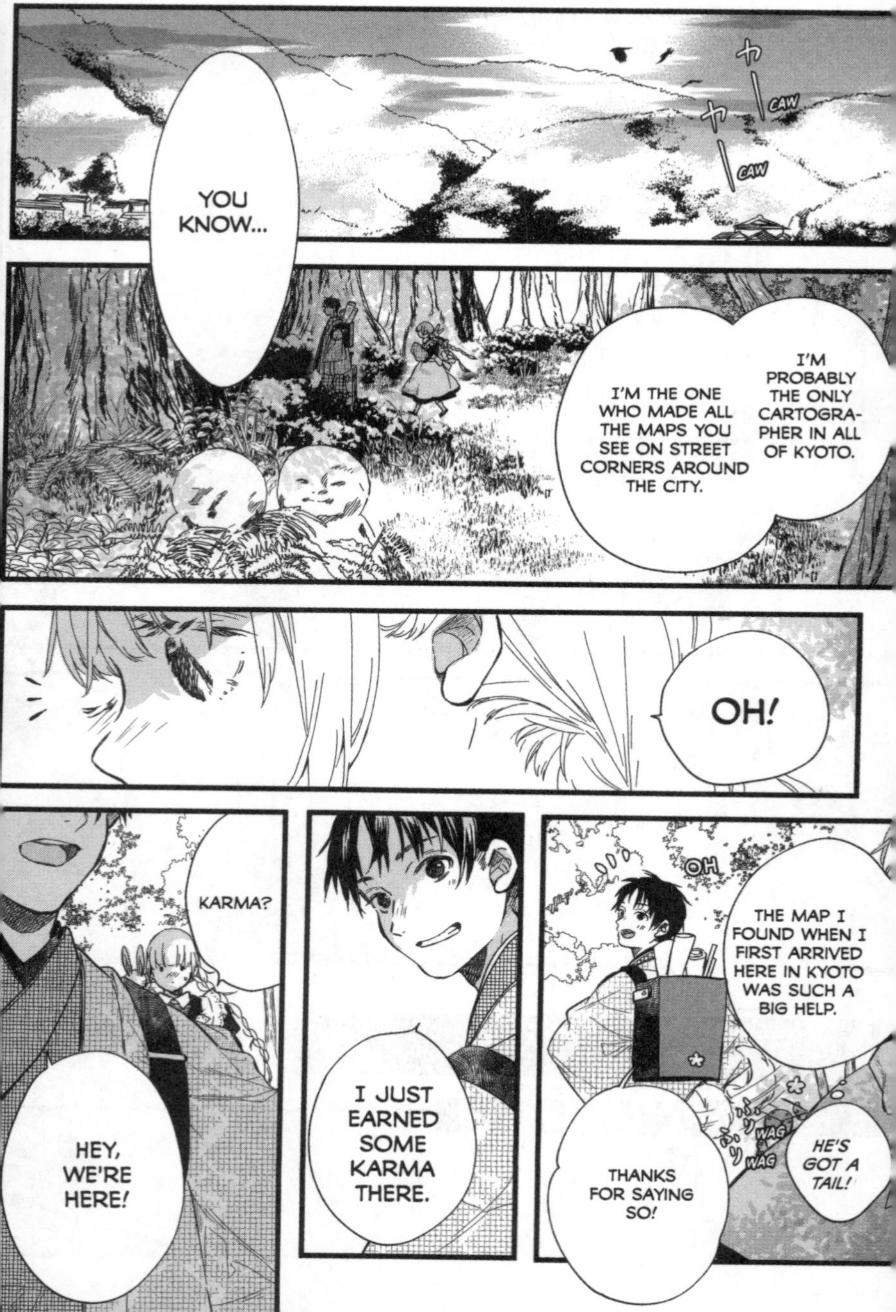
CAW
CAW
YOU KNOW...
I'M PROBABLY THE ONLY CARTOGRAPHER IN ALL OF KYOTO.
I'M THE ONE WHO MADE ALL THE MAPS YOU SEE ON STREET CORNERS AROUND THE CITY.
OH!
THE MAP I FOUND WHEN I FIRST ARRIVED HERE IN KYOTO WAS SUCH A BIG HELP.
OH
HE'S GOT A TAIL!
WAG WAG
THANKS FOR SAYING SO!
I JUST EARNED SOME KARMA THERE.
KARMA?
HEY, WE'RE HERE!

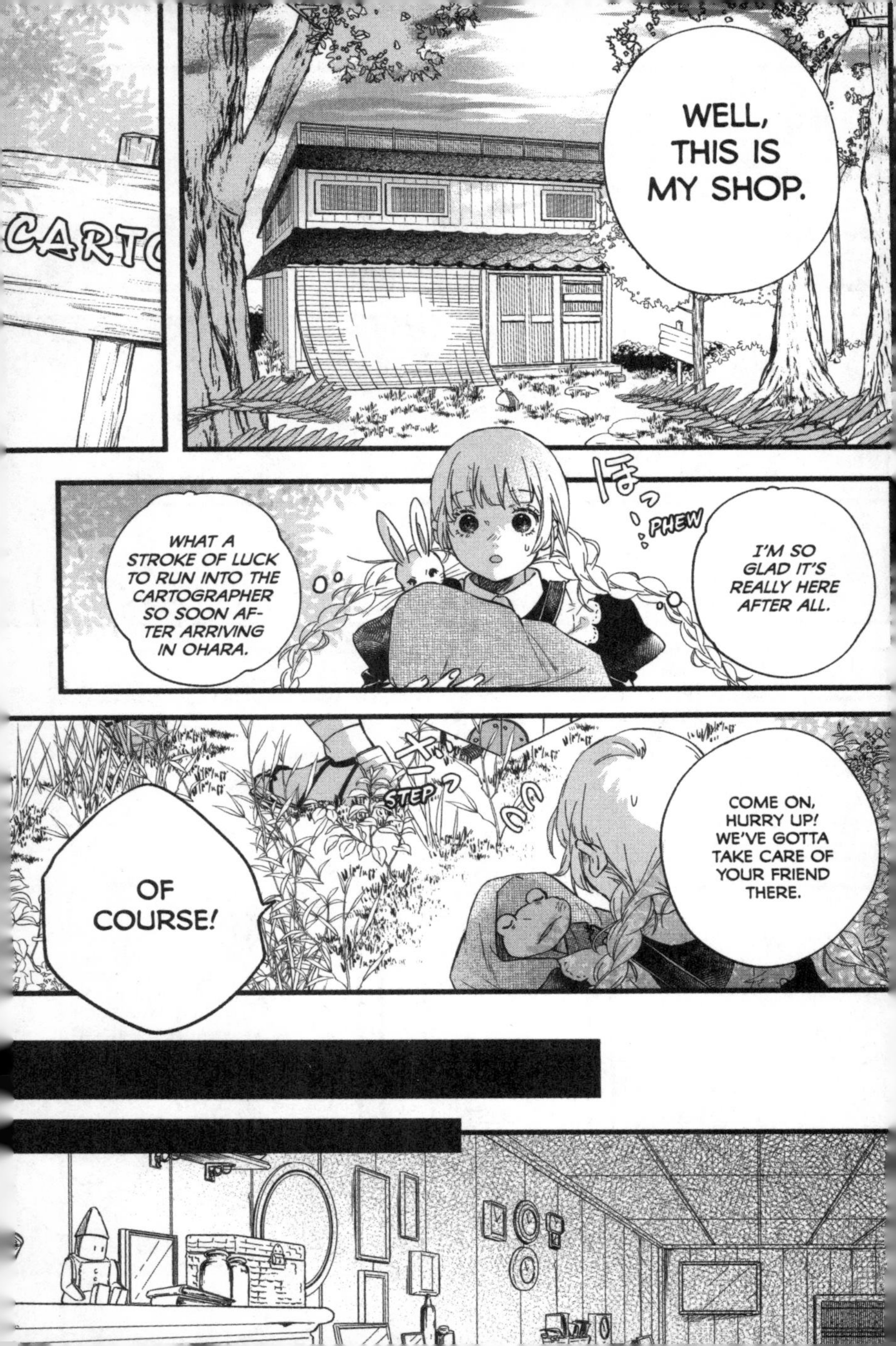
WELL, THIS IS MY SHOP.
CARTO
PHEW
I'M SO GLAD IT'S REALLY HERE AFTER ALL.
WHAT A STROKE OF LUCK TO RUN INTO THE CARTOGRAPHER SO SOON AFTER ARRIVING IN OHARA.
COME ON, HURRY UP! WE'VE GOTTA TAKE CARE OF YOUR FRIEND THERE.
STEP
OF COURSE!
[redacted]

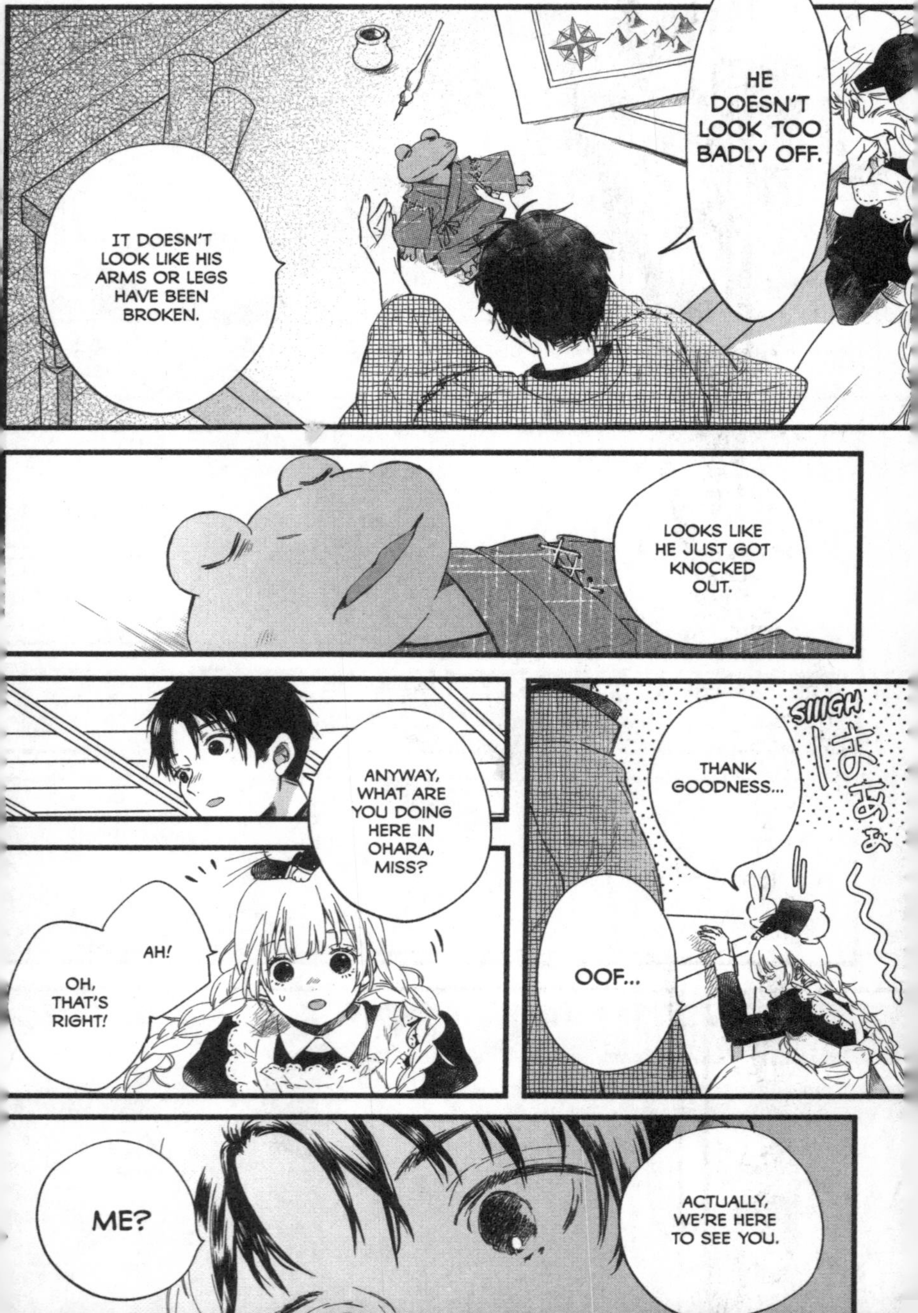
HE DOESN'T LOOK TOO BADLY OFF.
IT DOESN'T LOOK LIKE HIS ARMS OR LEGS HAVE BEEN BROKEN.
LOOKS LIKE HE JUST GOT KNOCKED OUT.
SIIIGH
はあぁ〜
THANK GOODNESS...
OOF...
ANYWAY, WHAT ARE YOU DOING HERE IN OHARA, MISS?
AH!
OH, THAT'S RIGHT!
ACTUALLY, WE'RE HERE TO SEE YOU.
ME?

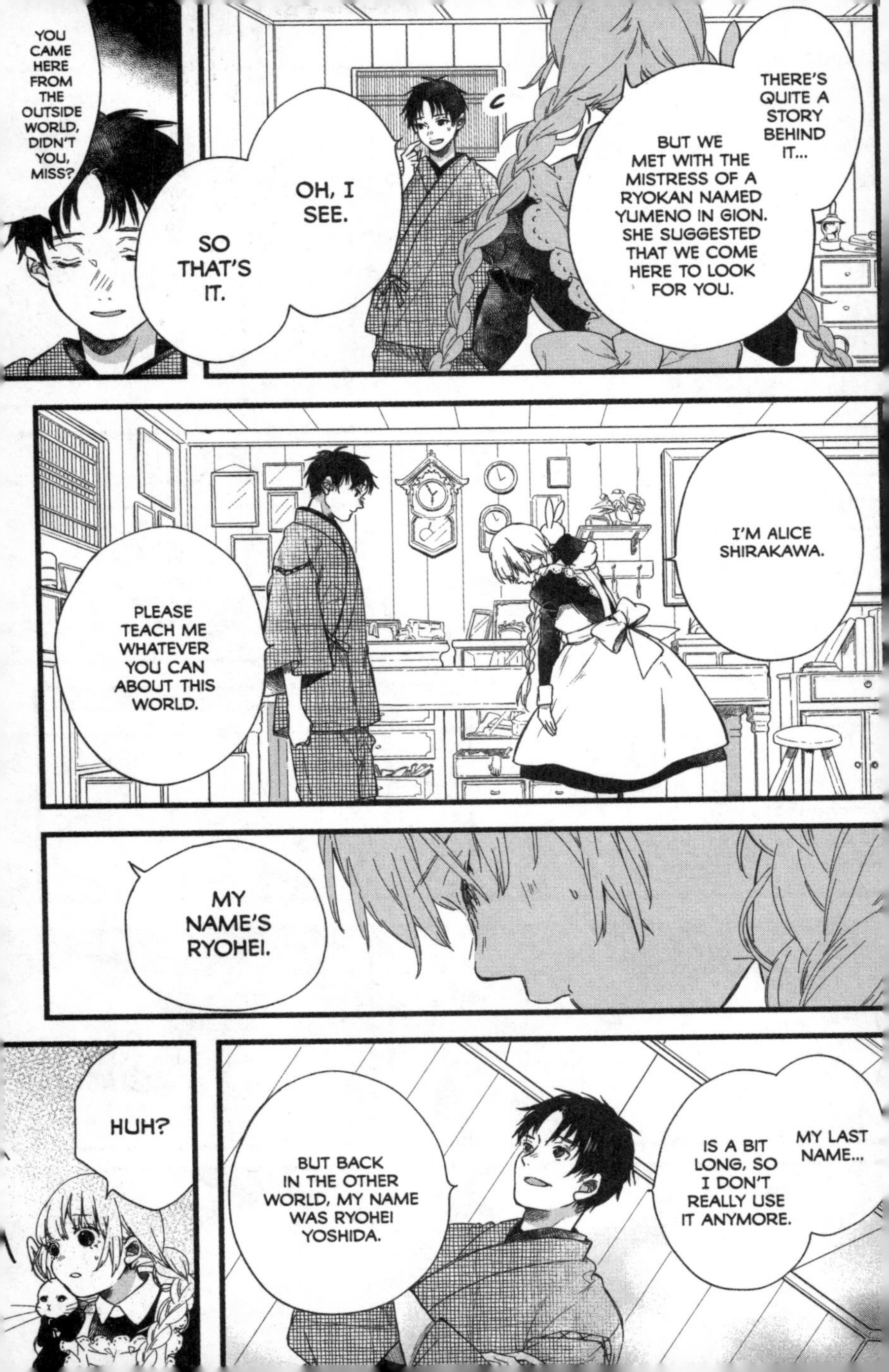
THERE'S QUITE A STORY BEHIND IT...
BUT WE MET WITH THE MISTRESS OF A RYOKAN NAMED YUMENO IN GION. SHE SUGGESTED THAT WE COME HERE TO LOOK FOR YOU.
OH, I SEE.
SO THAT'S IT.
YOU CAME HERE FROM THE OUTSIDE WORLD, DIDN'T YOU, MISS?
I'M ALICE SHIRAKAWA.
PLEASE TEACH ME WHATEVER YOU CAN ABOUT THIS WORLD.
MY NAME'S RYOHEI.
MY LAST NAME...
IS A BIT LONG, SO I DON'T REALLY USE IT ANYMORE.
BUT BACK IN THE OTHER WORLD, MY NAME WAS RYOHEI YOSHIDA.
HUH?

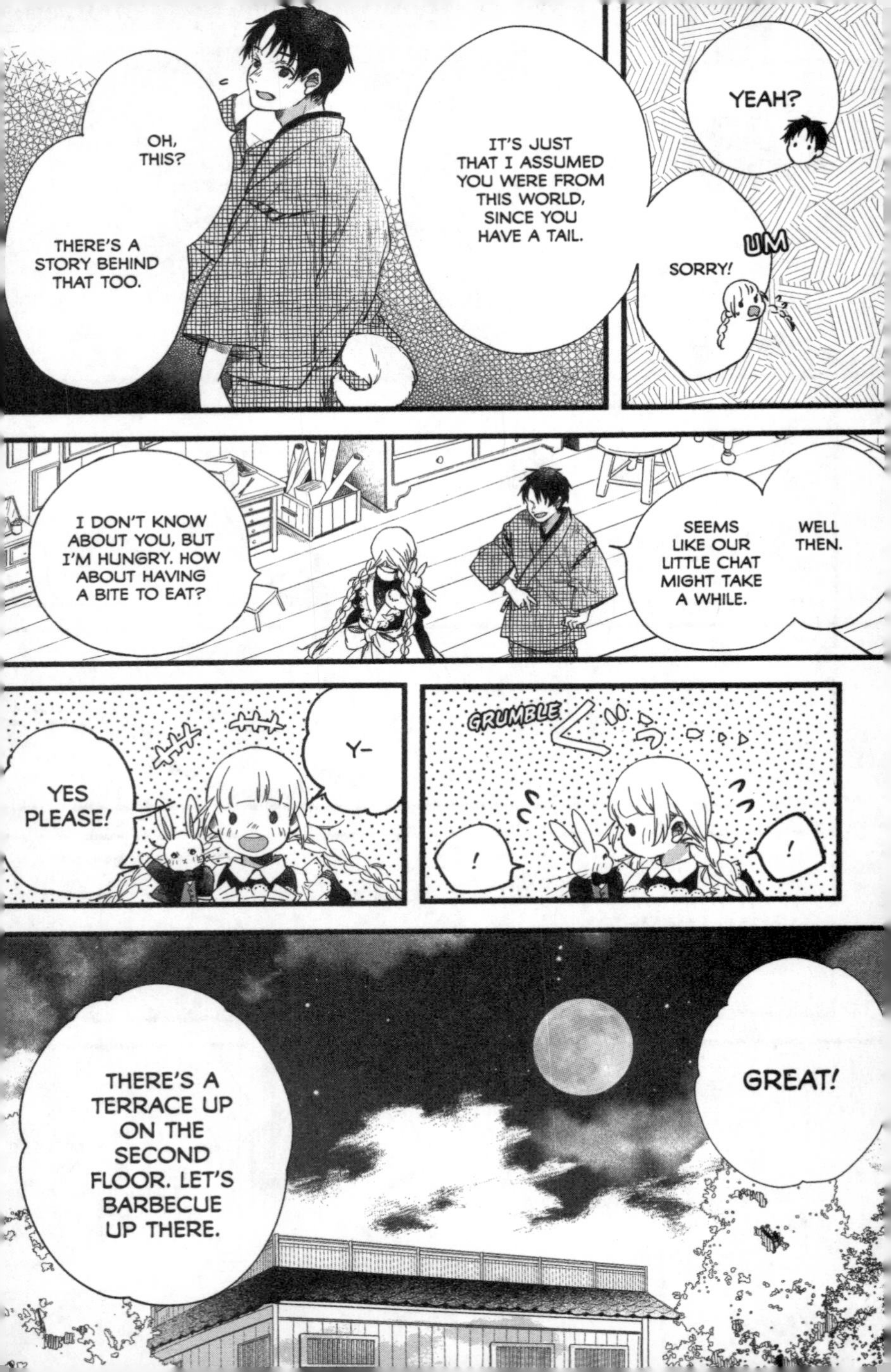
YEAH?
UM
SORRY!
IT'S JUST THAT I ASSUMED YOU WERE FROM THIS WORLD, SINCE YOU HAVE A TAIL.
OH, THIS?
THERE'S A STORY BEHIND THAT TOO.
WELL THEN.
SEEMS LIKE OUR LITTLE CHAT MIGHT TAKE A WHILE.
I DON'T KNOW ABOUT YOU, BUT I'M HUNGRY. HOW ABOUT HAVING A BITE TO EAT?
GRUMBLE
!
!
Y-
YES PLEASE!
GREAT!
THERE'S A TERRACE UP ON THE SECOND FLOOR. LET'S BARBECUE UP THERE.

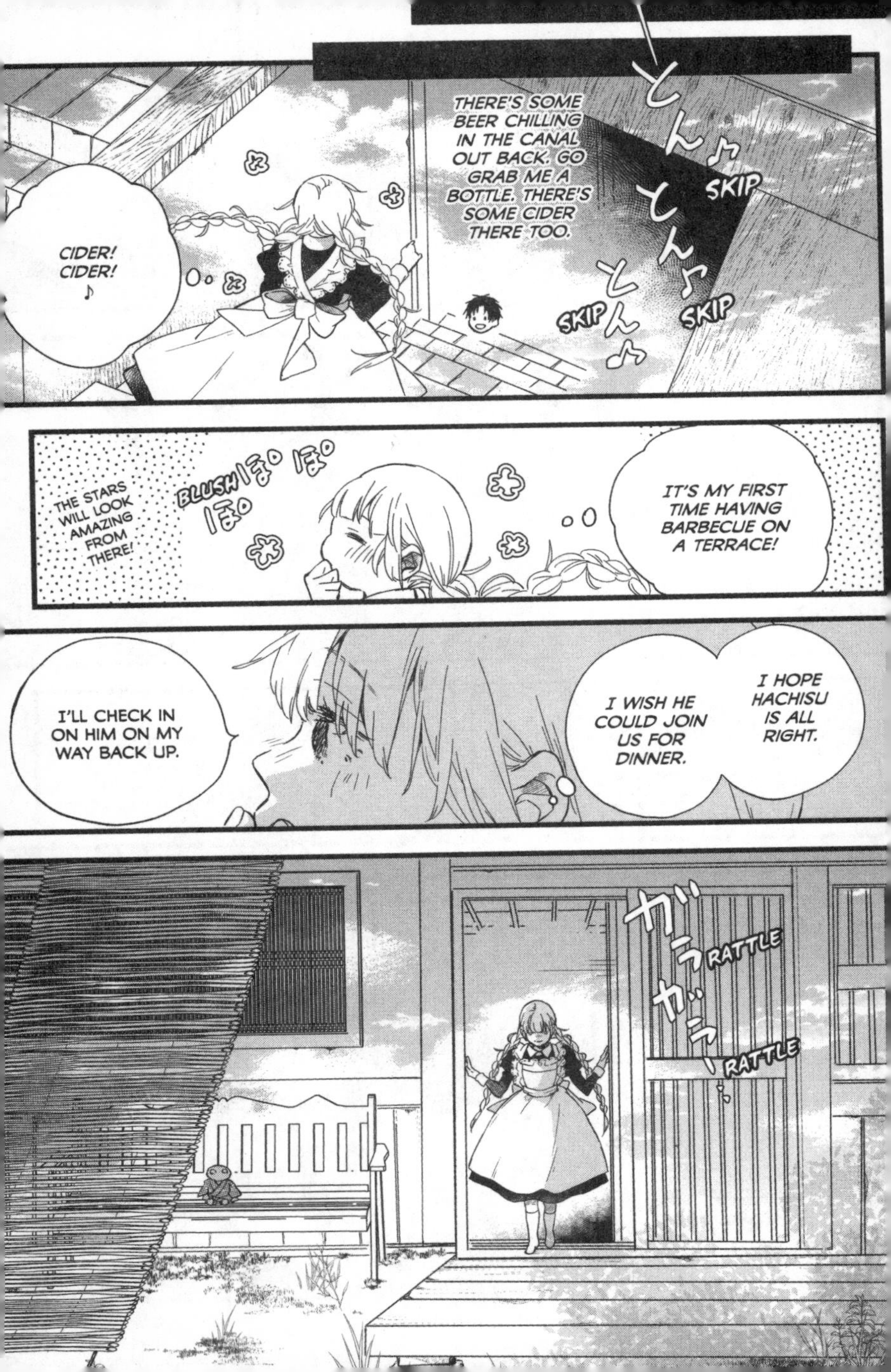

とん♪ SKIP
とん♪ SKIP
とん♪ SKIP
THERE'S SOME BEER CHILLING IN THE CANAL OUT BACK. GO GRAB ME A BOTTLE. THERE'S SOME CIDER THERE TOO.
CIDER! CIDER! ♪
IT'S MY FIRST TIME HAVING BARBECUE ON A TERRACE!
BLUSH ぽ ぽ ぽ
THE STARS WILL LOOK AMAZING FROM THERE!
I HOPE HACHISU IS ALL RIGHT.
I WISH HE COULD JOIN US FOR DINNER.
I'LL CHECK IN ON HIM ON MY WAY BACK UP.
RATTLE
RATTLE

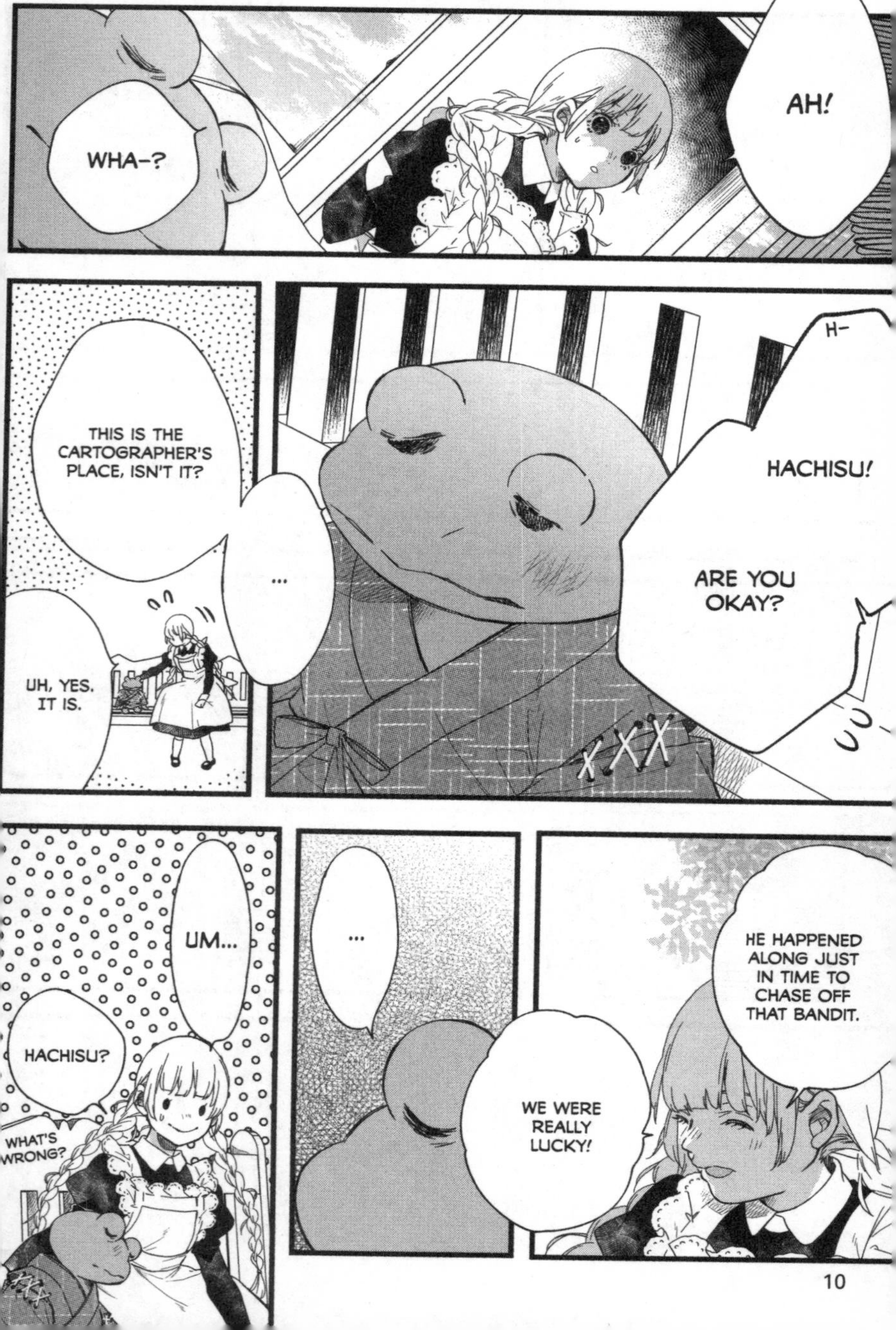
AH!
WHA-?
H-
HACHISU!
ARE YOU OKAY?
...
THIS IS THE CARTOGRAPHER'S PLACE, ISN'T IT?
UH, YES. IT IS.
HE HAPPENED ALONG JUST IN TIME TO CHASE OFF THAT BANDIT.
WE WERE REALLY LUCKY!
...
UM...
HACHISU?
WHAT'S WRONG?

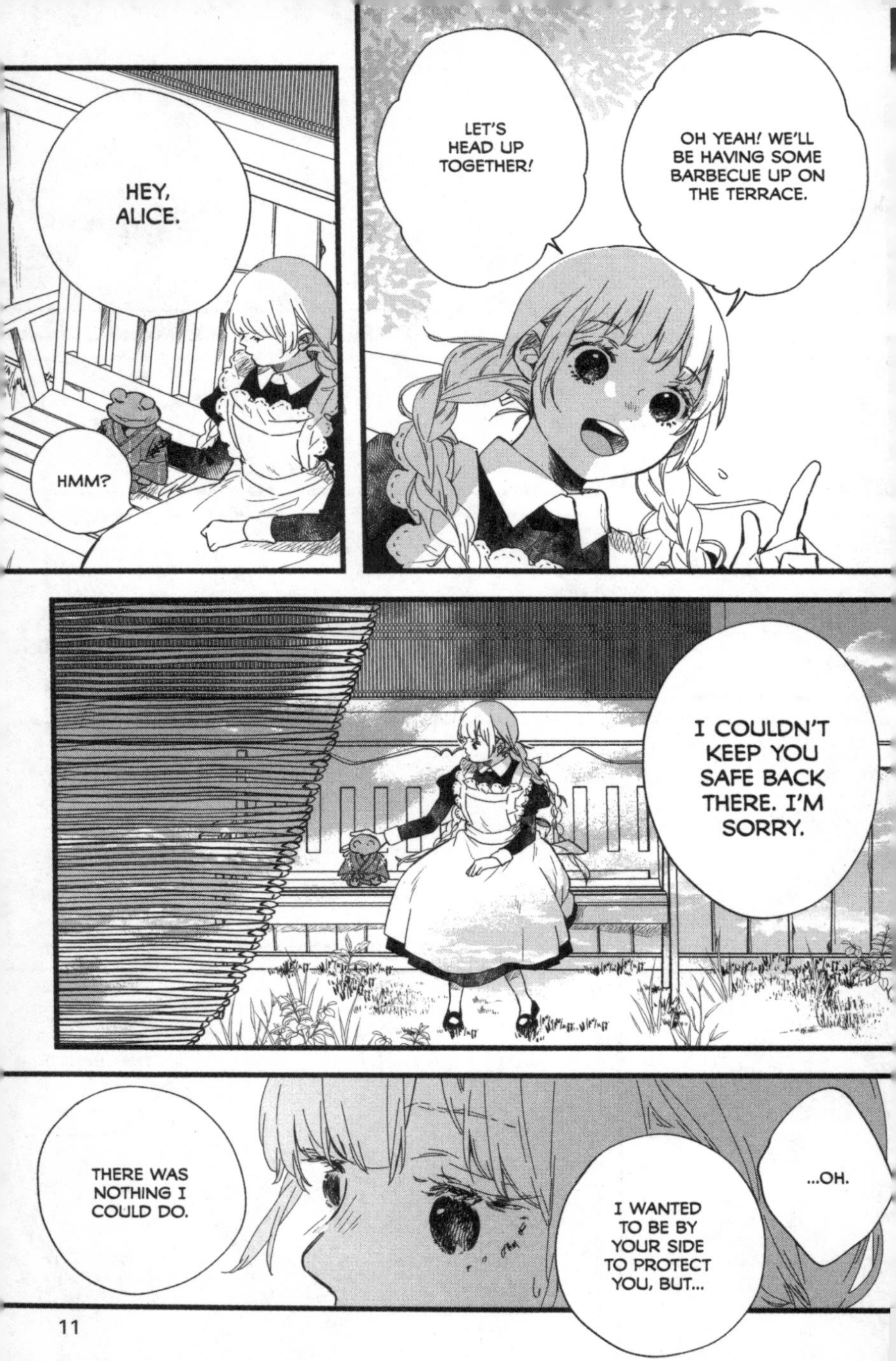
OH YEAH! WE'LL BE HAVING SOME BARBECUE UP ON THE TERRACE.
LET'S HEAD UP TOGETHER!
HEY, ALICE.
HMM?
I COULDN'T KEEP YOU SAFE BACK THERE. I'M SORRY.
...OH.
I WANTED TO BE BY YOUR SIDE TO PROTECT YOU, BUT...
THERE WAS NOTHING I COULD DO.

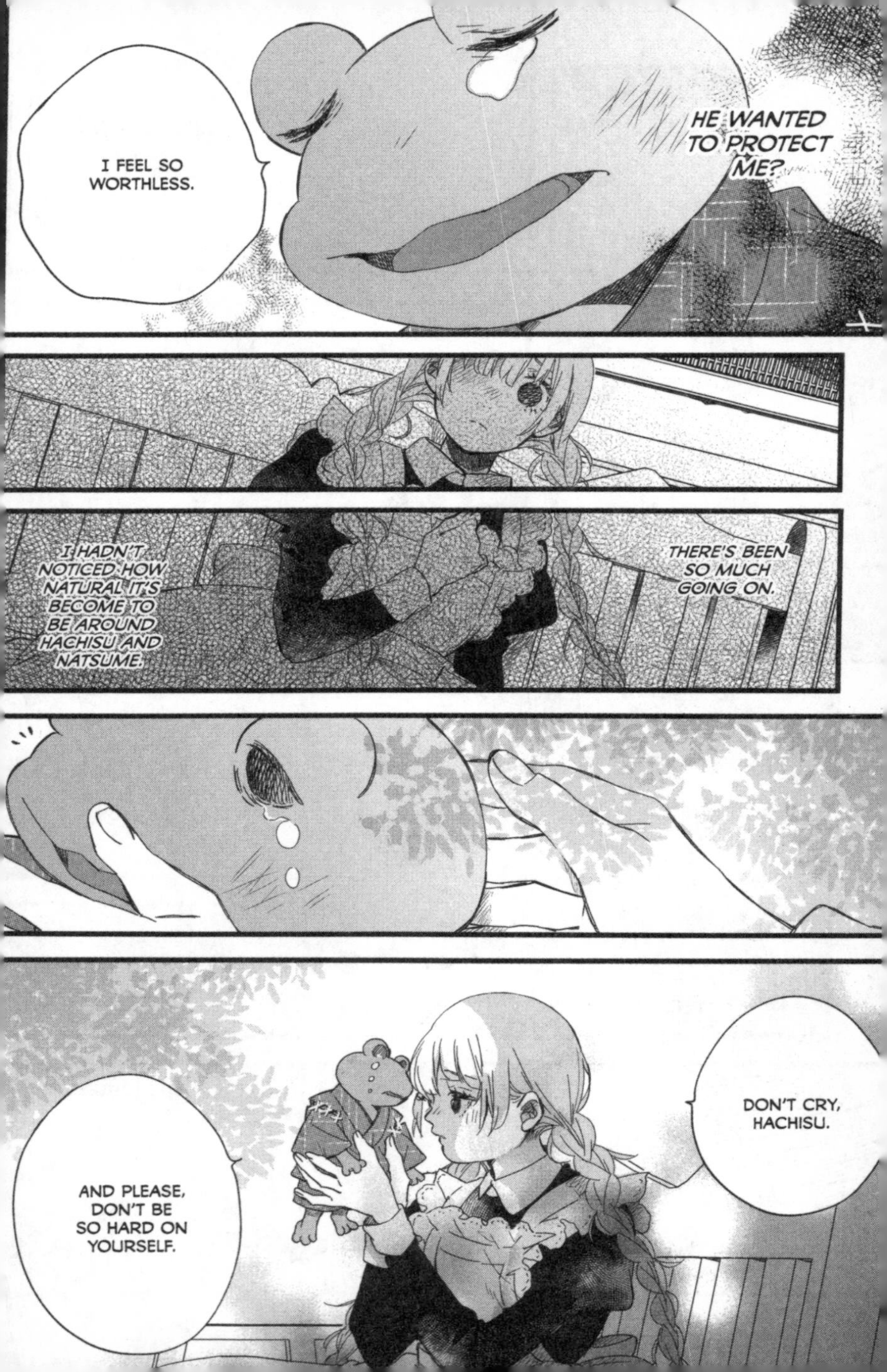
HE WANTED TO PROTECT ME?
I FEEL SO WORTHLESS.
THERE'S BEEN SO MUCH GOING ON.
I HADN'T NOTICED HOW NATURAL IT'S BECOME TO BE AROUND HACHISU AND NATSUME.
DON'T CRY, HACHISU.
AND PLEASE, DON'T BE SO HARD ON YOURSELF.

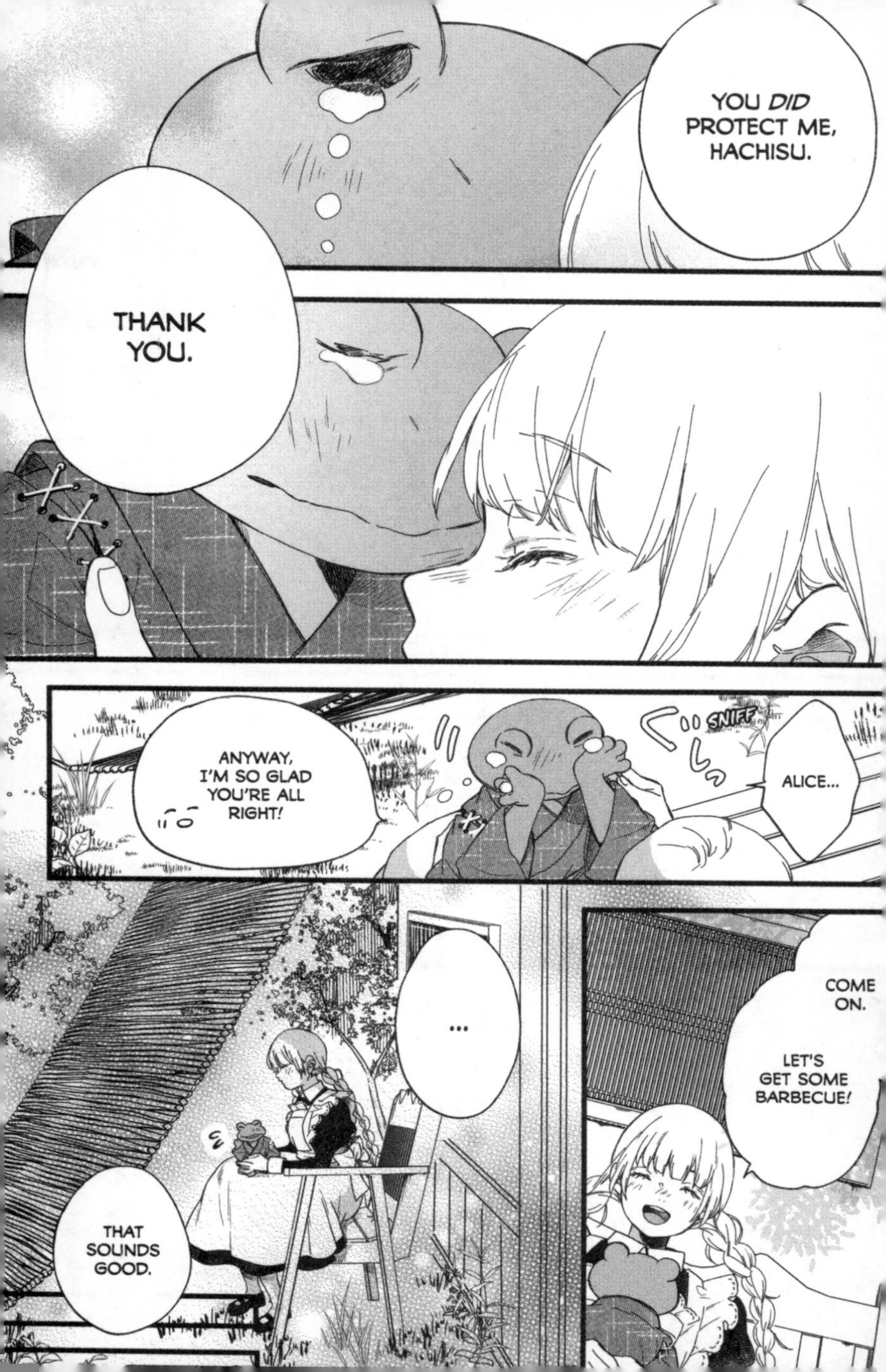
YOU *DID* PROTECT ME, HACHISU.
THANK YOU.
SNIFF
ALICE...
ANYWAY, I'M SO GLAD YOU'RE ALL RIGHT!
COME ON.
LET'S GET SOME BARBECUE!
...
THAT SOUNDS GOOD.

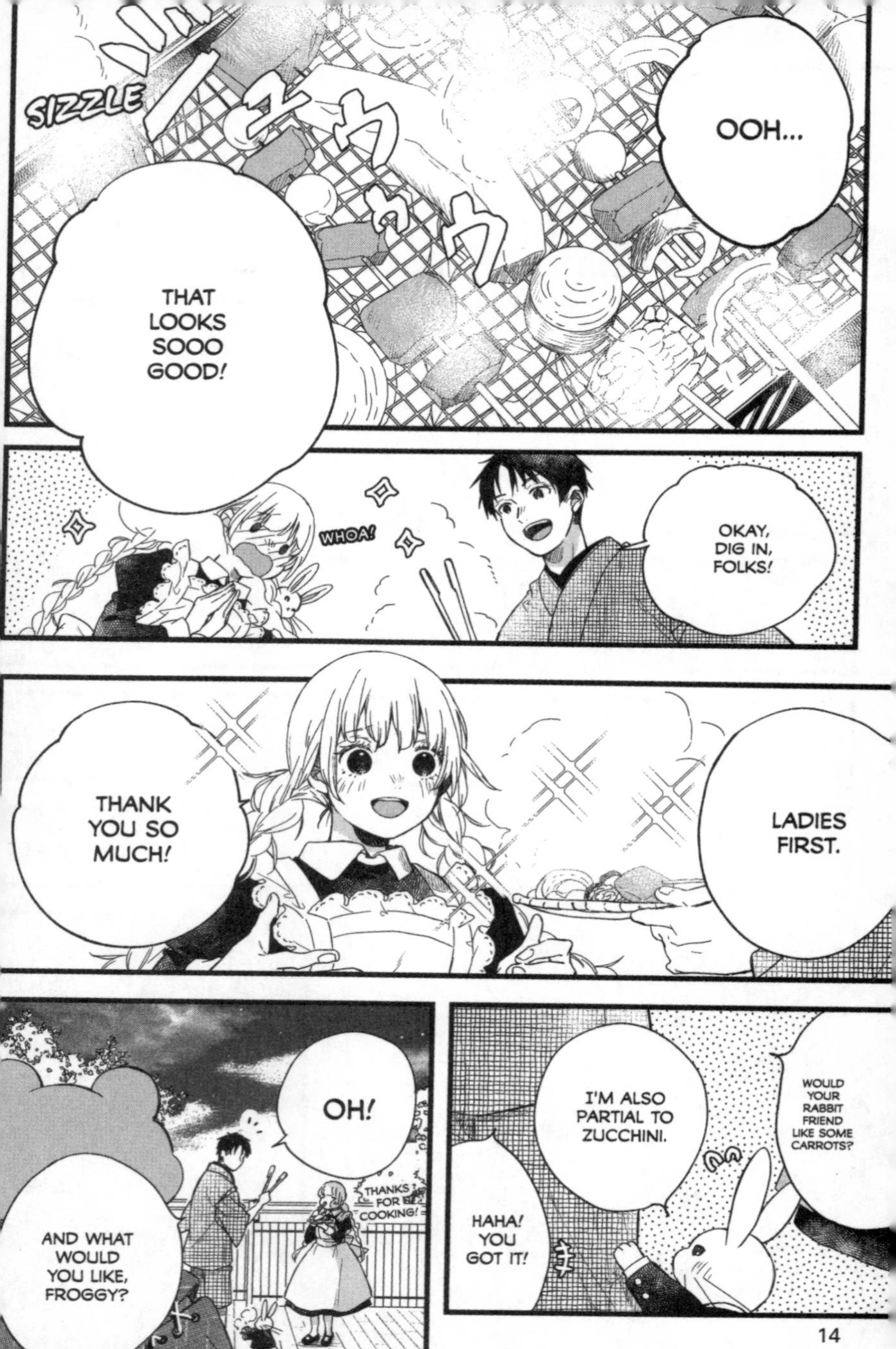
OOH...
SIZZLE
THAT LOOKS SOOO GOOD!
OKAY, DIG IN, FOLKS!
WHOA!
LADIES FIRST.
THANK YOU SO MUCH!
WOULD YOUR RABBIT FRIEND LIKE SOME CARROTS?
I'M ALSO PARTIAL TO ZUCCHINI.
HAHA! YOU GOT IT!
OH!
THANKS FOR COOKING!
AND WHAT WOULD YOU LIKE, FROGGY?

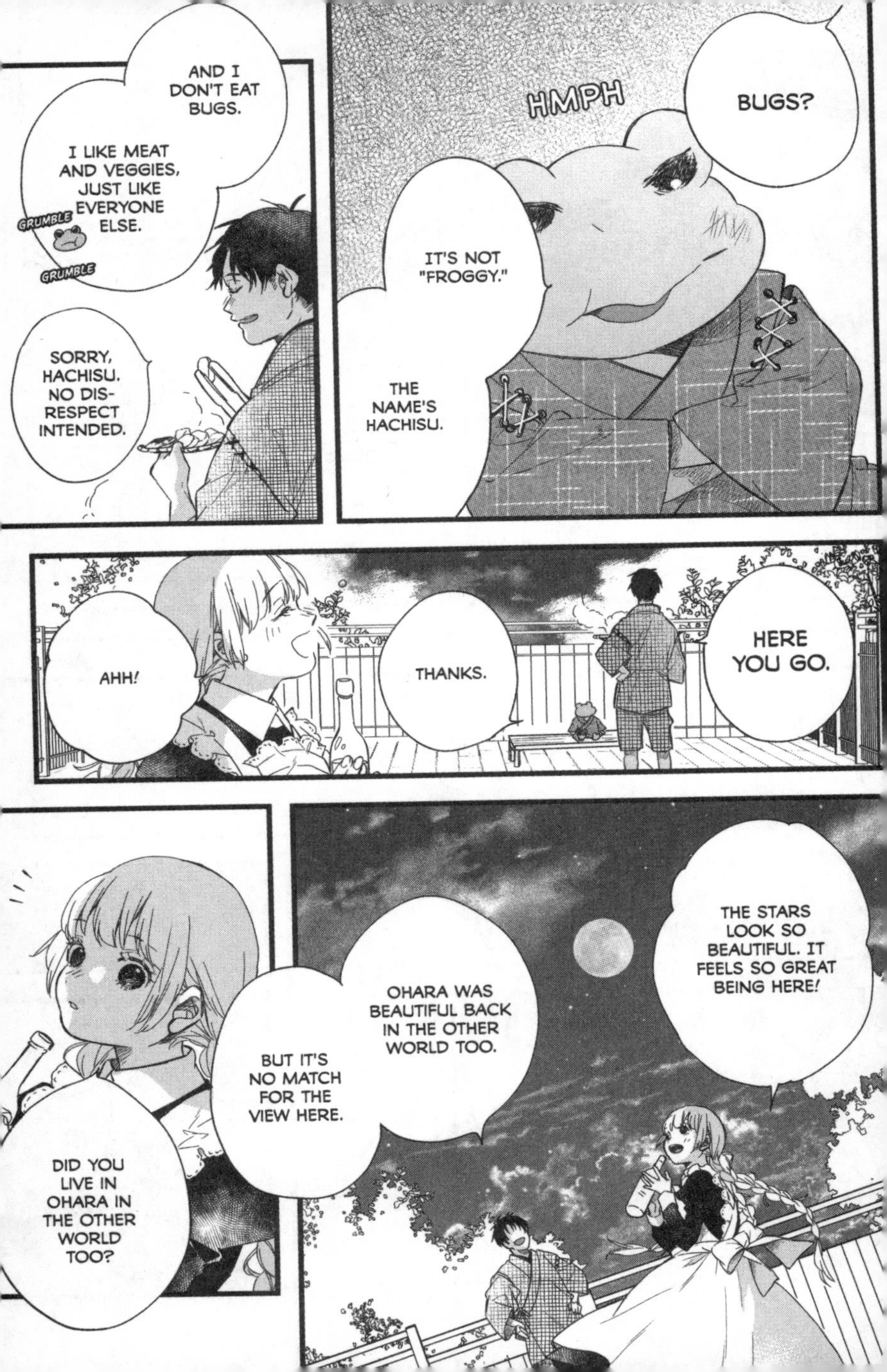
BUGS?
HMPH
IT'S NOT "FROGGY."
THE NAME'S HACHISU.
AND I DON'T EAT BUGS.
I LIKE MEAT AND VEGGIES, JUST LIKE EVERYONE ELSE.
GRUMBLE
GRUMBLE
SORRY, HACHISU. NO DIS- RESPECT INTENDED.
HERE YOU GO.
THANKS.
AHH!
THE STARS LOOK SO BEAUTIFUL. IT FEELS SO GREAT BEING HERE!
OHARA WAS BEAUTIFUL BACK IN THE OTHER WORLD TOO.
BUT IT'S NO MATCH FOR THE VIEW HERE.
DID YOU LIVE IN OHARA IN THE OTHER WORLD TOO?

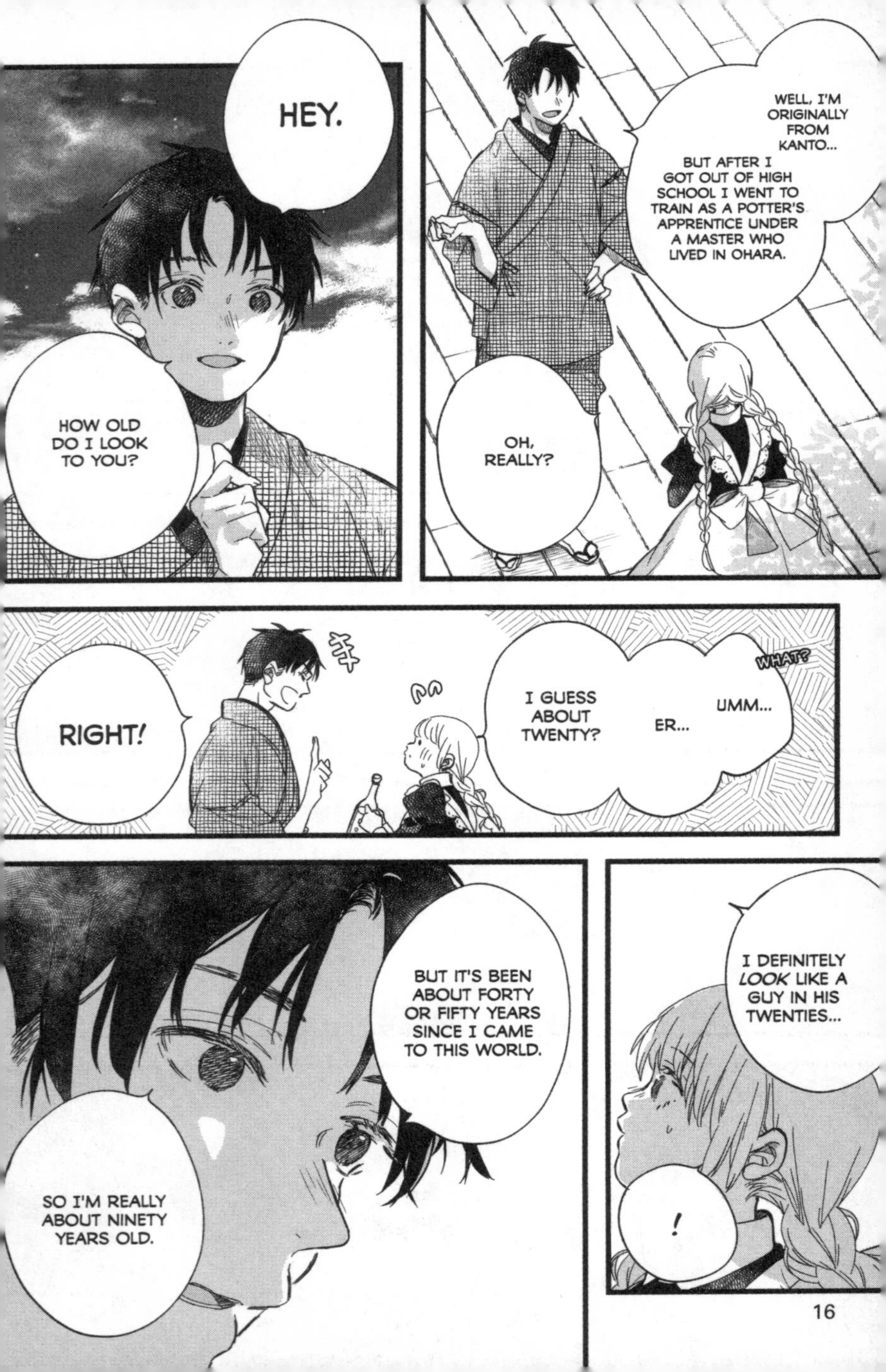
WELL, I'M ORIGINALLY FROM KANTO...
BUT AFTER I GOT OUT OF HIGH SCHOOL I WENT TO TRAIN AS A POTTER'S APPRENTICE UNDER A MASTER WHO LIVED IN OHARA.
OH, REALLY?
HEY.
HOW OLD DO I LOOK TO YOU?
WHAT?
UMM...
ER...
I GUESS ABOUT TWENTY?
RIGHT!
I DEFINITELY *LOOK* LIKE A GUY IN HIS TWENTIES...
!
BUT IT'S BEEN ABOUT FORTY OR FIFTY YEARS SINCE I CAME TO THIS WORLD.
SO I'M REALLY ABOUT NINETY YEARS OLD.

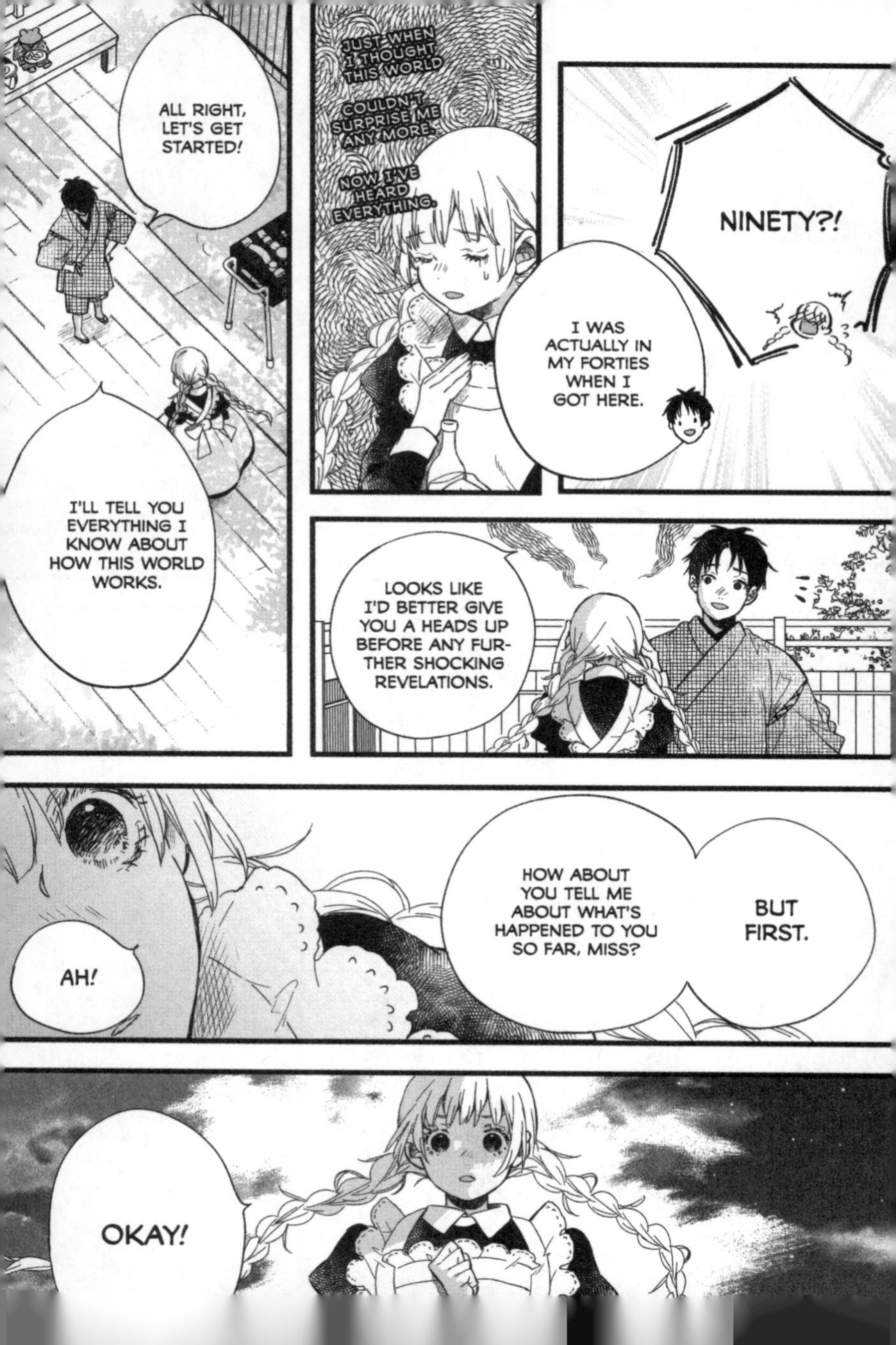
NINETY?!
I WAS ACTUALLY IN MY FORTIES WHEN I GOT HERE.
JUST WHEN I THOUGHT THIS WORLD
COULDN'T SURPRISE ME ANY MORE.
NOW I'VE HEARD EVERYTHING.
LOOKS LIKE I'D BETTER GIVE YOU A HEADS UP BEFORE ANY FURTHER SHOCKING REVELATIONS.
ALL RIGHT, LET'S GET STARTED!
I'LL TELL YOU EVERYTHING I KNOW ABOUT HOW THIS WORLD WORKS.
BUT FIRST.
HOW ABOUT YOU TELL ME ABOUT WHAT'S HAPPENED TO YOU SO FAR, MISS?
AH!
OKAY!

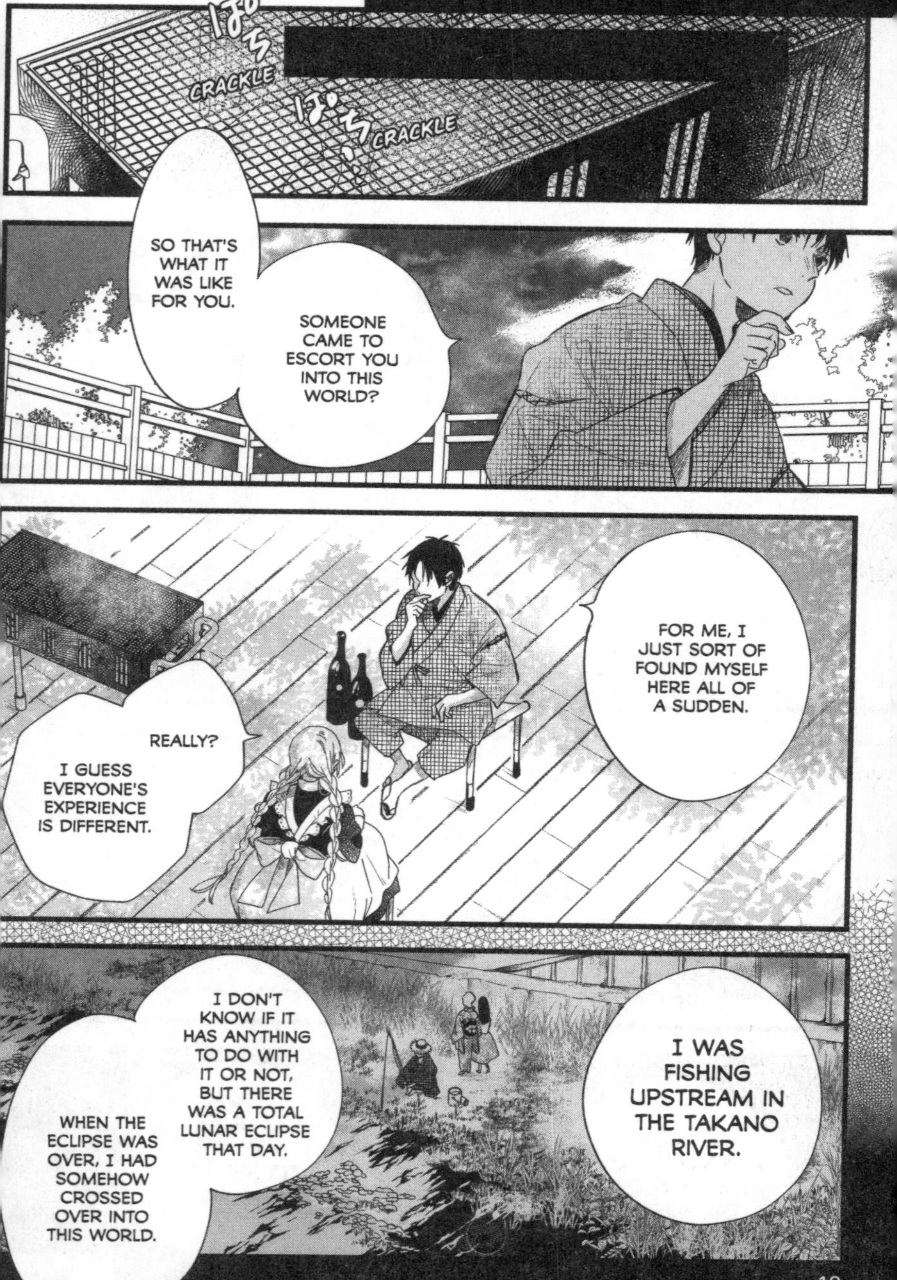

[redacted]
ぱち
CRACKLE
ぱち
CRACKLE
SO THAT'S WHAT IT WAS LIKE FOR YOU.
SOMEONE CAME TO ESCORT YOU INTO THIS WORLD?
FOR ME, I JUST SORT OF FOUND MYSELF HERE ALL OF A SUDDEN.
REALLY?
I GUESS EVERYONE'S EXPERIENCE IS DIFFERENT.
I WAS FISHING UPSTREAM IN THE TAKANO RIVER.
I DON'T KNOW IF IT HAS ANYTHING TO DO WITH IT OR NOT, BUT THERE WAS A TOTAL LUNAR ECLIPSE THAT DAY.
WHEN THE ECLIPSE WAS OVER, I HAD SOMEHOW CROSSED OVER INTO THIS WORLD.

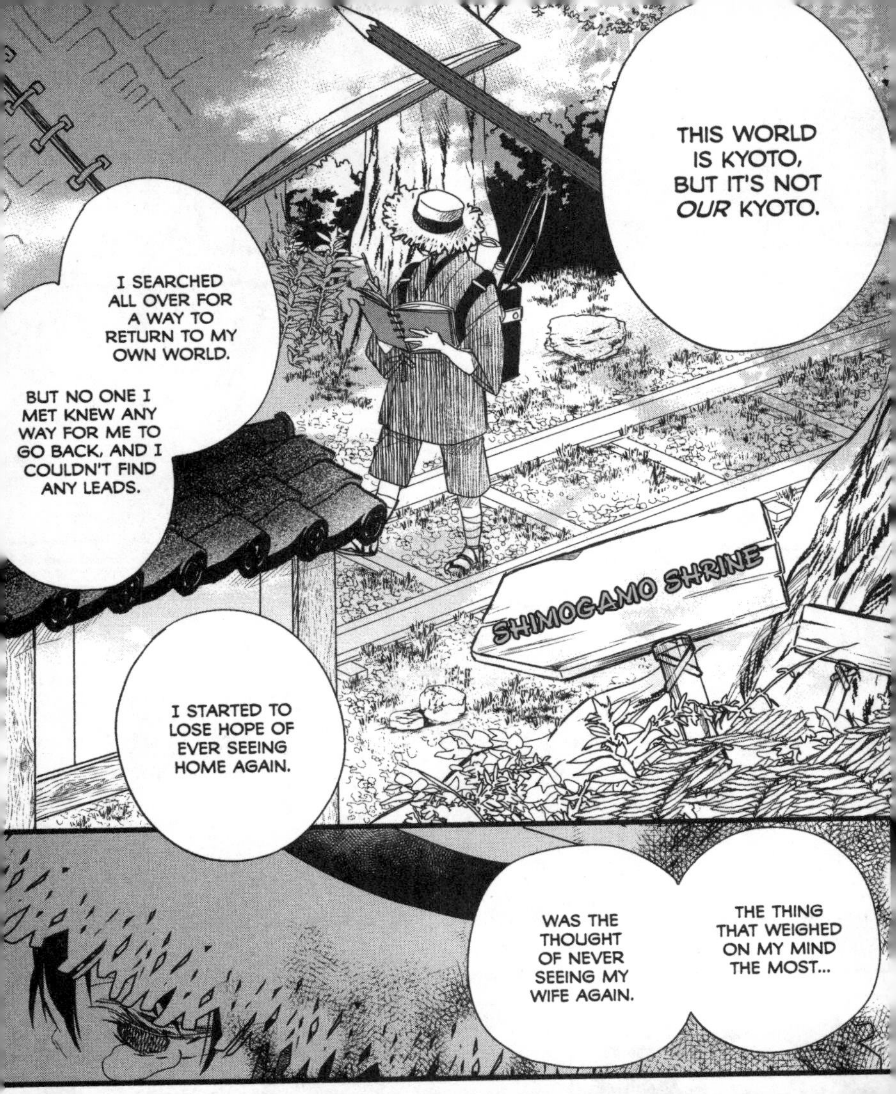
THIS WORLD IS KYOTO, BUT IT'S NOT *OUR* KYOTO.
I SEARCHED ALL OVER FOR A WAY TO RETURN TO MY OWN WORLD.
BUT NO ONE I MET KNEW ANY WAY FOR ME TO GO BACK, AND I COULDN'T FIND ANY LEADS.
SHIMOGAMO SHRINE
I STARTED TO LOSE HOPE OF EVER SEEING HOME AGAIN.
THE THING THAT WEIGHED ON MY MIND THE MOST...
WAS THE THOUGHT OF NEVER SEEING MY WIFE AGAIN.

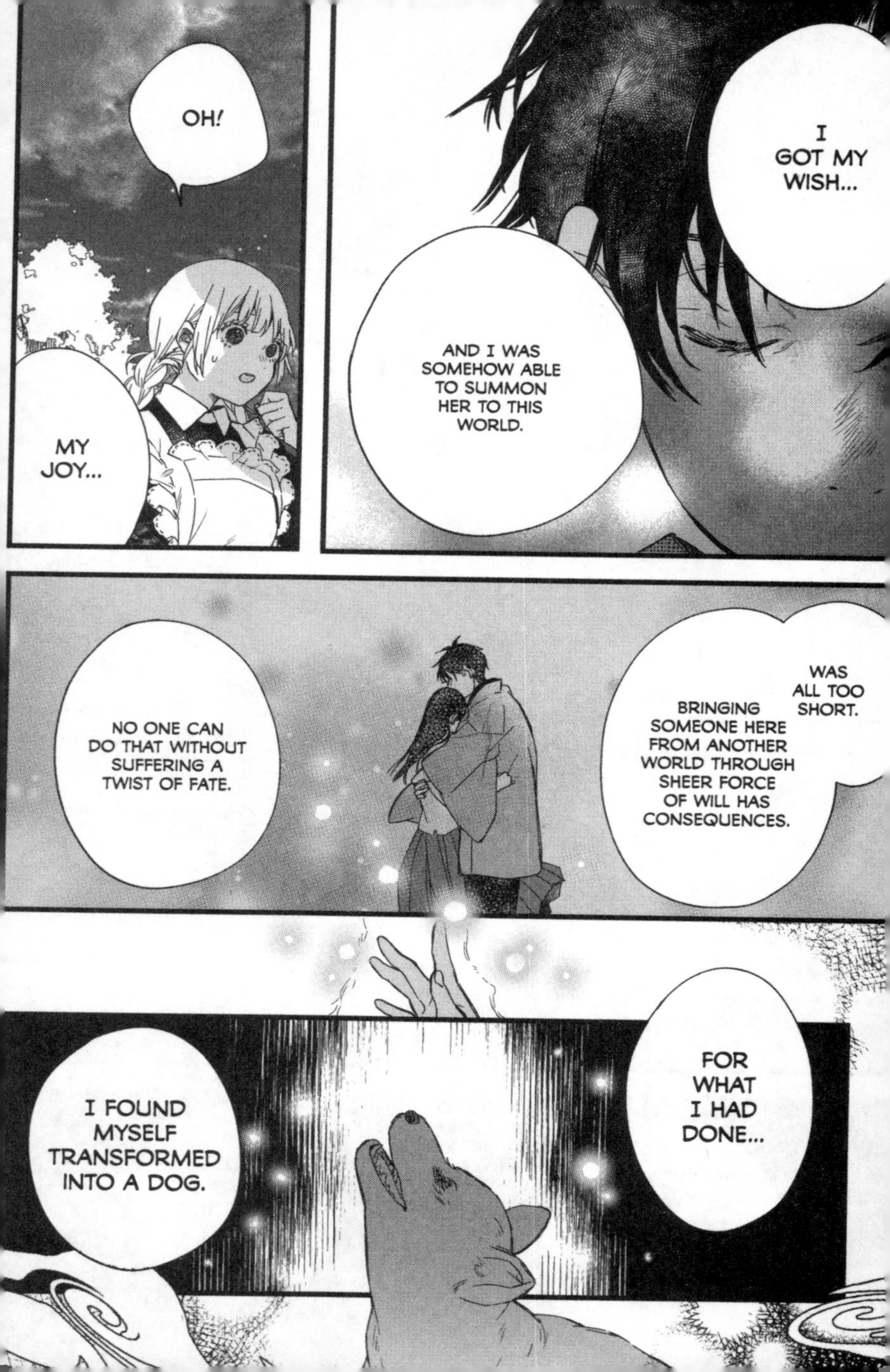
I GOT MY WISH...
AND I WAS SOMEHOW ABLE TO SUMMON HER TO THIS WORLD.
OH!
MY JOY...
WAS ALL TOO SHORT.
BRINGING SOMEONE HERE FROM ANOTHER WORLD THROUGH SHEER FORCE OF WILL HAS CONSEQUENCES.
NO ONE CAN DO THAT WITHOUT SUFFERING A TWIST OF FATE.
FOR WHAT I HAD DONE...
I FOUND MYSELF TRANSFORMED INTO A DOG.

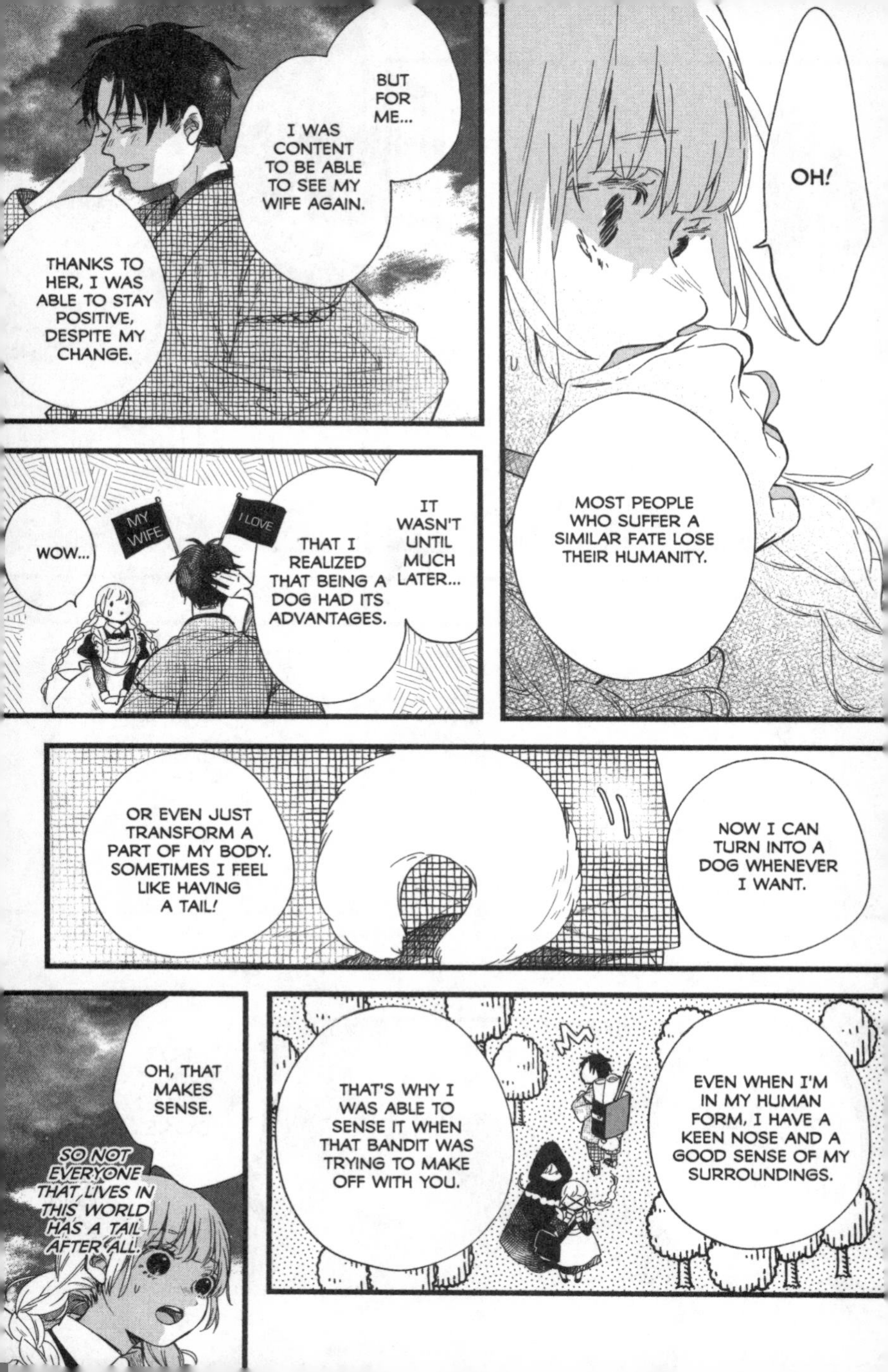

OH!
MOST PEOPLE WHO SUFFER A SIMILAR FATE LOSE THEIR HUMANITY.
BUT FOR ME...
I WAS CONTENT TO BE ABLE TO SEE MY WIFE AGAIN.
THANKS TO HER, I WAS ABLE TO STAY POSITIVE, DESPITE MY CHANGE.
IT WASN'T UNTIL MUCH LATER...
THAT I REALIZED THAT BEING A DOG HAD ITS ADVANTAGES.
I LOVE
MY WIFE
WOW...
NOW I CAN TURN INTO A DOG WHENEVER I WANT.
OR EVEN JUST TRANSFORM A PART OF MY BODY. SOMETIMES I FEEL LIKE HAVING A TAIL!
EVEN WHEN I'M IN MY HUMAN FORM, I HAVE A KEEN NOSE AND A GOOD SENSE OF MY SURROUNDINGS.
THAT'S WHY I WAS ABLE TO SENSE IT WHEN THAT BANDIT WAS TRYING TO MAKE OFF WITH YOU.
OH, THAT MAKES SENSE.
SO NOT EVERYONE THAT LIVES IN THIS WORLD HAS A TAIL AFTER ALL.

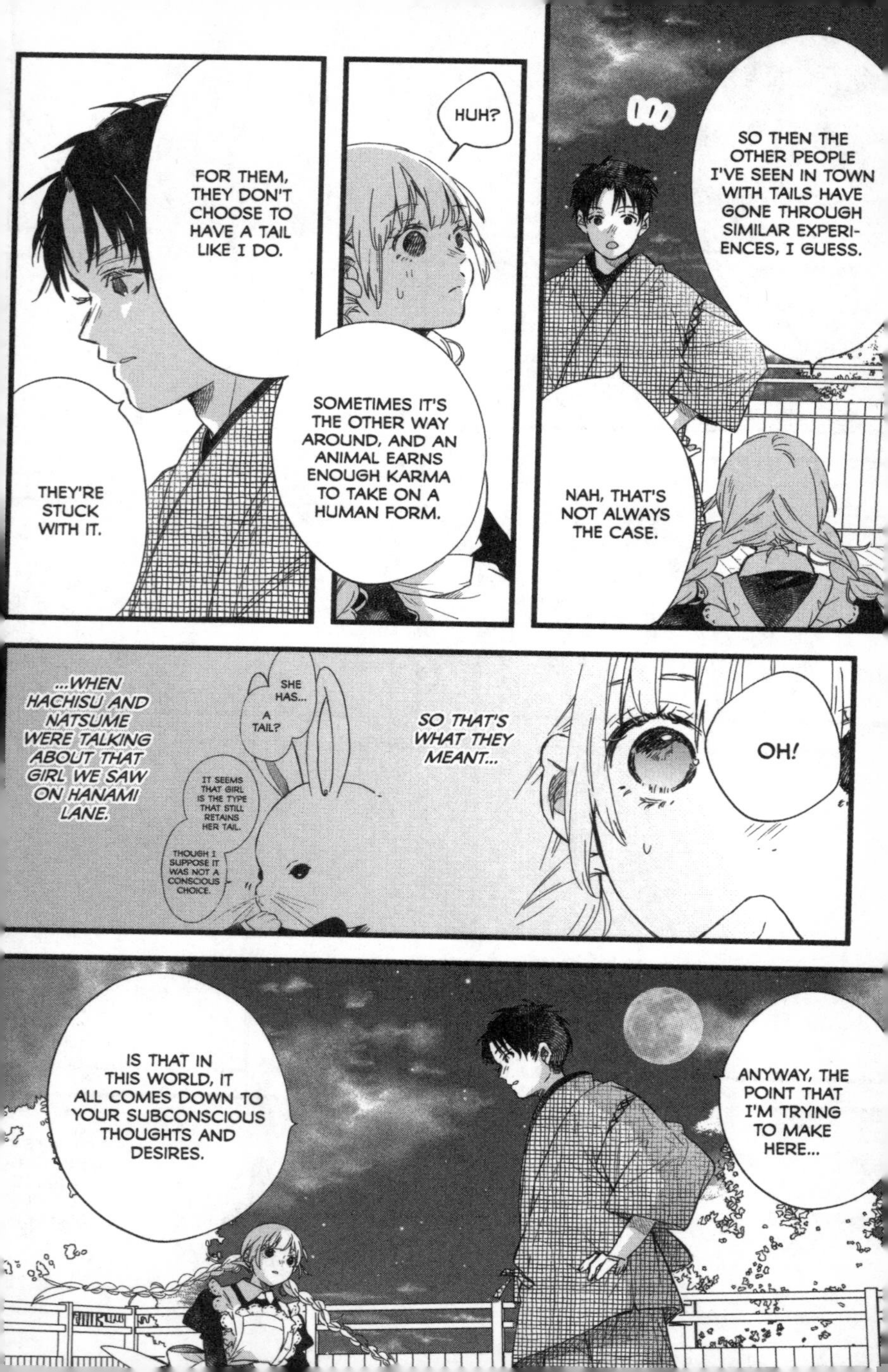
SO THEN THE OTHER PEOPLE I'VE SEEN IN TOWN WITH TAILS HAVE GONE THROUGH SIMILAR EXPERI-ENCES, I GUESS.
NAH, THAT'S NOT ALWAYS THE CASE.
HUH?
SOMETIMES IT'S THE OTHER WAY AROUND, AND AN ANIMAL EARNS ENOUGH KARMA TO TAKE ON A HUMAN FORM.
FOR THEM, THEY DON'T CHOOSE TO HAVE A TAIL LIKE I DO.
THEY'RE STUCK WITH IT.
OH!
SO THAT'S WHAT THEY MEANT...
SHE HAS...
A TAIL?
IT SEEMS THAT GIRL IS THE TYPE THAT STILL RETAINS HER TAIL.
THOUGH I SUPPOSE IT WAS NOT A CONSCIOUS CHOICE.
...WHEN HACHISU AND NATSUME WERE TALKING ABOUT THAT GIRL WE SAW ON HANAMI LANE.
ANYWAY, THE POINT THAT I'M TRYING TO MAKE HERE...
IS THAT IN THIS WORLD, IT ALL COMES DOWN TO YOUR SUBCONSCIOUS THOUGHTS AND DESIRES.

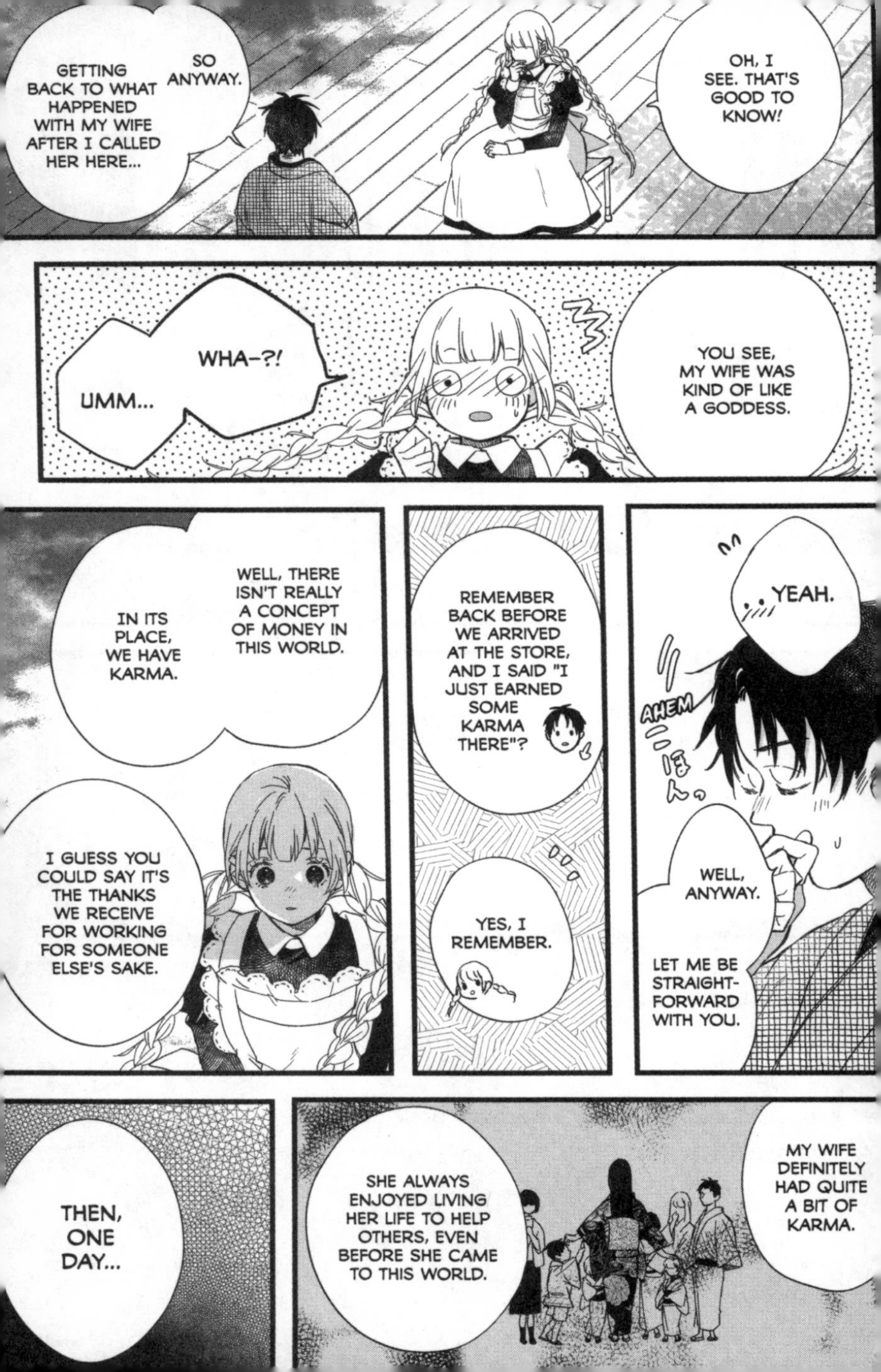
OH, I SEE. THAT'S GOOD TO KNOW!
SO ANYWAY.
GETTING BACK TO WHAT HAPPENED WITH MY WIFE AFTER I CALLED HER HERE...
YOU SEE, MY WIFE WAS KIND OF LIKE A GODDESS.
WHA-?!
UMM...
...YEAH.
AHEM
WELL, ANYWAY.
LET ME BE STRAIGHT-FORWARD WITH YOU.
REMEMBER BACK BEFORE WE ARRIVED AT THE STORE, AND I SAID "I JUST EARNED SOME KARMA THERE"?
YES, I REMEMBER.
WELL, THERE ISN'T REALLY A CONCEPT OF MONEY IN THIS WORLD.
IN ITS PLACE, WE HAVE KARMA.
I GUESS YOU COULD SAY IT'S THE THANKS WE RECEIVE FOR WORKING FOR SOMEONE ELSE'S SAKE.
MY WIFE DEFINITELY HAD QUITE A BIT OF KARMA.
SHE ALWAYS ENJOYED LIVING HER LIFE TO HELP OTHERS, EVEN BEFORE SHE CAME TO THIS WORLD.
THEN, ONE DAY...

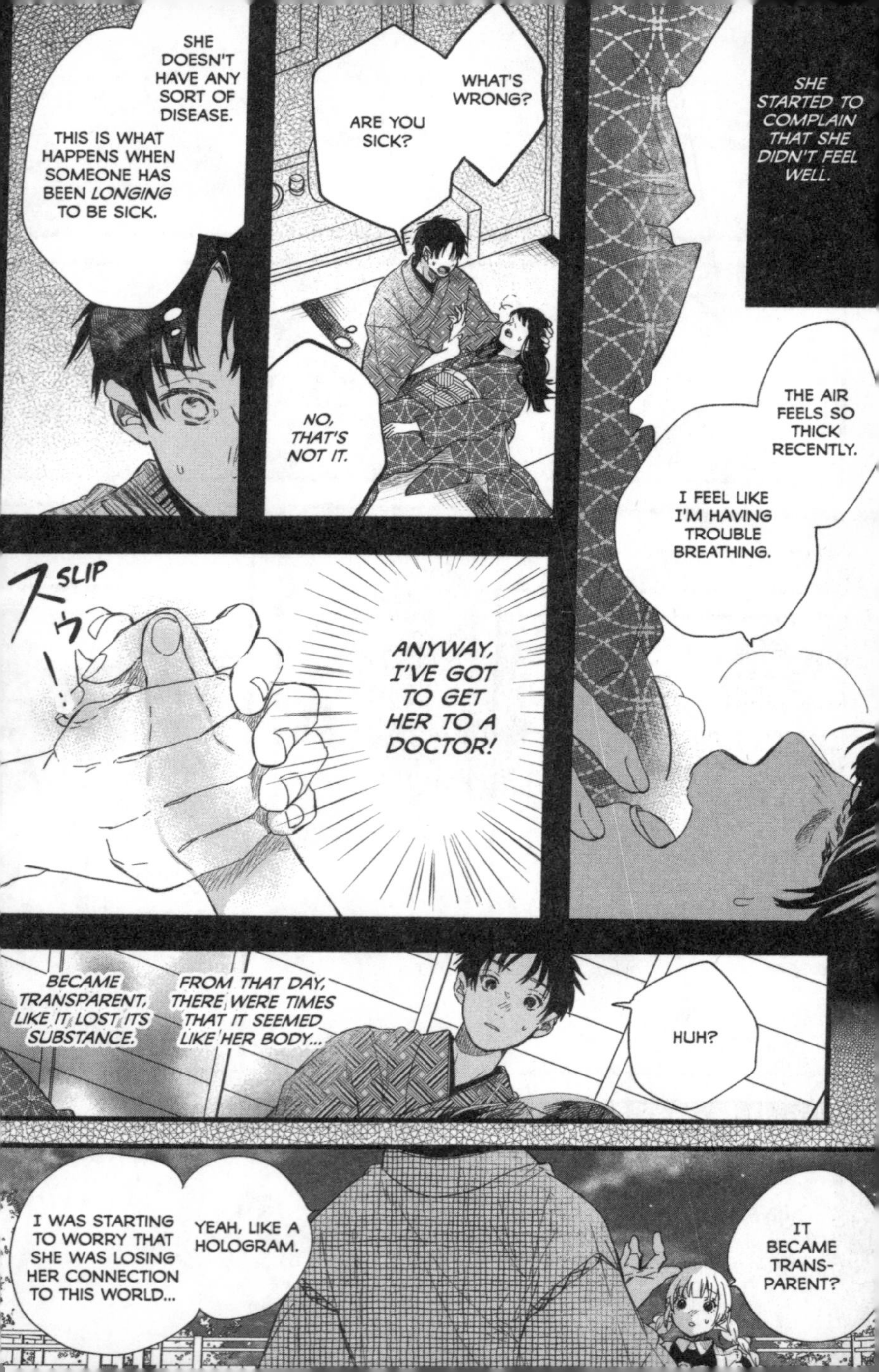
SHE STARTED TO COMPLAIN THAT SHE DIDN'T FEEL WELL.
THE AIR FEELS SO THICK RECENTLY.
I FEEL LIKE I'M HAVING TROUBLE BREATHING.
WHAT'S WRONG?
ARE YOU SICK?
NO, THAT'S NOT IT.
SHE DOESN'T HAVE ANY SORT OF DISEASE.
THIS IS WHAT HAPPENS WHEN SOMEONE HAS BEEN *LONGING* TO BE SICK.
スゥ!
SLIP
ANYWAY, I'VE GOT TO GET HER TO A DOCTOR!
HUH?
FROM THAT DAY, THERE WERE TIMES THAT IT SEEMED LIKE HER BODY...
BECAME TRANSPARENT, LIKE IT LOST ITS SUBSTANCE.
IT BECAME TRANS-PARENT?
YEAH, LIKE A HOLOGRAM.
I WAS STARTING TO WORRY THAT SHE WAS LOSING HER CONNECTION TO THIS WORLD...

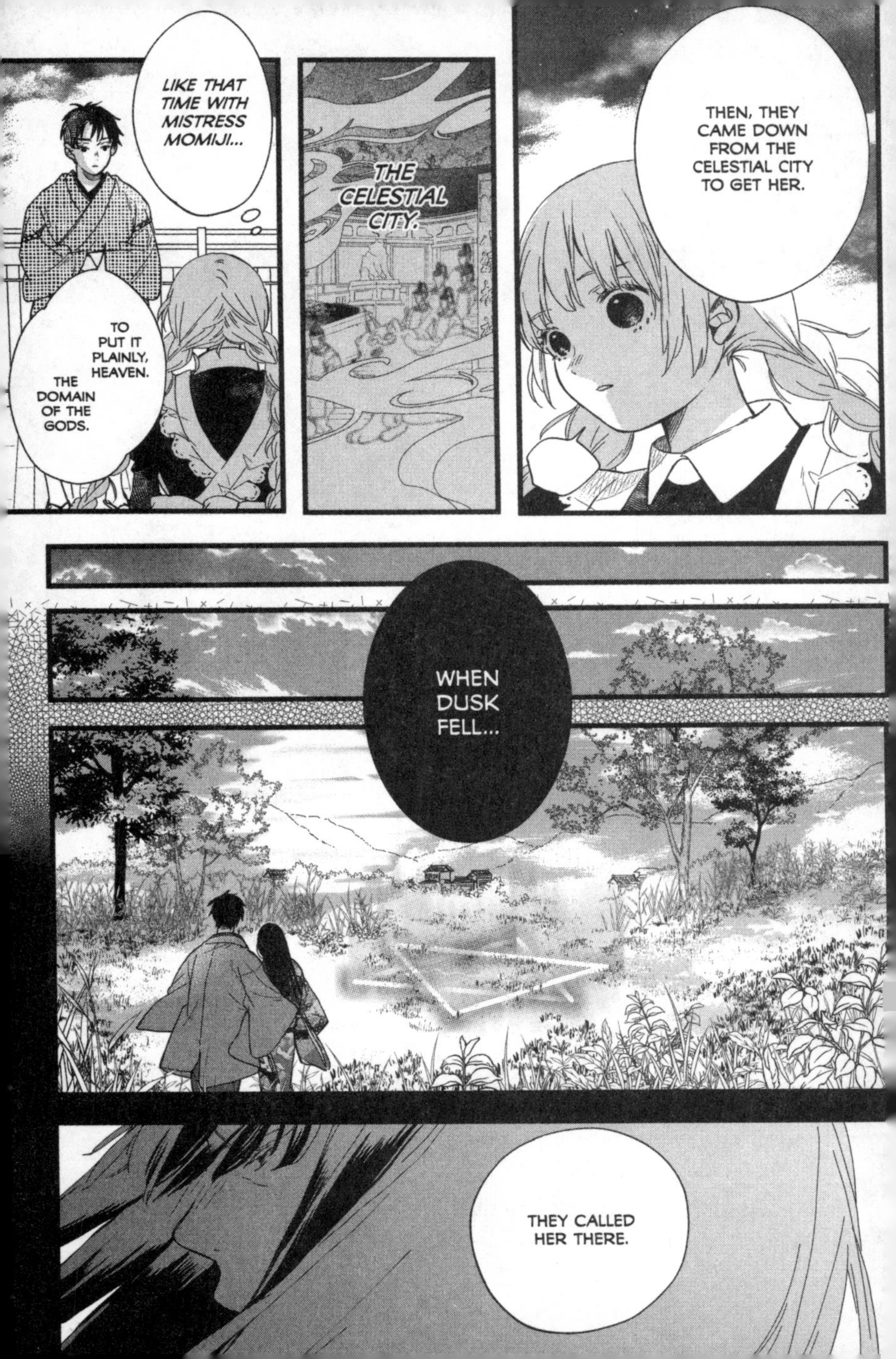
THEN, THEY CAME DOWN FROM THE CELESTIAL CITY TO GET HER.
THE CELESTIAL CITY.
LIKE THAT TIME WITH MISTRESS MOMIJI...
TO PUT IT PLAINLY, HEAVEN. THE DOMAIN OF THE GODS.
WHEN DUSK FELL...
THEY CALLED HER THERE.

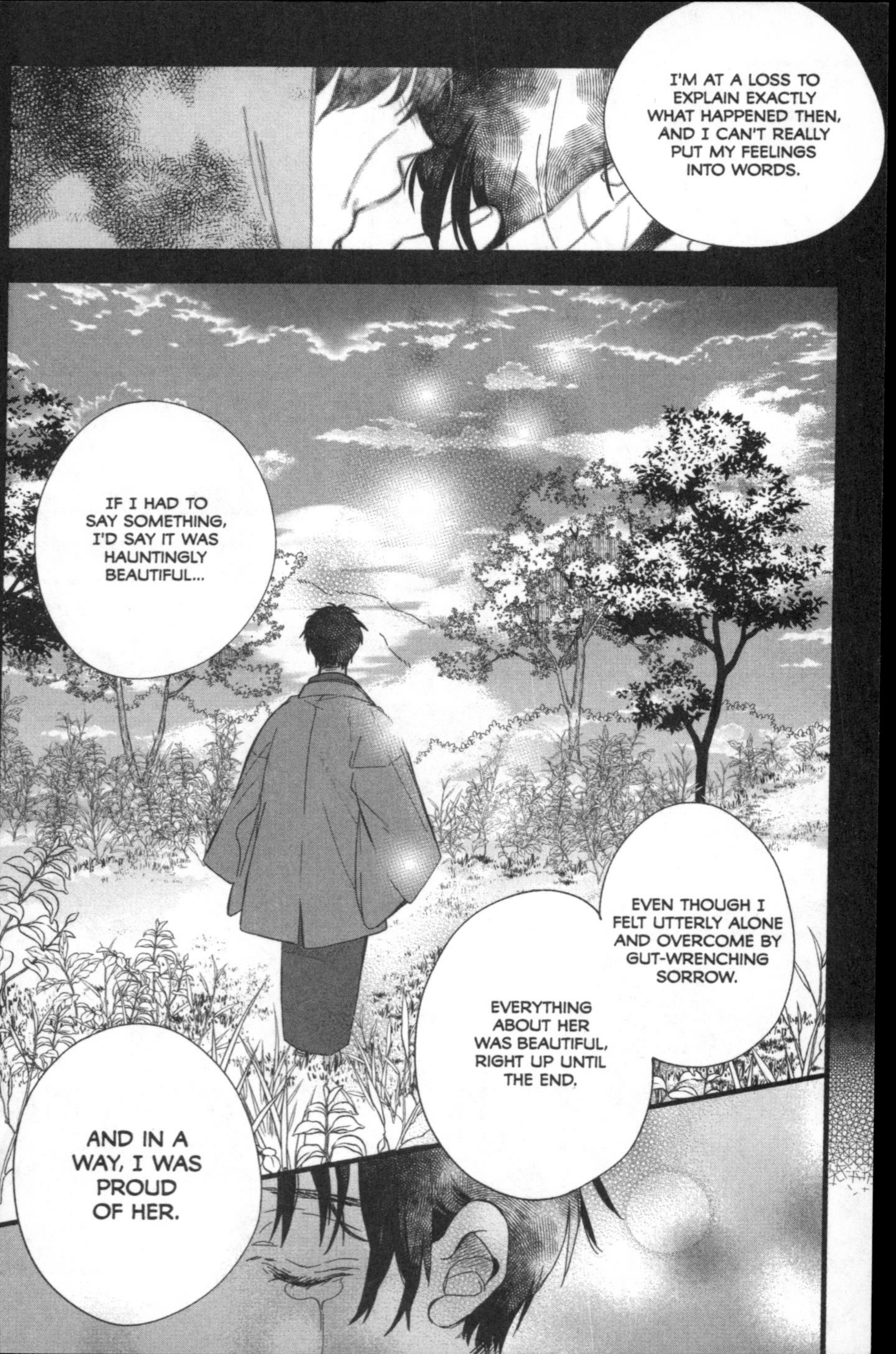
I'M AT A LOSS TO EXPLAIN EXACTLY WHAT HAPPENED THEN, AND I CAN'T REALLY PUT MY FEELINGS INTO WORDS.
IF I HAD TO SAY SOMETHING, I'D SAY IT WAS HAUNTINGLY BEAUTIFUL...
EVEN THOUGH I FELT UTTERLY ALONE AND OVERCOME BY GUT-WRENCHING SORROW.
EVERYTHING ABOUT HER WAS BEAUTIFUL, RIGHT UP UNTIL THE END.
AND IN A WAY, I WAS PROUD OF HER.

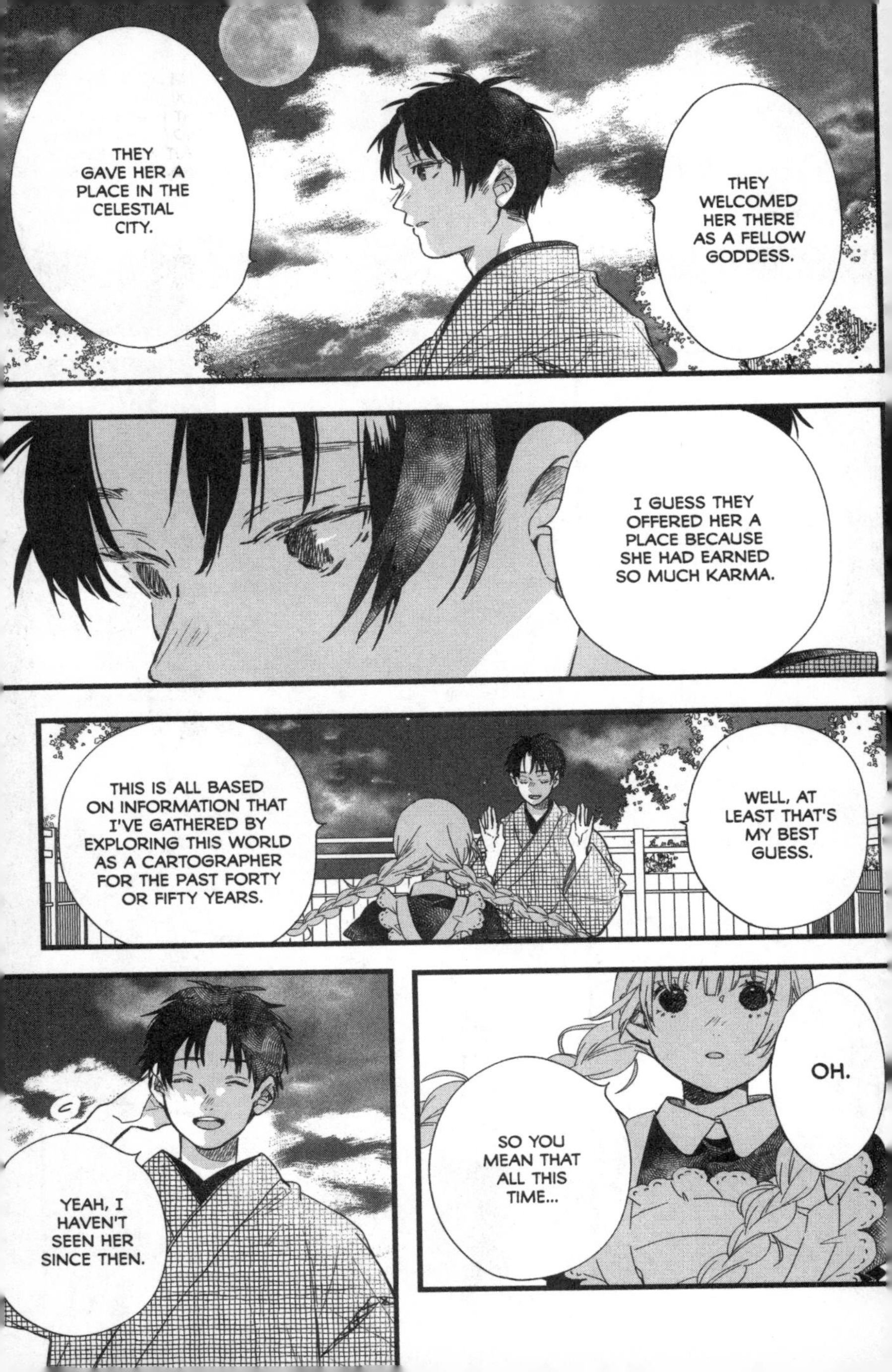
THEY WELCOMED HER THERE AS A FELLOW GODDESS.
THEY GAVE HER A PLACE IN THE CELESTIAL CITY.
I GUESS THEY OFFERED HER A PLACE BECAUSE SHE HAD EARNED SO MUCH KARMA.
WELL, AT LEAST THAT'S MY BEST GUESS.
THIS IS ALL BASED ON INFORMATION THAT I'VE GATHERED BY EXPLORING THIS WORLD AS A CARTOGRAPHER FOR THE PAST FORTY OR FIFTY YEARS.
OH.
SO YOU MEAN THAT ALL THIS TIME...
YEAH, I HAVEN'T SEEN HER SINCE THEN.

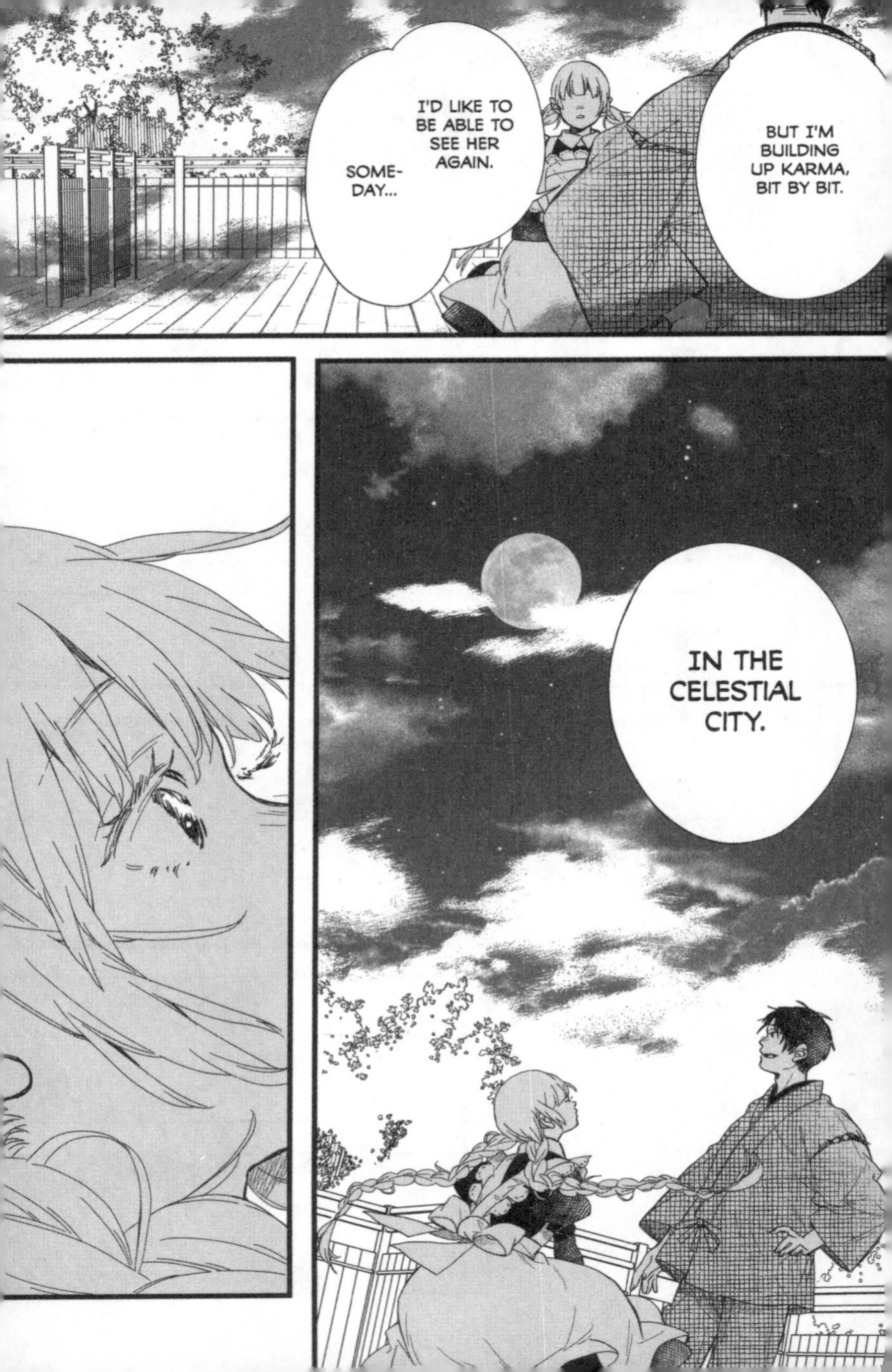
BUT I'M BUILDING UP KARMA, BIT BY BIT.
I'D LIKE TO BE ABLE TO SEE HER AGAIN.
SOME-DAY...
IN THE CELESTIAL CITY.

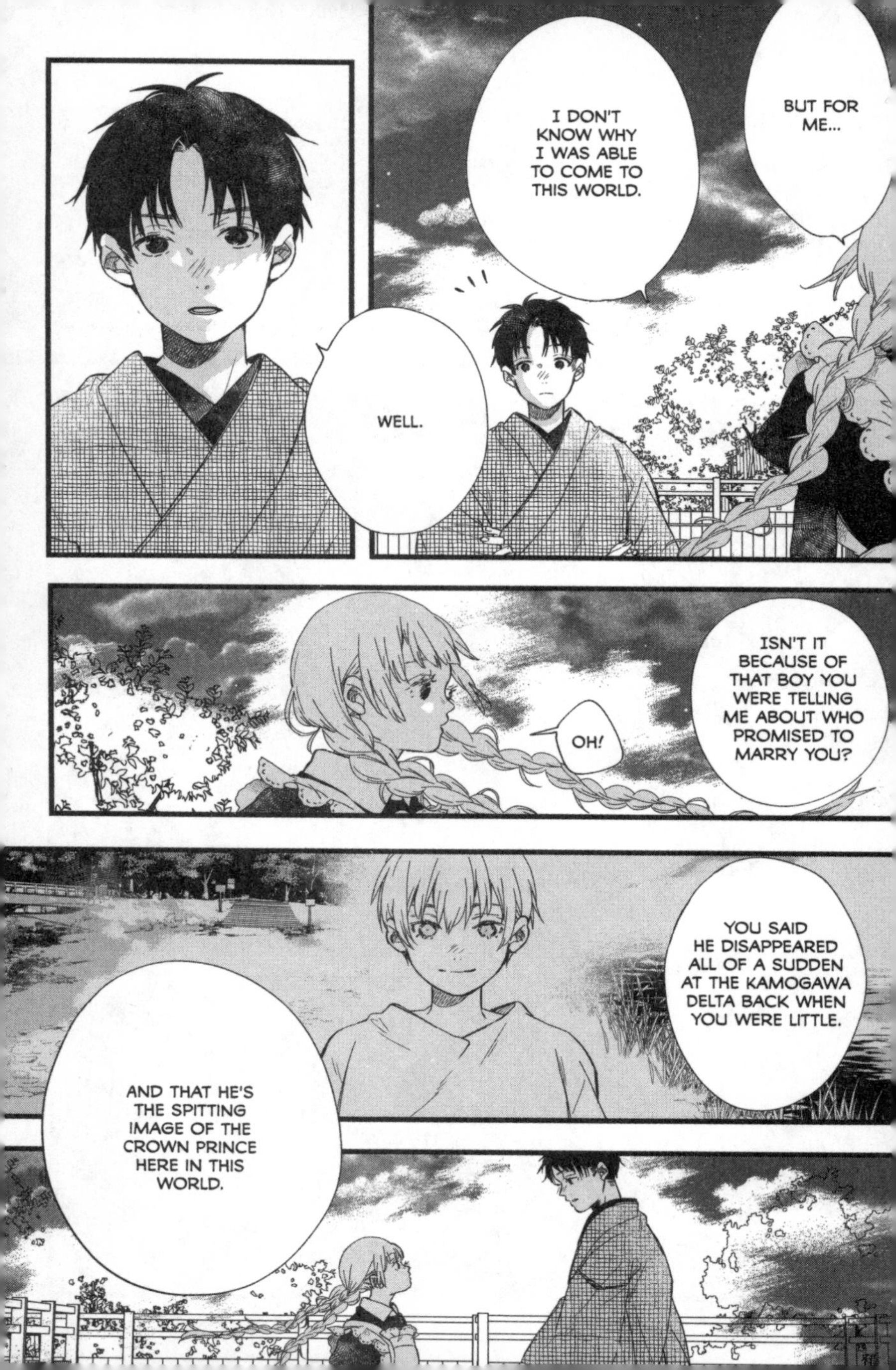
BUT FOR ME...
I DON'T KNOW WHY I WAS ABLE TO COME TO THIS WORLD.
WELL.
ISN'T IT BECAUSE OF THAT BOY YOU WERE TELLING ME ABOUT WHO PROMISED TO MARRY YOU?
OH!
YOU SAID HE DISAPPEARED ALL OF A SUDDEN AT THE KAMOGAWA DELTA BACK WHEN YOU WERE LITTLE.
AND THAT HE'S THE SPITTING IMAGE OF THE CROWN PRINCE HERE IN THIS WORLD.

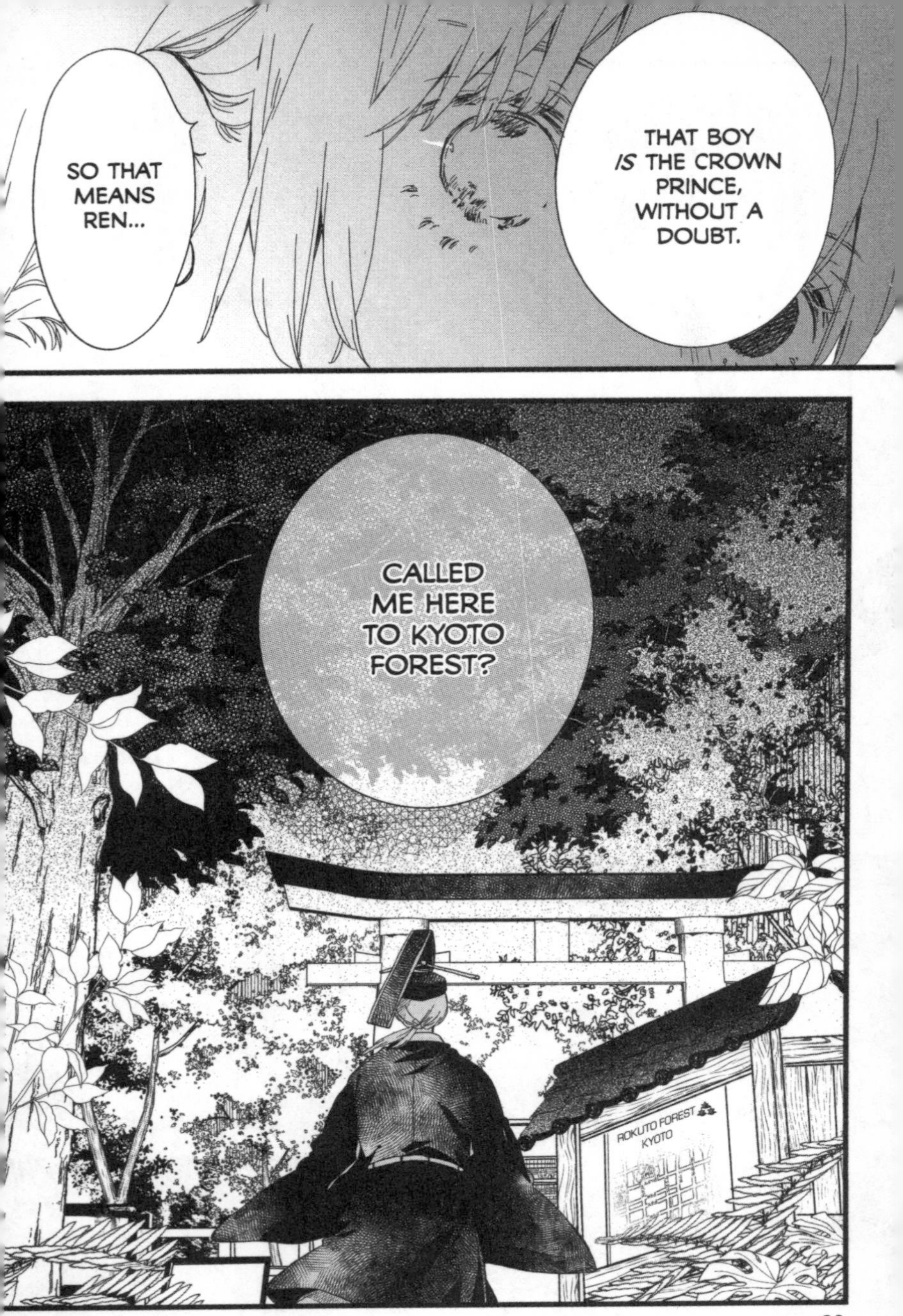
THAT BOY *IS* THE CROWN PRINCE, WITHOUT A DOUBT.
SO THAT MEANS REN...
CALLED ME HERE TO KYOTO FOREST?
ROKUTO FOREST KYOTO

Chapter 8

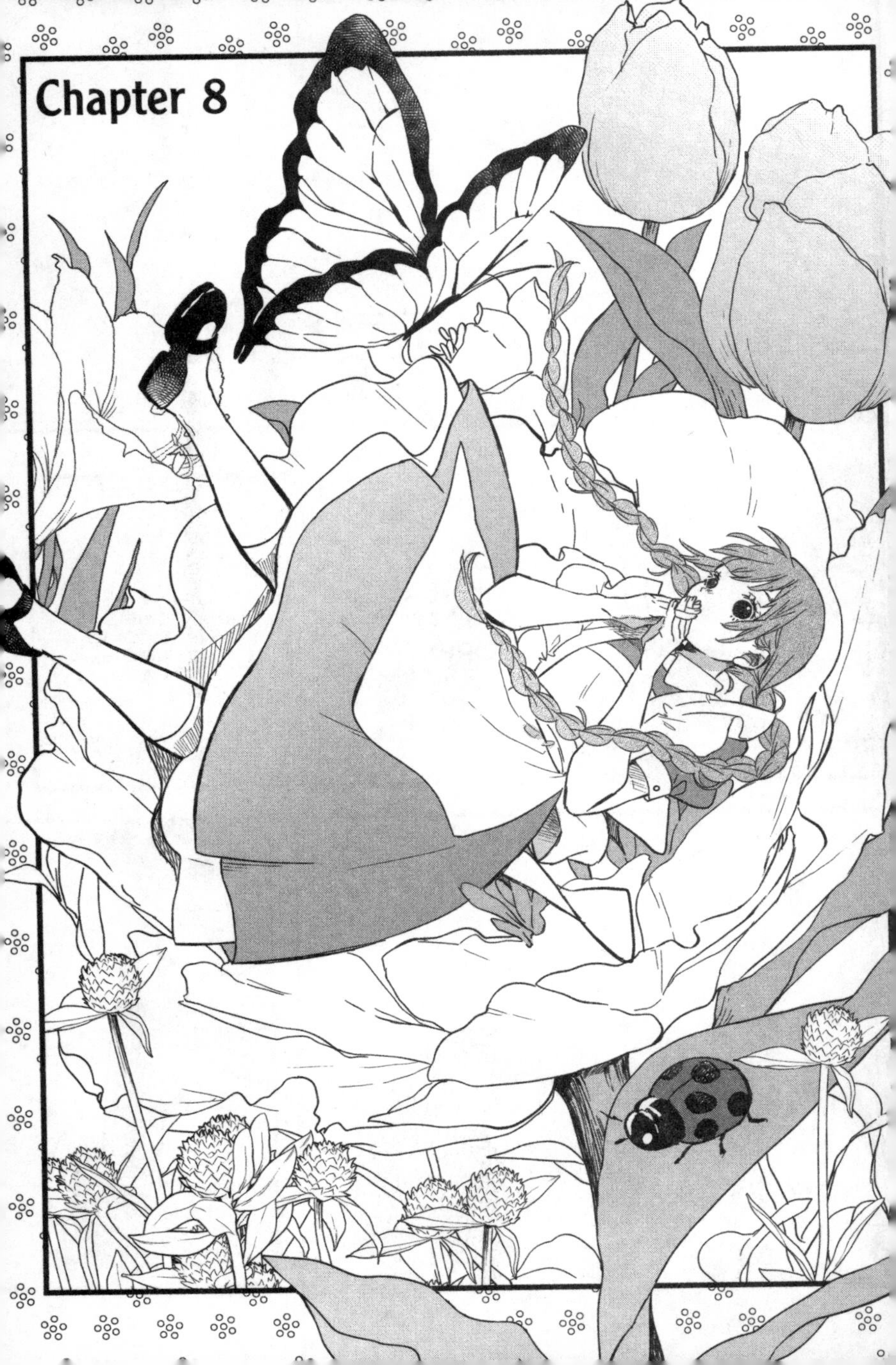

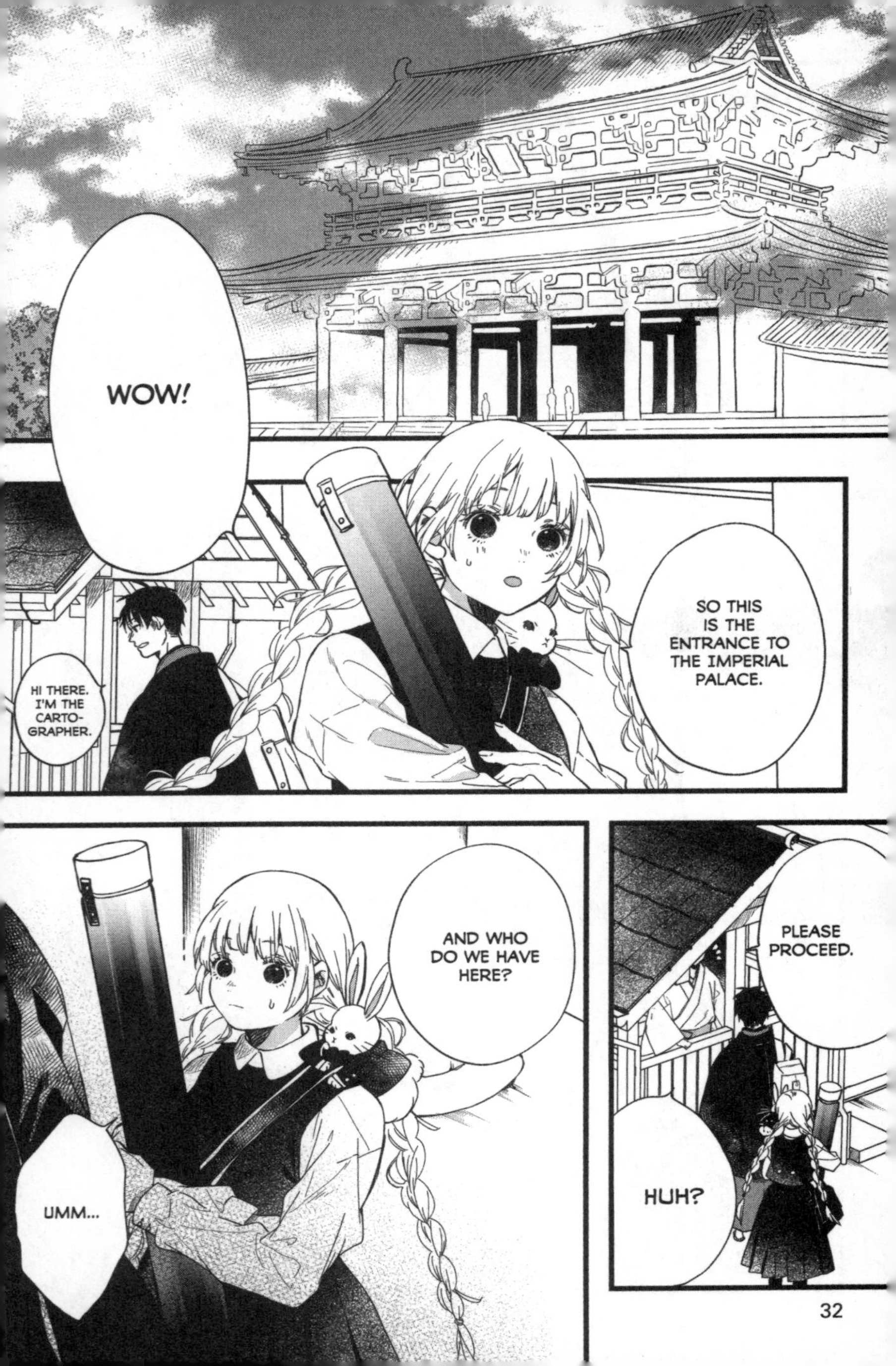
WOW!
SO THIS IS THE ENTRANCE TO THE IMPERIAL PALACE.
HI THERE. I'M THE CARTO-GRAPHER.
PLEASE PROCEED.
HUH?
AND WHO DO WE HAVE HERE?
UMM...

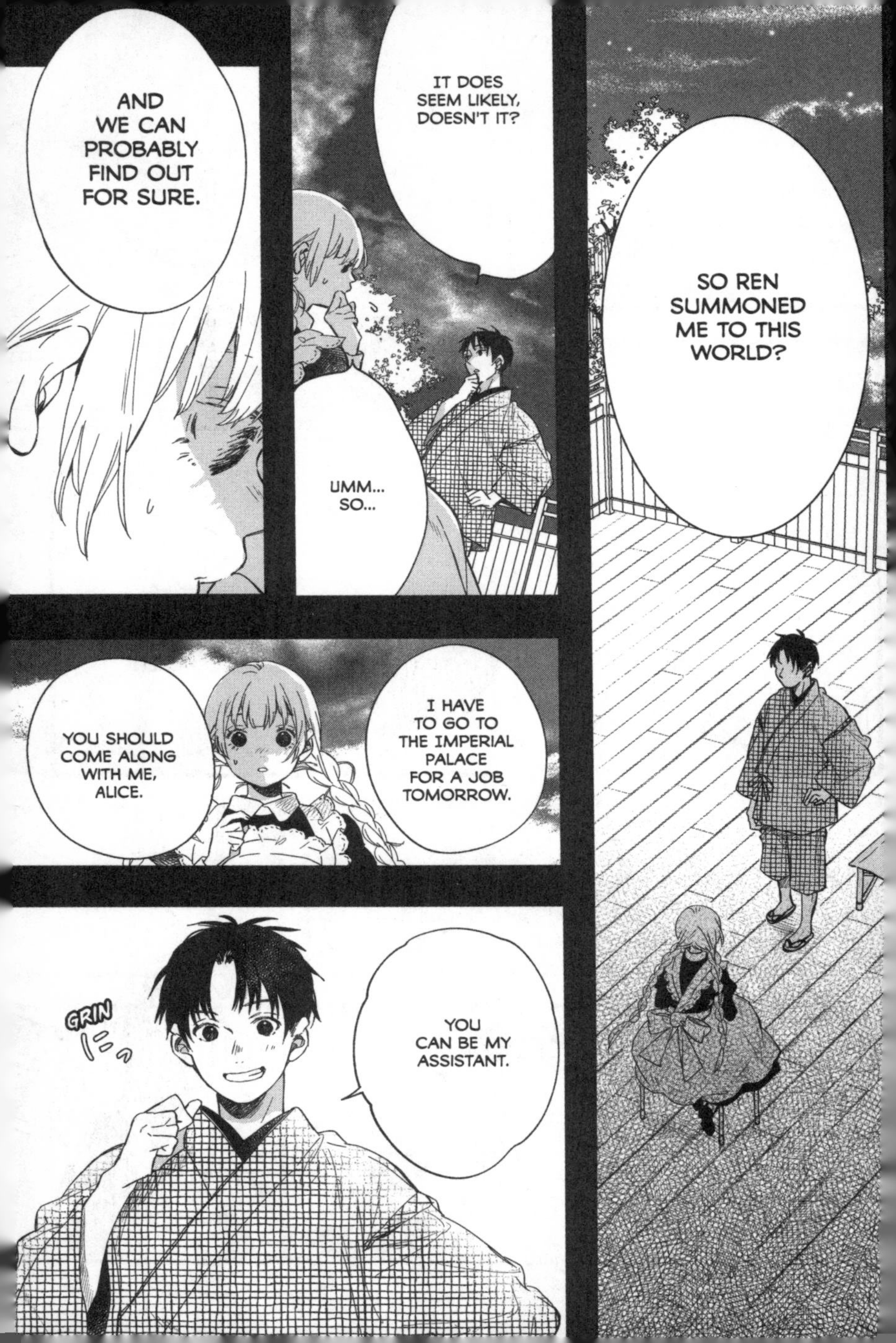
SO REN SUMMONED ME TO THIS WORLD?
IT DOES SEEM LIKELY, DOESN'T IT?
UMM... SO...
AND WE CAN PROBABLY FIND OUT FOR SURE.
I HAVE TO GO TO THE IMPERIAL PALACE FOR A JOB TOMORROW.
YOU SHOULD COME ALONG WITH ME, ALICE.
YOU CAN BE MY ASSISTANT.
GRIN

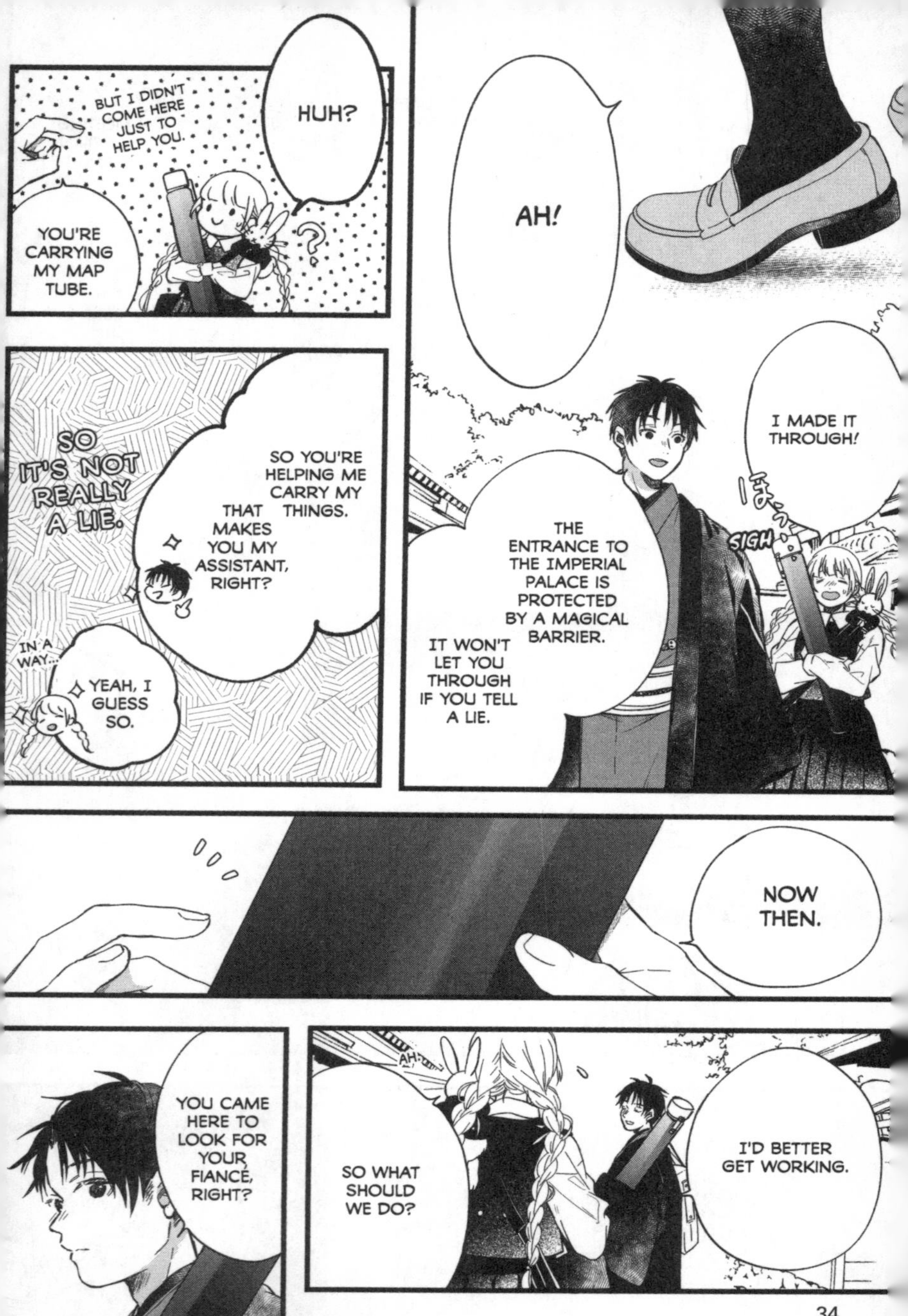
AH!
I MADE IT THROUGH!
ほっ
SIGH
THE ENTRANCE TO THE IMPERIAL PALACE IS PROTECTED BY A MAGICAL BARRIER.
IT WON'T LET YOU THROUGH IF YOU TELL A LIE.
HUH?
BUT I DIDN'T COME HERE JUST TO HELP YOU.
YOU'RE CARRYING MY MAP TUBE.
SO YOU'RE HELPING ME CARRY MY THINGS.
THAT MAKES YOU MY ASSISTANT, RIGHT?
SO IT'S NOT REALLY A LIE.
IN A WAY...
YEAH, I GUESS SO.
NOW THEN.
I'D BETTER GET WORKING.
SO WHAT SHOULD WE DO?
AH!
YOU CAME HERE TO LOOK FOR YOUR FIANCÉ, RIGHT?

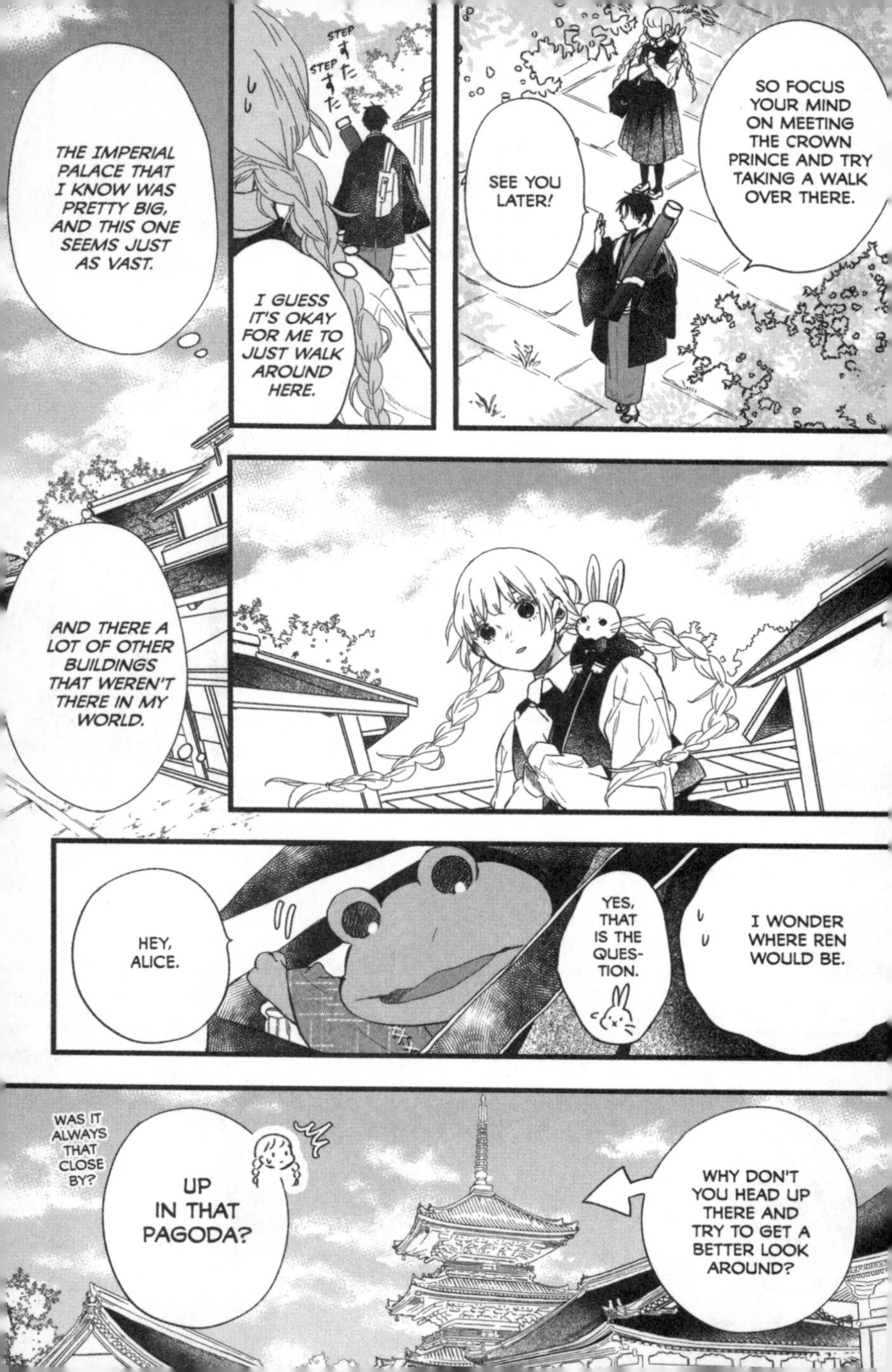
SO FOCUS YOUR MIND ON MEETING THE CROWN PRINCE AND TRY TAKING A WALK OVER THERE.
SEE YOU LATER!
STEP すた STEP すた
I GUESS IT'S OKAY FOR ME TO JUST WALK AROUND HERE.
THE IMPERIAL PALACE THAT I KNOW WAS PRETTY BIG, AND THIS ONE SEEMS JUST AS VAST.
AND THERE A LOT OF OTHER BUILDINGS THAT WEREN'T THERE IN MY WORLD.
I WONDER WHERE REN WOULD BE.
YES, THAT IS THE QUES-TION.
HEY, ALICE.
WHY DON'T YOU HEAD UP THERE AND TRY TO GET A BETTER LOOK AROUND?
UP IN THAT PAGODA?
WAS IT ALWAYS THAT CLOSE BY?

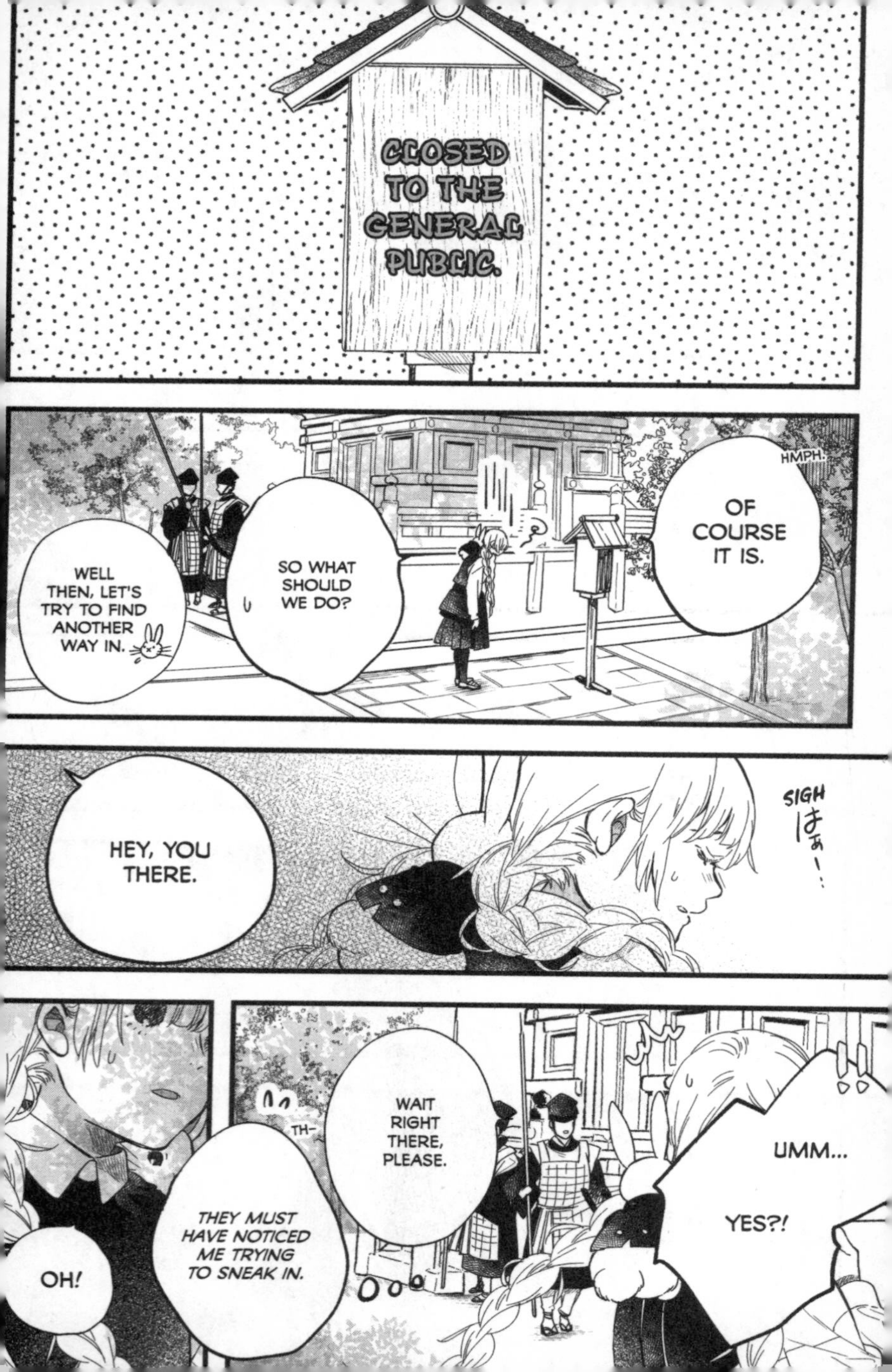
CLOSED TO THE GENERAL PUBLIC.
HMPH.
OF COURSE IT IS.
SO WHAT SHOULD WE DO?
WELL THEN, LET'S TRY TO FIND ANOTHER WAY IN.
SIGH
HEY, YOU THERE.
UMM...
YES?!
WAIT RIGHT THERE, PLEASE.
TH-
THEY MUST HAVE NOTICED ME TRYING TO SNEAK IN.
OH!

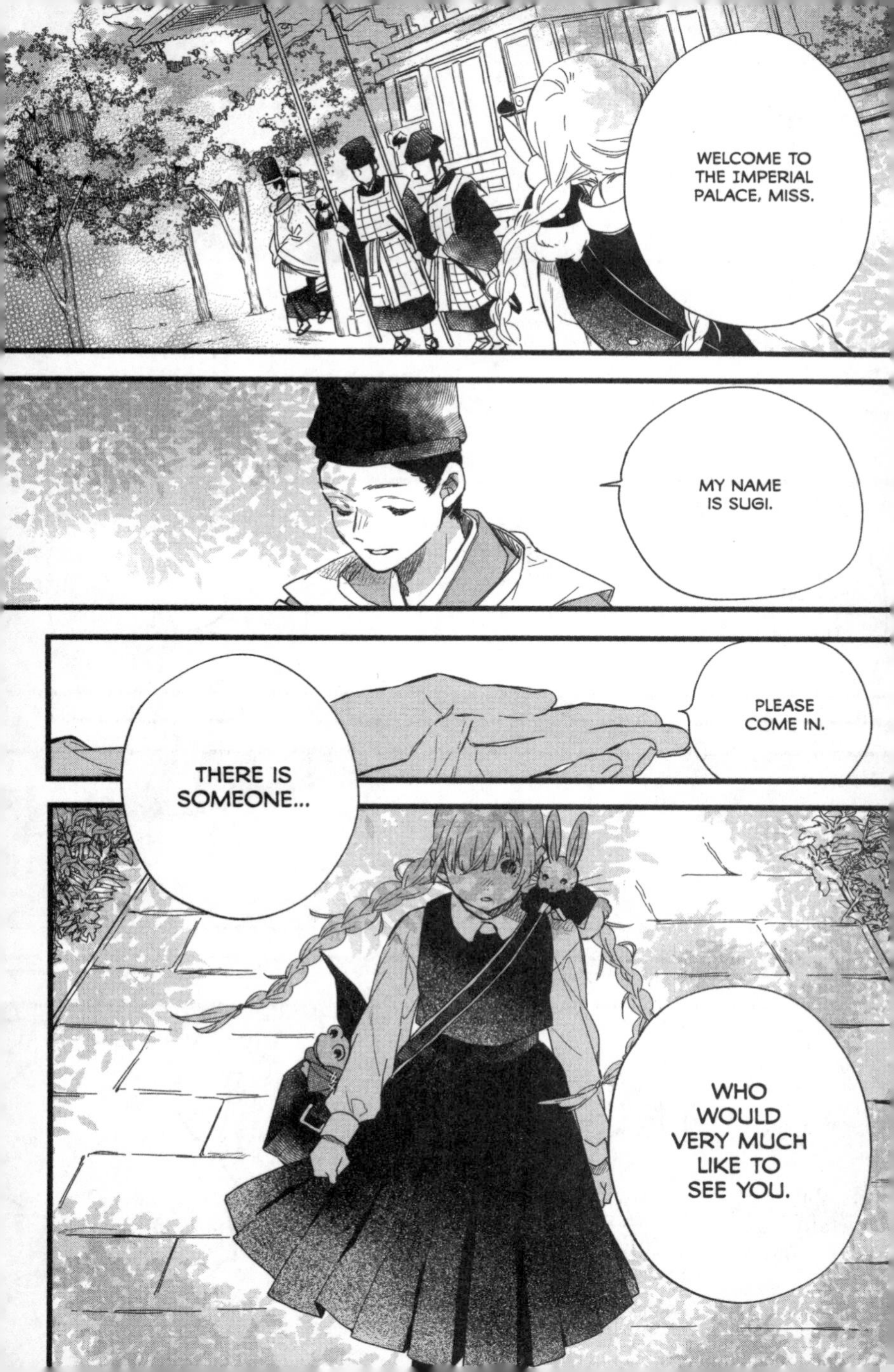
WELCOME TO THE IMPERIAL PALACE, MISS.
MY NAME IS SUGI.
PLEASE COME IN.
THERE IS SOMEONE...
WHO WOULD VERY MUCH LIKE TO SEE YOU.

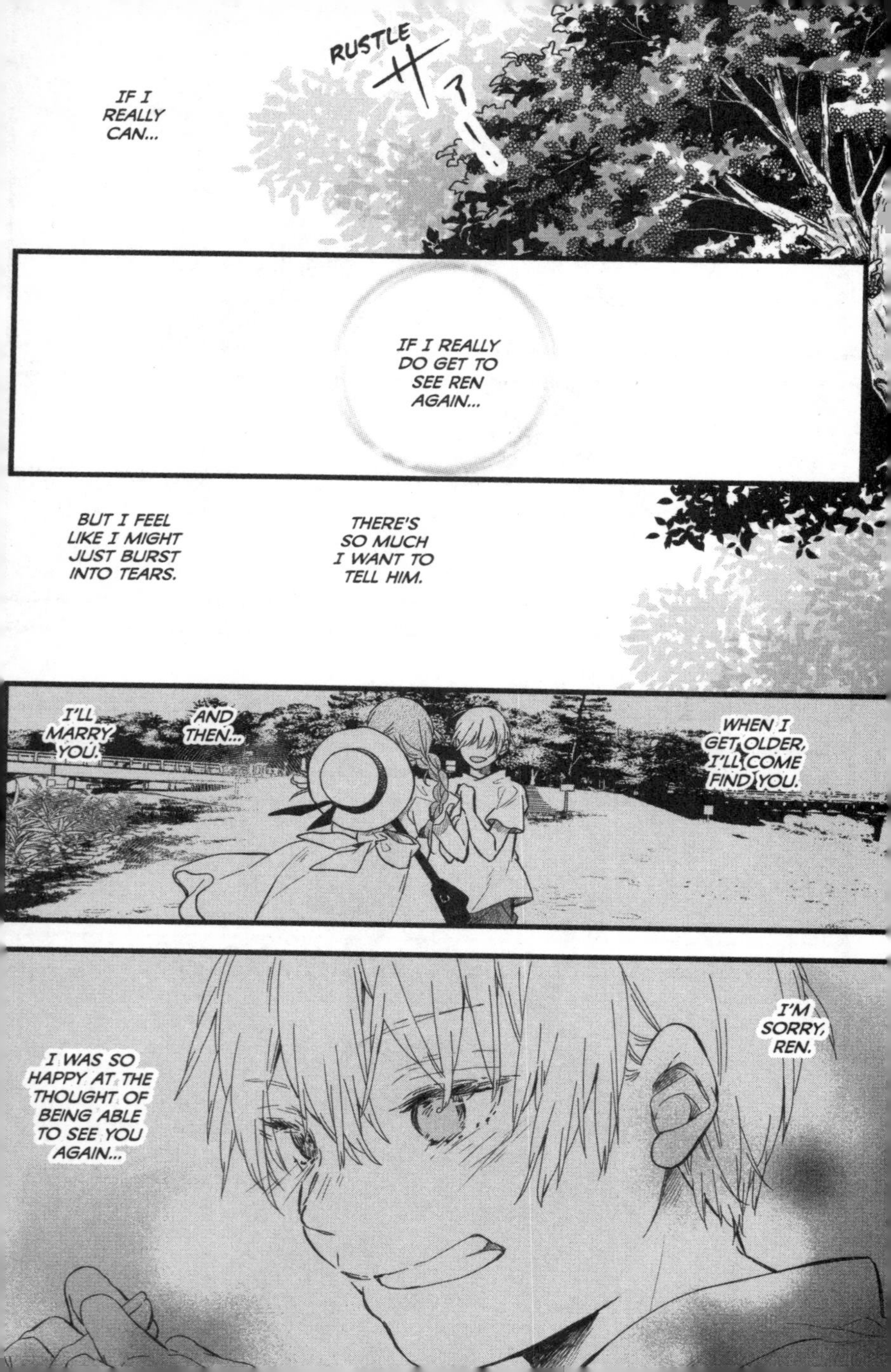
RUSTLE
IF I REALLY CAN...
IF I REALLY DO GET TO SEE REN AGAIN...
THERE'S SO MUCH I WANT TO TELL HIM.
BUT I FEEL LIKE I MIGHT JUST BURST INTO TEARS.
WHEN I GET OLDER, I'LL COME FIND YOU.
AND THEN...
I'LL MARRY YOU.
I'M SORRY, REN.
I WAS SO HAPPY AT THE THOUGHT OF BEING ABLE TO SEE YOU AGAIN...

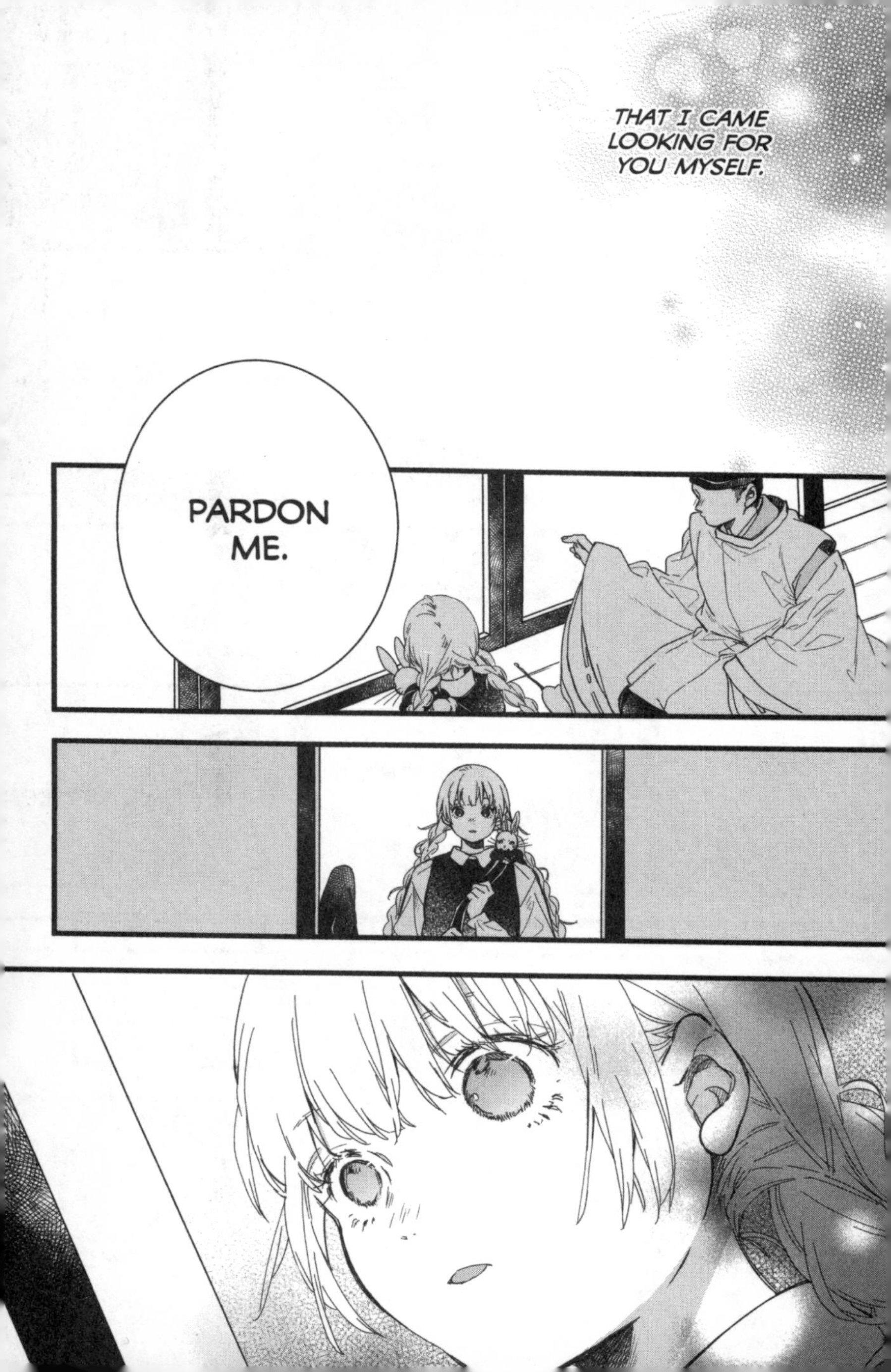
THAT I CAME LOOKING FOR YOU MYSELF.
PARDON ME.

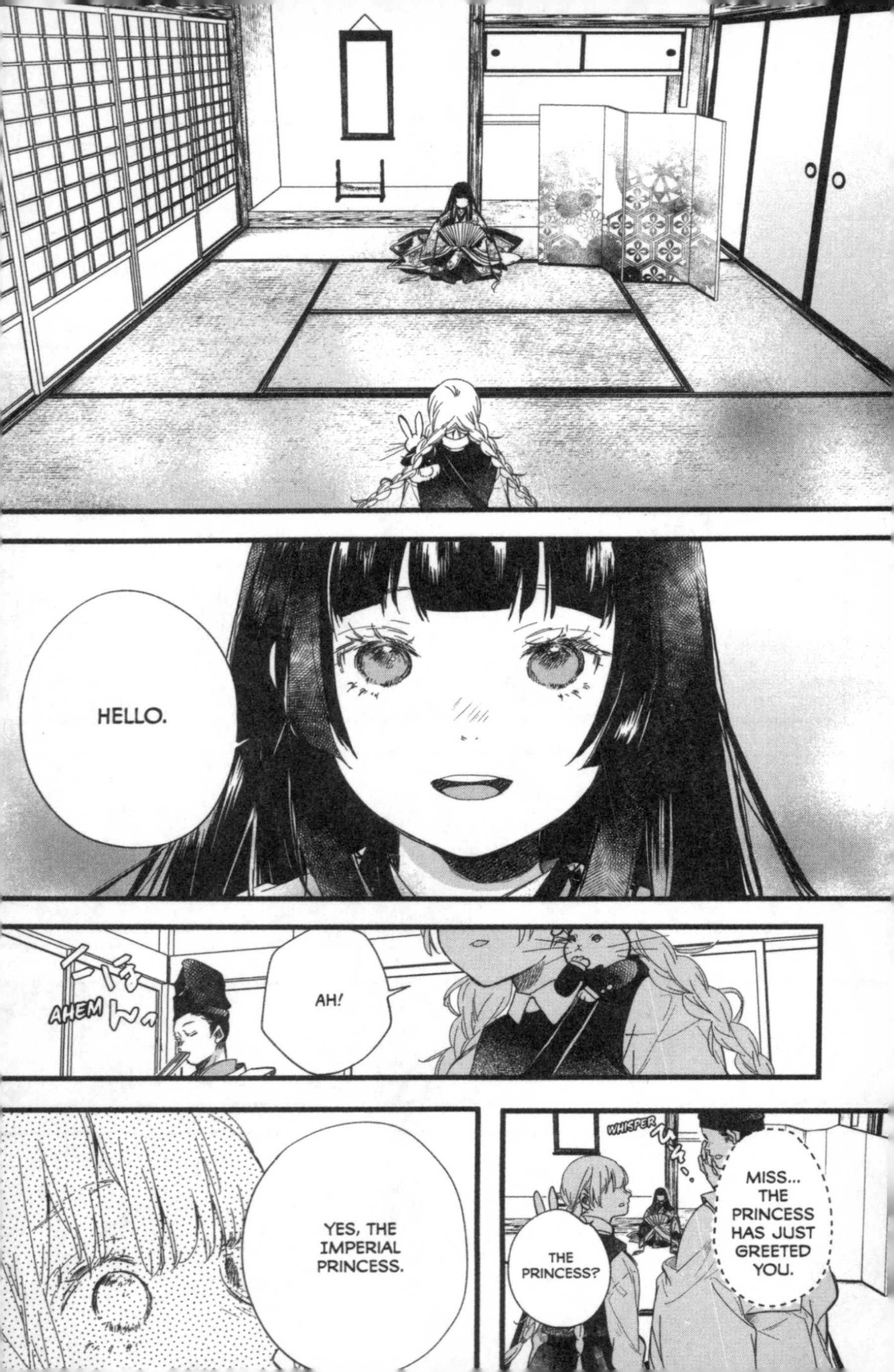
HELLO.
AH!
AHEM
WHISPER
MISS... THE PRINCESS HAS JUST GREETED YOU.
THE PRINCESS?
YES, THE IMPERIAL PRINCESS.

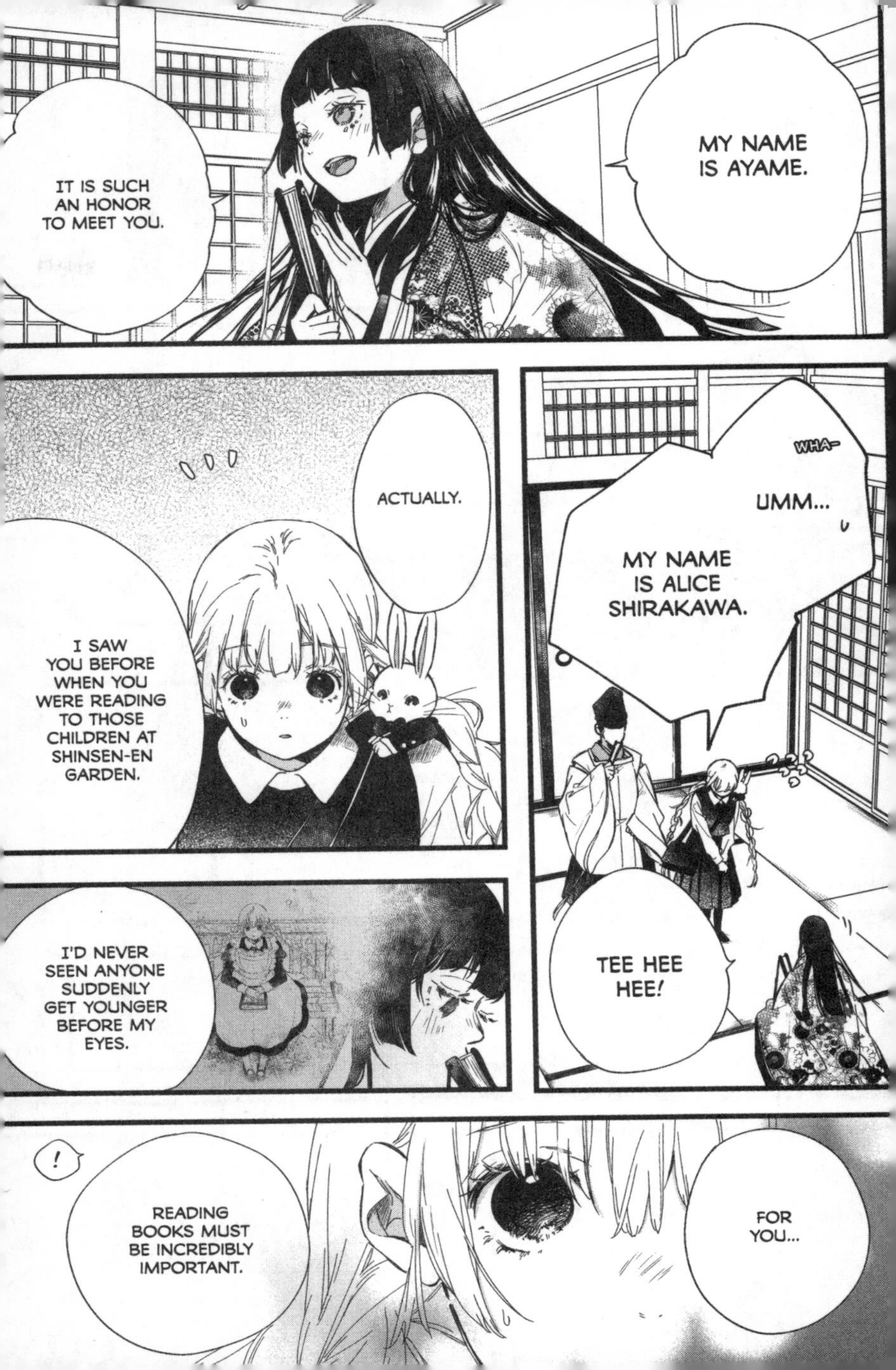
MY NAME IS AYAME.
IT IS SUCH AN HONOR TO MEET YOU.
WHA-
UMM...
MY NAME IS ALICE SHIRAKAWA.
TEE HEE HEE!
ACTUALLY.
I SAW YOU BEFORE WHEN YOU WERE READING TO THOSE CHILDREN AT SHINSEN-EN GARDEN.
I'D NEVER SEEN ANYONE SUDDENLY GET YOUNGER BEFORE MY EYES.
FOR YOU...
!
READING BOOKS MUST BE INCREDIBLY IMPORTANT.

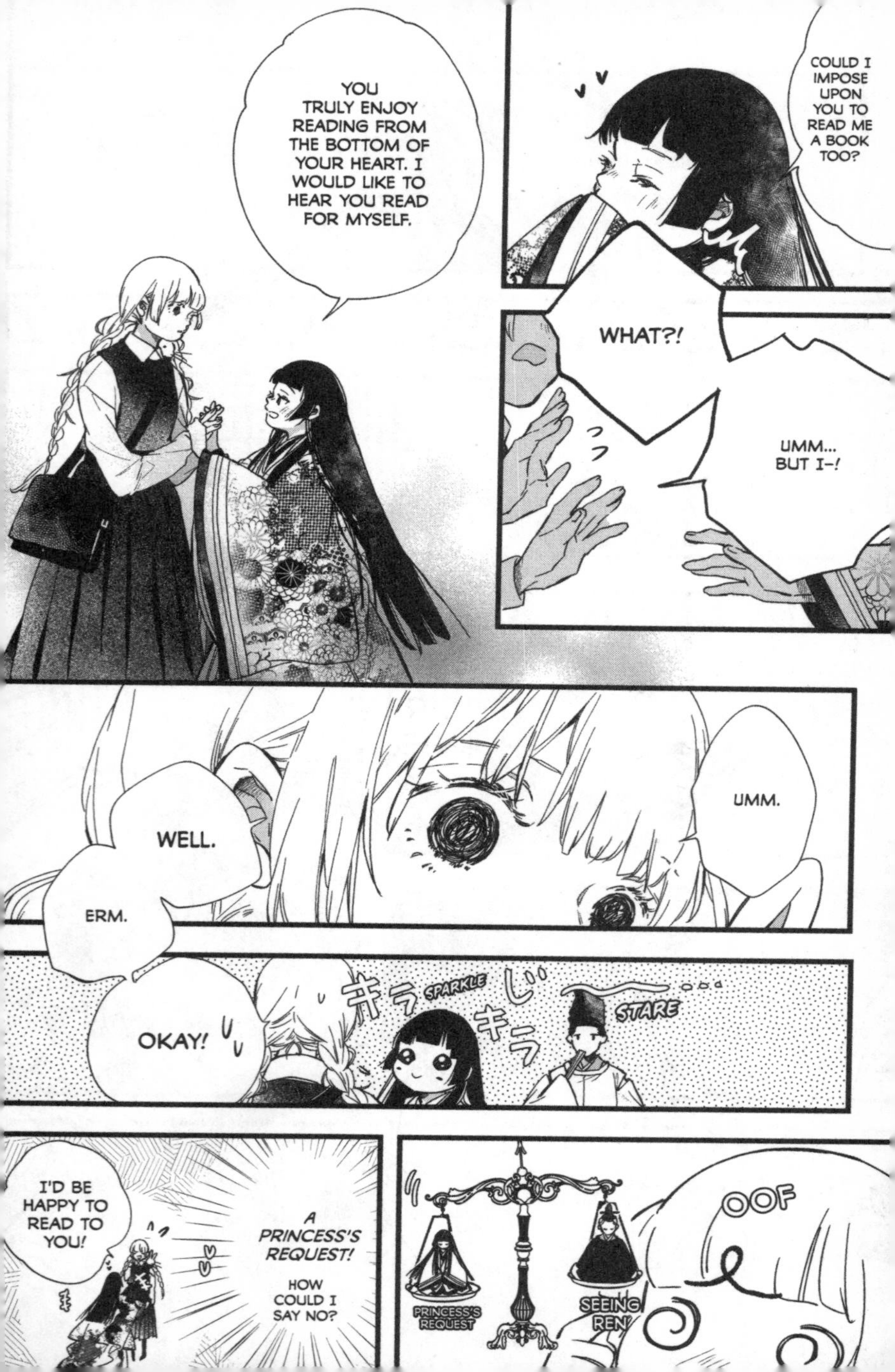
COULD I IMPOSE UPON YOU TO READ ME A BOOK TOO?
WHAT?!
UMM... BUT I–!
YOU TRULY ENJOY READING FROM THE BOTTOM OF YOUR HEART. I WOULD LIKE TO HEAR YOU READ FOR MYSELF.
UMM.
WELL.
ERM.
STARE
SPARKLE
OKAY!
OOF
SEEING REN
PRINCESS'S REQUEST
A PRINCESS'S REQUEST!
HOW COULD I SAY NO?
I'D BE HAPPY TO READ TO YOU!

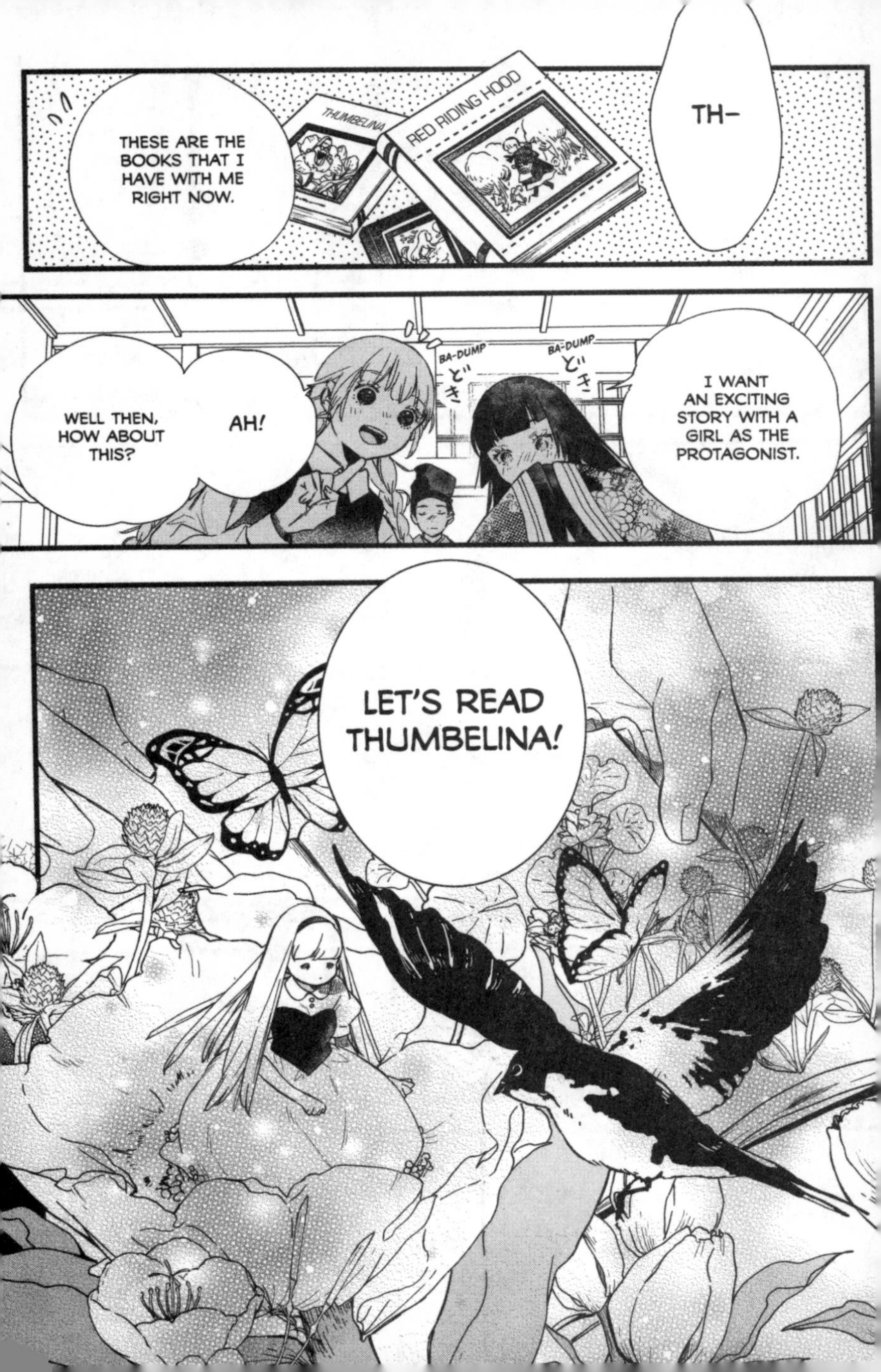
TH-
RED RIDING HOOD
THUMBELINA
THESE ARE THE BOOKS THAT I HAVE WITH ME RIGHT NOW.
I WANT AN EXCITING STORY WITH A GIRL AS THE PROTAGONIST.
BA-DUMP どき
BA-DUMP どき
AH!
WELL THEN, HOW ABOUT THIS?
LET'S READ THUMBELINA!

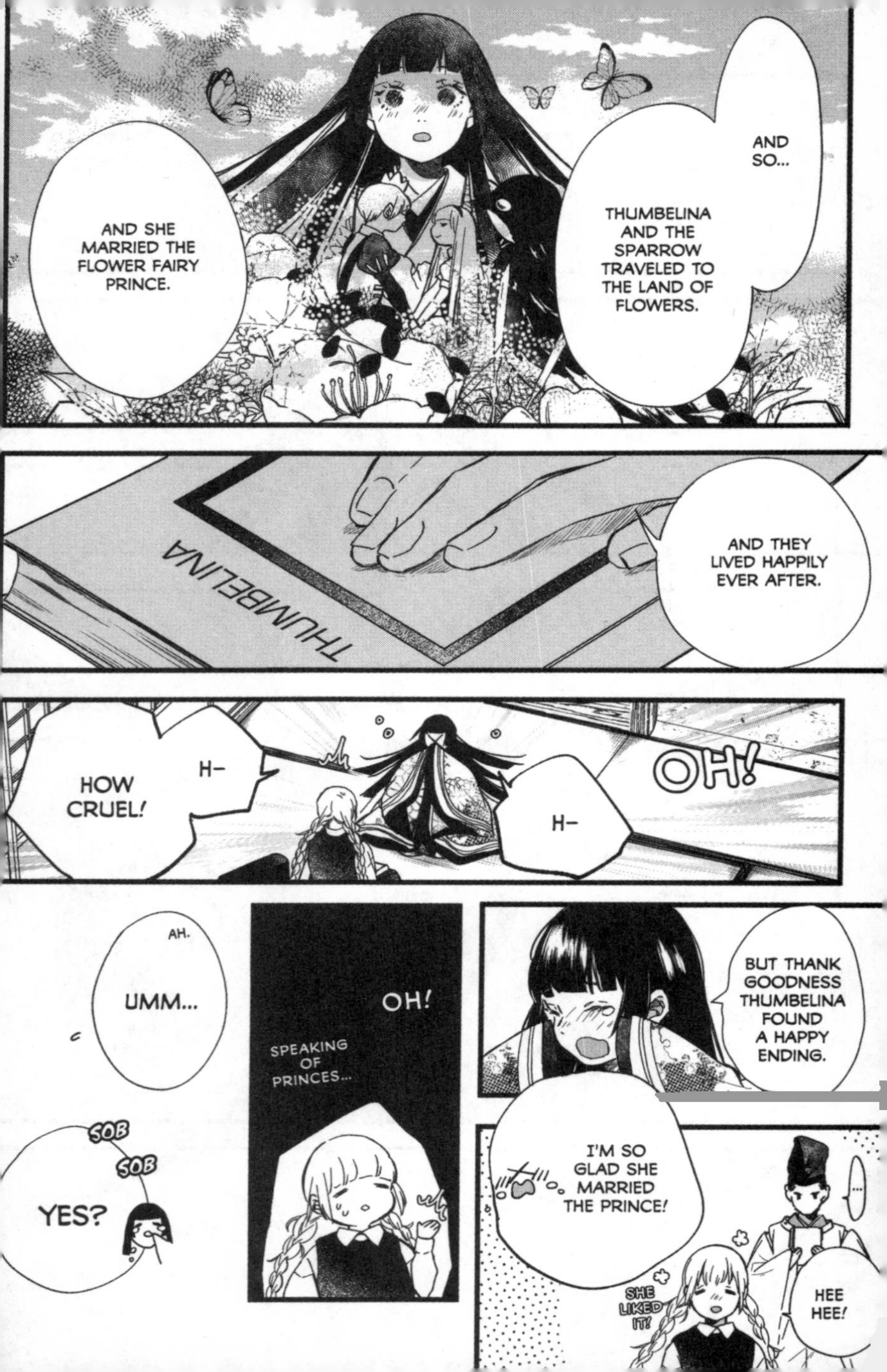
AND SO...
THUMBELINA AND THE SPARROW TRAVELED TO THE LAND OF FLOWERS.
AND SHE MARRIED THE FLOWER FAIRY PRINCE.
AND THEY LIVED HAPPILY EVER AFTER.
THUMBELINA
OH!
H-
H-
HOW CRUEL!
BUT THANK GOODNESS THUMBELINA FOUND A HAPPY ENDING.
I'M SO GLAD SHE MARRIED THE PRINCE!
...
HEE HEE!
SHE LIKED IT!
OH!
SPEAKING OF PRINCES...
AH.
UMM...
SOB
SOB
YES?

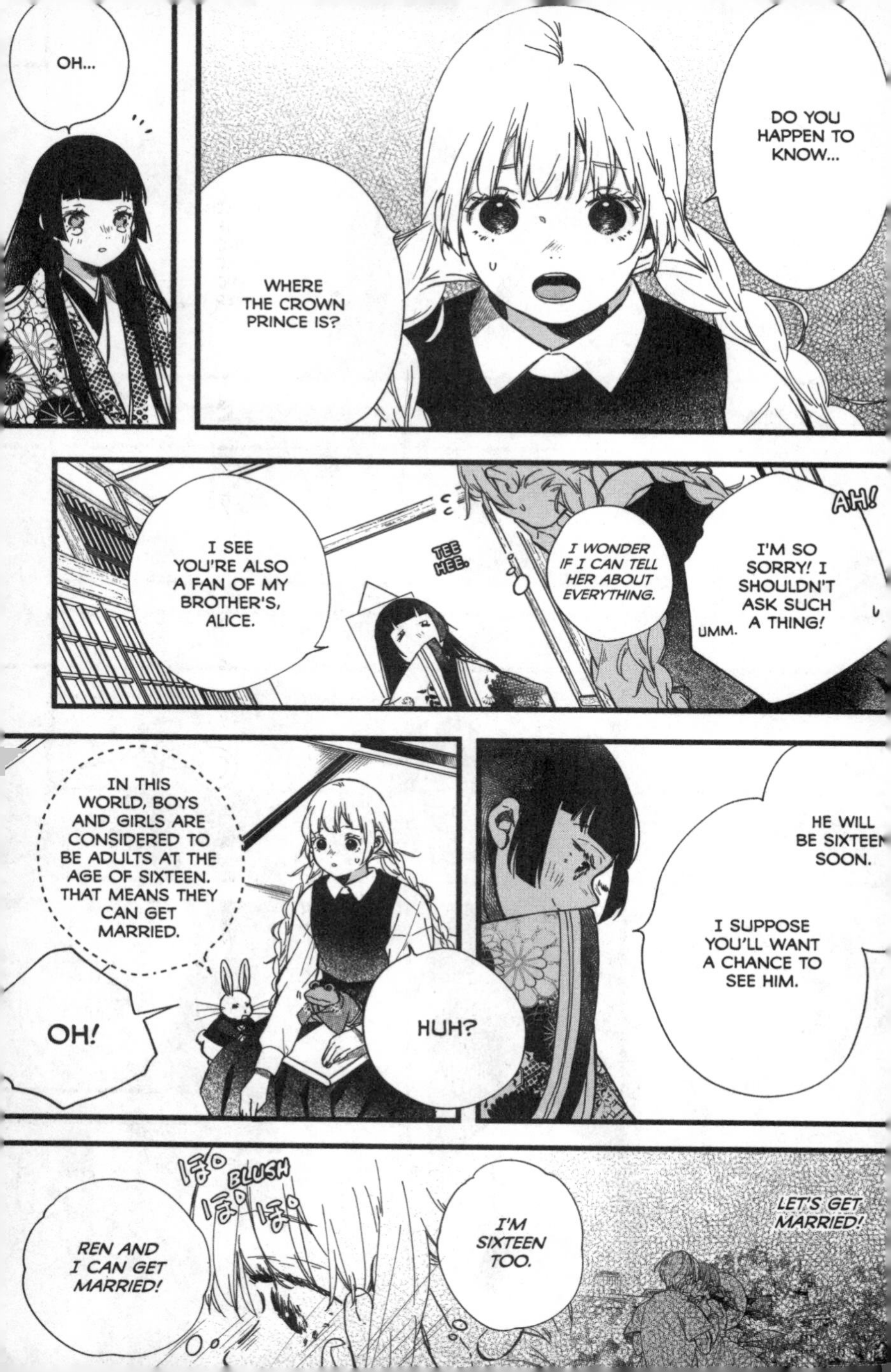
DO YOU HAPPEN TO KNOW...
WHERE THE CROWN PRINCE IS?
OH...
AH!
I'M SO SORRY! I SHOULDN'T ASK SUCH A THING!
UMM.
I WONDER IF I CAN TELL HER ABOUT EVERYTHING.
TEE HEE.
I SEE YOU'RE ALSO A FAN OF MY BROTHER'S, ALICE.
HE WILL BE SIXTEEN SOON.
I SUPPOSE YOU'LL WANT A CHANCE TO SEE HIM.
HUH?
IN THIS WORLD, BOYS AND GIRLS ARE CONSIDERED TO BE ADULTS AT THE AGE OF SIXTEEN. THAT MEANS THEY CAN GET MARRIED.
OH!
LET'S GET MARRIED!
I'M SIXTEEN TOO.
BLUSH
REN AND I CAN GET MARRIED!

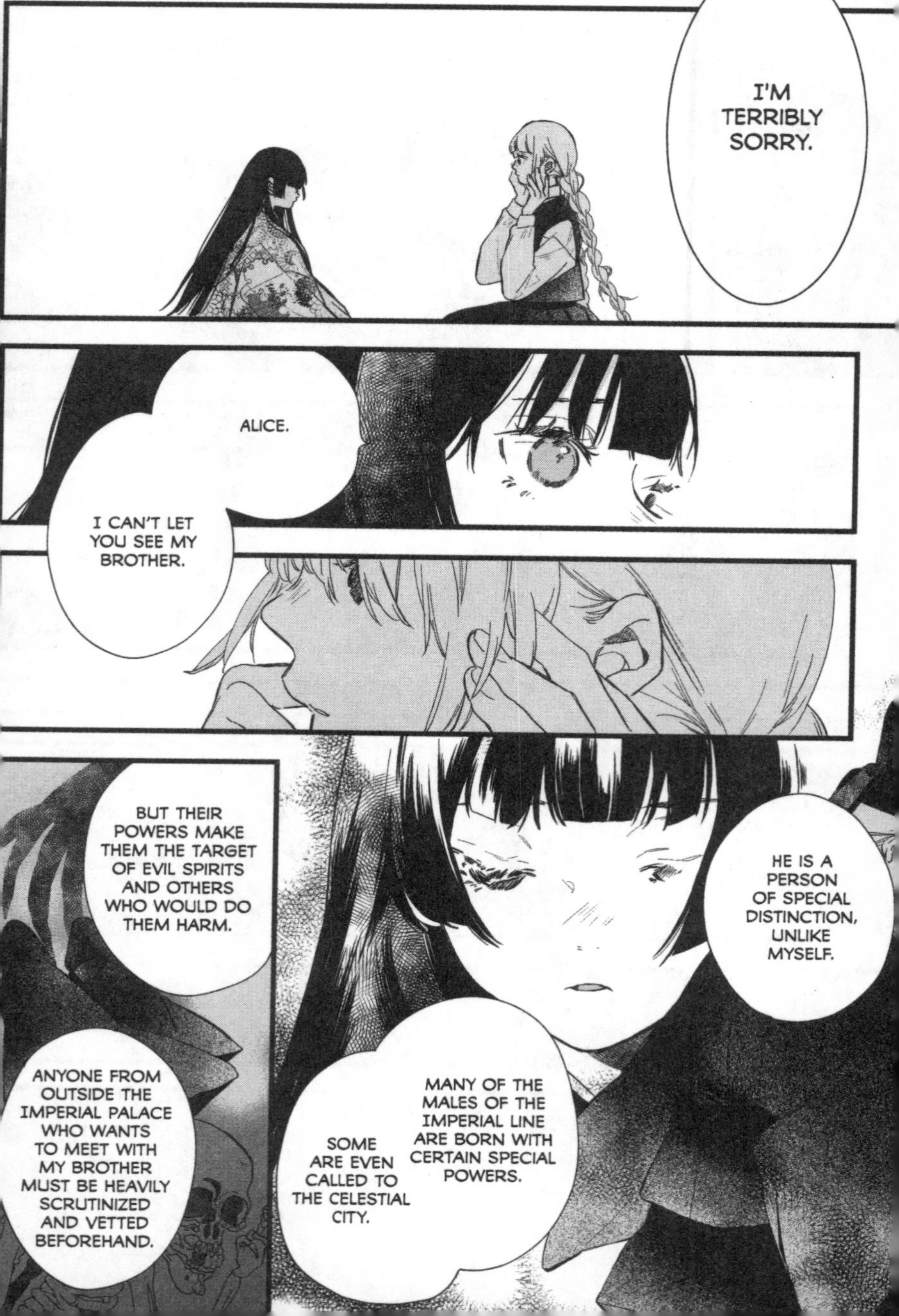
I'M TERRIBLY SORRY.
ALICE.
I CAN'T LET YOU SEE MY BROTHER.
HE IS A PERSON OF SPECIAL DISTINCTION, UNLIKE MYSELF.
MANY OF THE MALES OF THE IMPERIAL LINE ARE BORN WITH CERTAIN SPECIAL POWERS.
SOME ARE EVEN CALLED TO THE CELESTIAL CITY.
BUT THEIR POWERS MAKE THEM THE TARGET OF EVIL SPIRITS AND OTHERS WHO WOULD DO THEM HARM.
ANYONE FROM OUTSIDE THE IMPERIAL PALACE WHO WANTS TO MEET WITH MY BROTHER MUST BE HEAVILY SCRUTINIZED AND VETTED BEFOREHAND.

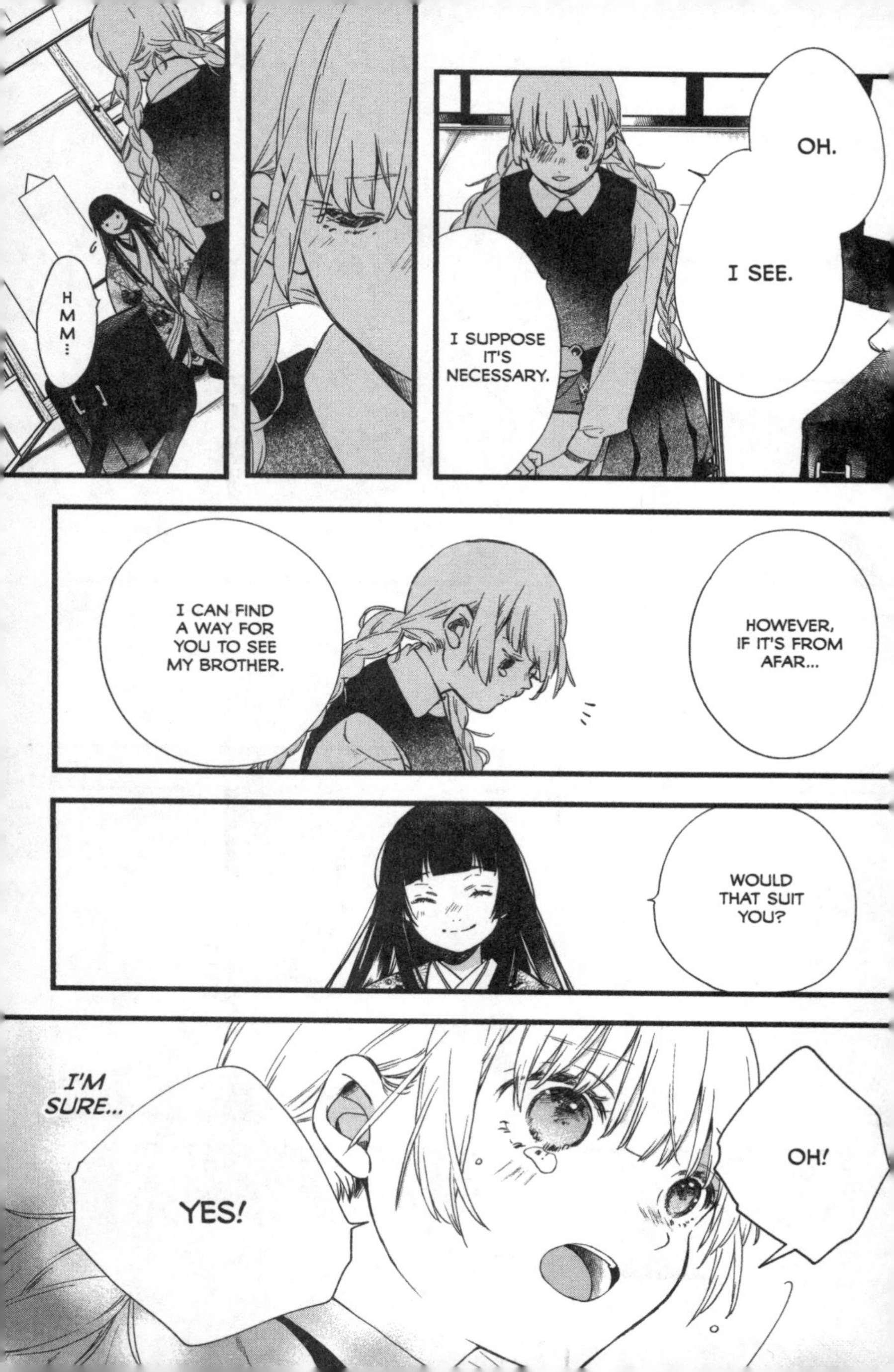
OH.
I SEE.
I SUPPOSE IT'S NECESSARY.
HMM...
HOWEVER, IF IT'S FROM AFAR...
I CAN FIND A WAY FOR YOU TO SEE MY BROTHER.
WOULD THAT SUIT YOU?
OH!
I'M SURE...
YES!

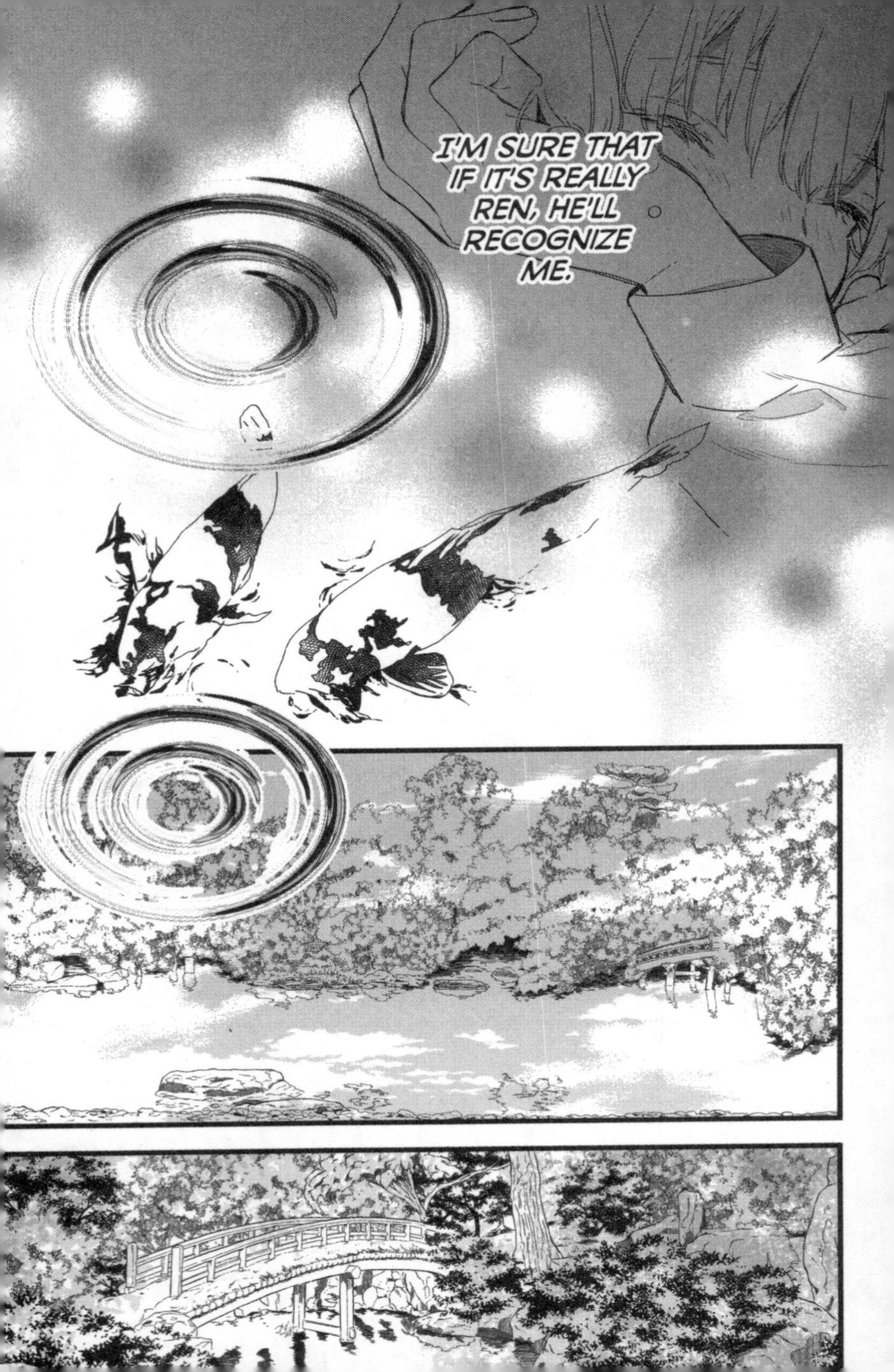
I'M SURE THAT IF IT'S REALLY REN, HE'LL RECOGNIZE ME.

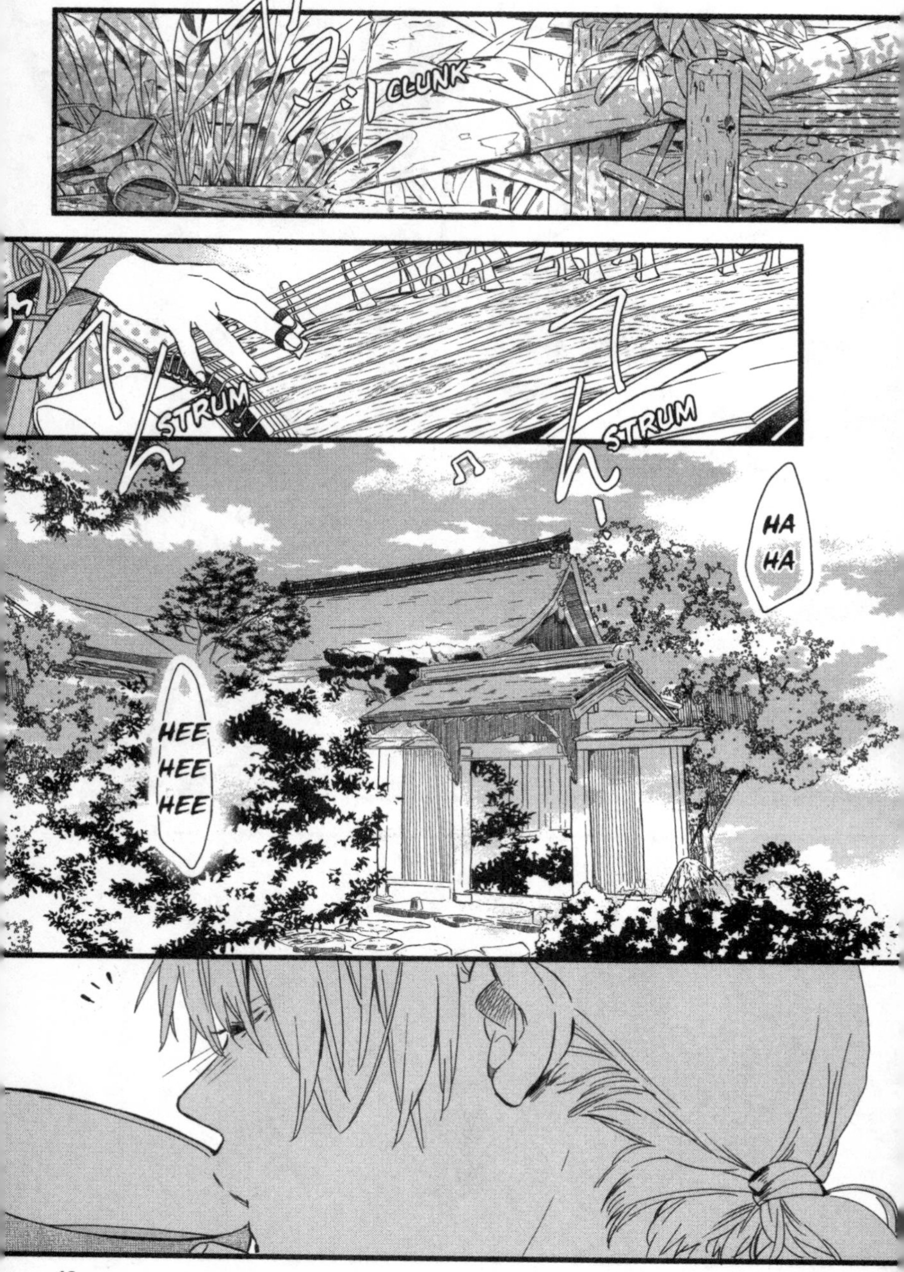
CLUNK
STRUM
STRUM
HA HA
HEE HEE HEE

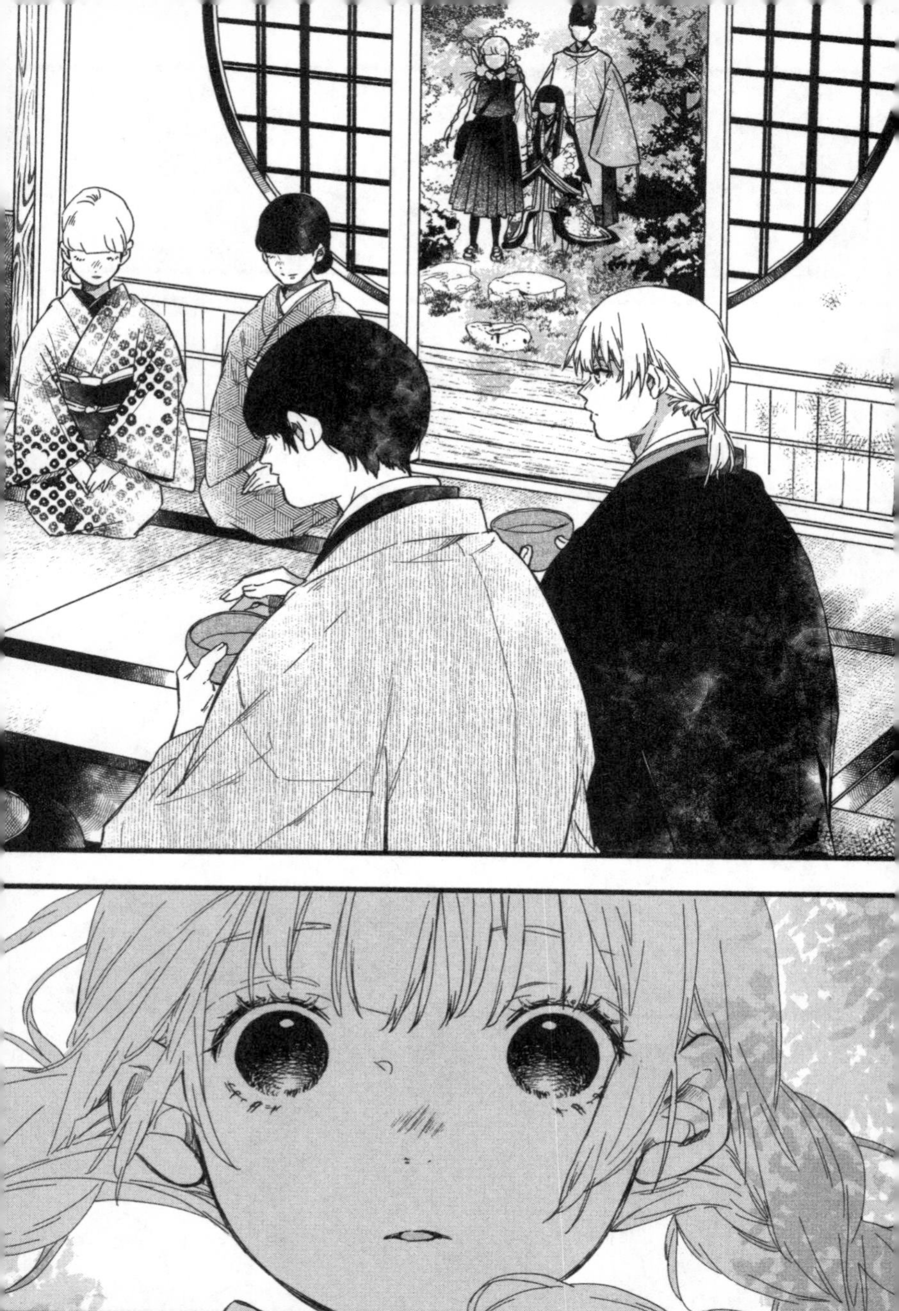

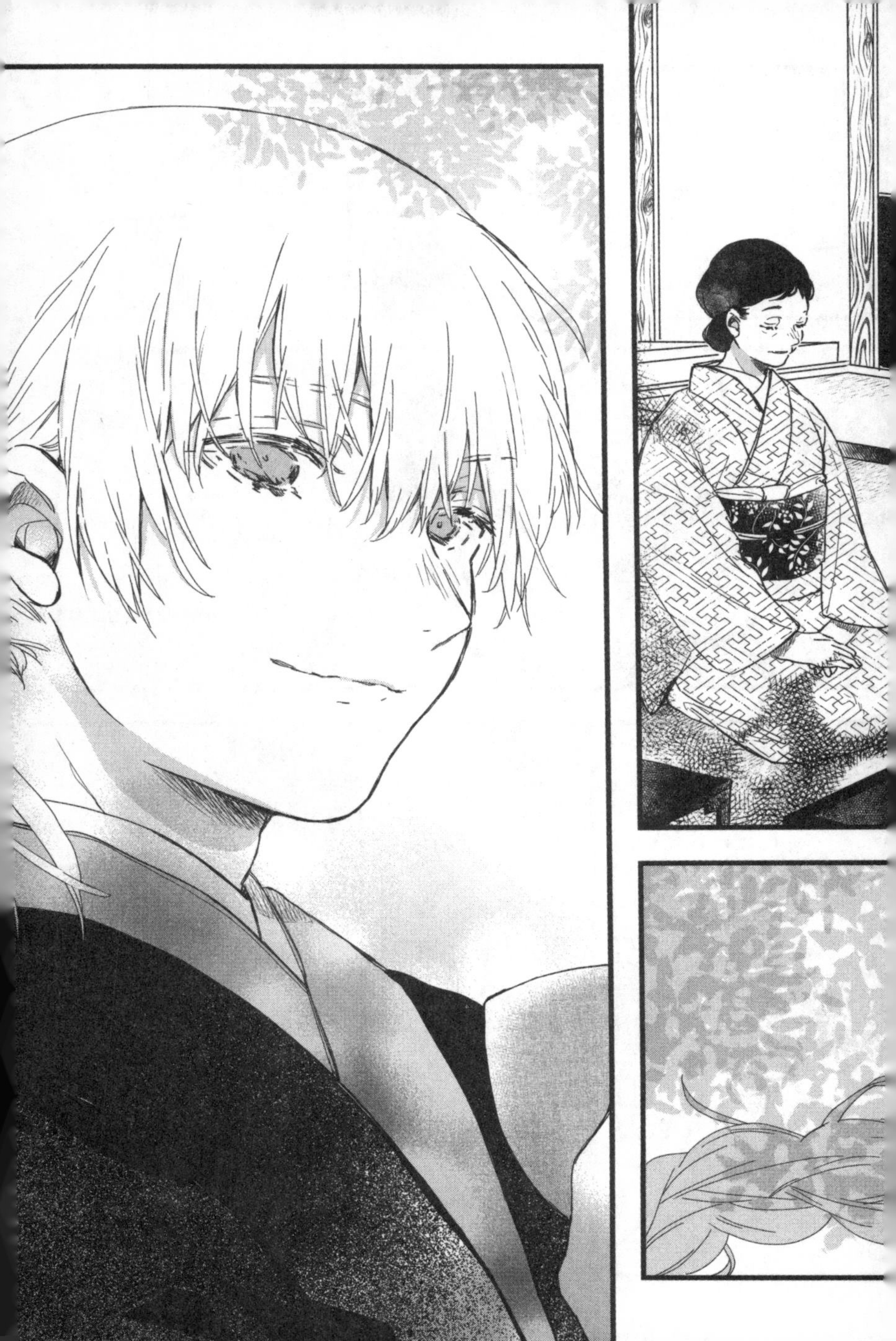

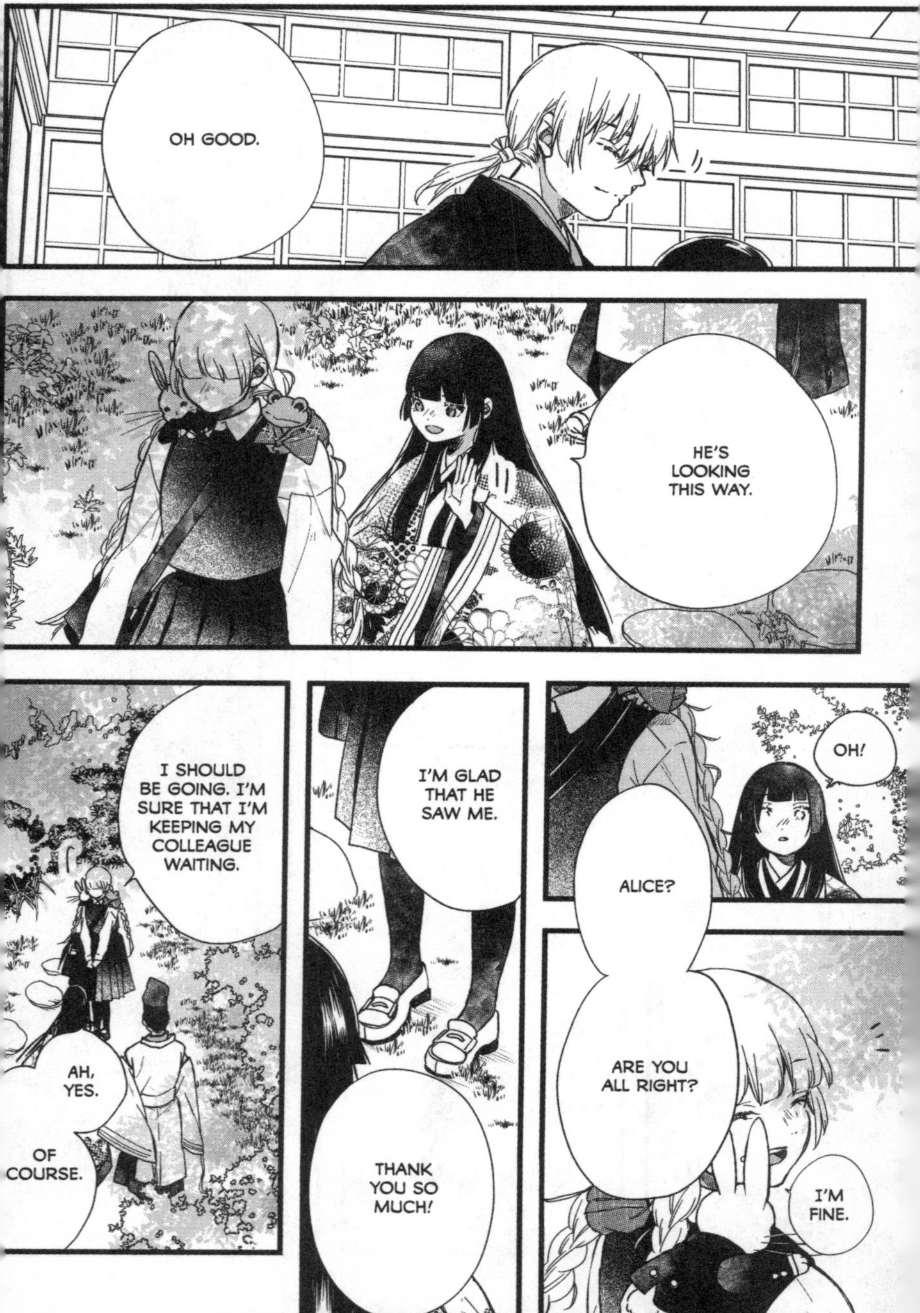
OH GOOD.
HE'S LOOKING THIS WAY.
OH!
ALICE?
ARE YOU ALL RIGHT?
I'M FINE.
I'M GLAD THAT HE SAW ME.
THANK YOU SO MUCH!
I SHOULD BE GOING. I'M SURE THAT I'M KEEPING MY COLLEAGUE WAITING.
AH, YES.
OF COURSE.

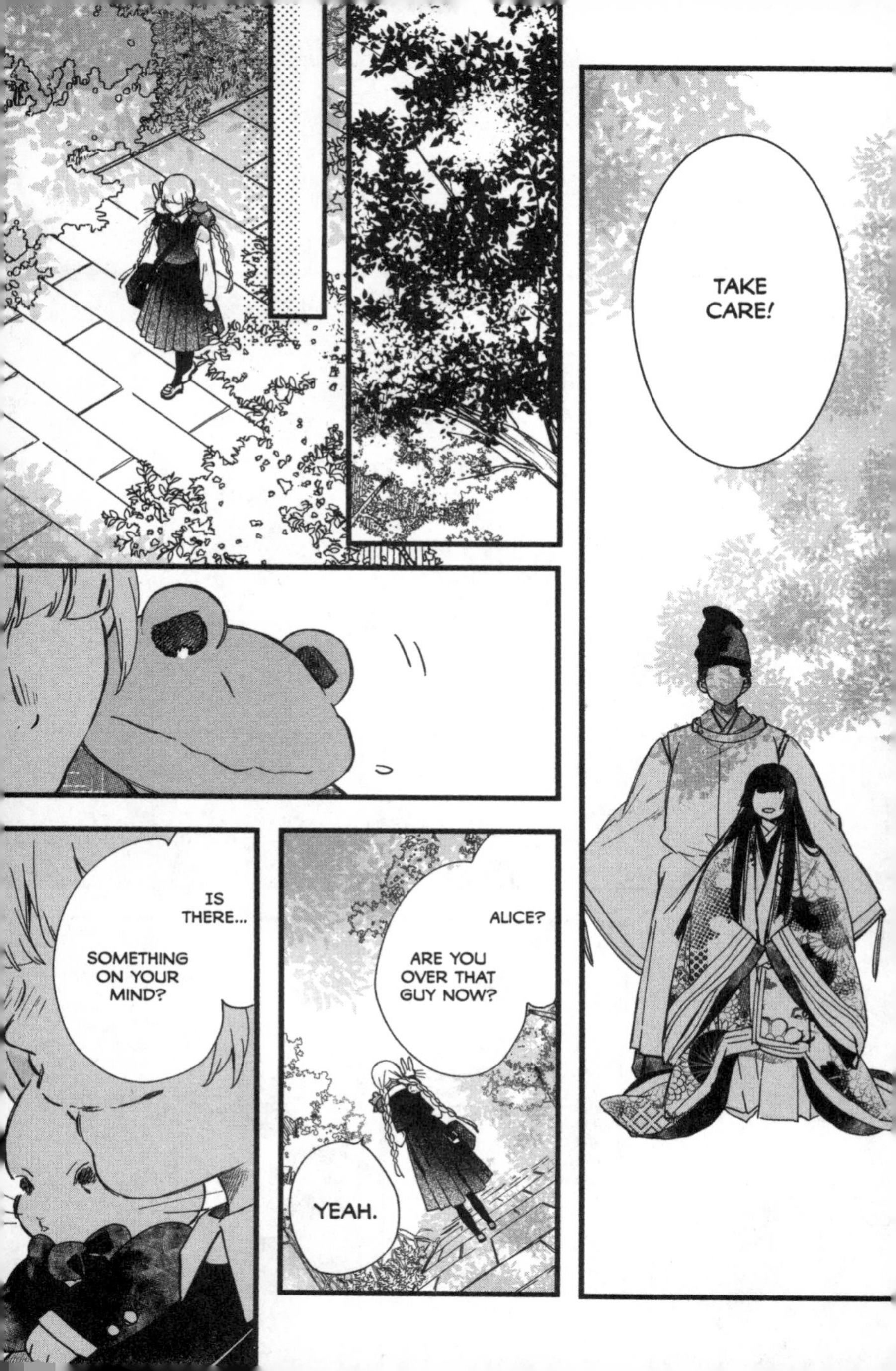
TAKE CARE!
ALICE?
ARE YOU OVER THAT GUY NOW?
YEAH.
IS THERE...
SOMETHING ON YOUR MIND?

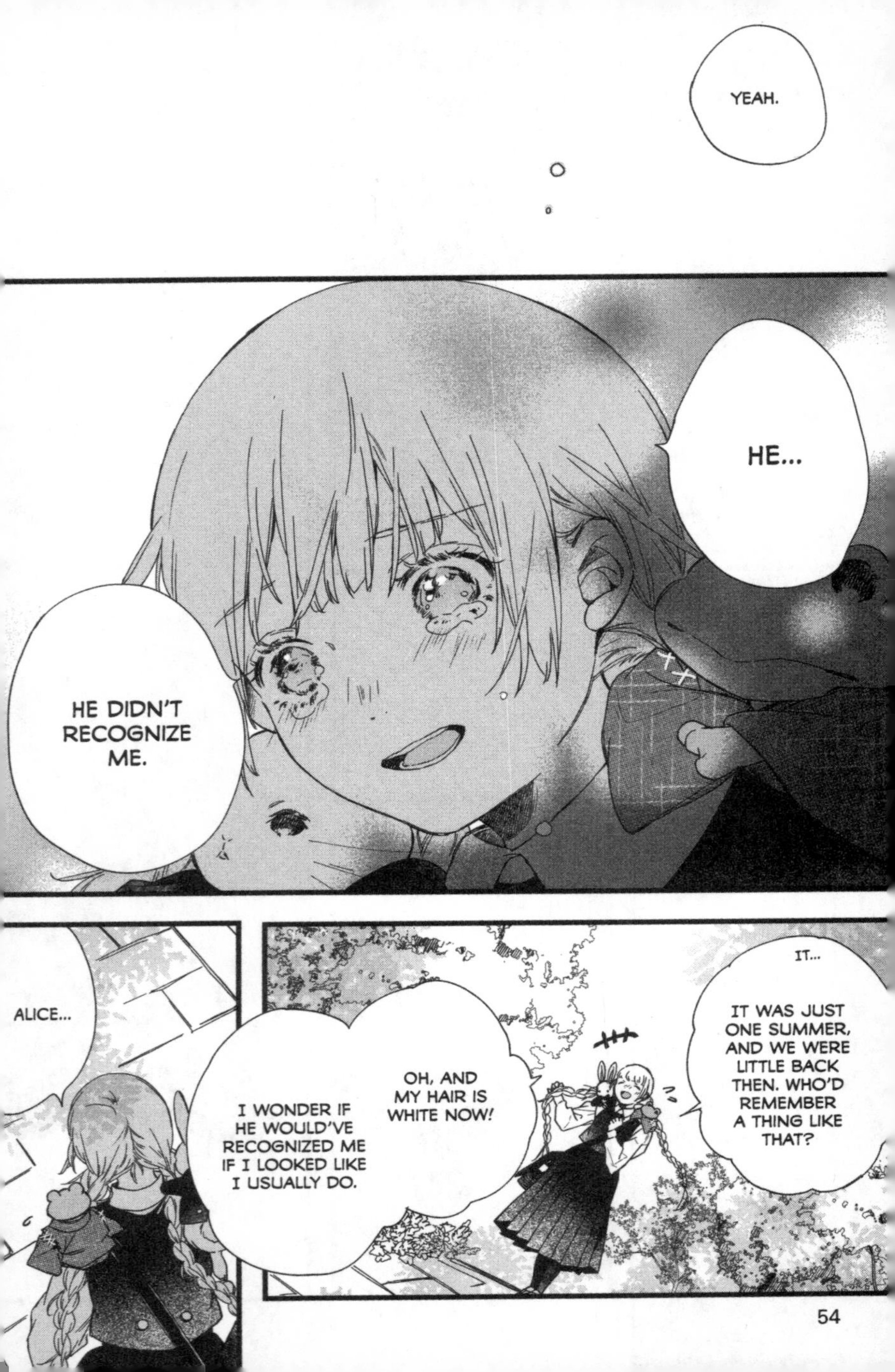
YEAH.
HE...
HE DIDN'T RECOGNIZE ME.
IT...
IT WAS JUST ONE SUMMER, AND WE WERE LITTLE BACK THEN. WHO'D REMEMBER A THING LIKE THAT?
OH, AND MY HAIR IS WHITE NOW!
I WONDER IF HE WOULD'VE RECOGNIZED ME IF I LOOKED LIKE I USUALLY DO.
ALICE...

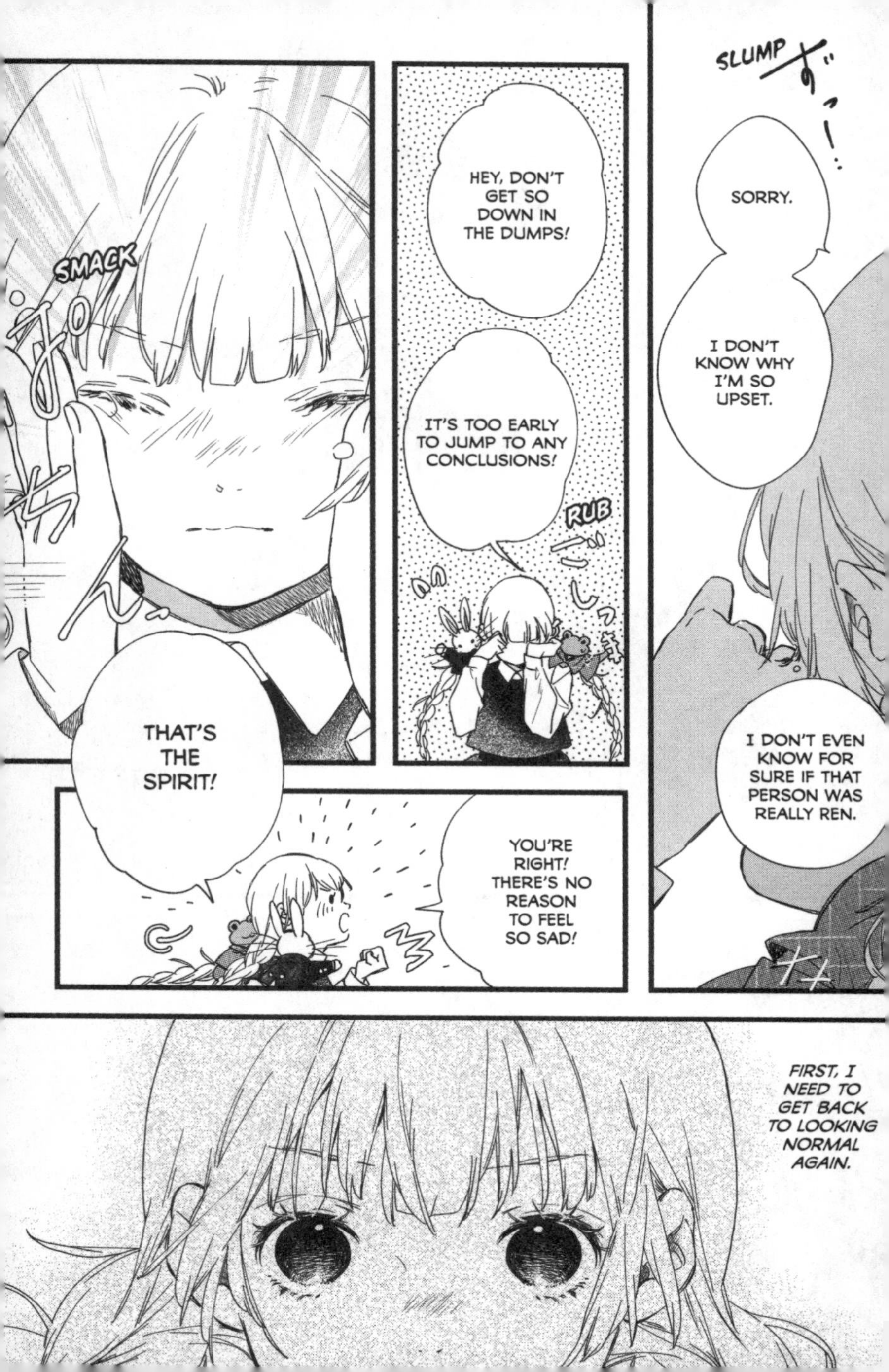
SLUMP
SORRY.
I DON'T KNOW WHY I'M SO UPSET.
I DON'T EVEN KNOW FOR SURE IF THAT PERSON WAS REALLY REN.
HEY, DON'T GET SO DOWN IN THE DUMPS!
IT'S TOO EARLY TO JUMP TO ANY CONCLUSIONS!
RUB
SMACK
YOU'RE RIGHT! THERE'S NO REASON TO FEEL SO SAD!
THAT'S THE SPIRIT!
FIRST, I NEED TO GET BACK TO LOOKING NORMAL AGAIN.

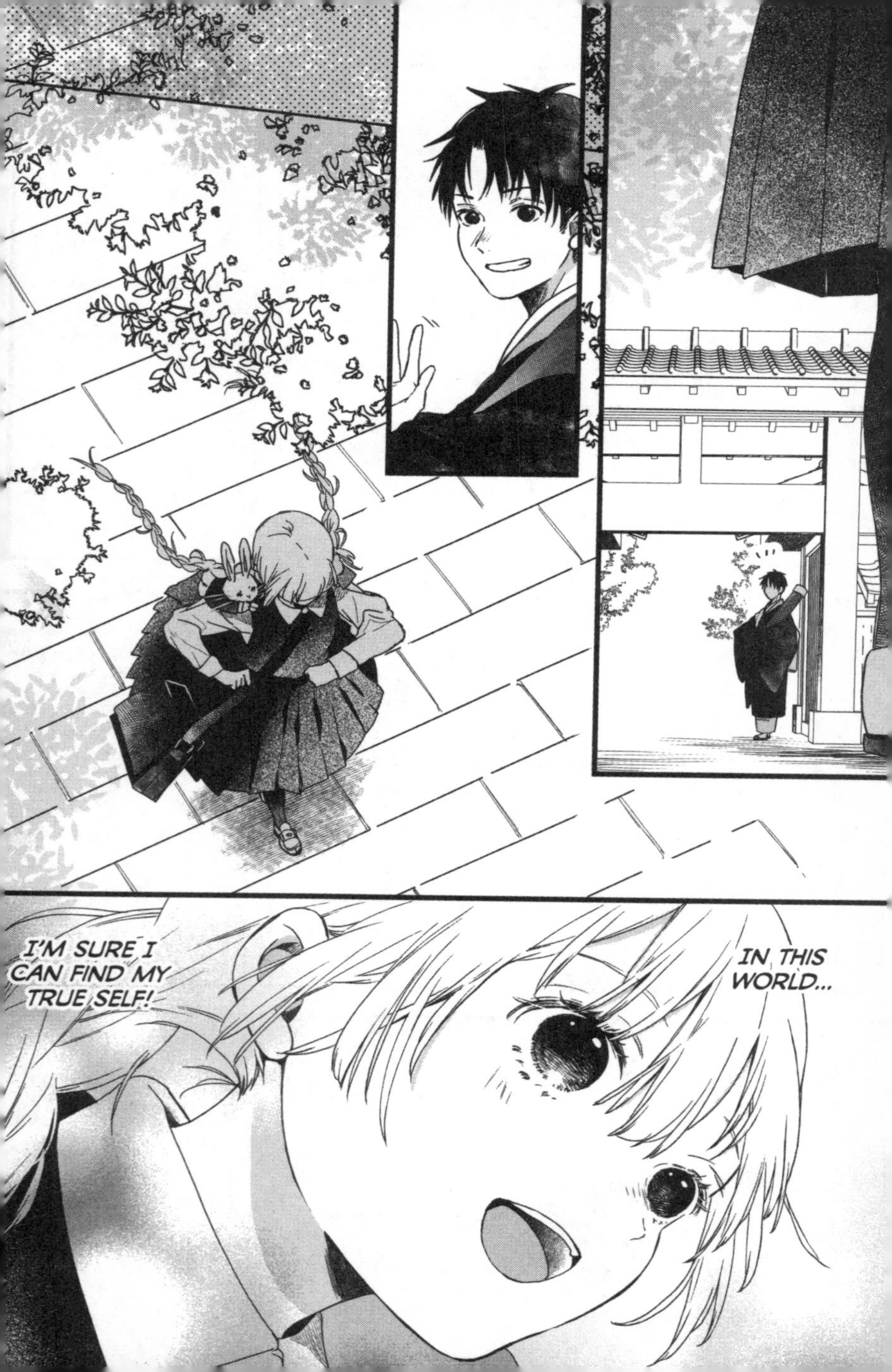
IN THIS WORLD...
I'M SURE I CAN FIND MY TRUE SELF!

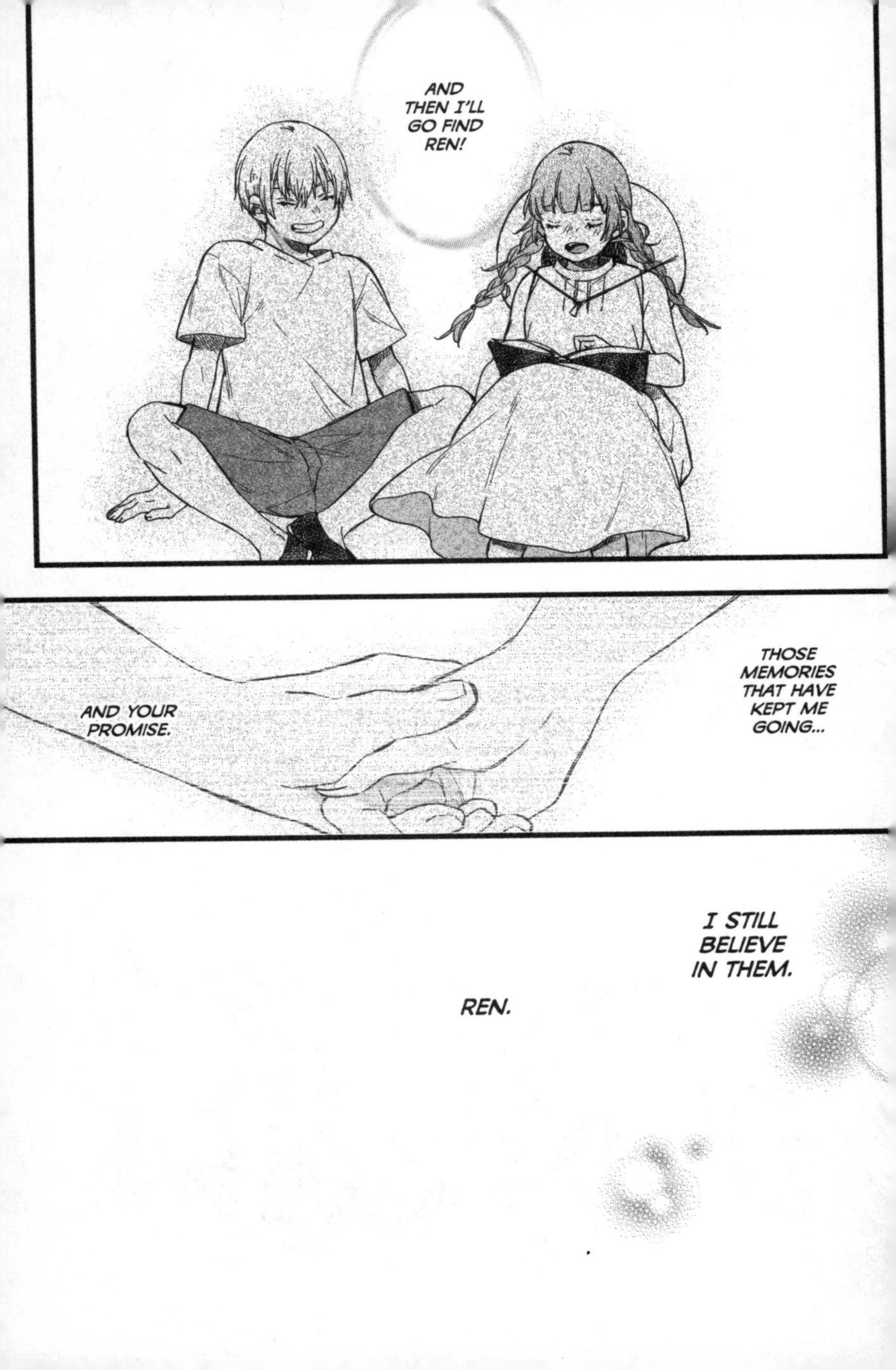
AND THEN I'LL GO FIND REN!
THOSE MEMORIES THAT HAVE KEPT ME GOING...
AND YOUR PROMISE.
I STILL BELIEVE IN THEM.
REN.

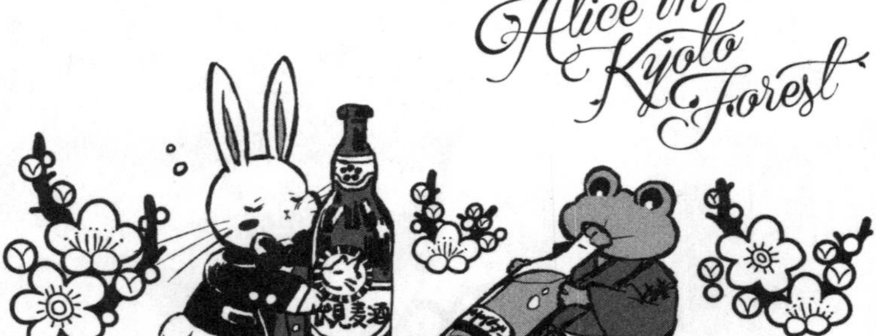
Alice in Kyoto Forest
伏見麦酒

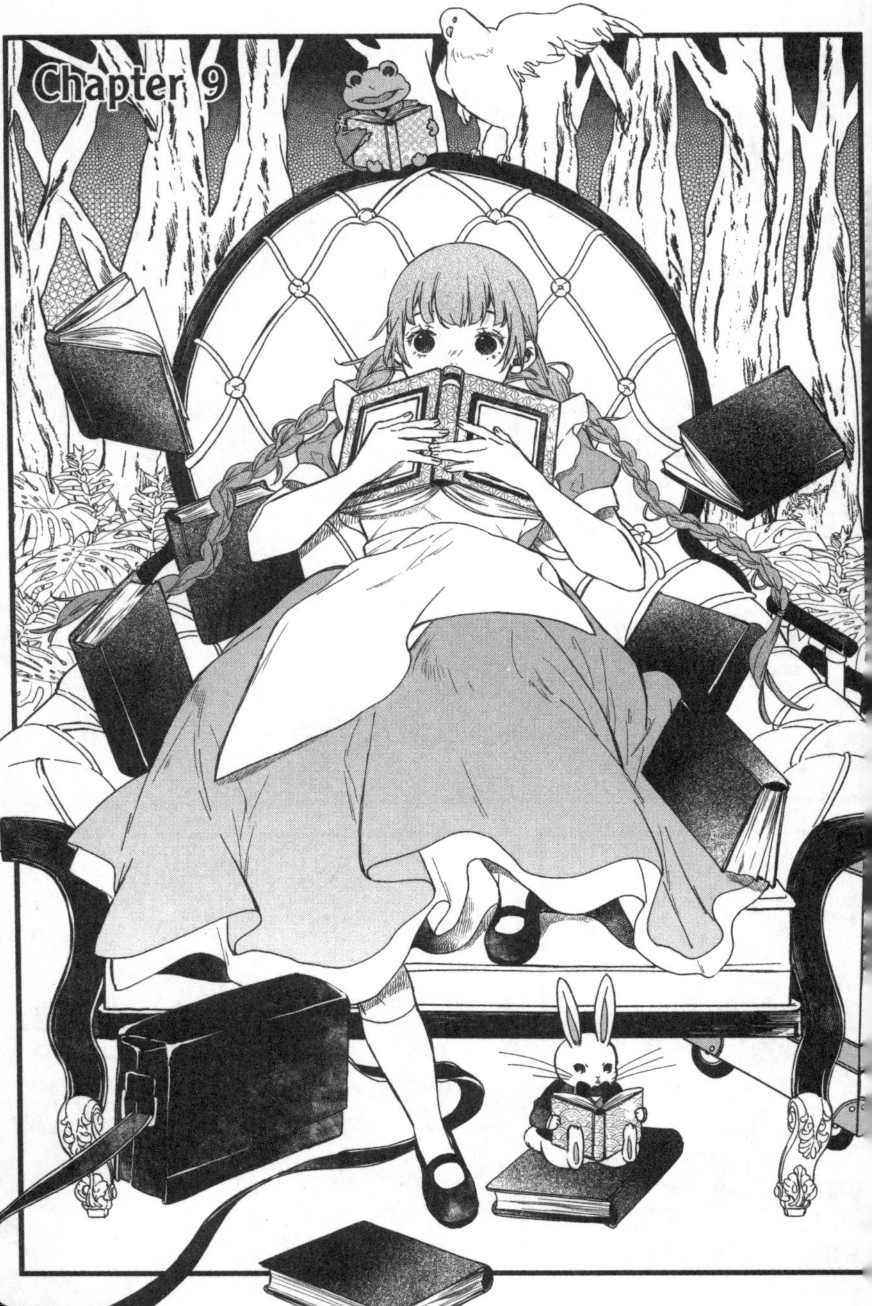
Chapter 9

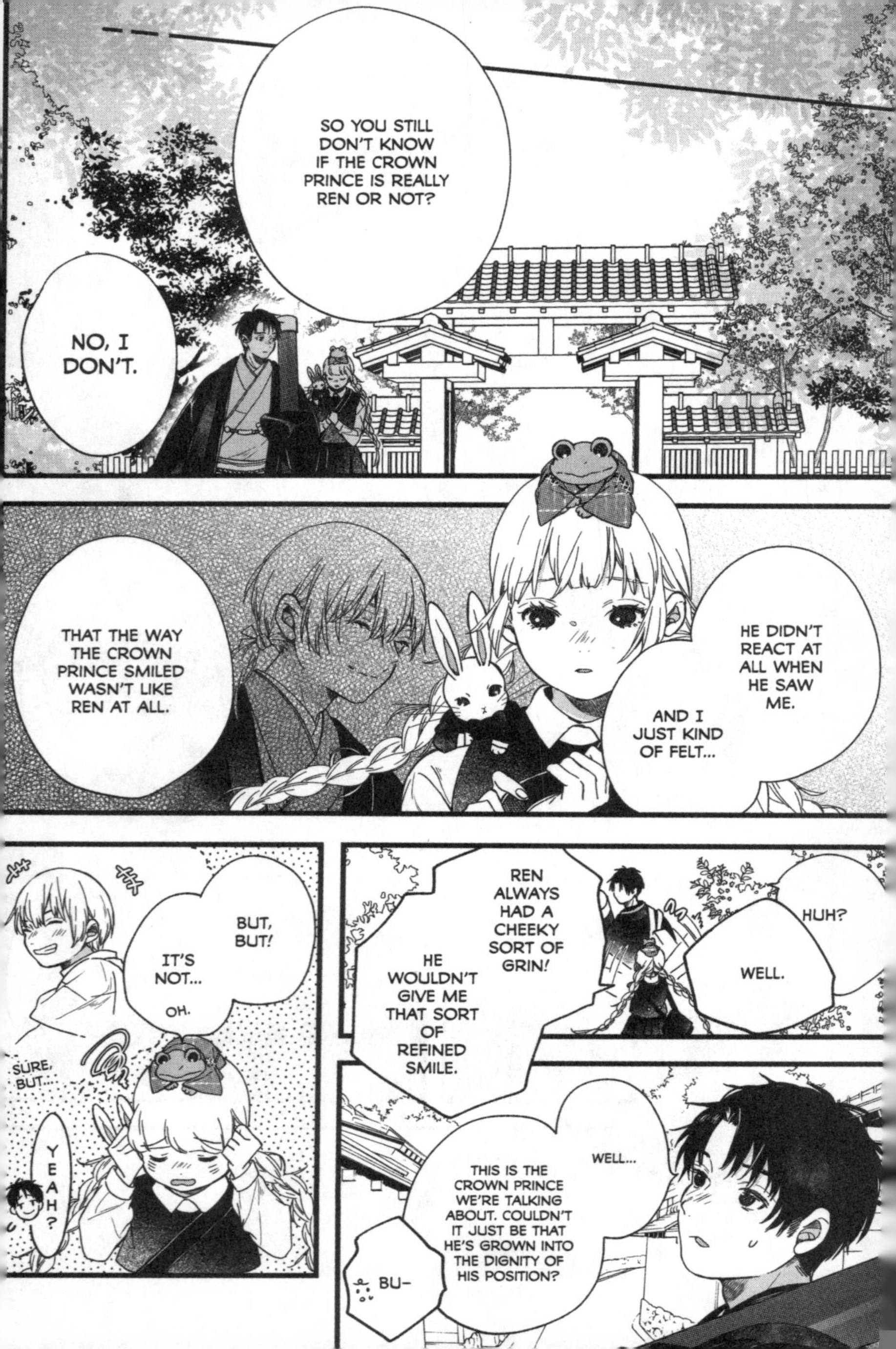
SO YOU STILL DON'T KNOW IF THE CROWN PRINCE IS REALLY REN OR NOT?
NO, I DON'T.
HE DIDN'T REACT AT ALL WHEN HE SAW ME.
AND I JUST KIND OF FELT...
THAT THE WAY THE CROWN PRINCE SMILED WASN'T LIKE REN AT ALL.
HUH?
WELL.
REN ALWAYS HAD A CHEEKY SORT OF GRIN!
HE WOULDN'T GIVE ME THAT SORT OF REFINED SMILE.
WELL...
THIS IS THE CROWN PRINCE WE'RE TALKING ABOUT. COULDN'T IT JUST BE THAT HE'S GROWN INTO THE DIGNITY OF HIS POSITION?
BU–
BUT, BUT!
IT'S NOT...
OH.
SURE, BUT...
YEAH?

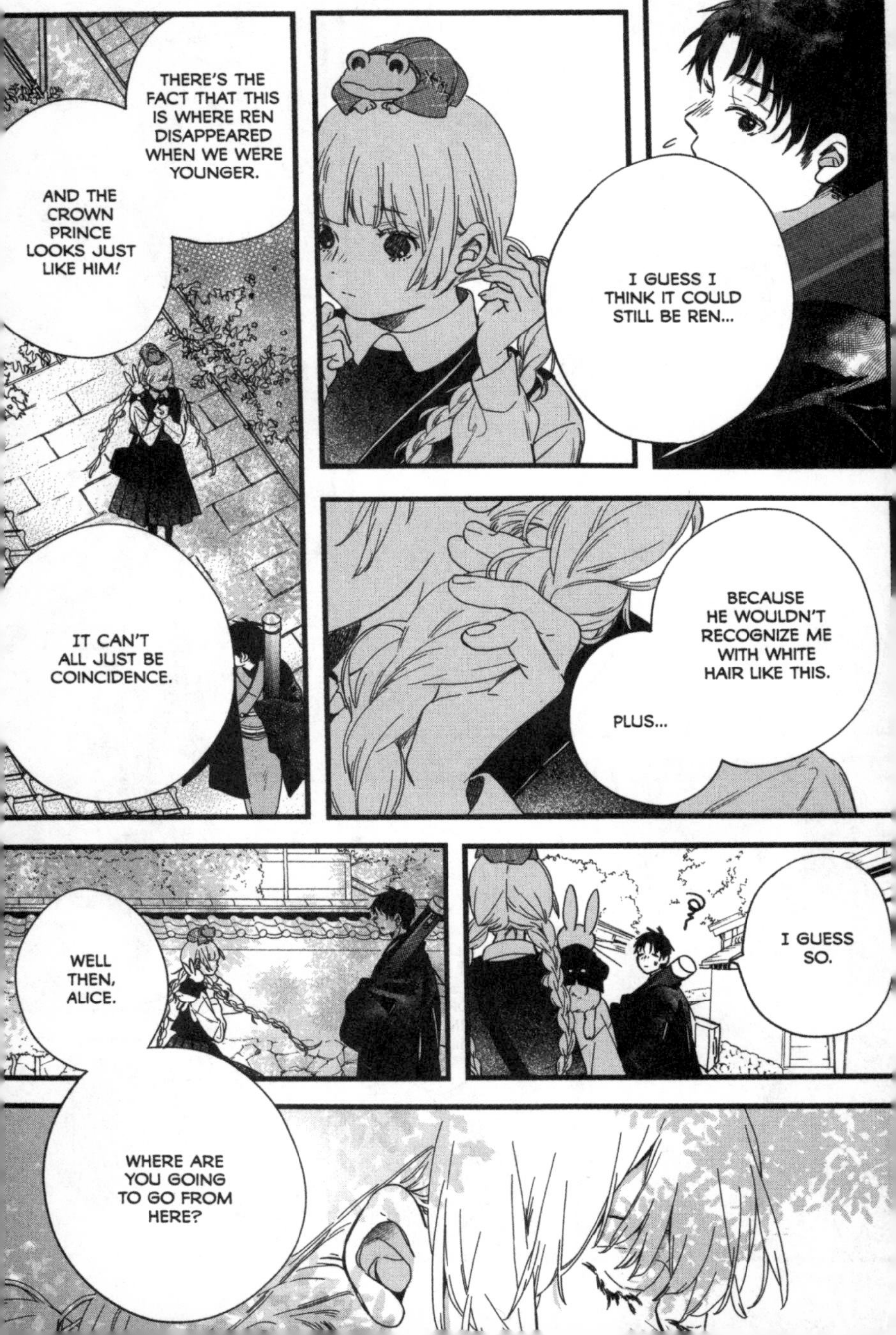
I GUESS I THINK IT COULD STILL BE REN...
BECAUSE HE WOULDN'T RECOGNIZE ME WITH WHITE HAIR LIKE THIS.
PLUS...
THERE'S THE FACT THAT THIS IS WHERE REN DISAPPEARED WHEN WE WERE YOUNGER.
AND THE CROWN PRINCE LOOKS JUST LIKE HIM!
IT CAN'T ALL JUST BE COINCIDENCE.
I GUESS SO.
WELL THEN, ALICE.
WHERE ARE YOU GOING TO GO FROM HERE?

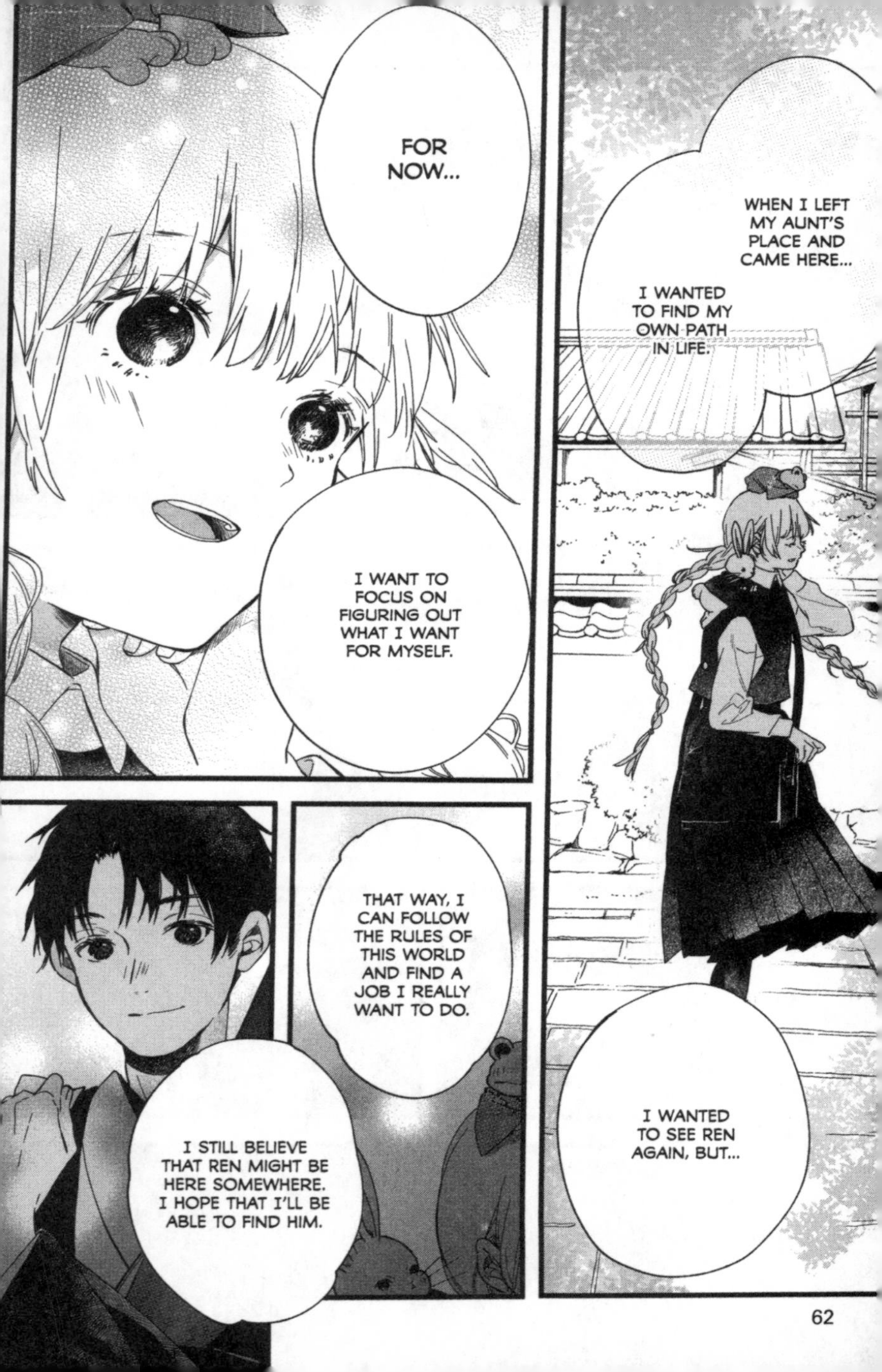
WHEN I LEFT MY AUNT'S PLACE AND CAME HERE...
I WANTED TO FIND MY OWN PATH IN LIFE.
I WANTED TO SEE REN AGAIN, BUT...
FOR NOW...
I WANT TO FOCUS ON FIGURING OUT WHAT I WANT FOR MYSELF.
THAT WAY, I CAN FOLLOW THE RULES OF THIS WORLD AND FIND A JOB I REALLY WANT TO DO.
I STILL BELIEVE THAT REN MIGHT BE HERE SOMEWHERE. I HOPE THAT I'LL BE ABLE TO FIND HIM.

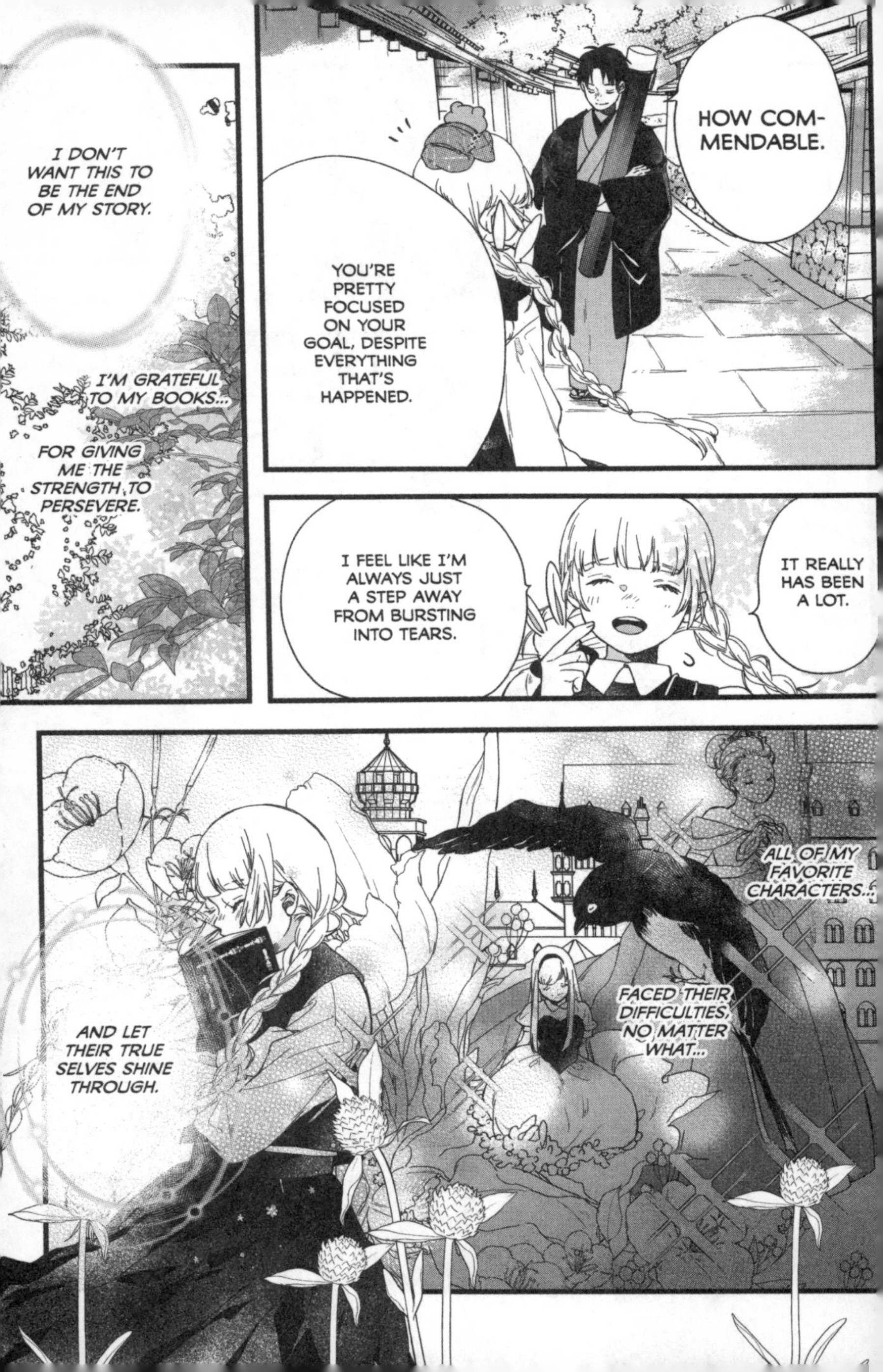
HOW COM-MENDABLE.
YOU'RE PRETTY FOCUSED ON YOUR GOAL, DESPITE EVERYTHING THAT'S HAPPENED.
IT REALLY HAS BEEN A LOT.
I FEEL LIKE I'M ALWAYS JUST A STEP AWAY FROM BURSTING INTO TEARS.
I DON'T WANT THIS TO BE THE END OF MY STORY.
I'M GRATEFUL TO MY BOOKS...
FOR GIVING ME THE STRENGTH TO PERSEVERE.
ALL OF MY FAVORITE CHARACTERS...
FACED THEIR DIFFICULTIES, NO MATTER WHAT...
AND LET THEIR TRUE SELVES SHINE THROUGH.

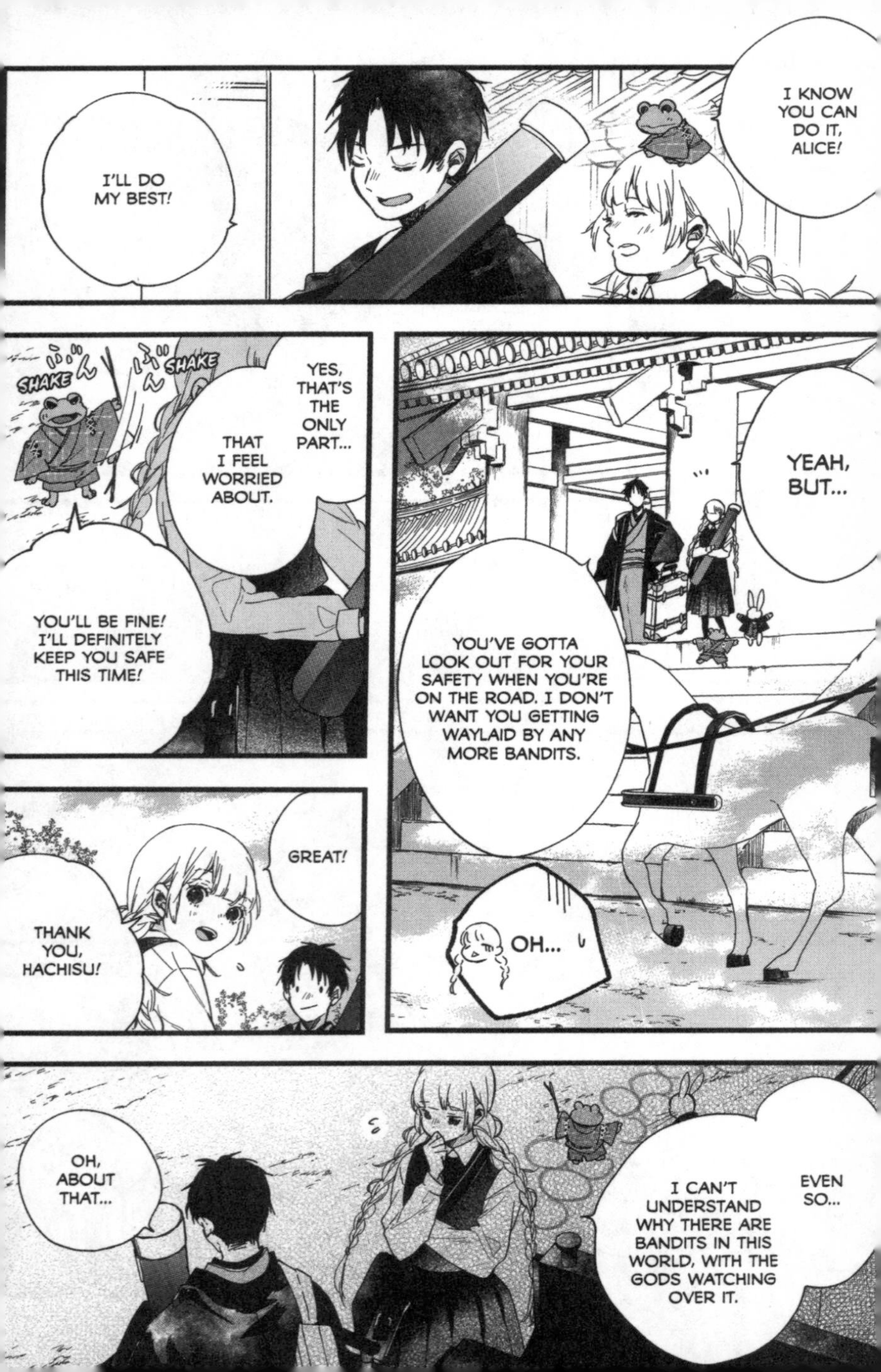
I KNOW YOU CAN DO IT, ALICE!
I'LL DO MY BEST!
YEAH, BUT...
YOU'VE GOTTA LOOK OUT FOR YOUR SAFETY WHEN YOU'RE ON THE ROAD. I DON'T WANT YOU GETTING WAYLAID BY ANY MORE BANDITS.
OH...
YES, THAT'S THE ONLY PART...
THAT I FEEL WORRIED ABOUT.
SHAKE
SHAKE
YOU'LL BE FINE! I'LL DEFINITELY KEEP YOU SAFE THIS TIME!
GREAT!
THANK YOU, HACHISU!
EVEN SO...
I CAN'T UNDERSTAND WHY THERE ARE BANDITS IN THIS WORLD, WITH THE GODS WATCHING OVER IT.
OH, ABOUT THAT...

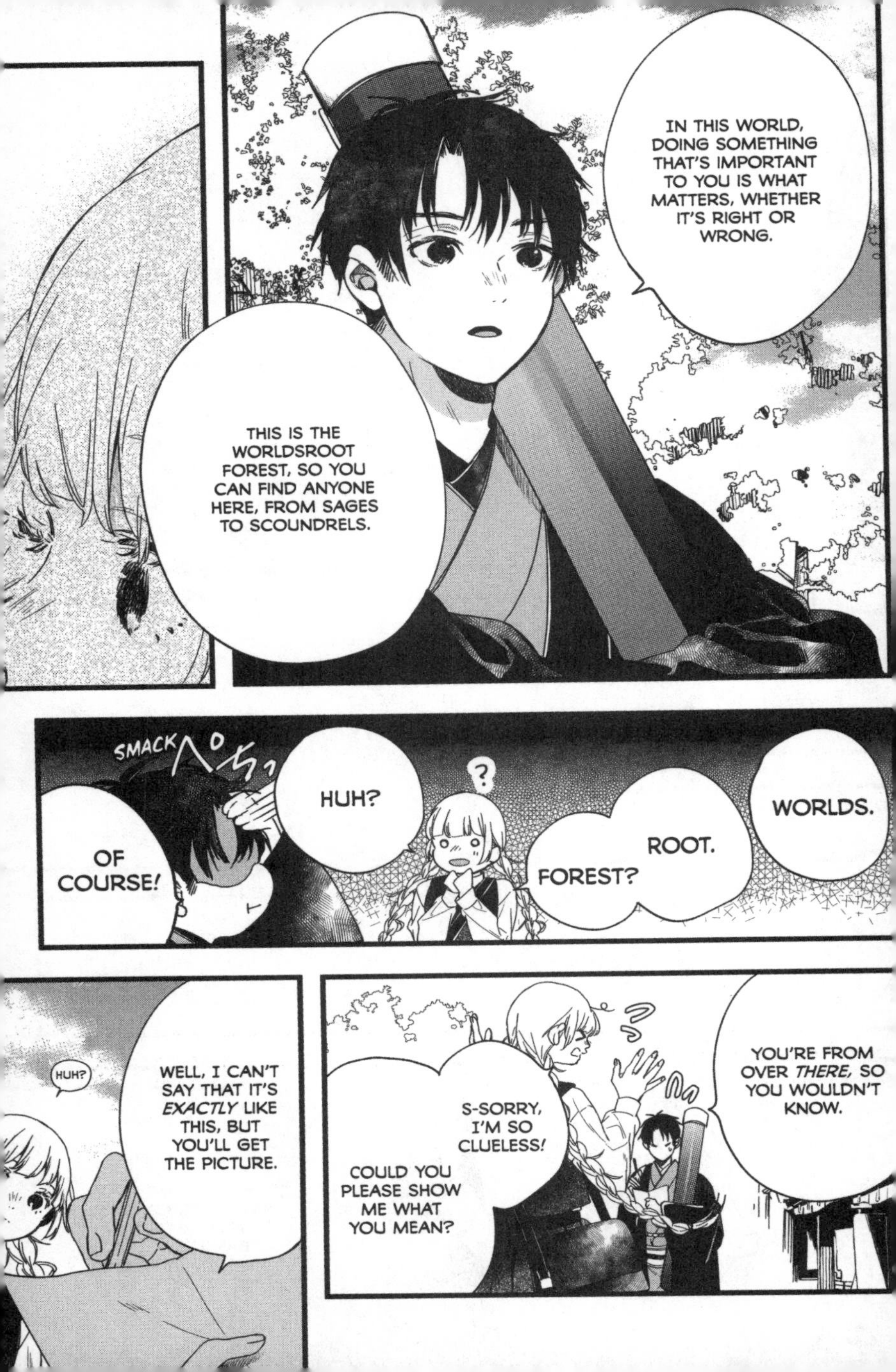
IN THIS WORLD, DOING SOMETHING THAT'S IMPORTANT TO YOU IS WHAT MATTERS, WHETHER IT'S RIGHT OR WRONG.
THIS IS THE WORLDSROOT FOREST, SO YOU CAN FIND ANYONE HERE, FROM SAGES TO SCOUNDRELS.
WORLDS.
ROOT.
FOREST?
?
HUH?
SMACK
OF COURSE!
YOU'RE FROM OVER *THERE,* SO YOU WOULDN'T KNOW.
S-SORRY, I'M SO CLUELESS!
COULD YOU PLEASE SHOW ME WHAT YOU MEAN?
WELL, I CAN'T SAY THAT IT'S *EXACTLY* LIKE THIS, BUT YOU'LL GET THE PICTURE.
HUH?

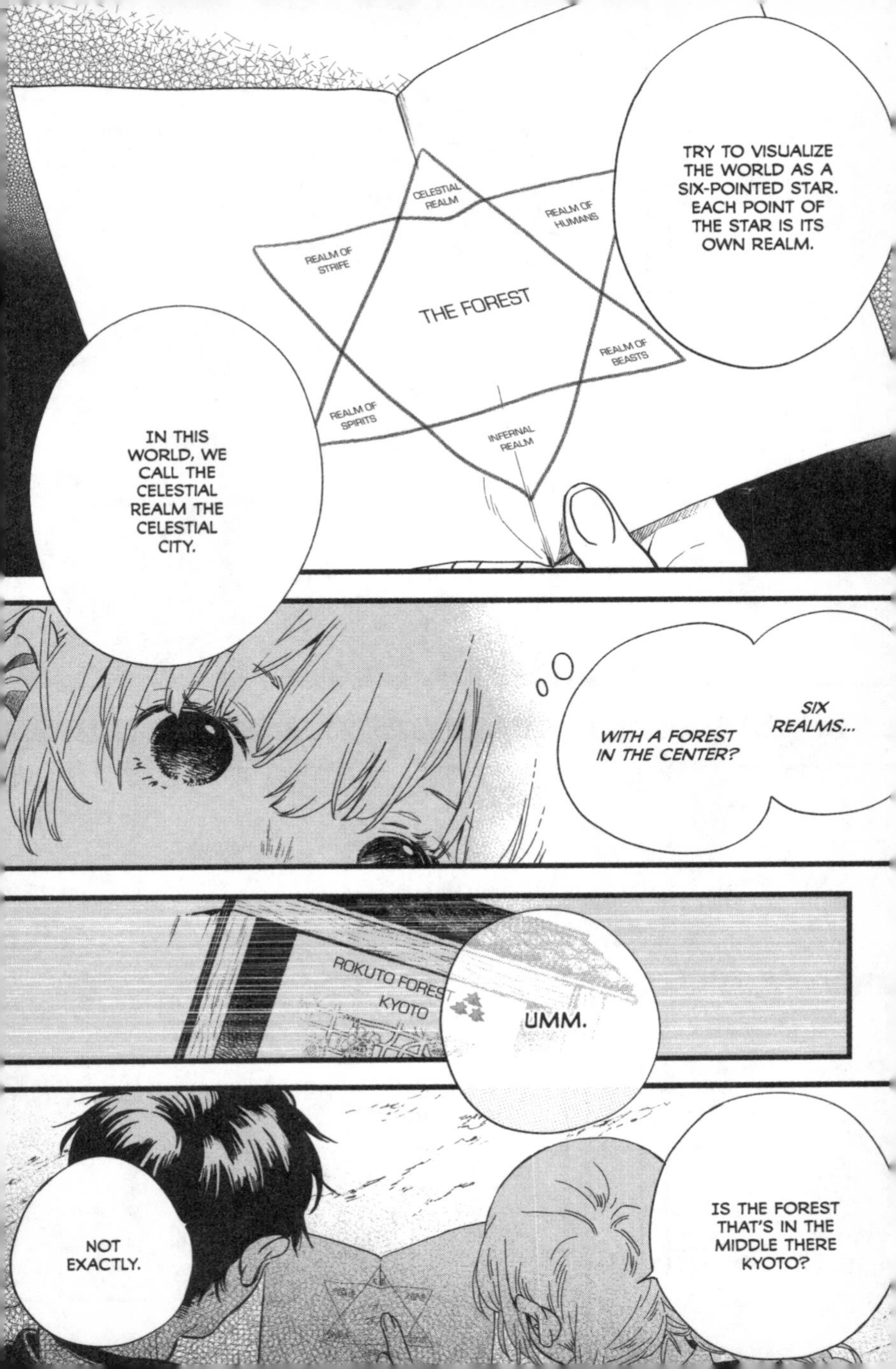
TRY TO VISUALIZE THE WORLD AS A SIX-POINTED STAR. EACH POINT OF THE STAR IS ITS OWN REALM.
CELESTIAL REALM
REALM OF HUMANS
REALM OF STRIFE
THE FOREST
REALM OF BEASTS
REALM OF SPIRITS
INFERNAL REALM
IN THIS WORLD, WE CALL THE CELESTIAL REALM THE CELESTIAL CITY.
SIX REALMS...
WITH A FOREST IN THE CENTER?
ROKUTO FOREST
KYOTO
UMM.
IS THE FOREST THAT'S IN THE MIDDLE THERE KYOTO?
NOT EXACTLY.

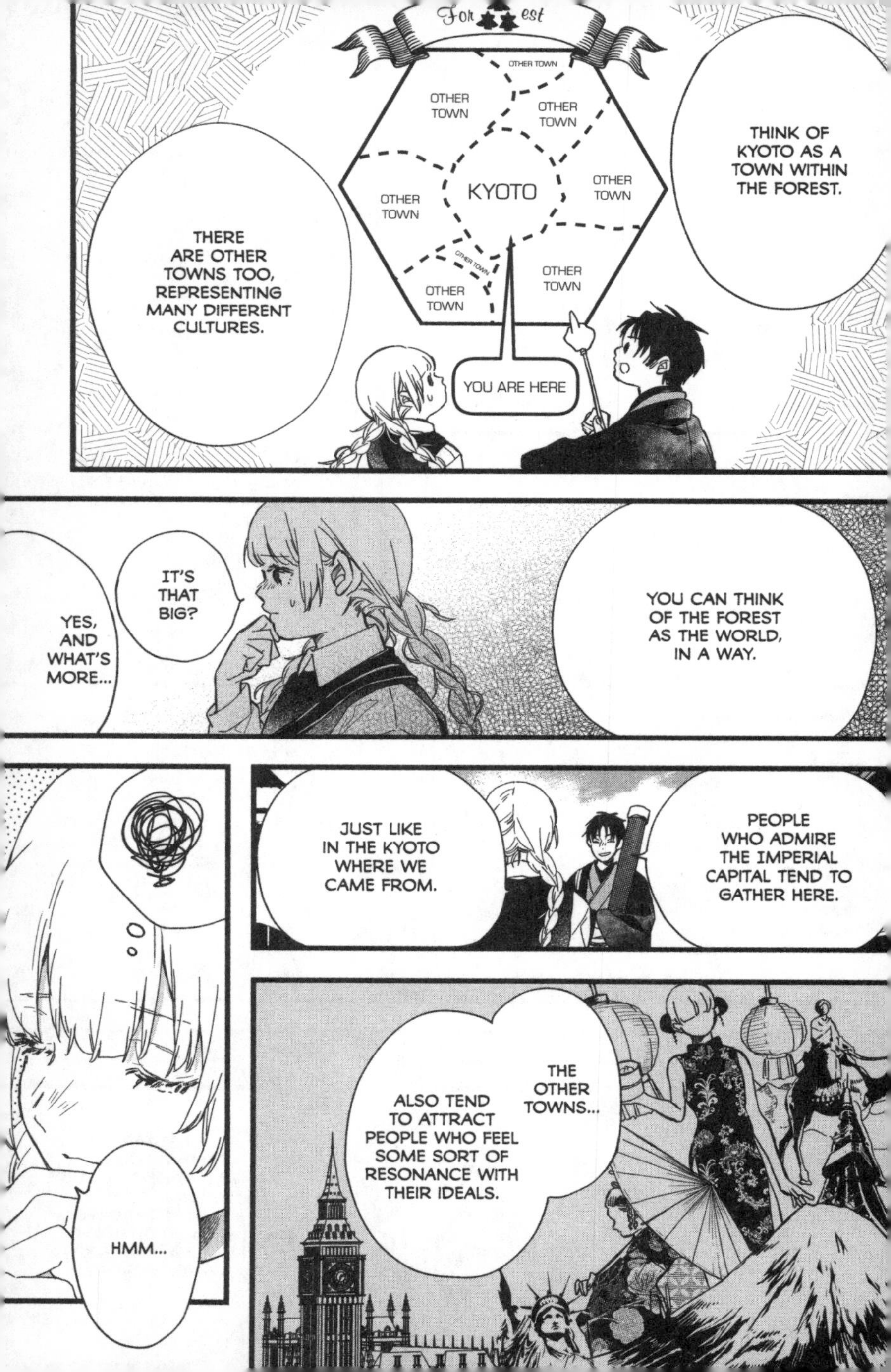
THINK OF KYOTO AS A TOWN WITHIN THE FOREST.
For est
OTHER TOWN
OTHER TOWN
OTHER TOWN
OTHER TOWN
KYOTO
OTHER TOWN
OTHER TOWN
OTHER TOWN
OTHER TOWN
YOU ARE HERE
THERE ARE OTHER TOWNS TOO, REPRESENTING MANY DIFFERENT CULTURES.
YOU CAN THINK OF THE FOREST AS THE WORLD, IN A WAY.
IT'S THAT BIG?
YES, AND WHAT'S MORE...
PEOPLE WHO ADMIRE THE IMPERIAL CAPITAL TEND TO GATHER HERE.
JUST LIKE IN THE KYOTO WHERE WE CAME FROM.
THE OTHER TOWNS...
ALSO TEND TO ATTRACT PEOPLE WHO FEEL SOME SORT OF RESONANCE WITH THEIR IDEALS.
HMM...

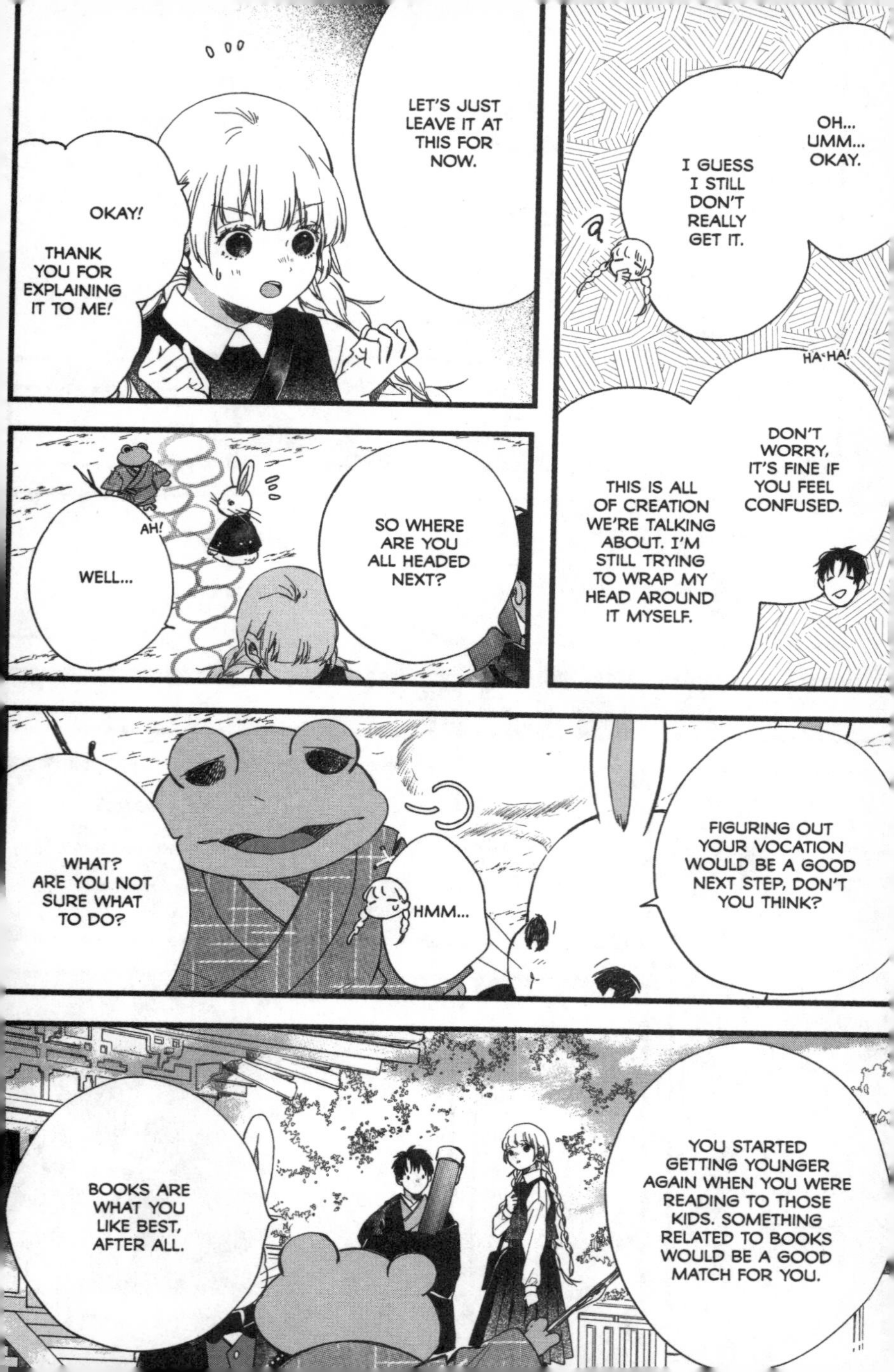
OH... UMM... OKAY.
I GUESS I STILL DON'T REALLY GET IT.
HA-HA!
DON'T WORRY, IT'S FINE IF YOU FEEL CONFUSED.
THIS IS ALL OF CREATION WE'RE TALKING ABOUT. I'M STILL TRYING TO WRAP MY HEAD AROUND IT MYSELF.
LET'S JUST LEAVE IT AT THIS FOR NOW.
OKAY!
THANK YOU FOR EXPLAINING IT TO ME!
SO WHERE ARE YOU ALL HEADED NEXT?
AH!
WELL...
FIGURING OUT YOUR VOCATION WOULD BE A GOOD NEXT STEP, DON'T YOU THINK?
HMM...
WHAT? ARE YOU NOT SURE WHAT TO DO?
YOU STARTED GETTING YOUNGER AGAIN WHEN YOU WERE READING TO THOSE KIDS. SOMETHING RELATED TO BOOKS WOULD BE A GOOD MATCH FOR YOU.
BOOKS ARE WHAT YOU LIKE BEST, AFTER ALL.

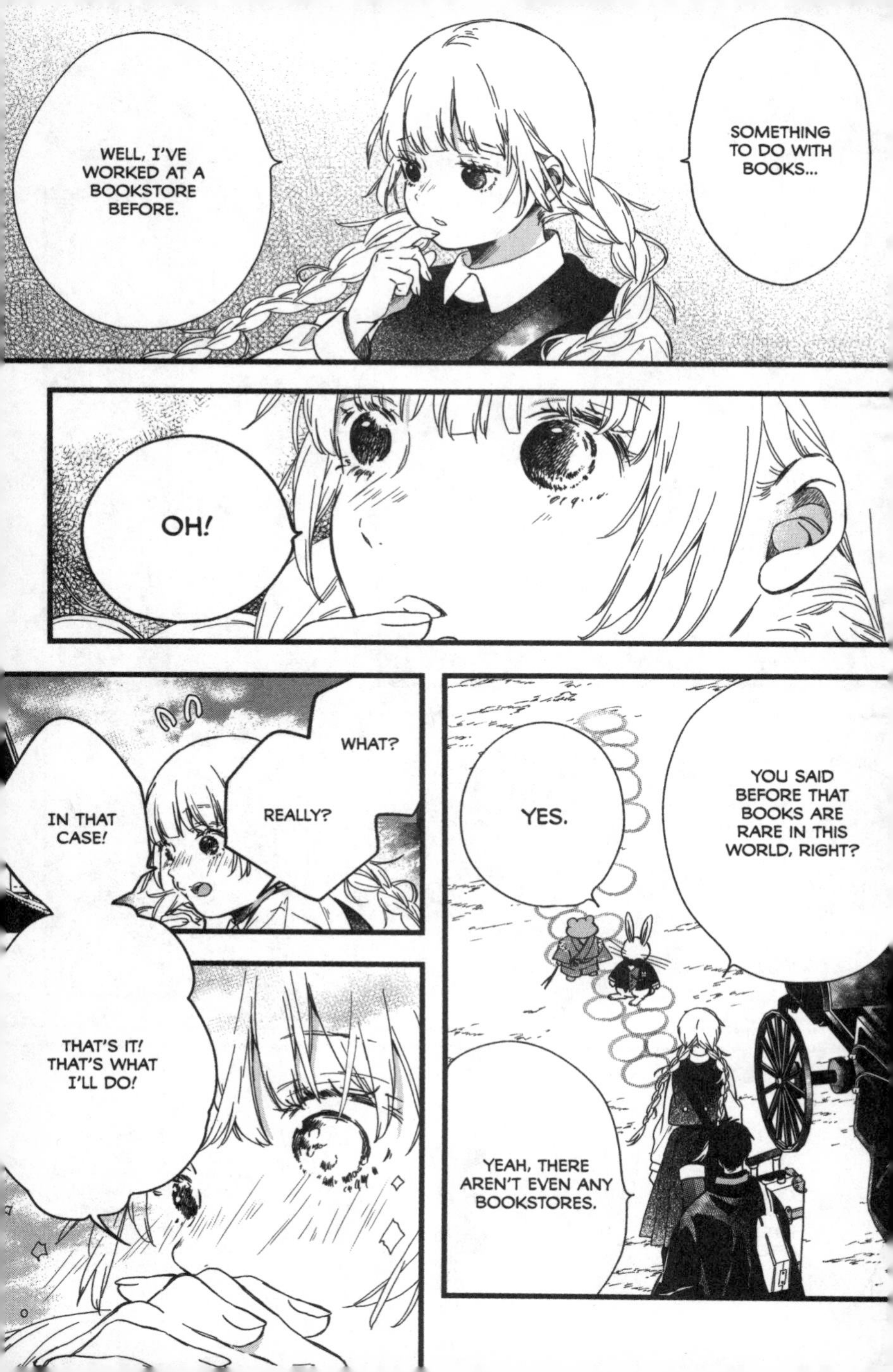
SOMETHING TO DO WITH BOOKS...
WELL, I'VE WORKED AT A BOOKSTORE BEFORE.
OH!
YOU SAID BEFORE THAT BOOKS ARE RARE IN THIS WORLD, RIGHT?
YES.
YEAH, THERE AREN'T EVEN ANY BOOKSTORES.
WHAT?
REALLY?
IN THAT CASE!
THAT'S IT! THAT'S WHAT I'LL DO!

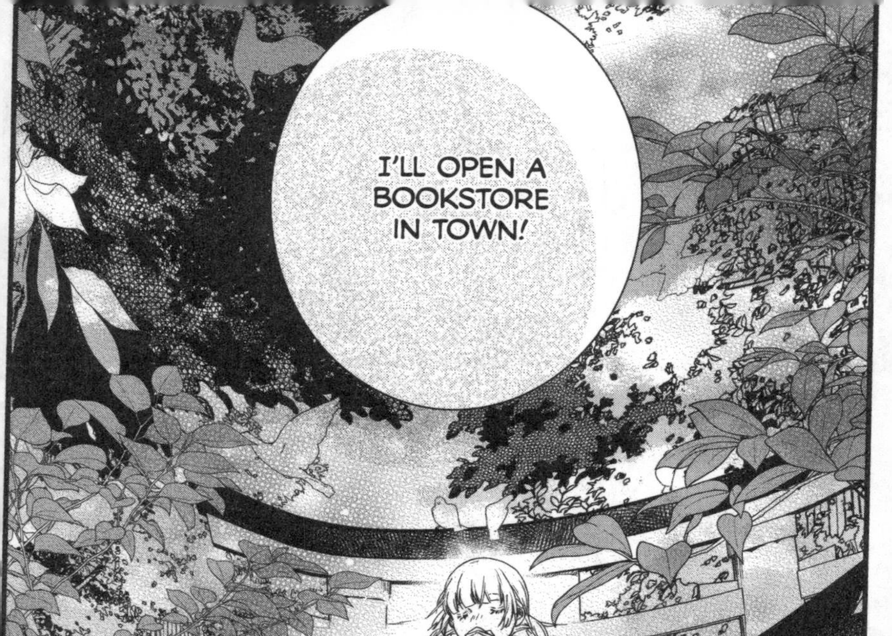
I'LL OPEN A BOOKSTORE IN TOWN!
ROKUTO FOREST
KYOTO
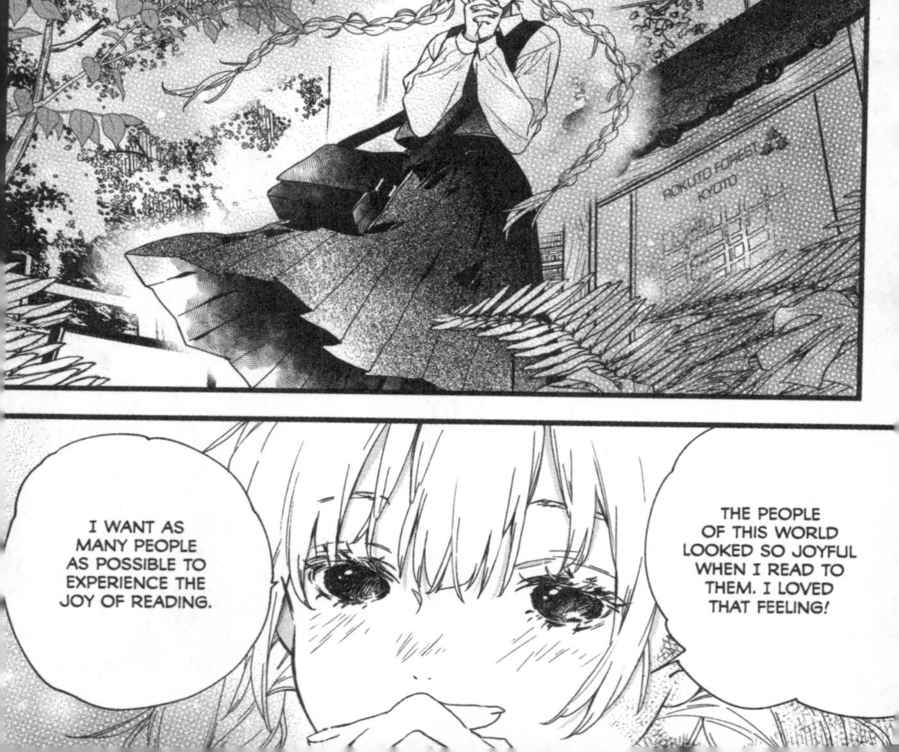
THE PEOPLE OF THIS WORLD LOOKED SO JOYFUL WHEN I READ TO THEM. I LOVED THAT FEELING!
I WANT AS MANY PEOPLE AS POSSIBLE TO EXPERIENCE THE JOY OF READING.

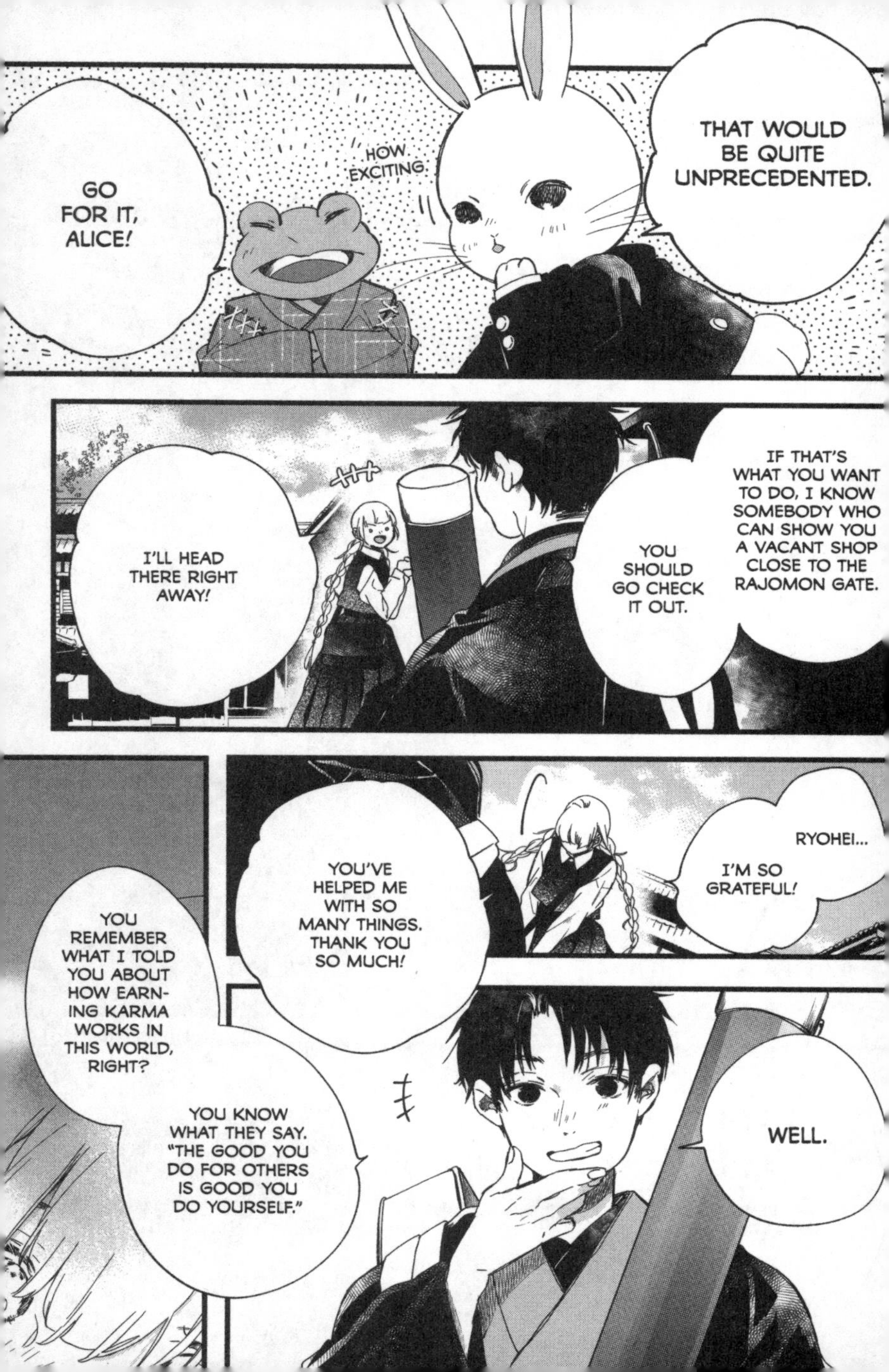
THAT WOULD BE QUITE UNPRECEDENTED.
HOW EXCITING.
GO FOR IT, ALICE!
IF THAT'S WHAT YOU WANT TO DO, I KNOW SOMEBODY WHO CAN SHOW YOU A VACANT SHOP CLOSE TO THE RAJOMON GATE.
YOU SHOULD GO CHECK IT OUT.
I'LL HEAD THERE RIGHT AWAY!
RYOHEI...
I'M SO GRATEFUL!
YOU'VE HELPED ME WITH SO MANY THINGS. THANK YOU SO MUCH!
WELL.
YOU KNOW WHAT THEY SAY. "THE GOOD YOU DO FOR OTHERS IS GOOD YOU DO YOURSELF."
YOU REMEMBER WHAT I TOLD YOU ABOUT HOW EARNING KARMA WORKS IN THIS WORLD, RIGHT?

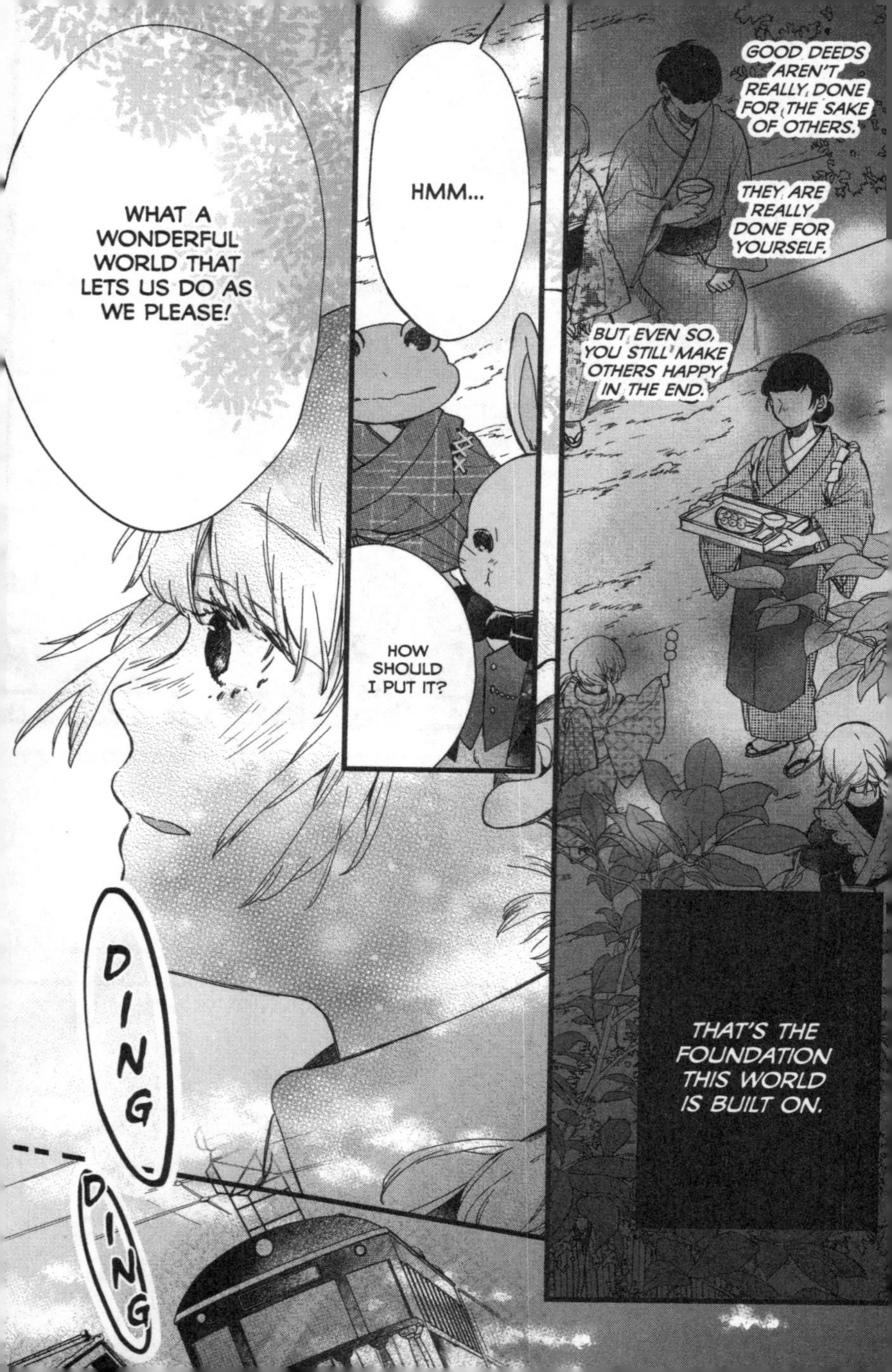
GOOD DEEDS AREN'T REALLY DONE FOR THE SAKE OF OTHERS.
THEY ARE REALLY DONE FOR YOURSELF.
BUT EVEN SO, YOU STILL MAKE OTHERS HAPPY IN THE END.
THAT'S THE FOUNDATION THIS WORLD IS BUILT ON.
HMM...
HOW SHOULD I PUT IT?
WHAT A WONDERFUL WORLD THAT LETS US DO AS WE PLEASE!
DING
DING

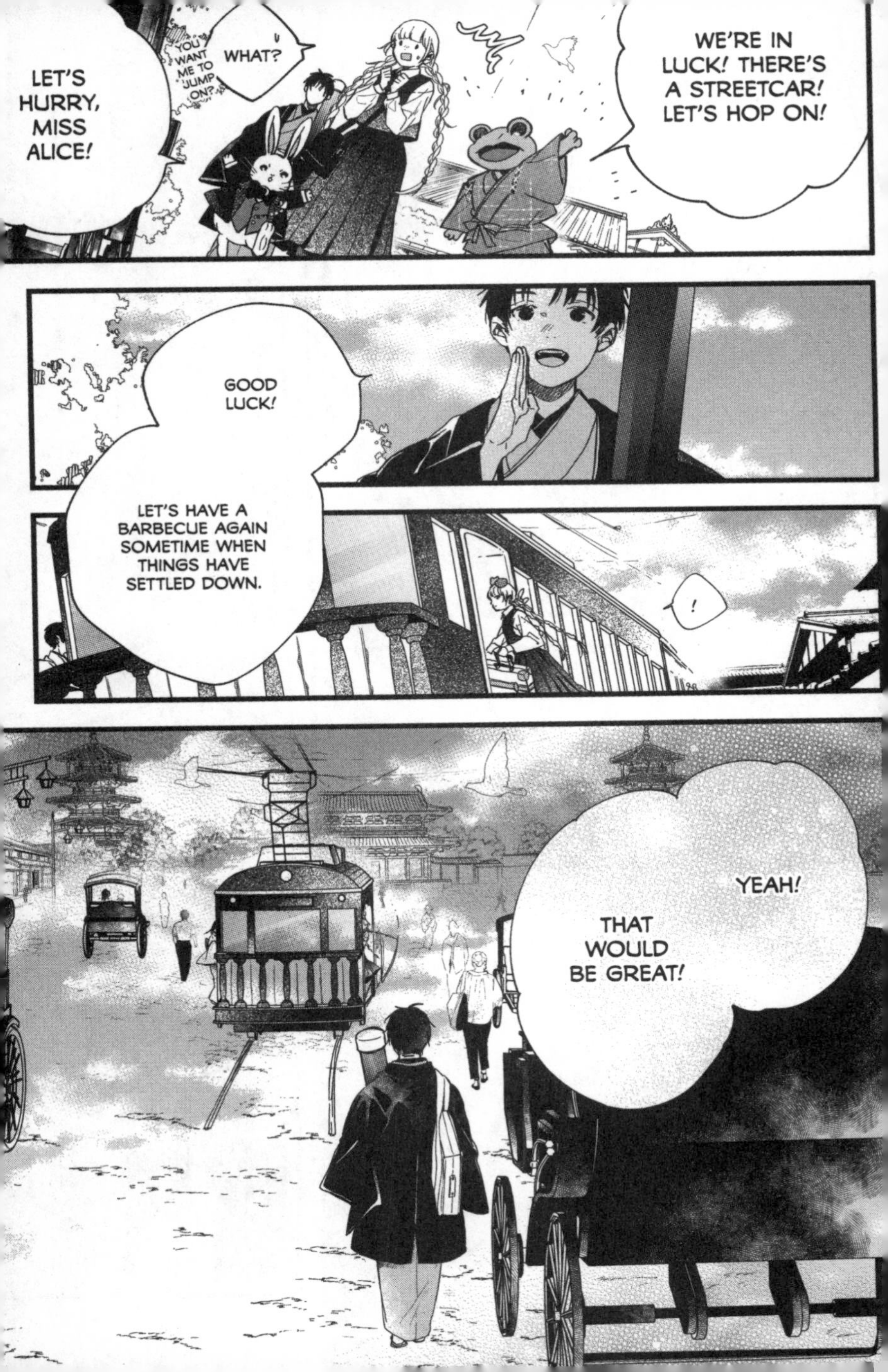
WE'RE IN LUCK! THERE'S A STREETCAR! LET'S HOP ON!
WHAT?
YOU WANT ME TO JUMP ON?
LET'S HURRY, MISS ALICE!
GOOD LUCK!
LET'S HAVE A BARBECUE AGAIN SOMETIME WHEN THINGS HAVE SETTLED DOWN.
!
YEAH!
THAT WOULD BE GREAT!

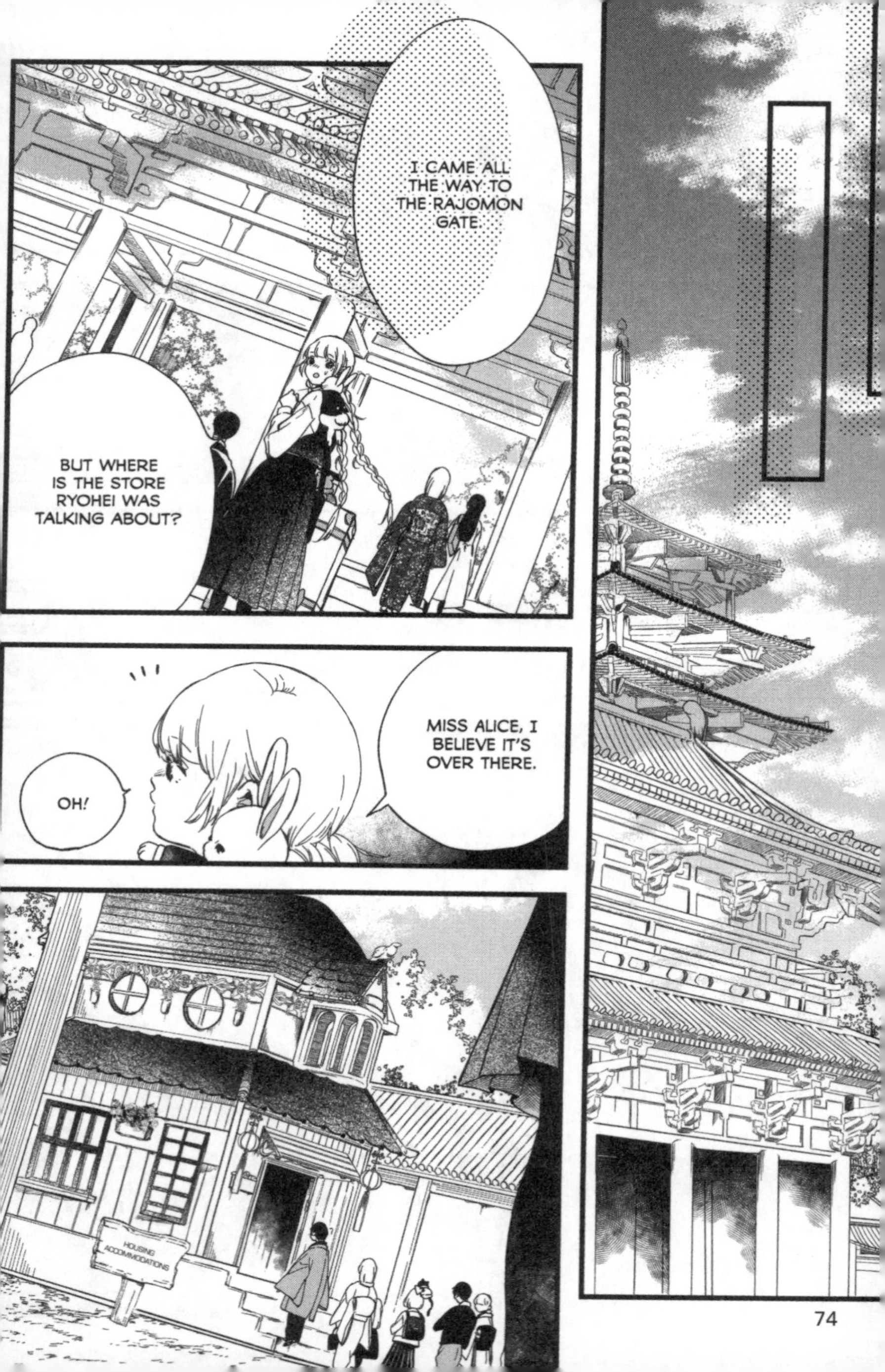
I CAME ALL THE WAY TO THE RAJOMON GATE.
BUT WHERE IS THE STORE RYOHEI WAS TALKING ABOUT?
MISS ALICE, I BELIEVE IT'S OVER THERE.
OH!
HOUSING ACCOMMODATIONS

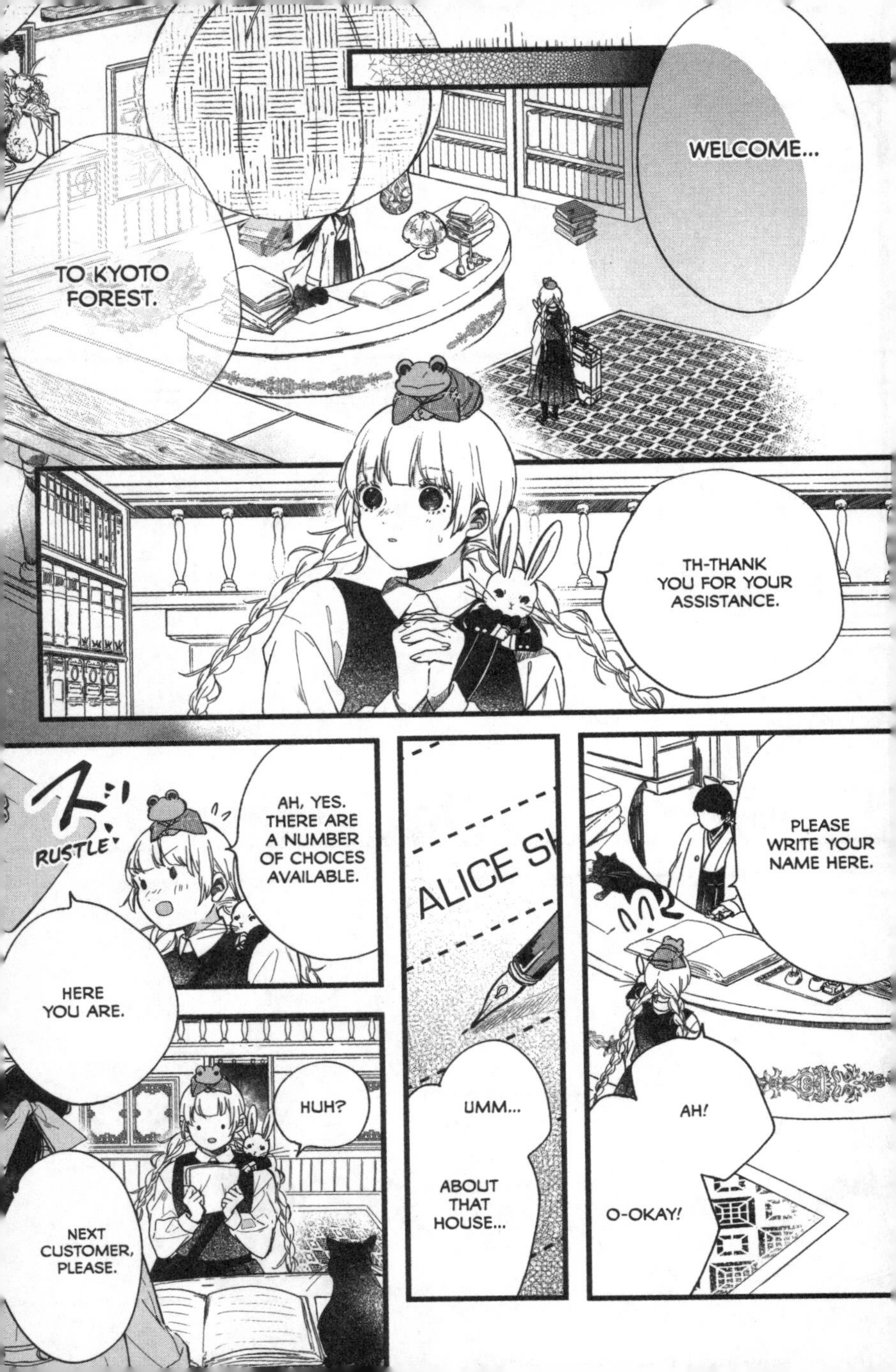
WELCOME...
TO KYOTO FOREST.
TH-THANK YOU FOR YOUR ASSISTANCE.
PLEASE WRITE YOUR NAME HERE.
AH!
O-OKAY!
ALICE S
UMM...
ABOUT THAT HOUSE...
AH, YES. THERE ARE A NUMBER OF CHOICES AVAILABLE.
RUSTLE
HERE YOU ARE.
HUH?
NEXT CUSTOMER, PLEASE.

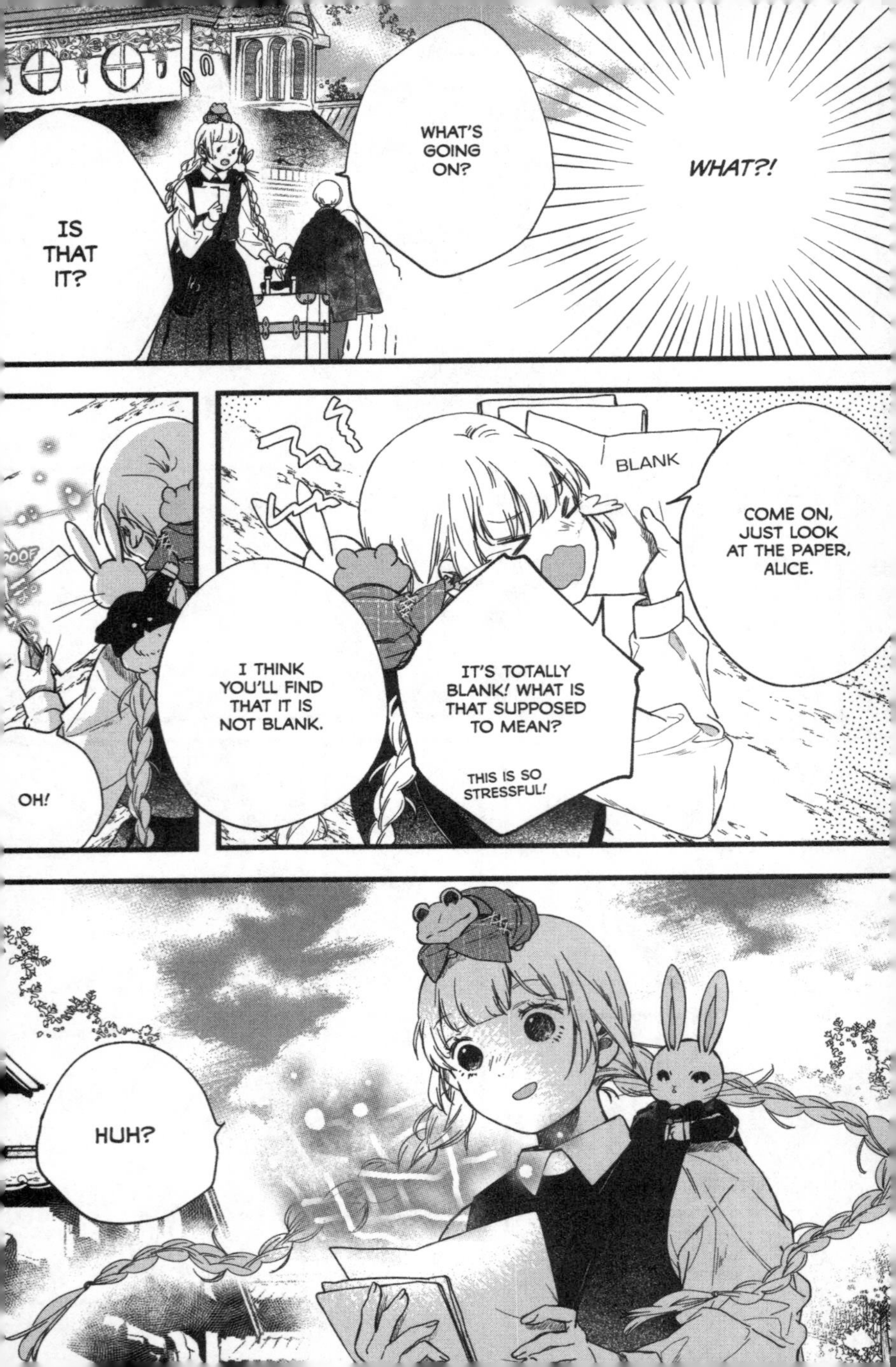
WHAT?!
WHAT'S GOING ON?
IS THAT IT?
BLANK
COME ON, JUST LOOK AT THE PAPER, ALICE.
IT'S TOTALLY BLANK! WHAT IS THAT SUPPOSED TO MEAN?
THIS IS SO STRESSFUL!
I THINK YOU'LL FIND THAT IT IS NOT BLANK.
OH!
HUH?

Chapter 10

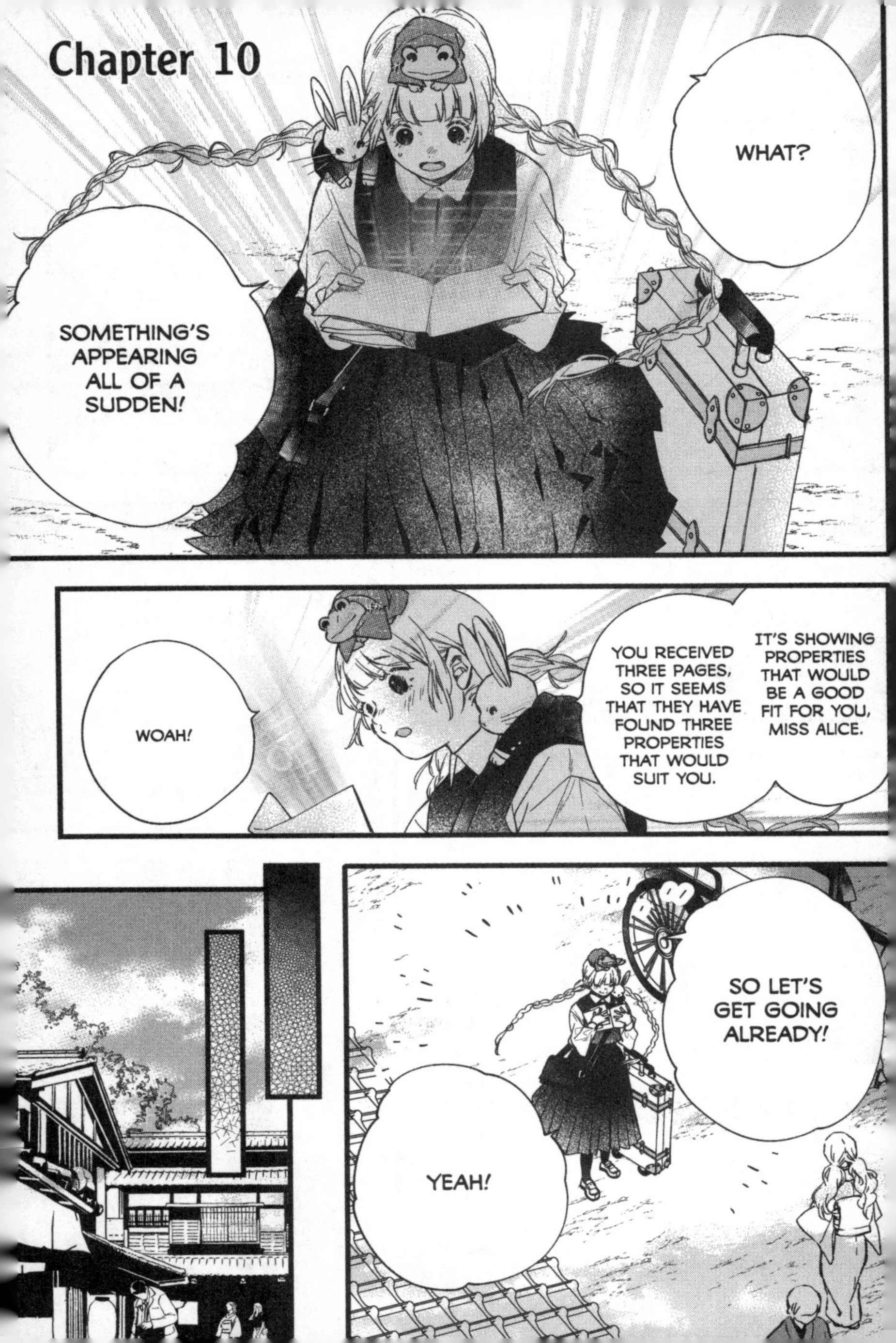

WHAT?
SOMETHING'S APPEARING ALL OF A SUDDEN!
IT'S SHOWING PROPERTIES THAT WOULD BE A GOOD FIT FOR YOU, MISS ALICE.
YOU RECEIVED THREE PAGES, SO IT SEEMS THAT THEY HAVE FOUND THREE PROPERTIES THAT WOULD SUIT YOU.
WOAH!
SO LET'S GET GOING ALREADY!
YEAH!

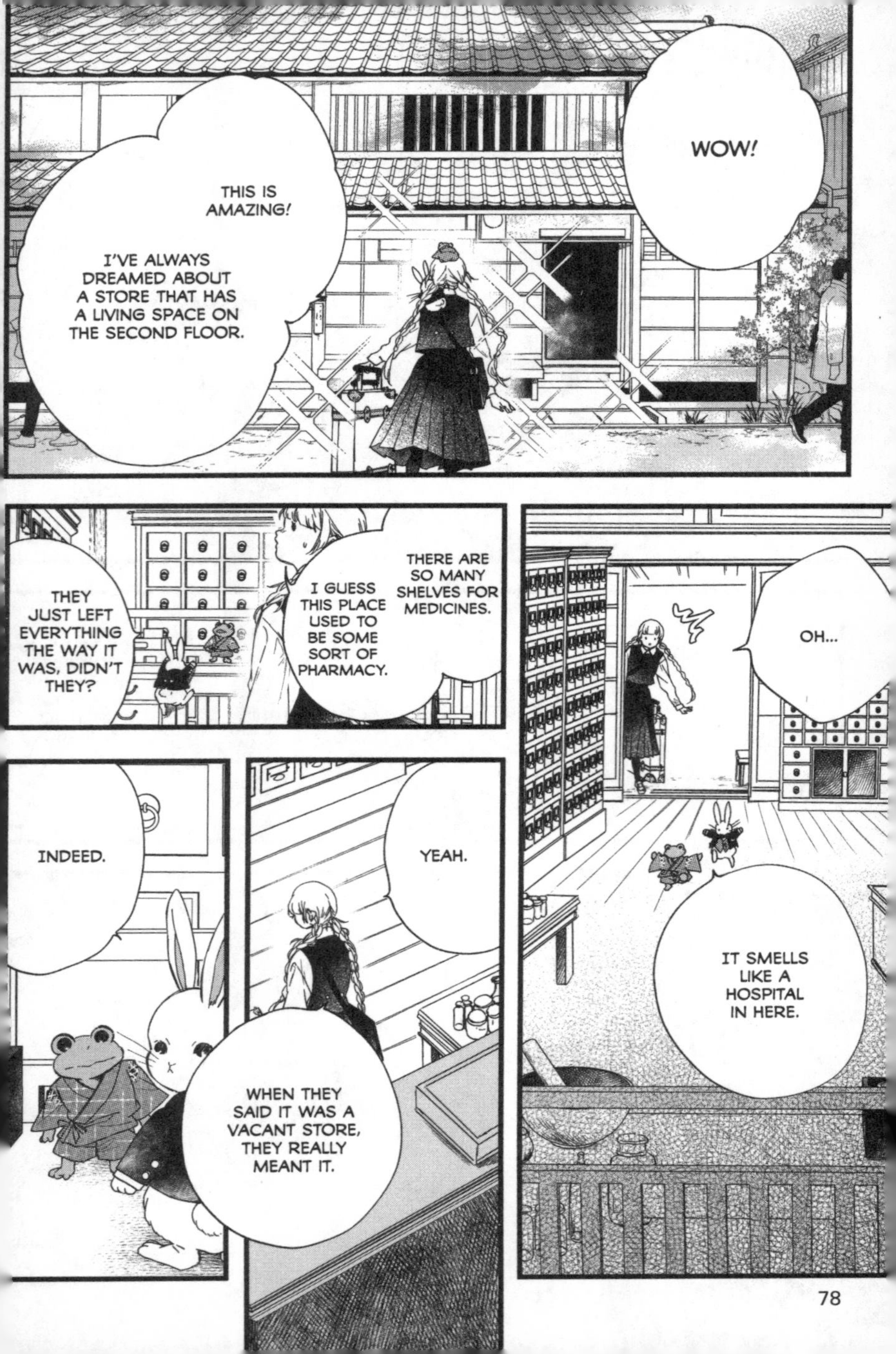
WOW!
THIS IS AMAZING! I'VE ALWAYS DREAMED ABOUT A STORE THAT HAS A LIVING SPACE ON THE SECOND FLOOR.
OH...
IT SMELLS LIKE A HOSPITAL IN HERE.
THERE ARE SO MANY SHELVES FOR MEDICINES.
I GUESS THIS PLACE USED TO BE SOME SORT OF PHARMACY.
THEY JUST LEFT EVERYTHING THE WAY IT WAS, DIDN'T THEY?
YEAH.
WHEN THEY SAID IT WAS A VACANT STORE, THEY REALLY MEANT IT.
INDEED.

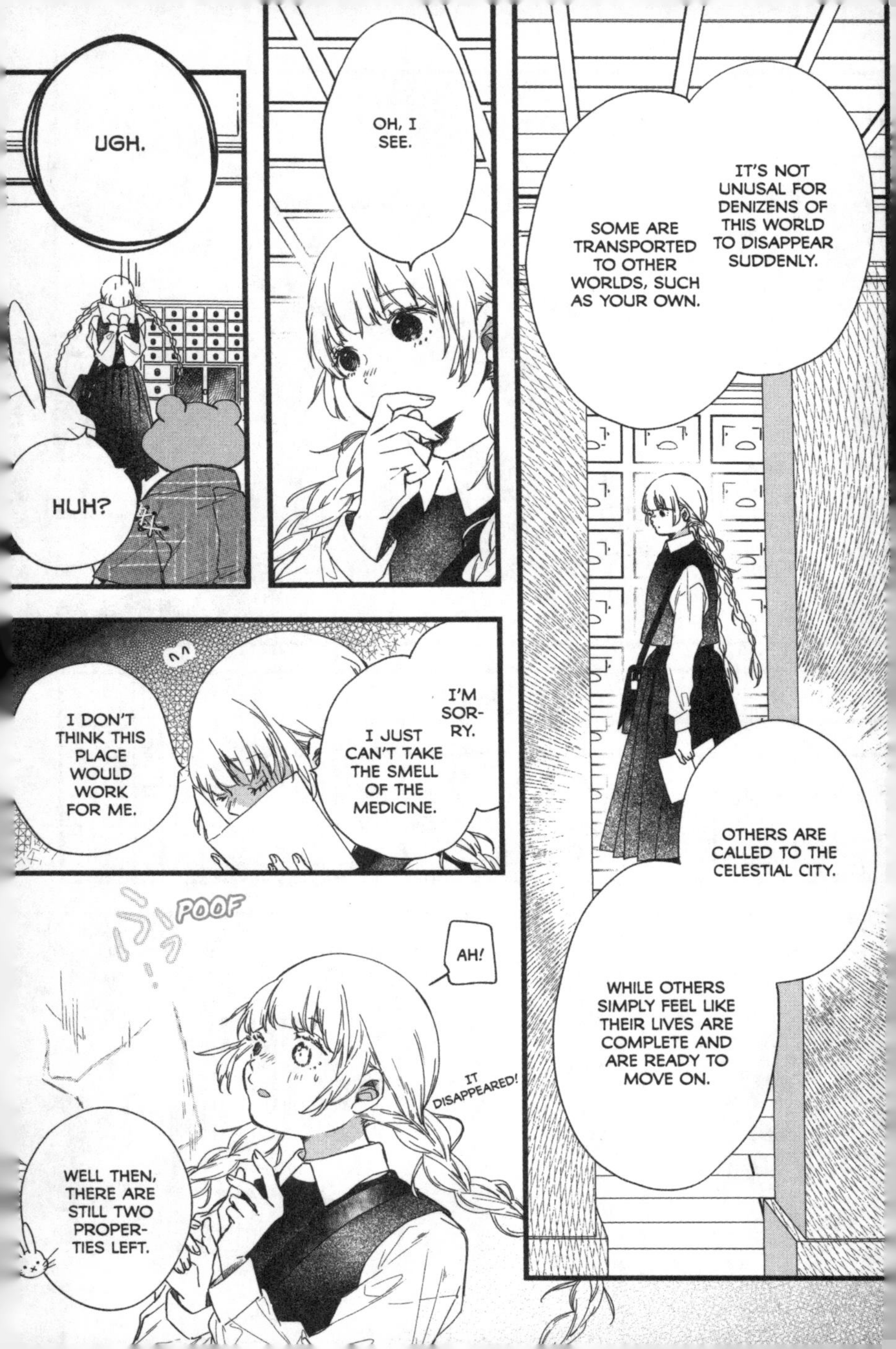
IT'S NOT UNUSUAL FOR DENIZENS OF THIS WORLD TO DISAPPEAR SUDDENLY.
SOME ARE TRANSPORTED TO OTHER WORLDS, SUCH AS YOUR OWN.
OTHERS ARE CALLED TO THE CELESTIAL CITY.
WHILE OTHERS SIMPLY FEEL LIKE THEIR LIVES ARE COMPLETE AND ARE READY TO MOVE ON.
OH, I SEE.
UGH.
HUH?
I'M SORRY.
I JUST CAN'T TAKE THE SMELL OF THE MEDICINE.
I DON'T THINK THIS PLACE WOULD WORK FOR ME.
POOF
AH!
IT DISAPPEARED!
WELL THEN, THERE ARE STILL TWO PROPERTIES LEFT.

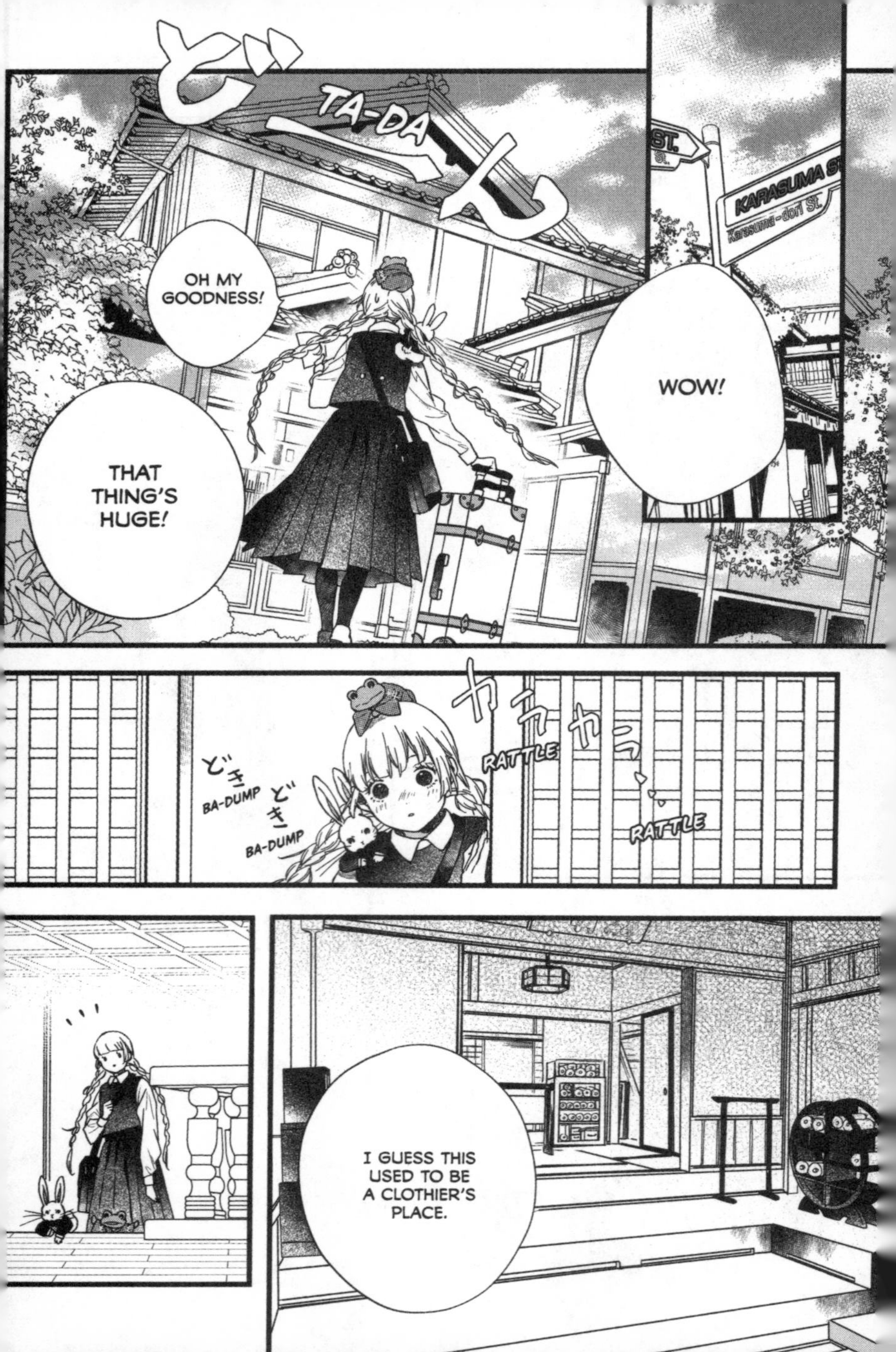
どーん
TA-DA
KARASUMA ST.
Karasuma-dori St.
WOW!
OH MY GOODNESS!
THAT THING'S HUGE!
カラカラ
RATTLE
RATTLE
どきどき
BA-DUMP
BA-DUMP
I GUESS THIS USED TO BE A CLOTHIER'S PLACE.

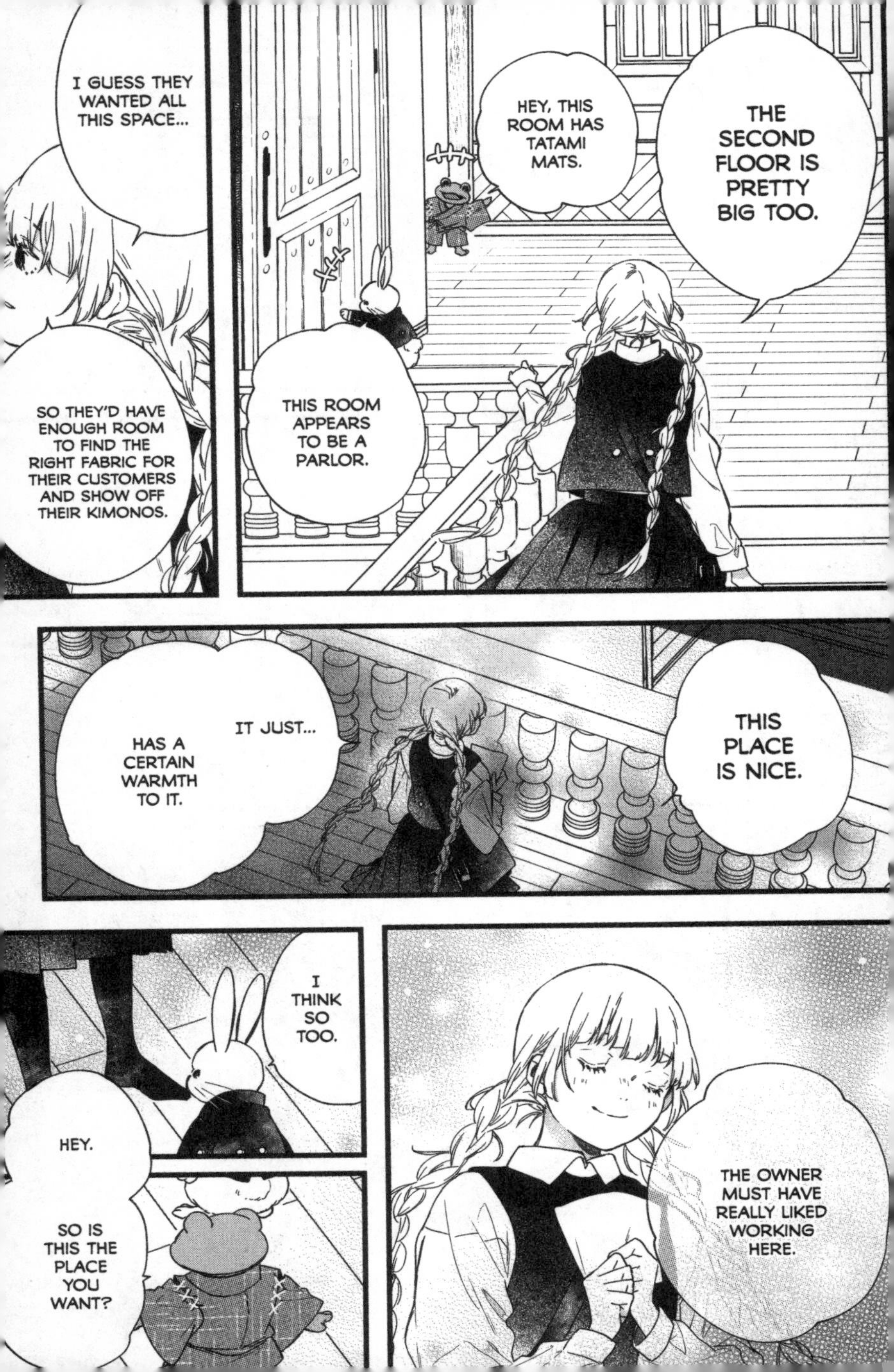
THE SECOND FLOOR IS PRETTY BIG TOO.
HEY, THIS ROOM HAS TATAMI MATS.
THIS ROOM APPEARS TO BE A PARLOR.
I GUESS THEY WANTED ALL THIS SPACE...
SO THEY'D HAVE ENOUGH ROOM TO FIND THE RIGHT FABRIC FOR THEIR CUSTOMERS AND SHOW OFF THEIR KIMONOS.
THIS PLACE IS NICE.
IT JUST...
HAS A CERTAIN WARMTH TO IT.
THE OWNER MUST HAVE REALLY LIKED WORKING HERE.
I THINK SO TOO.
HEY.
SO IS THIS THE PLACE YOU WANT?

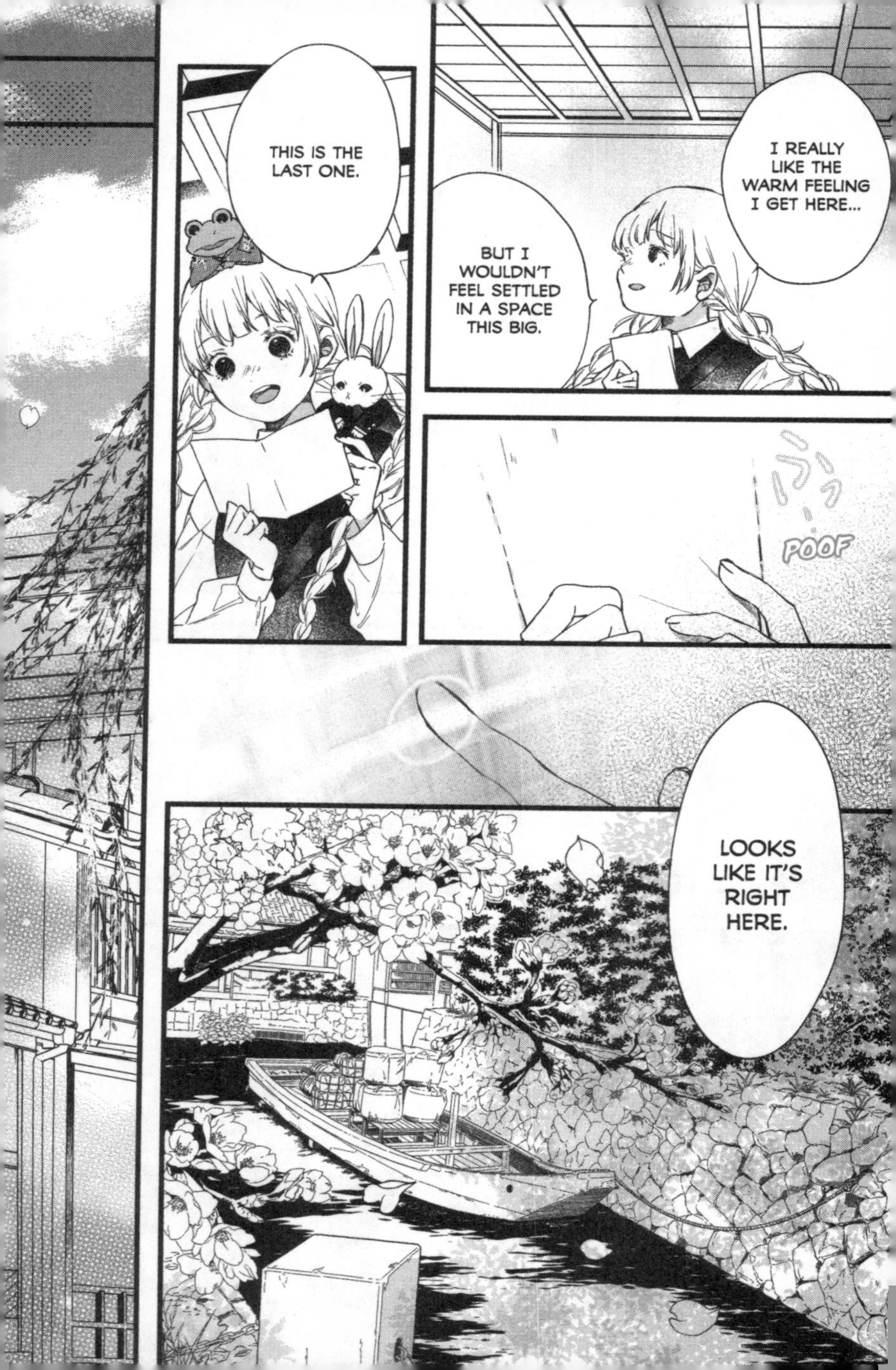
I REALLY LIKE THE WARM FEELING I GET HERE...
BUT I WOULDN'T FEEL SETTLED IN A SPACE THIS BIG.
THIS IS THE LAST ONE.
POOF
LOOKS LIKE IT'S RIGHT HERE.

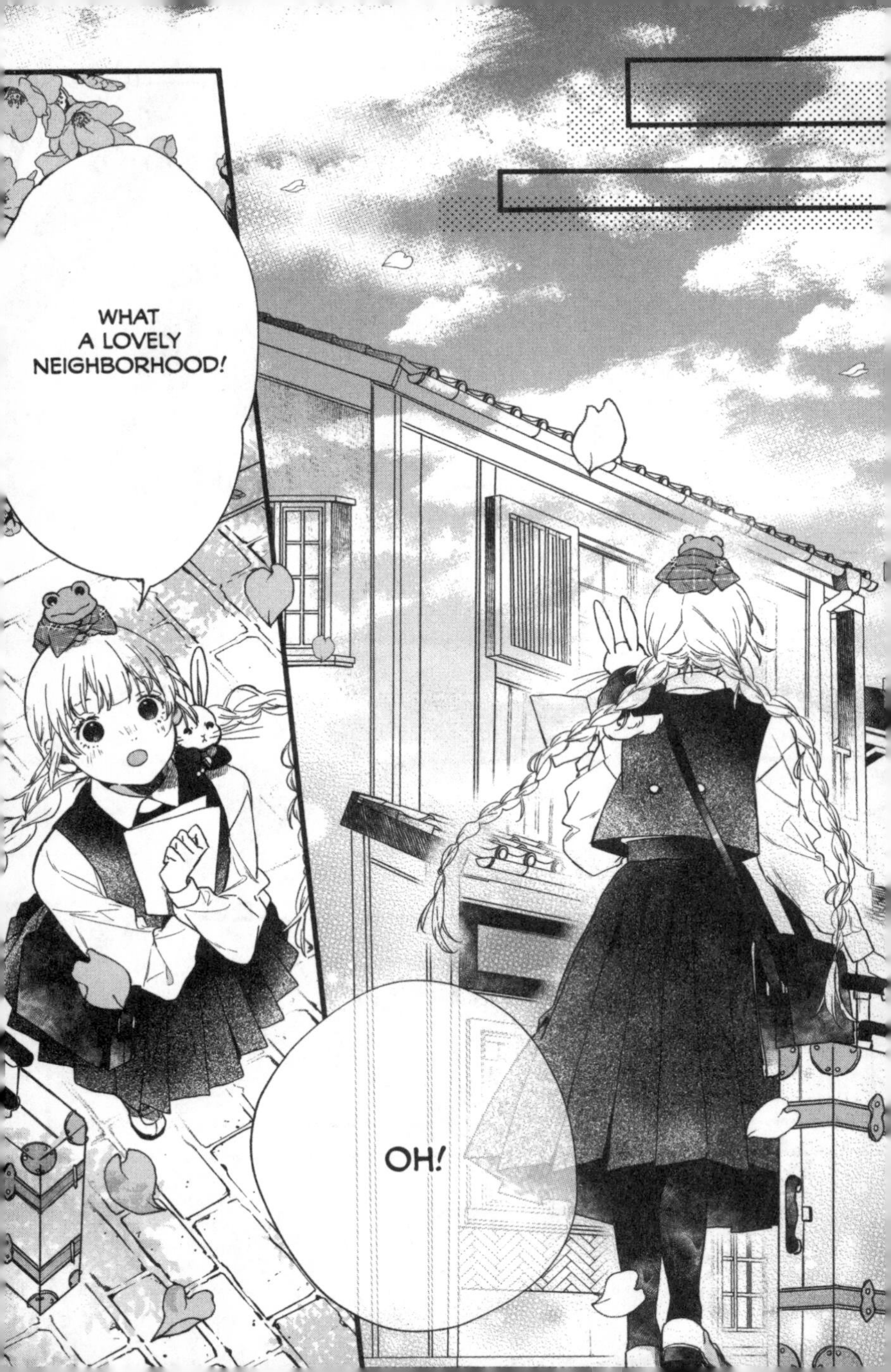
OH!
WHAT A LOVELY NEIGHBORHOOD!

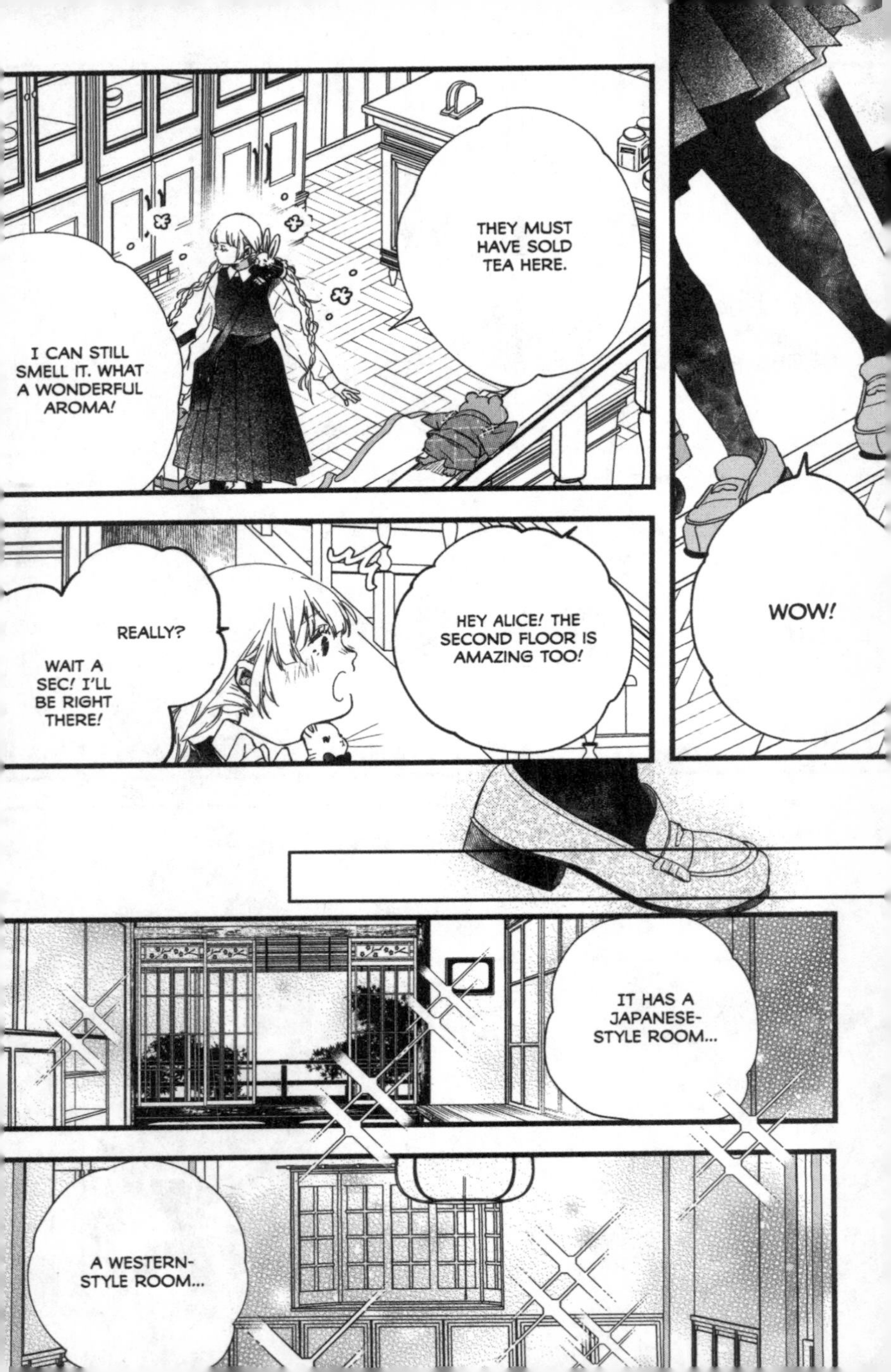
WOW!
THEY MUST HAVE SOLD TEA HERE.
I CAN STILL SMELL IT. WHAT A WONDERFUL AROMA!
HEY ALICE! THE SECOND FLOOR IS AMAZING TOO!
REALLY?
WAIT A SEC! I'LL BE RIGHT THERE!
IT HAS A JAPANESE-STYLE ROOM...
A WESTERN-STYLE ROOM...

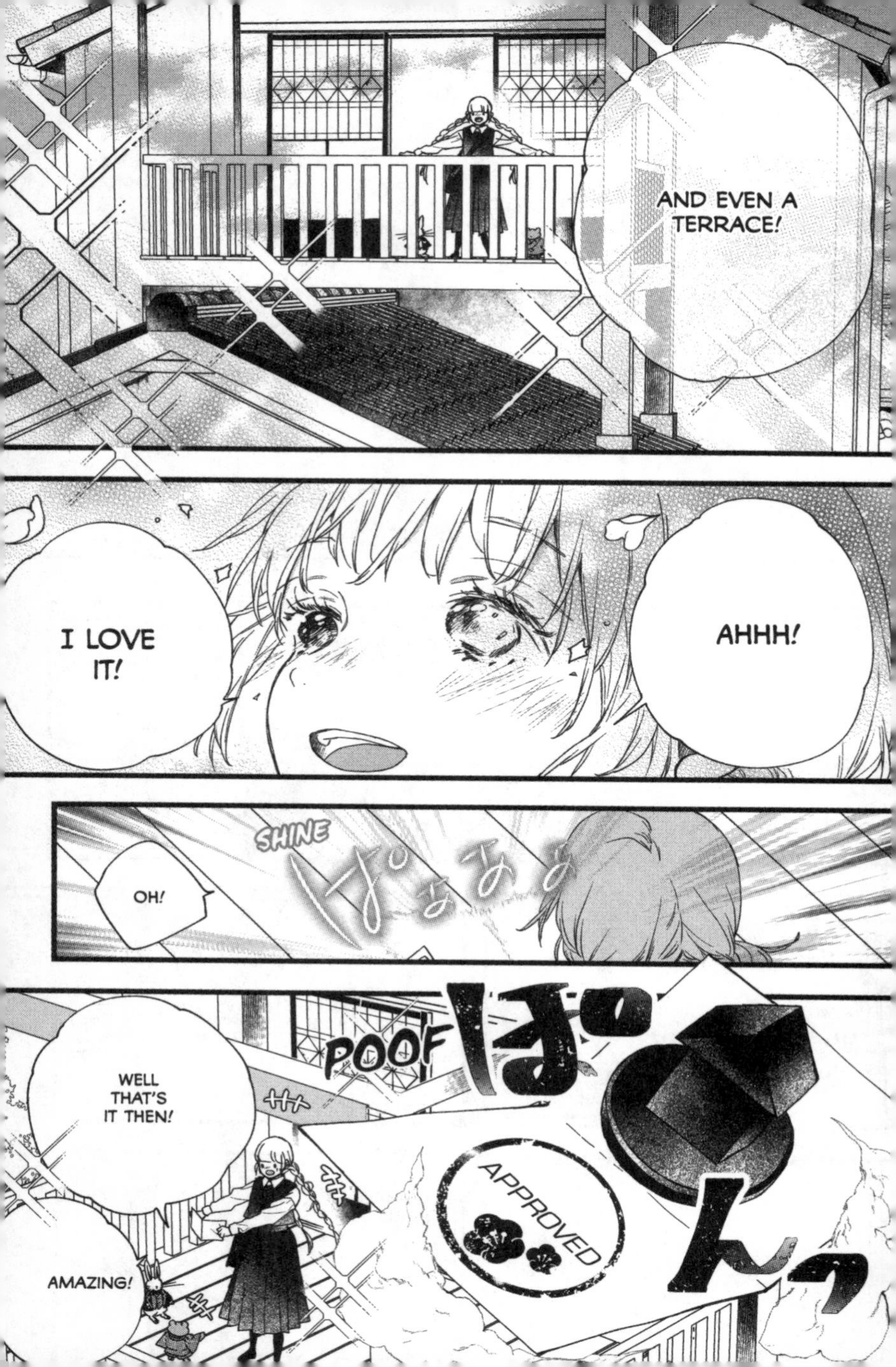
AND EVEN A TERRACE!
AHHH!
I LOVE IT!
SHINE
OH!
POOF
APPROVED
WELL THAT'S IT THEN!
AMAZING!

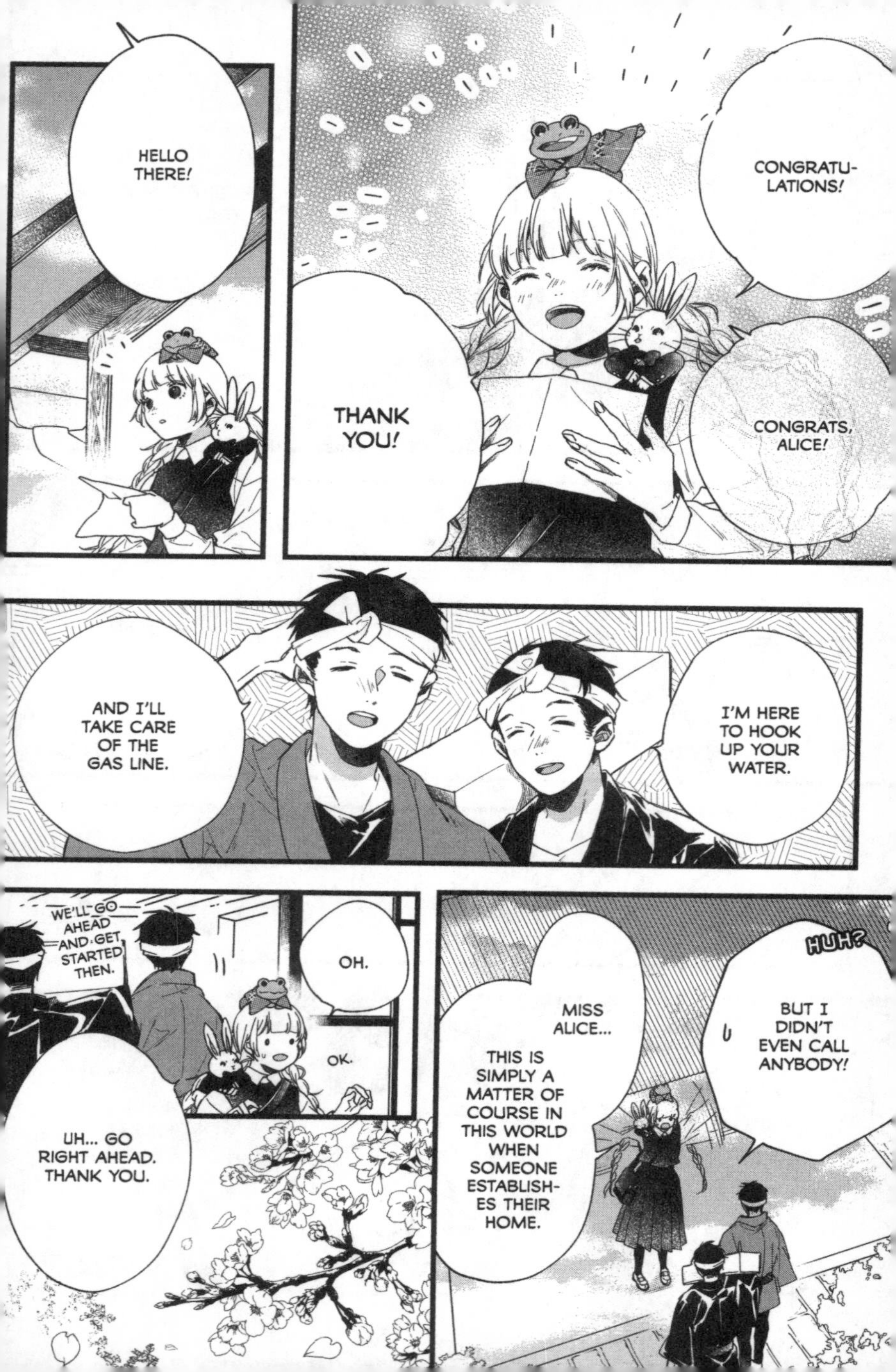
CONGRATULATIONS!
CONGRATS, ALICE!
THANK YOU!
HELLO THERE!
I'M HERE TO HOOK UP YOUR WATER.
AND I'LL TAKE CARE OF THE GAS LINE.
HUH?
BUT I DIDN'T EVEN CALL ANYBODY!
MISS ALICE...
THIS IS SIMPLY A MATTER OF COURSE IN THIS WORLD WHEN SOMEONE ESTABLISHES THEIR HOME.
OH.
WE'LL GO AHEAD AND GET STARTED THEN.
OK.
UH... GO RIGHT AHEAD. THANK YOU.

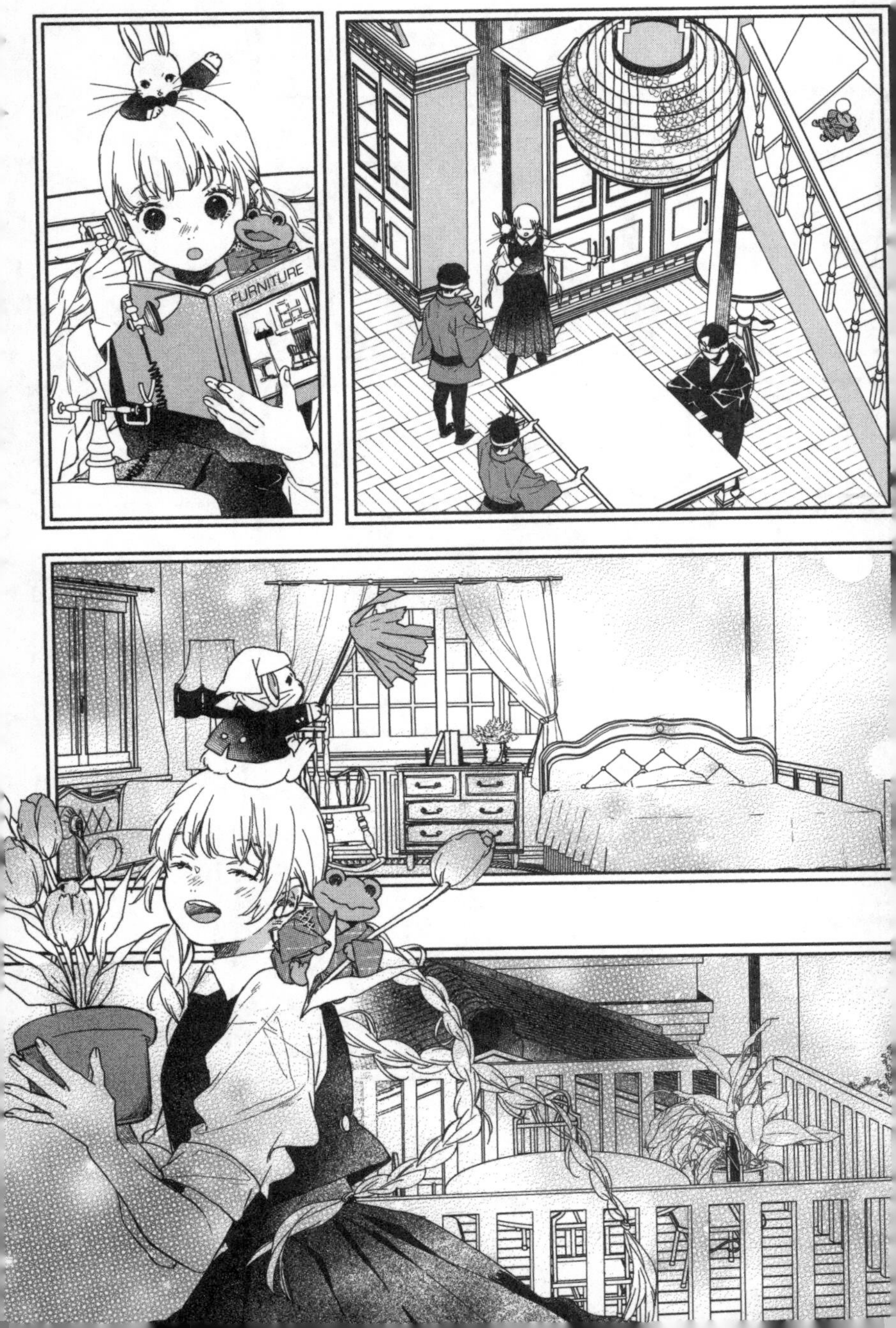
FURNITURE
FURNITURE

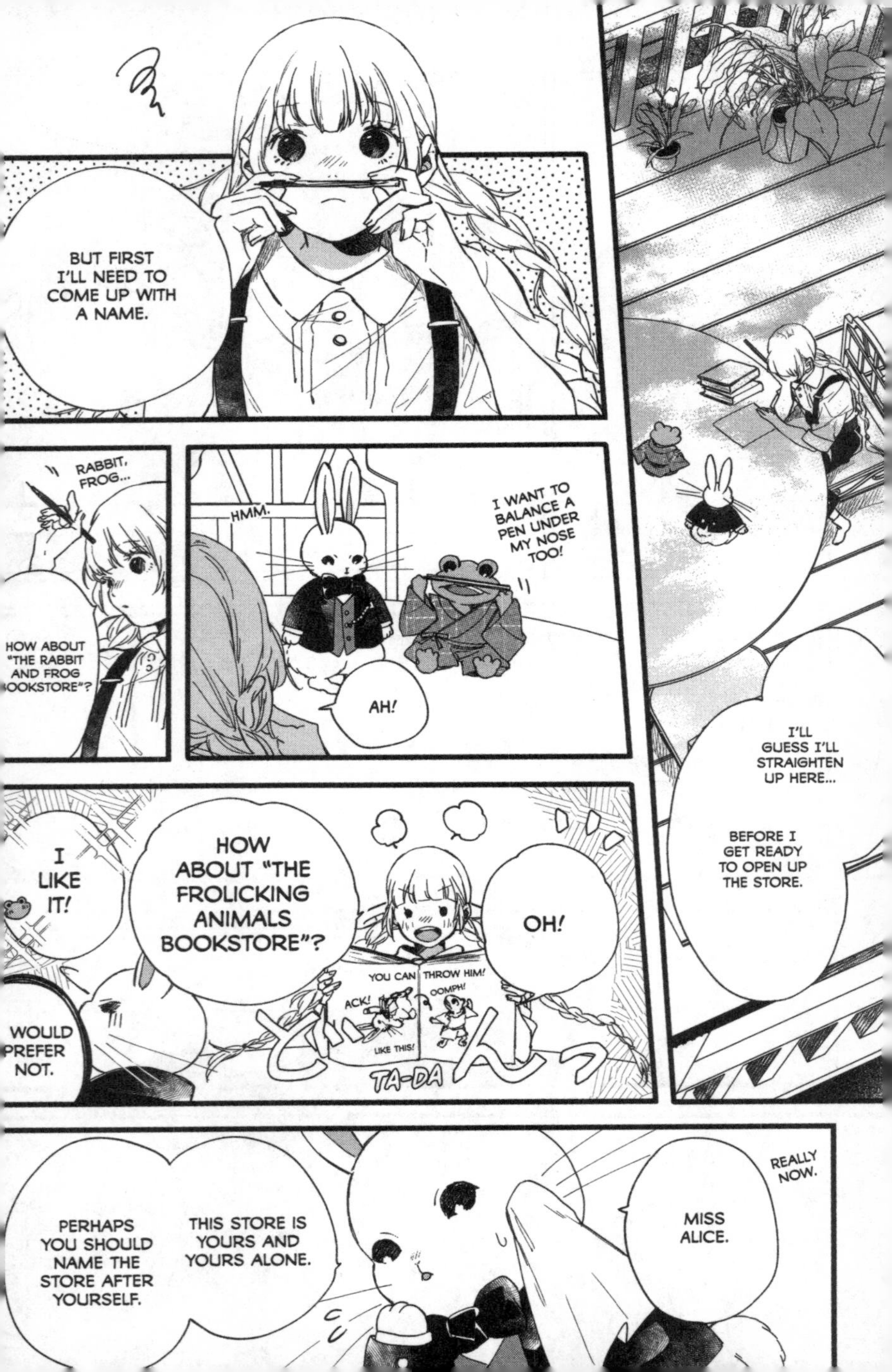
I'LL GUESS I'LL STRAIGHTEN UP HERE...
BEFORE I GET READY TO OPEN UP THE STORE.
BUT FIRST I'LL NEED TO COME UP WITH A NAME.
I WANT TO BALANCE A PEN UNDER MY NOSE TOO!
HMM.
AH!
RABBIT, FROG...
HOW ABOUT "THE RABBIT AND FROG OOKSTORE"?
OH!
HOW ABOUT "THE FROLICKING ANIMALS BOOKSTORE"?
YOU CAN THROW HIM!
OOMPH!
ACK!
LIKE THIS!
TA-DA
I LIKE IT!
WOULD PREFER NOT.
REALLY NOW.
MISS ALICE.
THIS STORE IS YOURS AND YOURS ALONE.
PERHAPS YOU SHOULD NAME THE STORE AFTER YOURSELF.

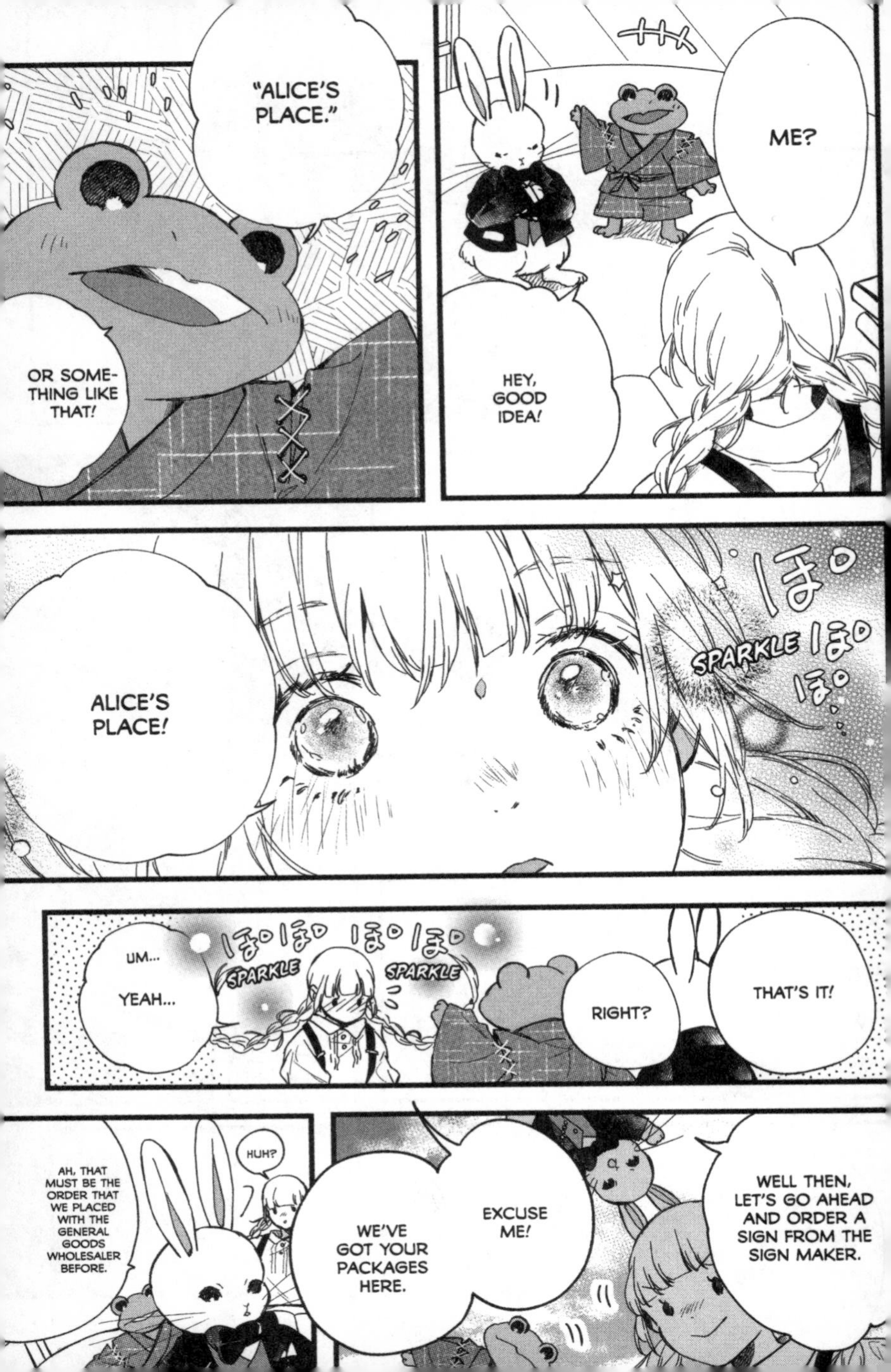
ME?
HEY, GOOD IDEA!
"ALICE'S PLACE."
OR SOME-THING LIKE THAT!
SPARKLE
ALICE'S PLACE!
THAT'S IT!
RIGHT?
SPARKLE
SPARKLE
UM... YEAH...
WELL THEN, LET'S GO AHEAD AND ORDER A SIGN FROM THE SIGN MAKER.
EXCUSE ME!
WE'VE GOT YOUR PACKAGES HERE.
HUH?
AH, THAT MUST BE THE ORDER THAT WE PLACED WITH THE GENERAL GOODS WHOLESALER BEFORE.

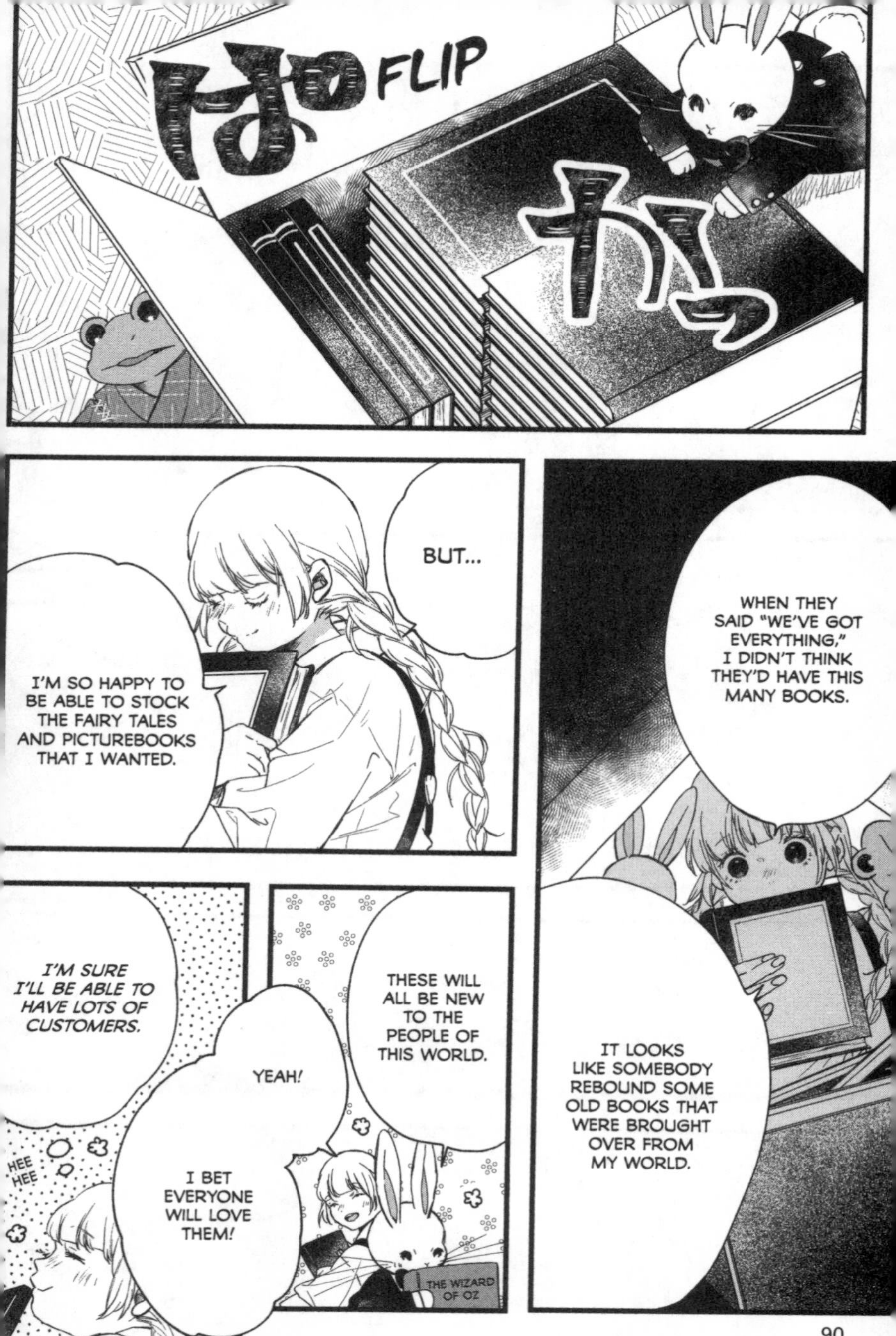
FLIP
WHEN THEY SAID "WE'VE GOT EVERYTHING," I DIDN'T THINK THEY'D HAVE THIS MANY BOOKS.
IT LOOKS LIKE SOMEBODY REBOUND SOME OLD BOOKS THAT WERE BROUGHT OVER FROM MY WORLD.
BUT...
I'M SO HAPPY TO BE ABLE TO STOCK THE FAIRY TALES AND PICTUREBOOKS THAT I WANTED.
THESE WILL ALL BE NEW TO THE PEOPLE OF THIS WORLD.
YEAH!
I BET EVERYONE WILL LOVE THEM!
THE WIZARD OF OZ
I'M SURE I'LL BE ABLE TO HAVE LOTS OF CUSTOMERS.
HEE HEE

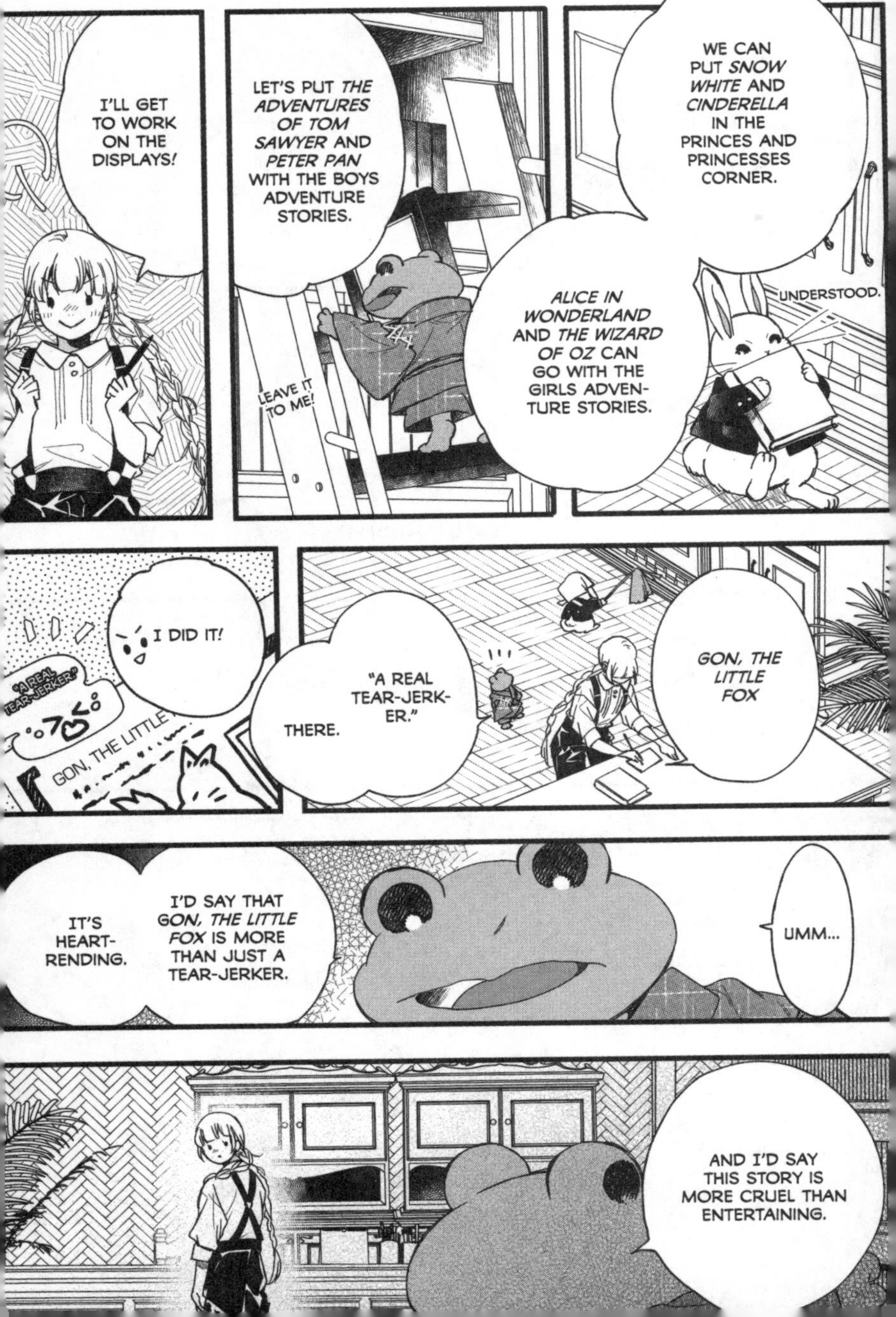
WE CAN PUT *SNOW WHITE* AND *CINDERELLA* IN THE PRINCES AND PRINCESSES CORNER.
UNDERSTOOD.
ALICE IN WONDERLAND AND *THE WIZARD OF OZ* CAN GO WITH THE GIRLS ADVENTURE STORIES.
LET'S PUT *THE ADVENTURES OF TOM SAWYER* AND *PETER PAN* WITH THE BOYS ADVENTURE STORIES.
LEAVE IT TO ME!
I'LL GET TO WORK ON THE DISPLAYS!
GON, THE LITTLE FOX
"A REAL TEAR-JERKER."
THERE.
I DID IT!
"A REAL TEAR-JERKER."
GON, THE LITTLE
UMM...
I'D SAY THAT *GON, THE LITTLE FOX* IS MORE THAN JUST A TEAR-JERKER.
IT'S HEART-RENDING.
AND I'D SAY THIS STORY IS MORE CRUEL THAN ENTERTAINING.

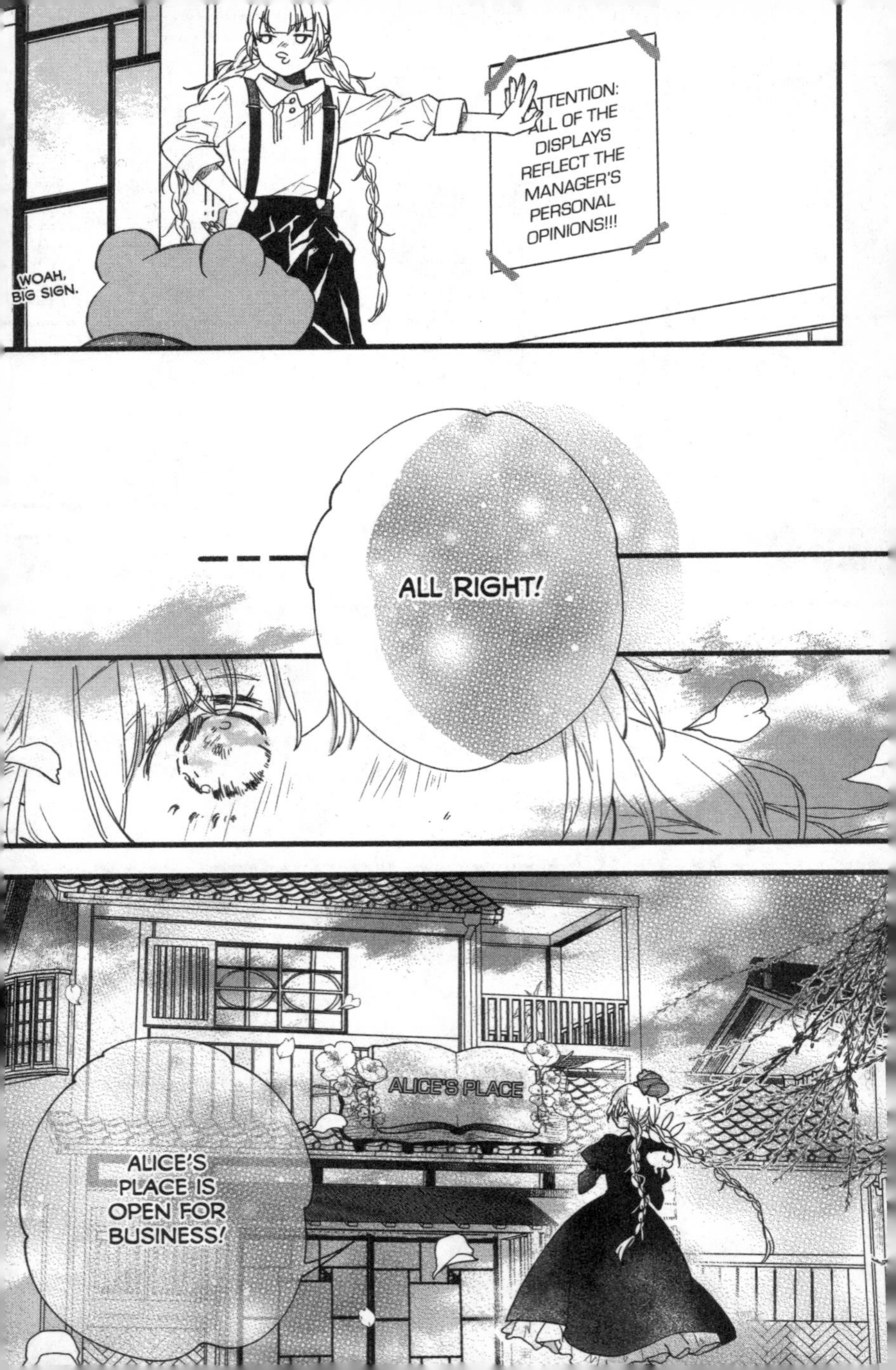
ATTENTION: ALL OF THE DISPLAYS REFLECT THE MANAGER'S PERSONAL OPINIONS!!!
WOAH, BIG SIGN.
ALL RIGHT!
ALICE'S PLACE
ALICE'S PLACE IS OPEN FOR BUSINESS!

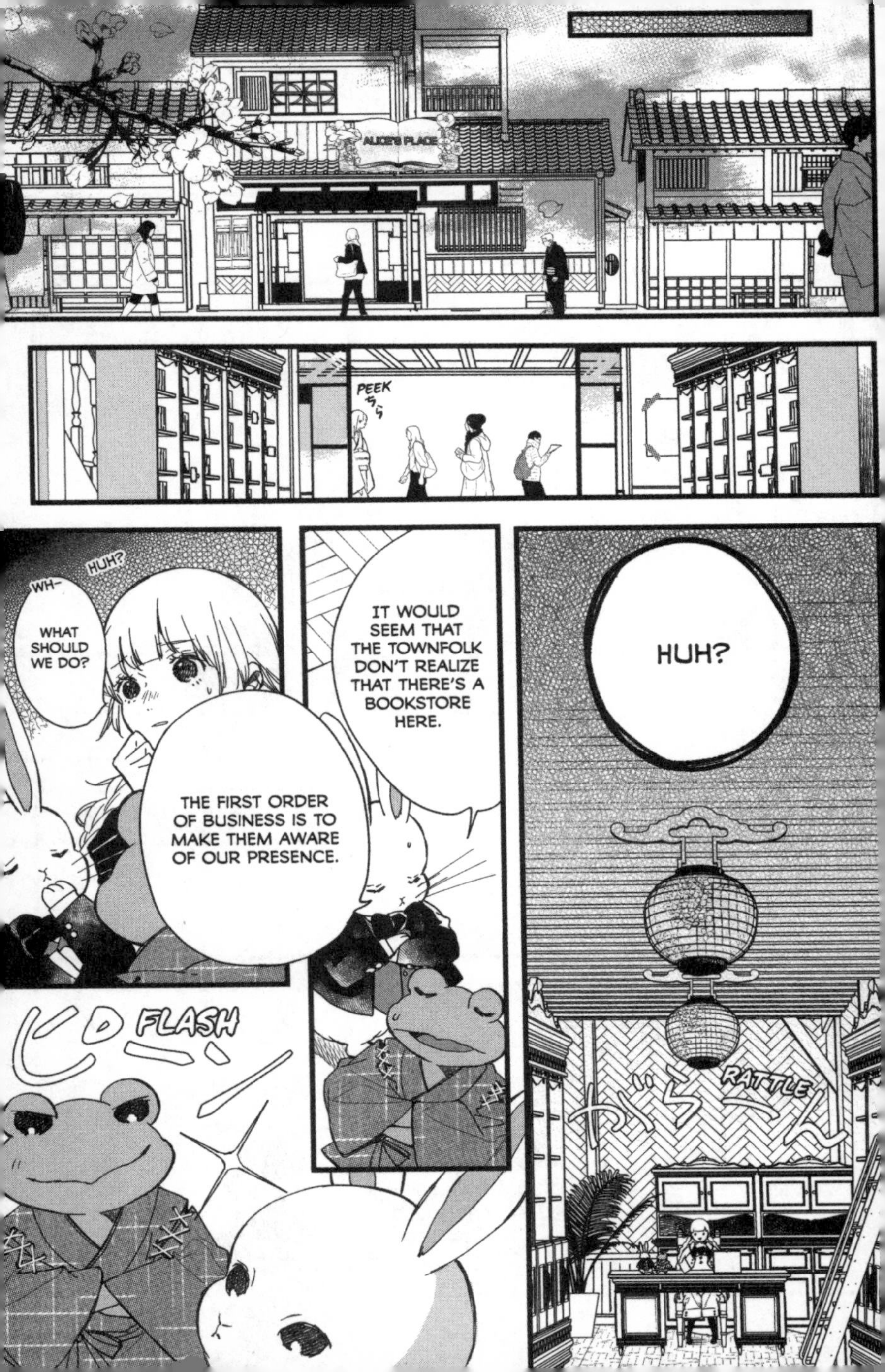
ALICE'S PLACE
PEEK
ちら
HUH?
RATTLE
IT WOULD SEEM THAT THE TOWNFOLK DON'T REALIZE THAT THERE'S A BOOKSTORE HERE.
HUH?
WH-
WHAT SHOULD WE DO?
THE FIRST ORDER OF BUSINESS IS TO MAKE THEM AWARE OF OUR PRESENCE.
FLASH

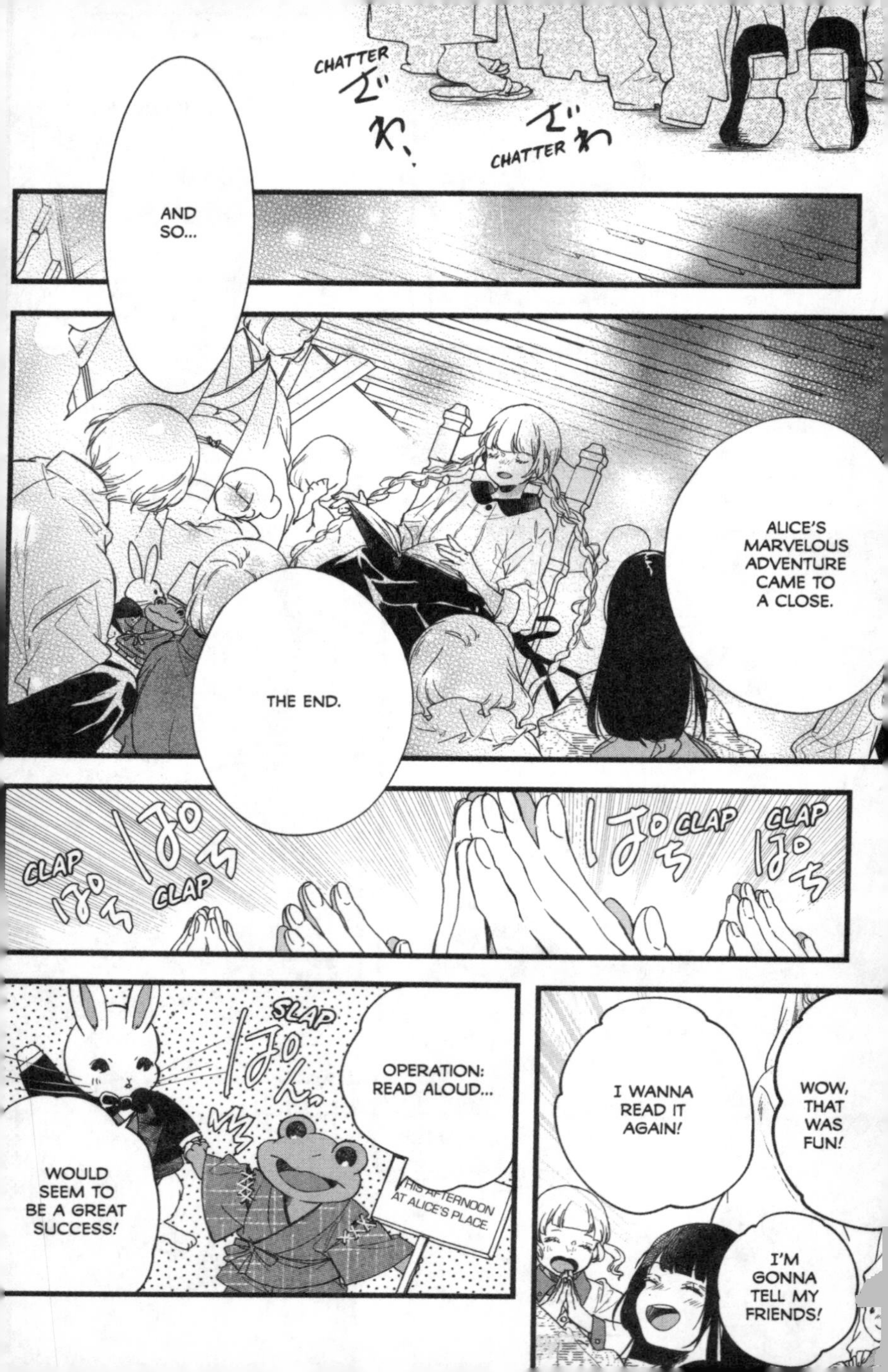

CHATTER ざわ
CHATTER ざわ
AND SO...
ALICE'S MARVELOUS ADVENTURE CAME TO A CLOSE.
THE END.
CLAP ぱち
CLAP ぱち
CLAP ぱち
CLAP ぱち
WOW, THAT WAS FUN!
I WANNA READ IT AGAIN!
I'M GONNA TELL MY FRIENDS!
OPERATION: READ ALOUD...
SLAP ぽん
HIS AFTERNOON AT ALICE'S PLACE.
WOULD SEEM TO BE A GREAT SUCCESS!

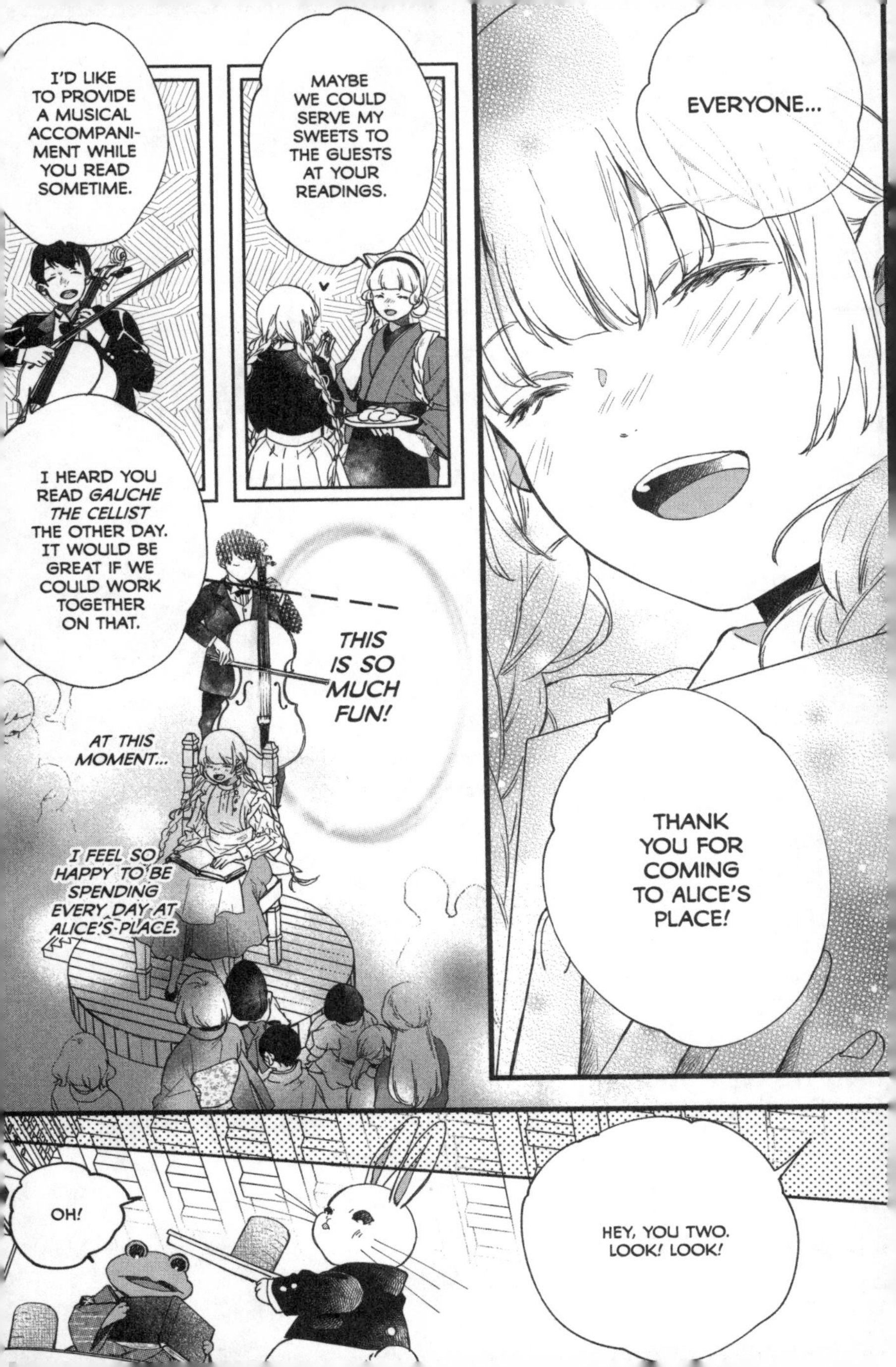
EVERYONE...
THANK YOU FOR COMING TO ALICE'S PLACE!
MAYBE WE COULD SERVE MY SWEETS TO THE GUESTS AT YOUR READINGS.
I'D LIKE TO PROVIDE A MUSICAL ACCOMPANI-MENT WHILE YOU READ SOMETIME.
I HEARD YOU READ *GAUCHE THE CELLIST* THE OTHER DAY. IT WOULD BE GREAT IF WE COULD WORK TOGETHER ON THAT.
THIS IS SO MUCH FUN!
AT THIS MOMENT...
I FEEL SO HAPPY TO BE SPENDING EVERY DAY AT ALICE'S PLACE.
HEY, YOU TWO. LOOK! LOOK!
OH!

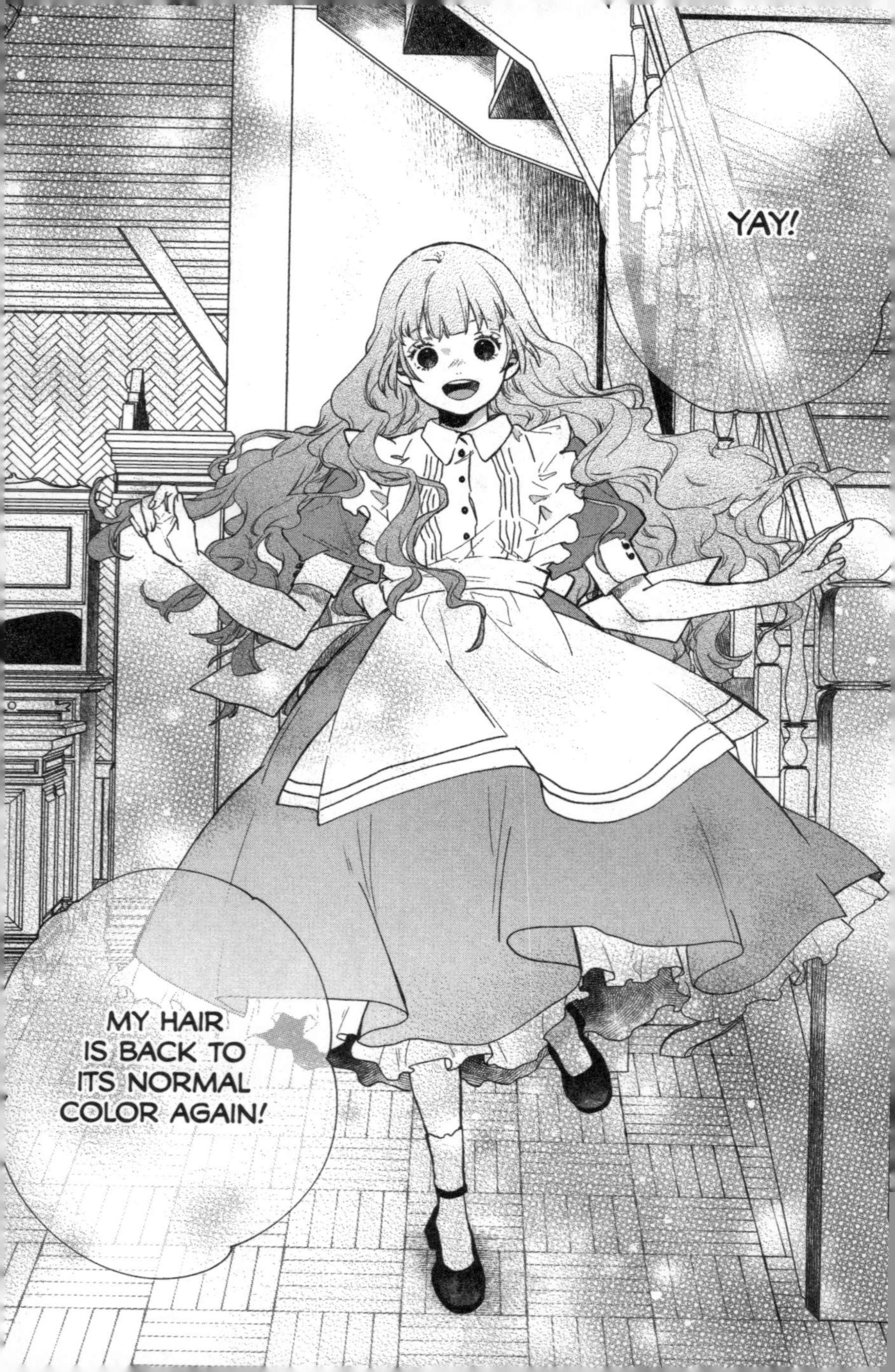
YAY!
MY HAIR IS BACK TO ITS NORMAL COLOR AGAIN!

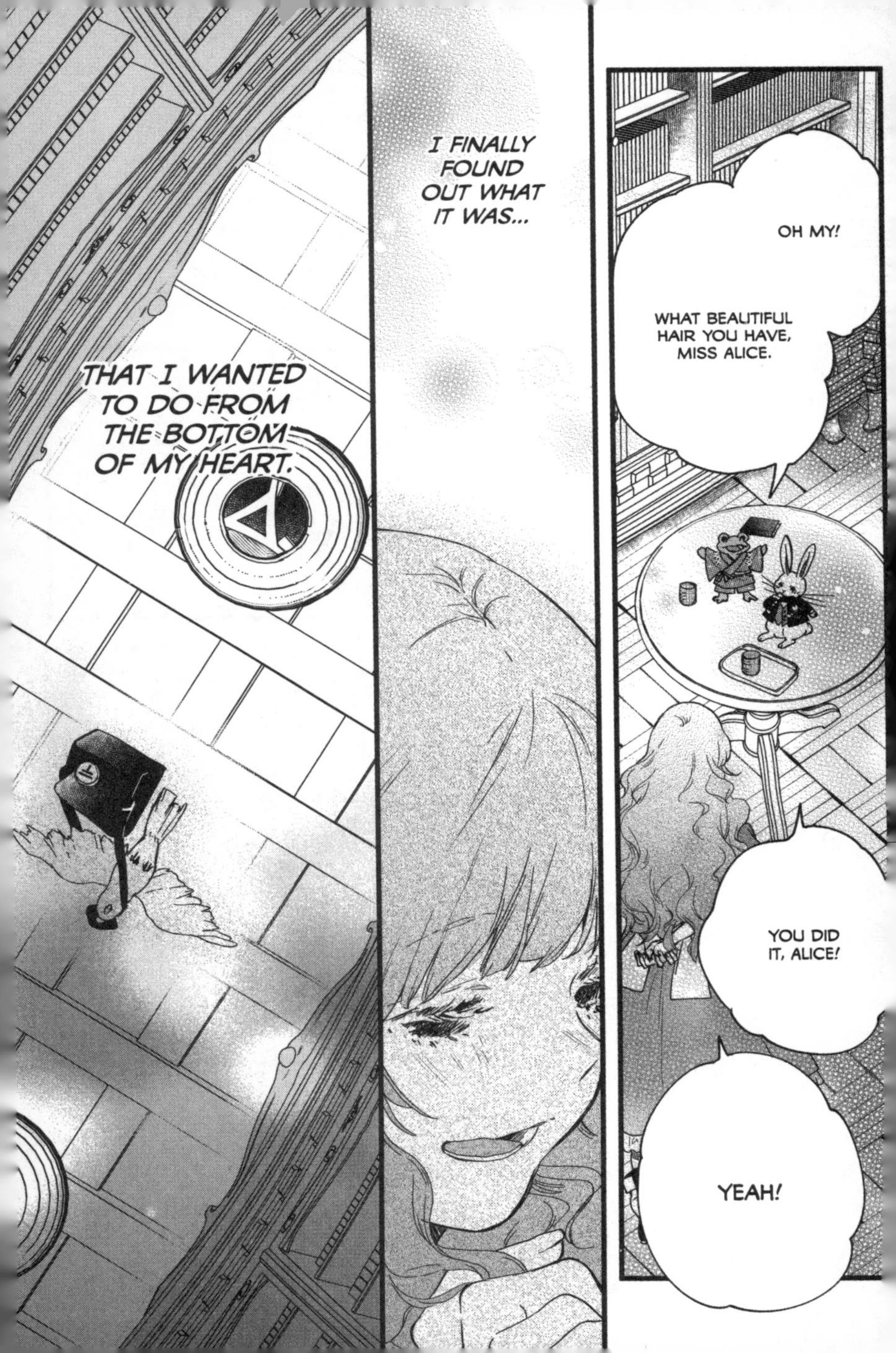
OH MY!
WHAT BEAUTIFUL HAIR YOU HAVE, MISS ALICE.
YOU DID IT, ALICE!
YEAH!
I FINALLY FOUND OUT WHAT IT WAS...
THAT I WANTED TO DO FROM THE BOTTOM OF MY HEART.

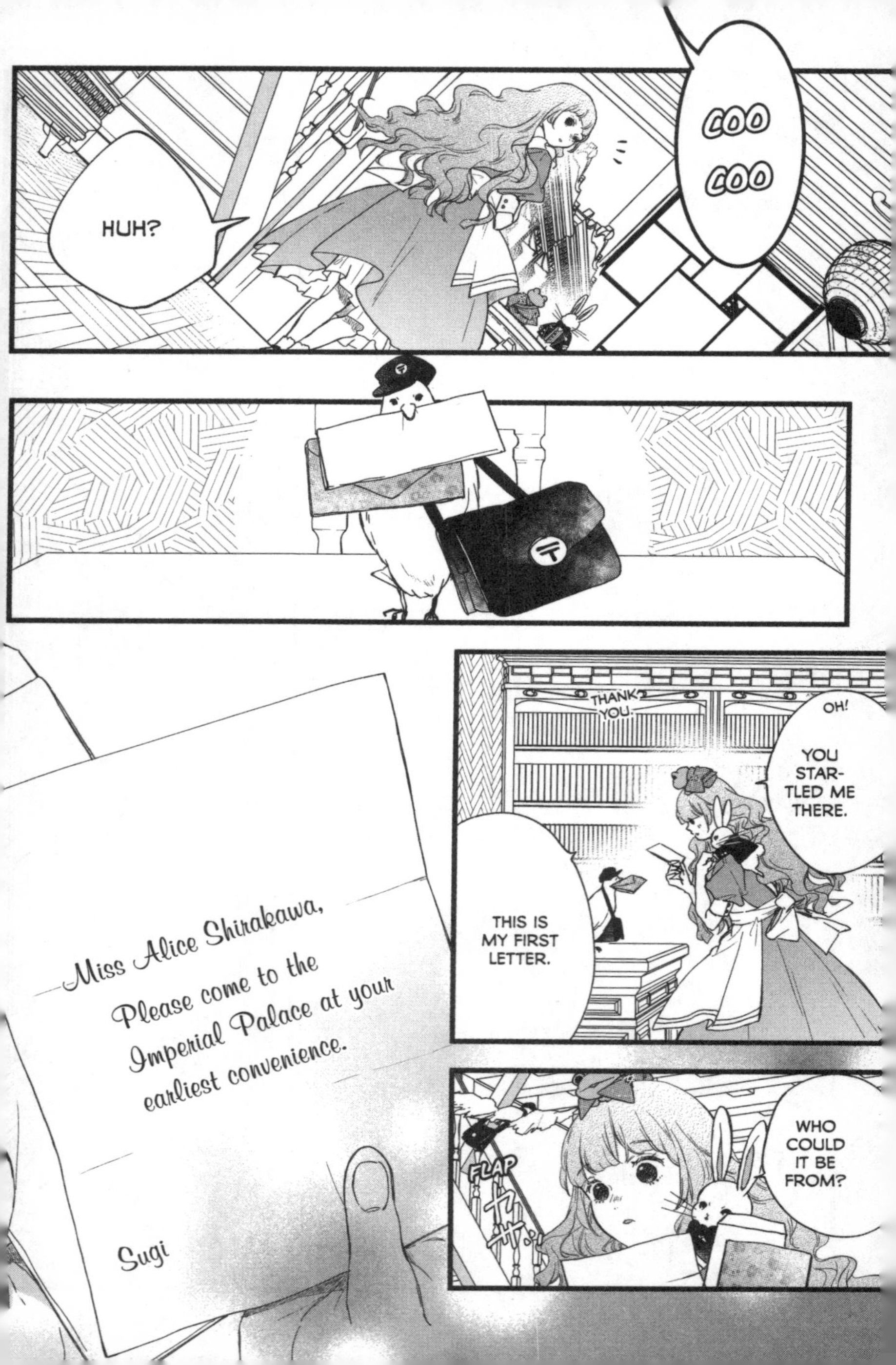
COO COO
HUH?
OH!
YOU STARTLED ME THERE.
THANK YOU.
THIS IS MY FIRST LETTER.
WHO COULD IT BE FROM?
FLAP
Miss Alice Shirakawa,
Please come to the Imperial Palace at your earliest convenience.
Sugi

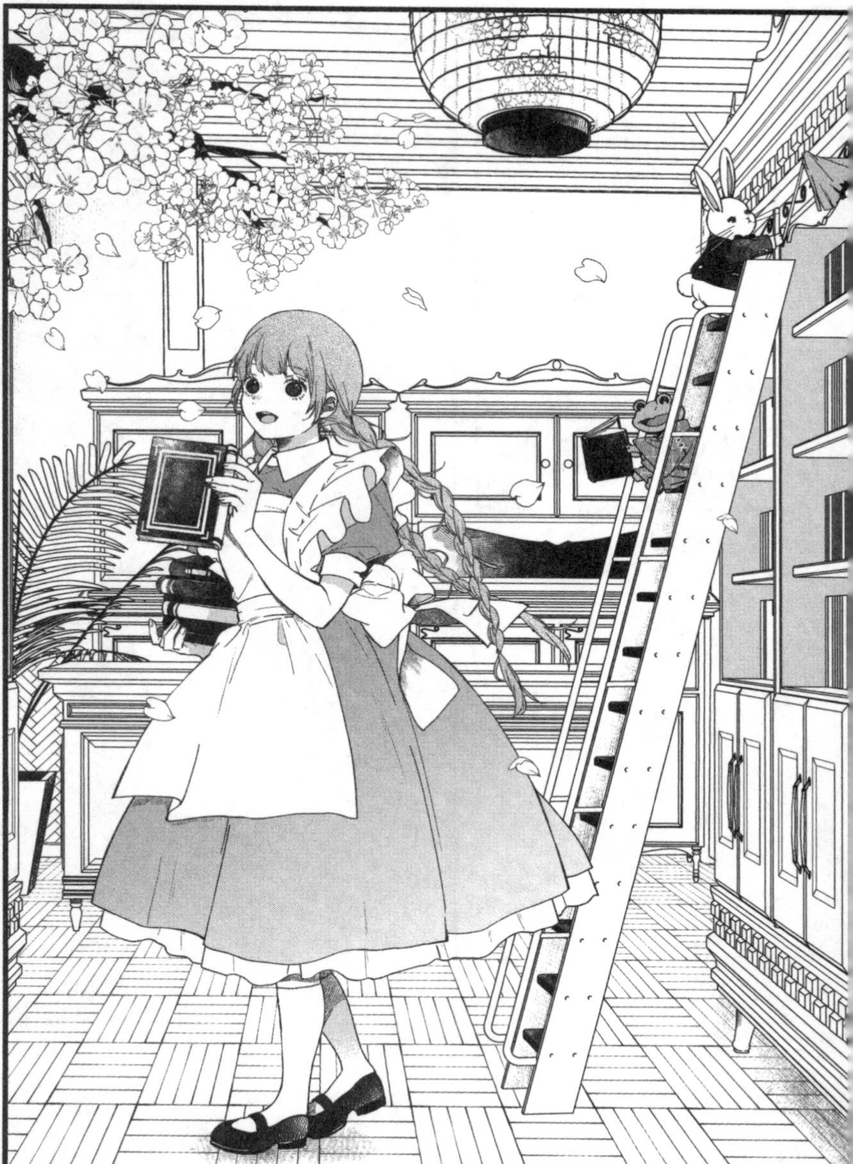
Chapter 11

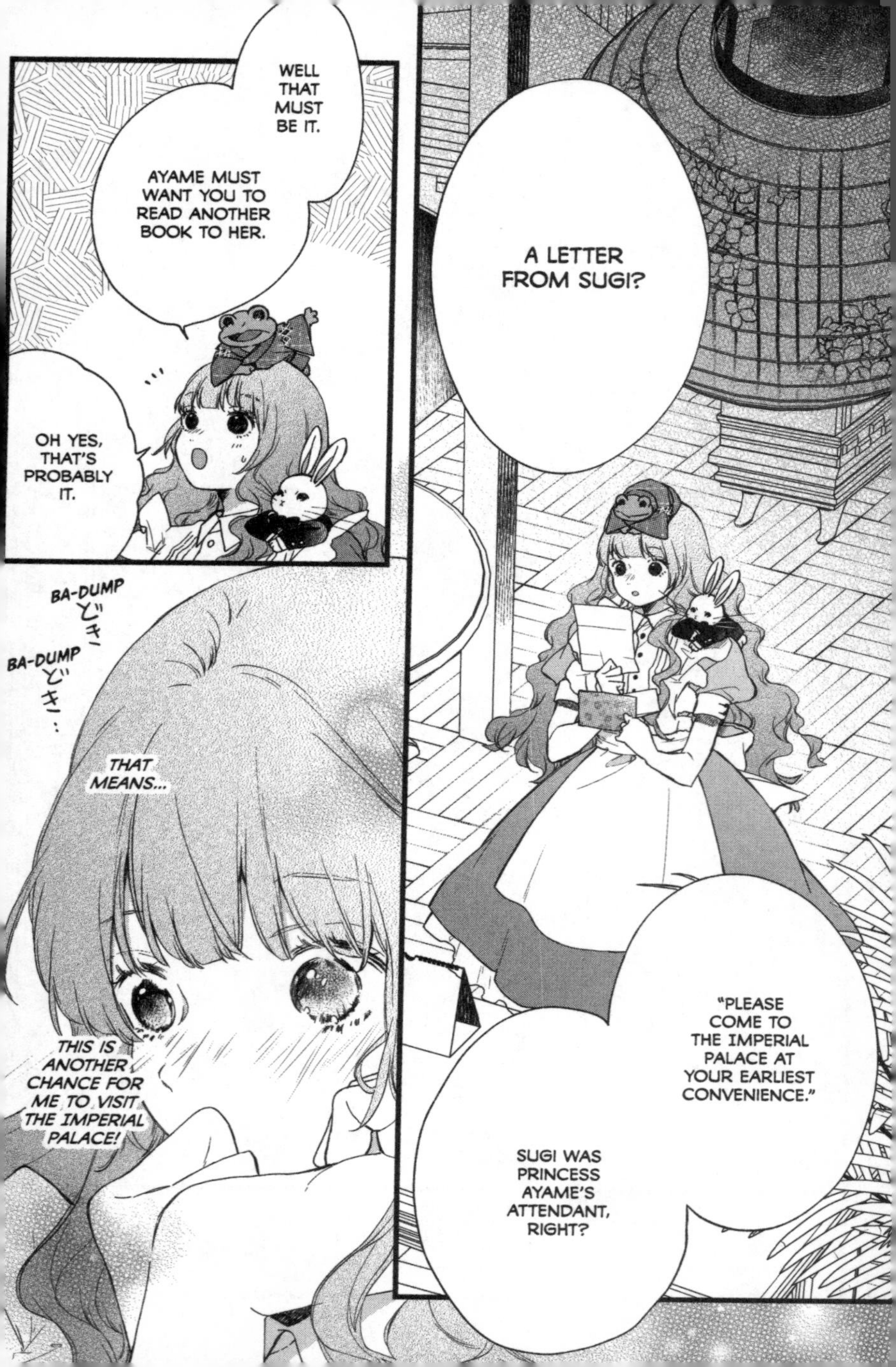
A LETTER FROM SUGI?
"PLEASE COME TO THE IMPERIAL PALACE AT YOUR EARLIEST CONVENIENCE."
SUGI WAS PRINCESS AYAME'S ATTENDANT, RIGHT?
WELL THAT MUST BE IT.
AYAME MUST WANT YOU TO READ ANOTHER BOOK TO HER.
OH YES, THAT'S PROBABLY IT.
BA-DUMP どき
BA-DUMP どき…
THAT MEANS...
THIS IS ANOTHER CHANCE FOR ME TO VISIT THE IMPERIAL PALACE!

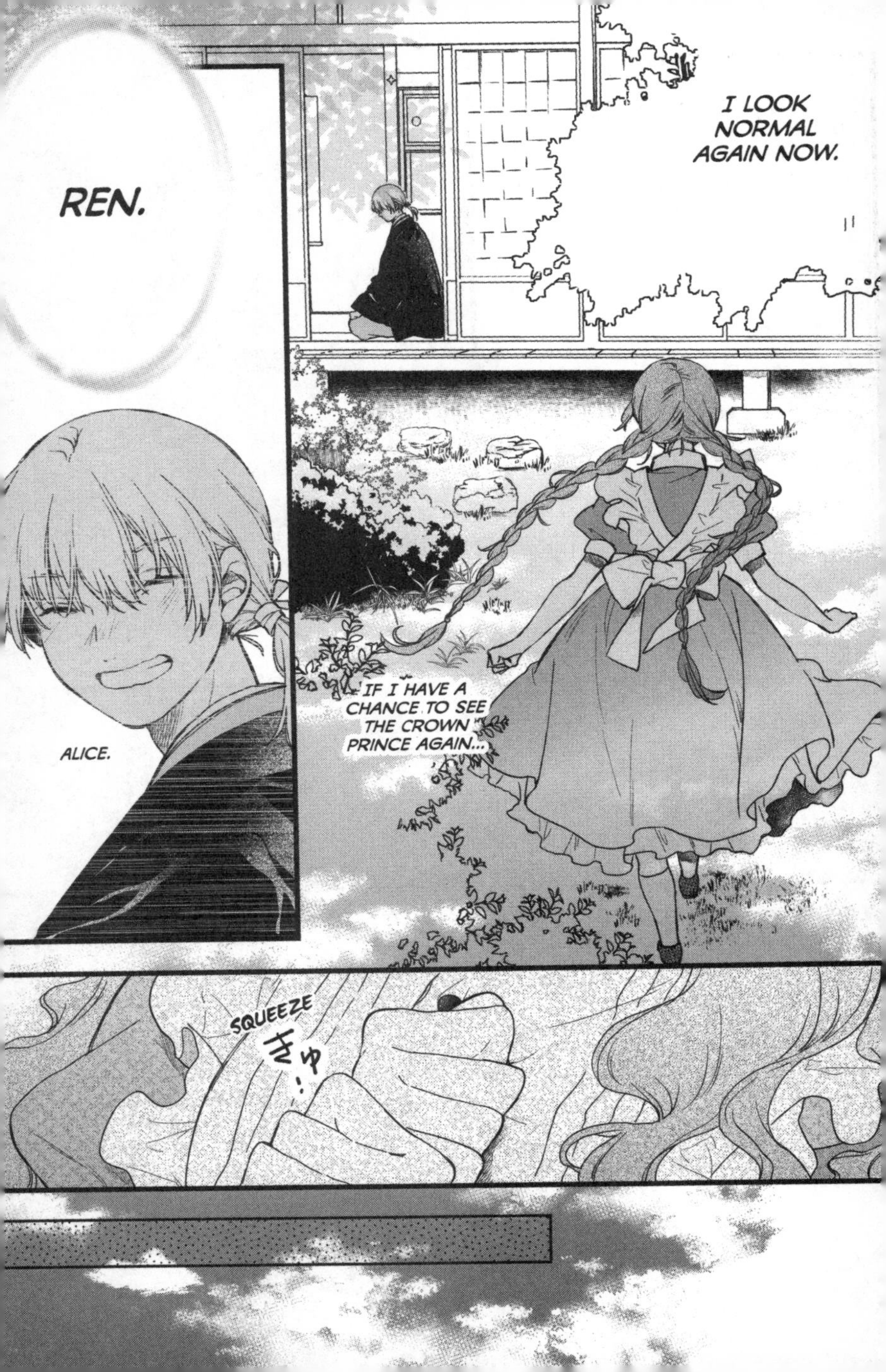
I LOOK NORMAL AGAIN NOW.
IF I HAVE A CHANCE TO SEE THE CROWN PRINCE AGAIN...
REN.
ALICE.
SQUEEZE
きゅ!

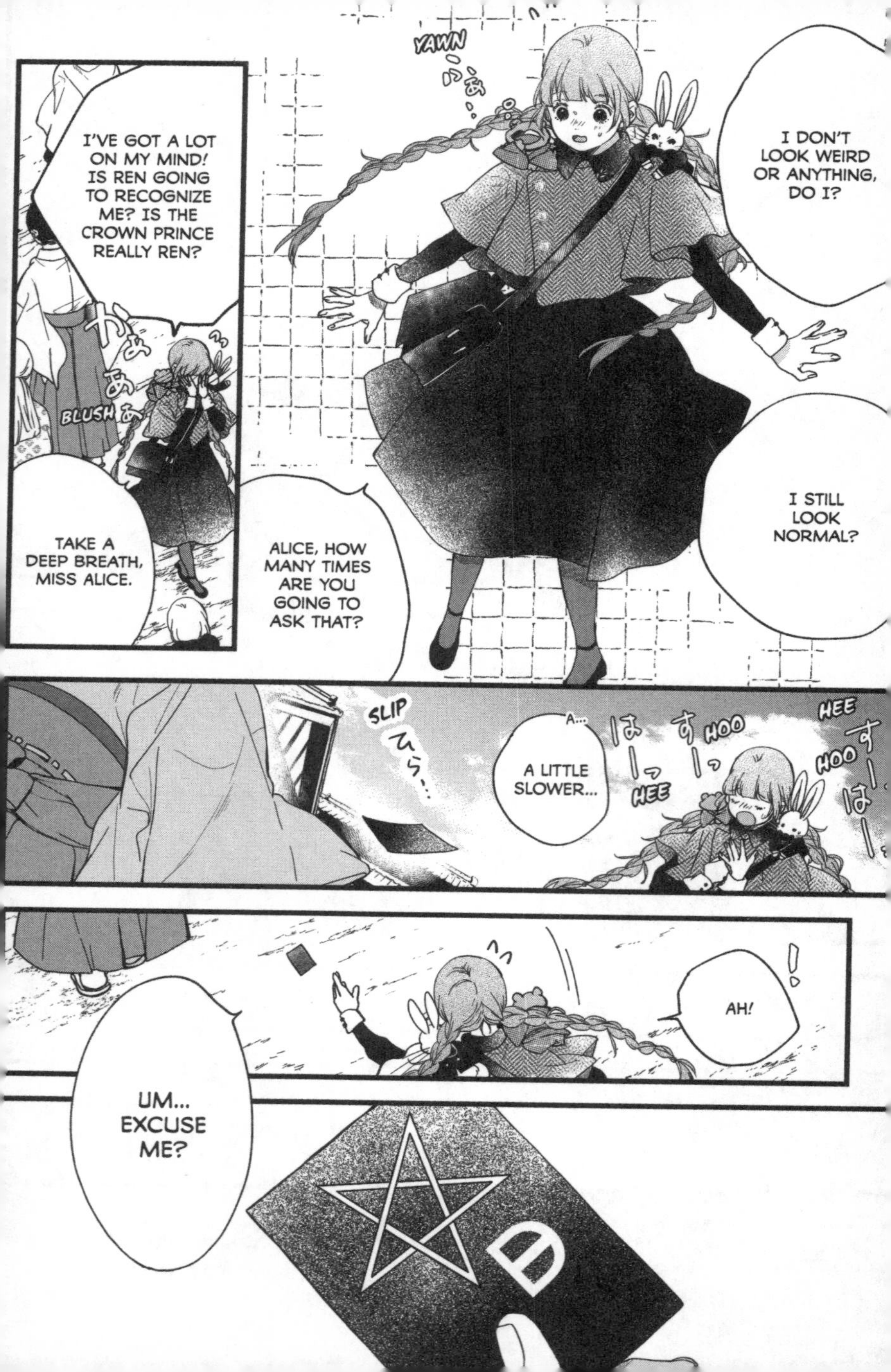
YAWN
I DON'T LOOK WEIRD OR ANYTHING, DO I?
I STILL LOOK NORMAL?
ALICE, HOW MANY TIMES ARE YOU GOING TO ASK THAT?
I'VE GOT A LOT ON MY MIND! IS REN GOING TO RECOGNIZE ME? IS THE CROWN PRINCE REALLY REN?
BLUSH
TAKE A DEEP BREATH, MISS ALICE.
HEE HOO
HOO HEE
A... A LITTLE SLOWER...
SLIP
AH!
UM... EXCUSE ME?

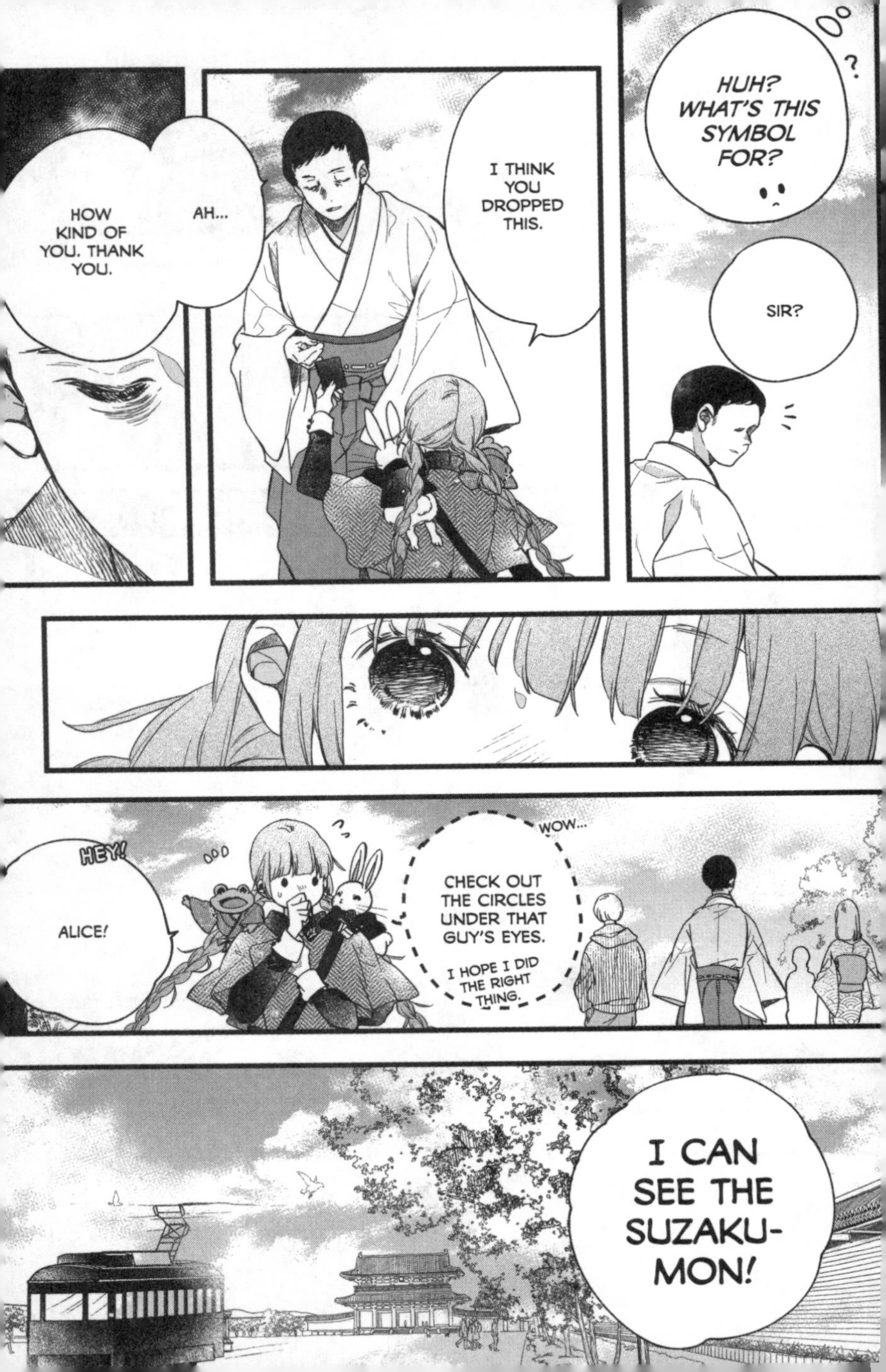
HUH? WHAT'S THIS SYMBOL FOR?
SIR?
I THINK YOU DROPPED THIS.
AH...
HOW KIND OF YOU. THANK YOU.
WOW...
CHECK OUT THE CIRCLES UNDER THAT GUY'S EYES.
I HOPE I DID THE RIGHT THING.
HEY!
ALICE!
I CAN SEE THE SUZAKU-MON!

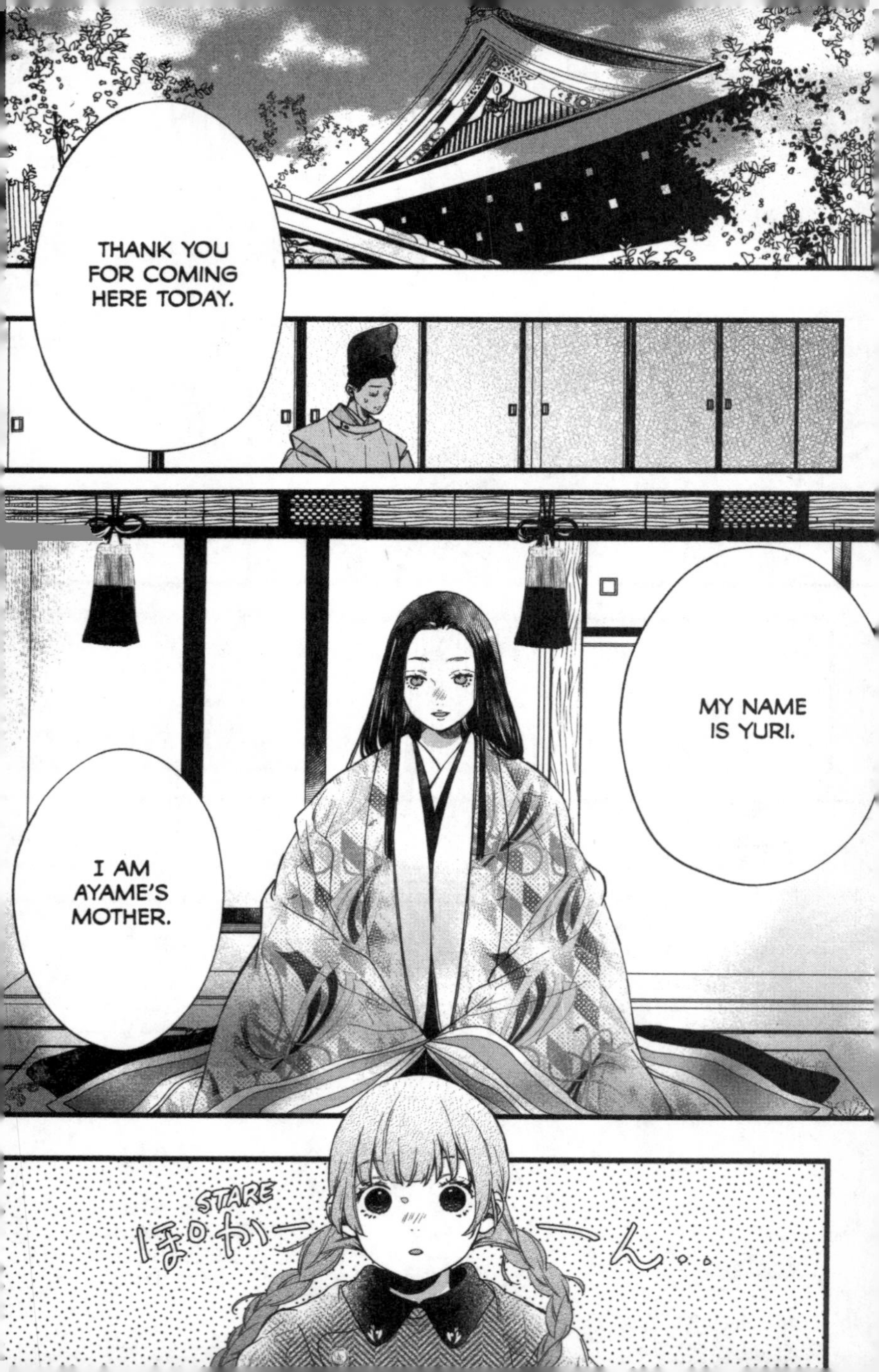
THANK YOU FOR COMING HERE TODAY.
MY NAME IS YURI.
I AM AYAME'S MOTHER.
STARE

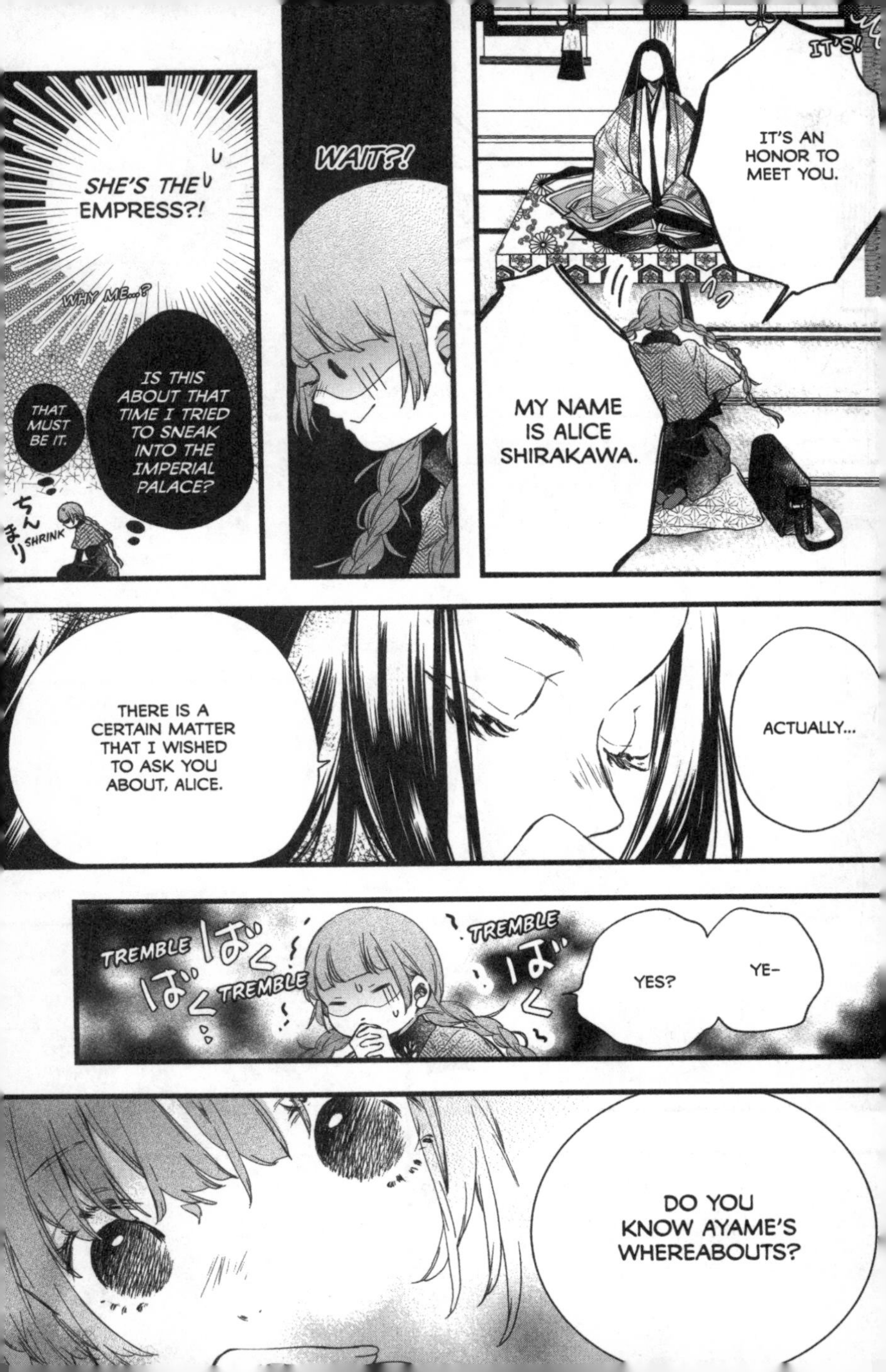
IT'S!
IT'S AN HONOR TO MEET YOU.
MY NAME IS ALICE SHIRAKAWA.
WAIT?!
SHE'S THE EMPRESS?!
WHY ME...?
IS THIS ABOUT THAT TIME I TRIED TO SNEAK INTO THE IMPERIAL PALACE?
THAT MUST BE IT.
ちんまり
SHRINK
ACTUALLY...
THERE IS A CERTAIN MATTER THAT I WISHED TO ASK YOU ABOUT, ALICE.
YE-
YES?
ばく
TREMBLE
ばくばく
TREMBLE
TREMBLE
DO YOU KNOW AYAME'S WHEREABOUTS?

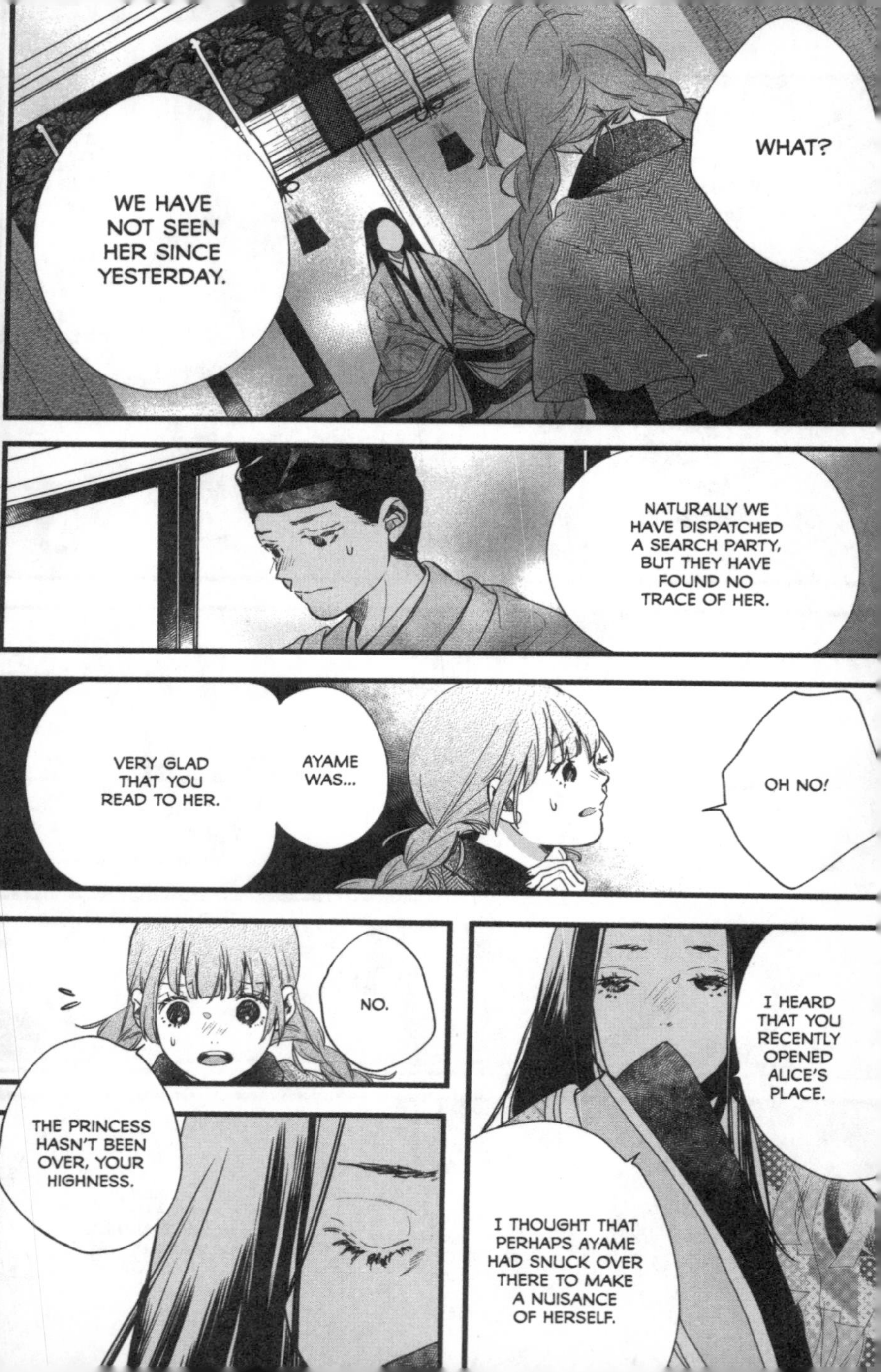
WHAT?
WE HAVE NOT SEEN HER SINCE YESTERDAY.
NATURALLY WE HAVE DISPATCHED A SEARCH PARTY, BUT THEY HAVE FOUND NO TRACE OF HER.
OH NO!
AYAME WAS...
VERY GLAD THAT YOU READ TO HER.
I HEARD THAT YOU RECENTLY OPENED ALICE'S PLACE.
I THOUGHT THAT PERHAPS AYAME HAD SNUCK OVER THERE TO MAKE A NUISANCE OF HERSELF.
NO.
THE PRINCESS HASN'T BEEN OVER, YOUR HIGHNESS.

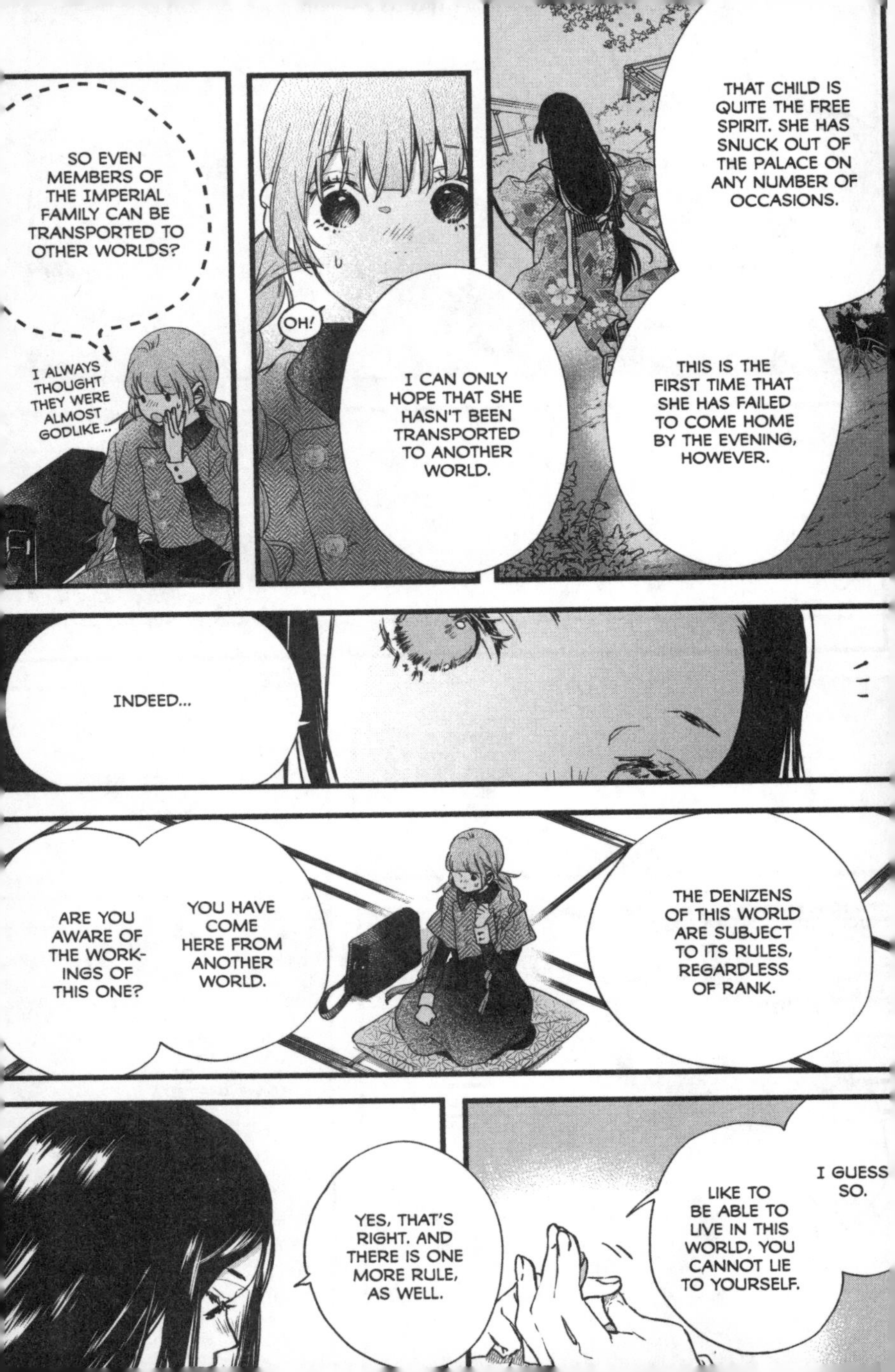
THAT CHILD IS QUITE THE FREE SPIRIT. SHE HAS SNUCK OUT OF THE PALACE ON ANY NUMBER OF OCCASIONS.
THIS IS THE FIRST TIME THAT SHE HAS FAILED TO COME HOME BY THE EVENING, HOWEVER.
I CAN ONLY HOPE THAT SHE HASN'T BEEN TRANSPORTED TO ANOTHER WORLD.
OH!
SO EVEN MEMBERS OF THE IMPERIAL FAMILY CAN BE TRANSPORTED TO OTHER WORLDS?
I ALWAYS THOUGHT THEY WERE ALMOST GODLIKE...
INDEED...
THE DENIZENS OF THIS WORLD ARE SUBJECT TO ITS RULES, REGARDLESS OF RANK.
YOU HAVE COME HERE FROM ANOTHER WORLD.
ARE YOU AWARE OF THE WORK-INGS OF THIS ONE?
I GUESS SO.
LIKE TO BE ABLE TO LIVE IN THIS WORLD, YOU CANNOT LIE TO YOURSELF.
YES, THAT'S RIGHT. AND THERE IS ONE MORE RULE, AS WELL.

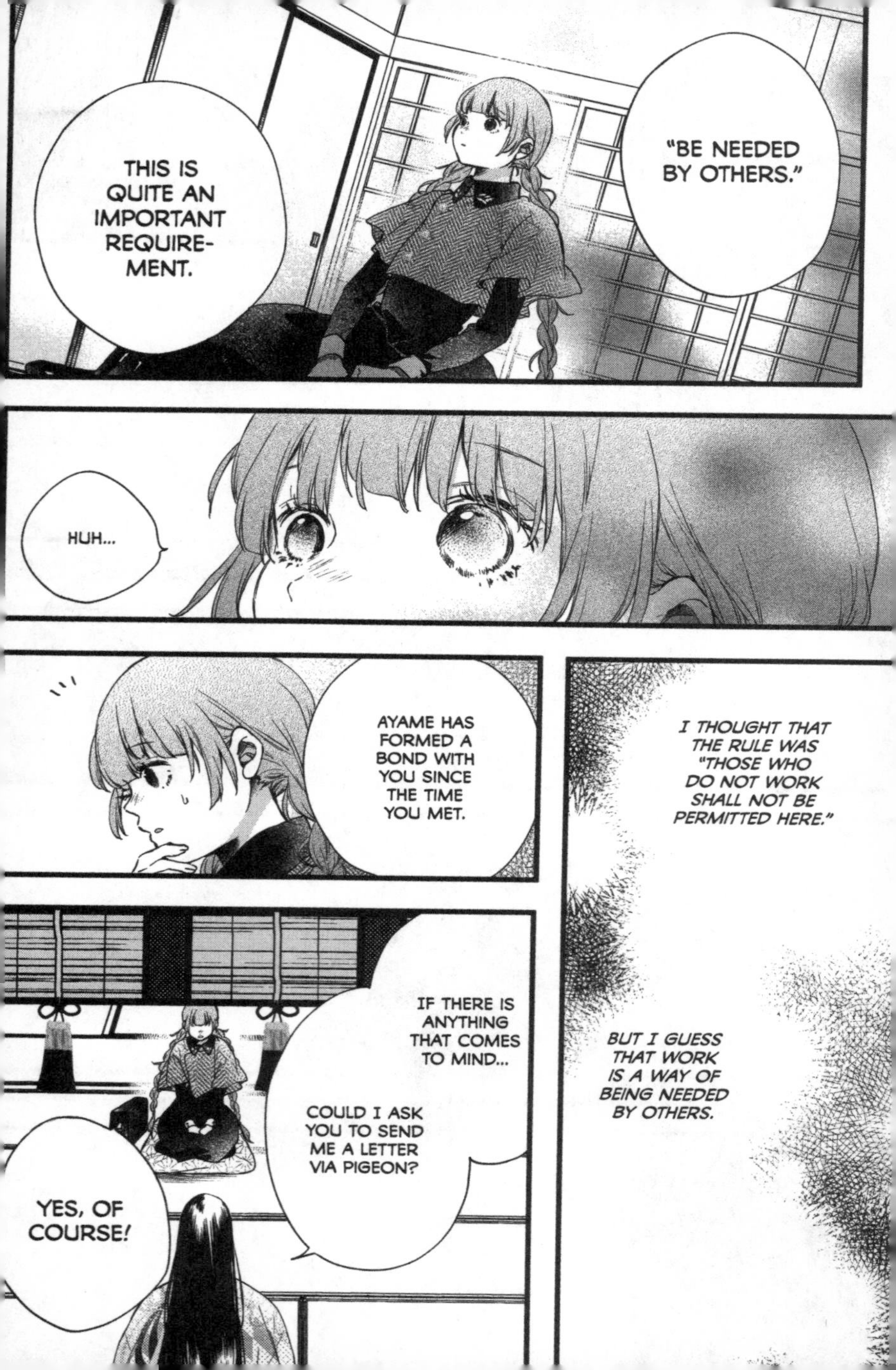
"BE NEEDED BY OTHERS."
THIS IS QUITE AN IMPORTANT REQUIRE-MENT.
HUH...
I THOUGHT THAT THE RULE WAS "THOSE WHO DO NOT WORK SHALL NOT BE PERMITTED HERE."
BUT I GUESS THAT WORK IS A WAY OF BEING NEEDED BY OTHERS.
AYAME HAS FORMED A BOND WITH YOU SINCE THE TIME YOU MET.
IF THERE IS ANYTHING THAT COMES TO MIND...
COULD I ASK YOU TO SEND ME A LETTER VIA PIGEON?
YES, OF COURSE!

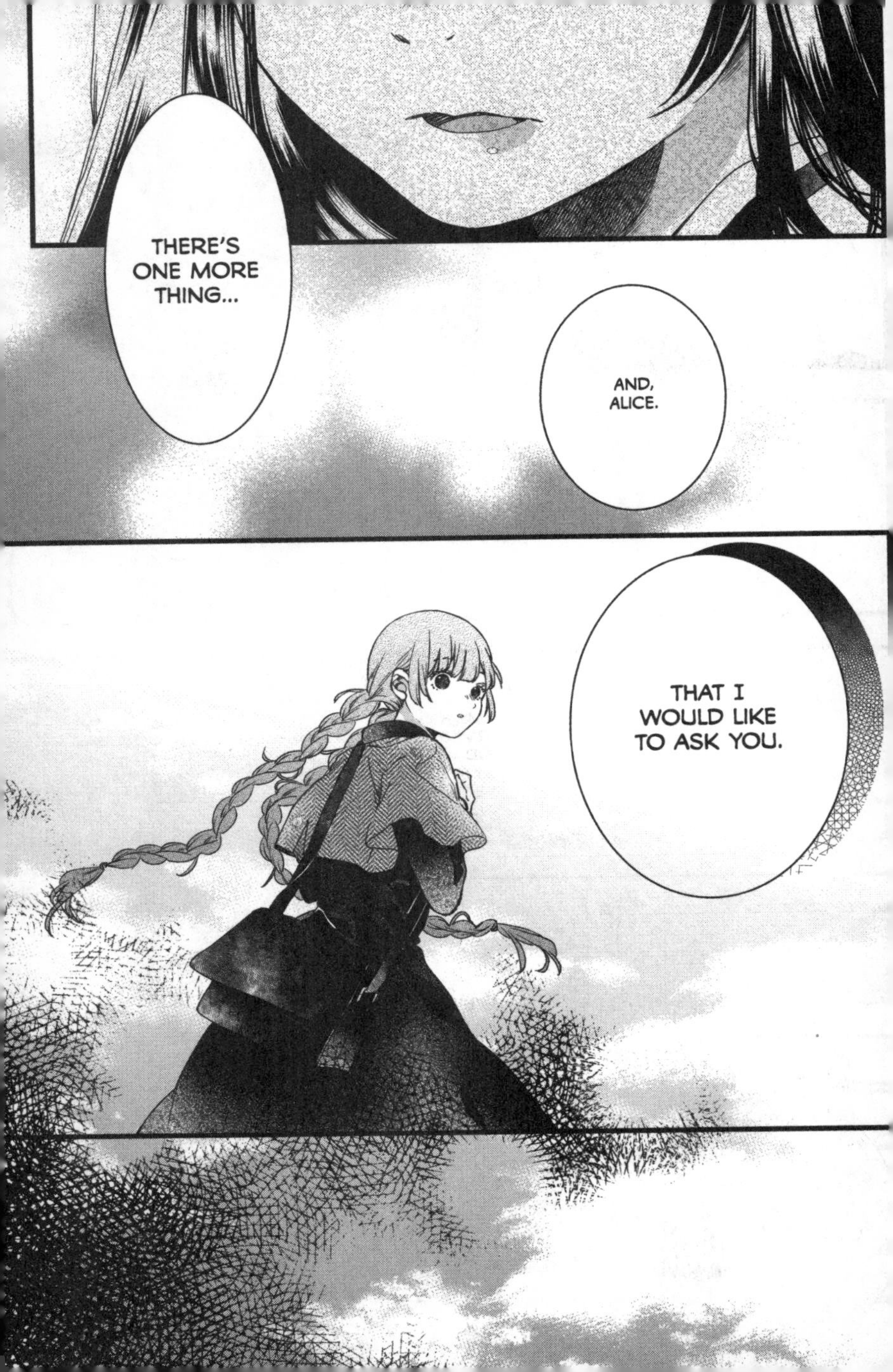
AND, ALICE.
THERE'S ONE MORE THING...
THAT I WOULD LIKE TO ASK YOU.

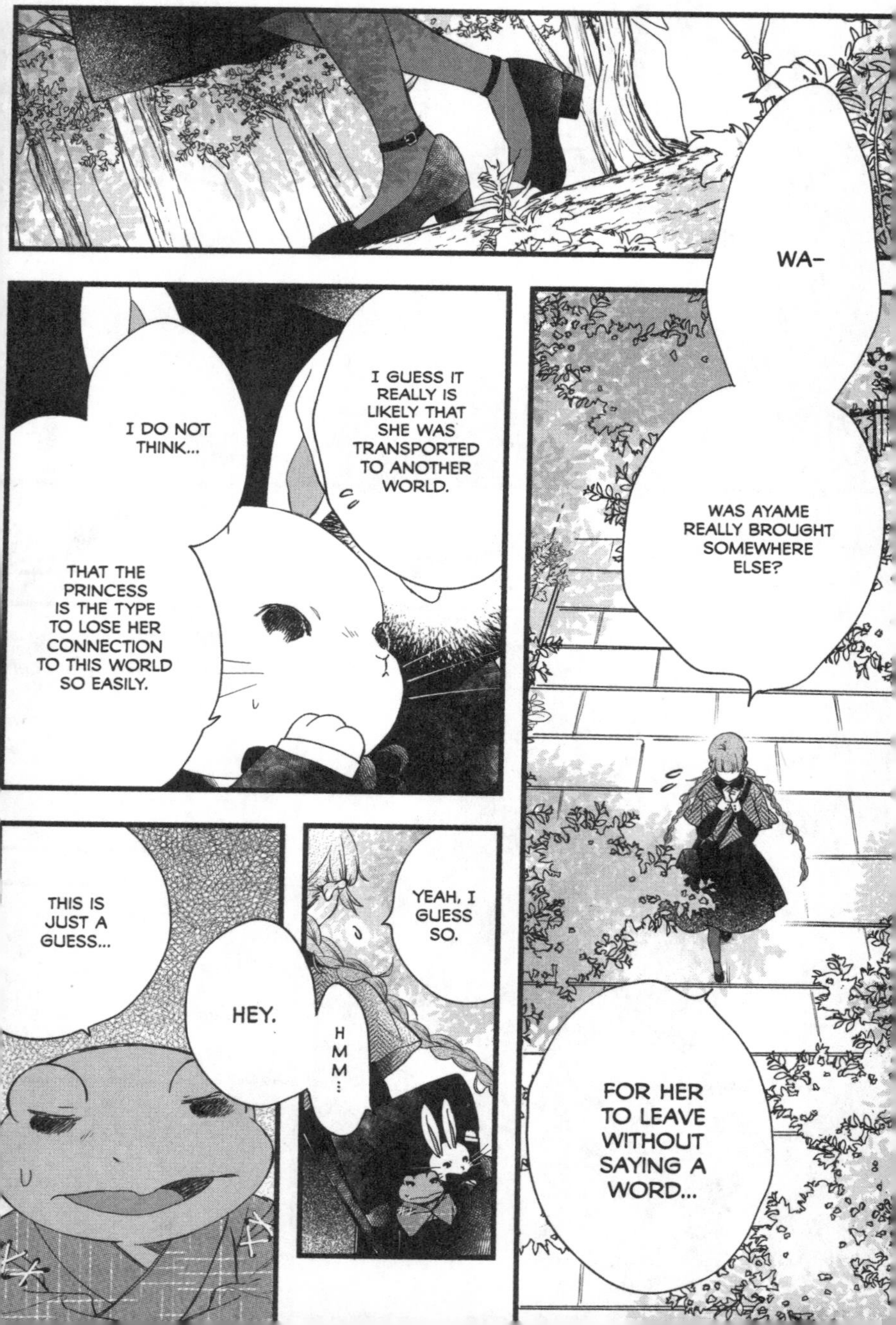
WA-
WAS AYAME REALLY BROUGHT SOMEWHERE ELSE?
FOR HER TO LEAVE WITHOUT SAYING A WORD...
I GUESS IT REALLY IS LIKELY THAT SHE WAS TRANSPORTED TO ANOTHER WORLD.
I DO NOT THINK...
THAT THE PRINCESS IS THE TYPE TO LOSE HER CONNECTION TO THIS WORLD SO EASILY.
YEAH, I GUESS SO.
HMM...
THIS IS JUST A GUESS...
HEY.

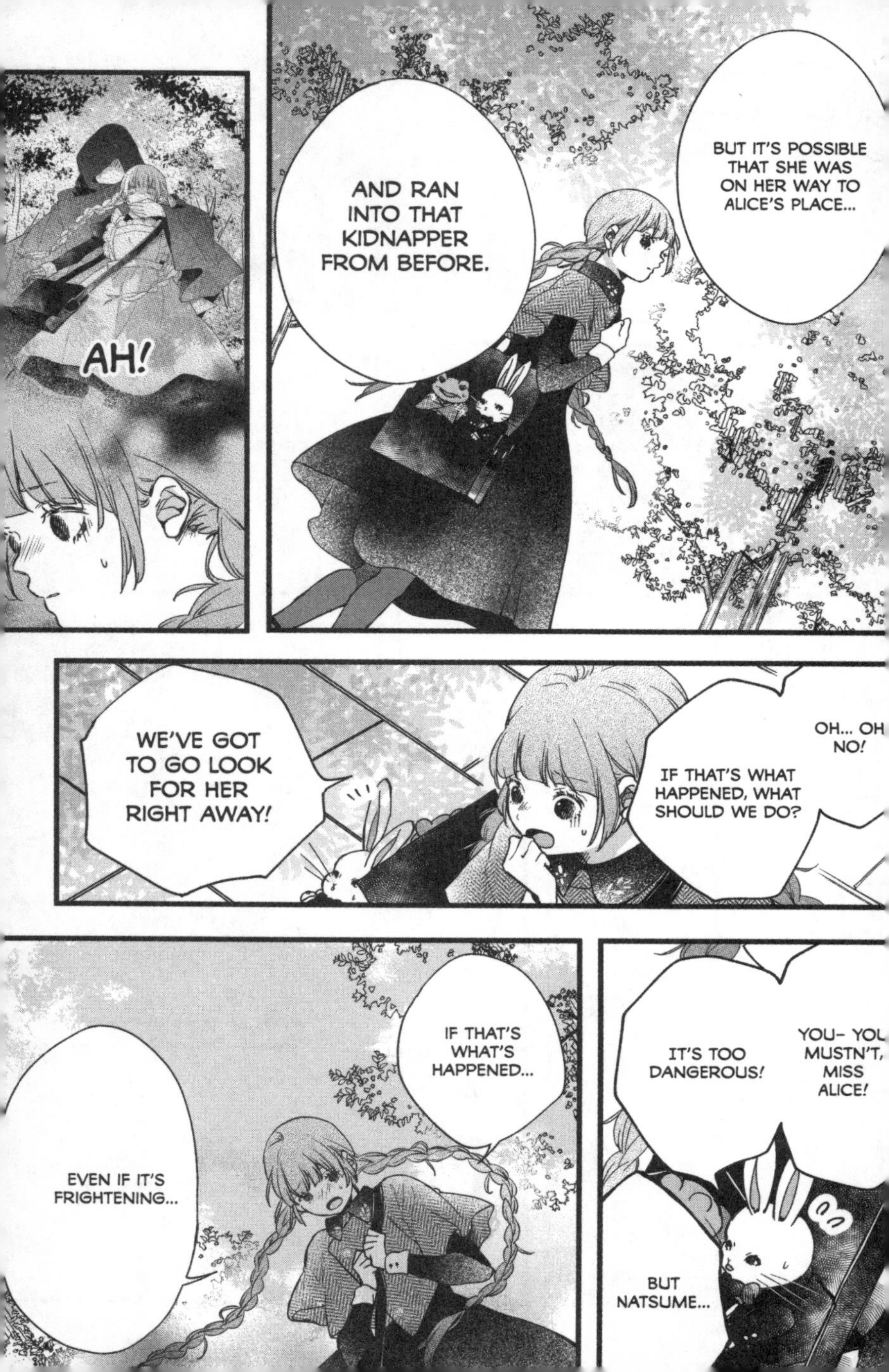
BUT IT'S POSSIBLE THAT SHE WAS ON HER WAY TO ALICE'S PLACE...
AND RAN INTO THAT KIDNAPPER FROM BEFORE.
AH!
OH... OH NO!
IF THAT'S WHAT HAPPENED, WHAT SHOULD WE DO?
WE'VE GOT TO GO LOOK FOR HER RIGHT AWAY!
YOU- YOU MUSTN'T, MISS ALICE!
IT'S TOO DANGEROUS!
BUT NATSUME...
IF THAT'S WHAT'S HAPPENED...
EVEN IF IT'S FRIGHTENING...

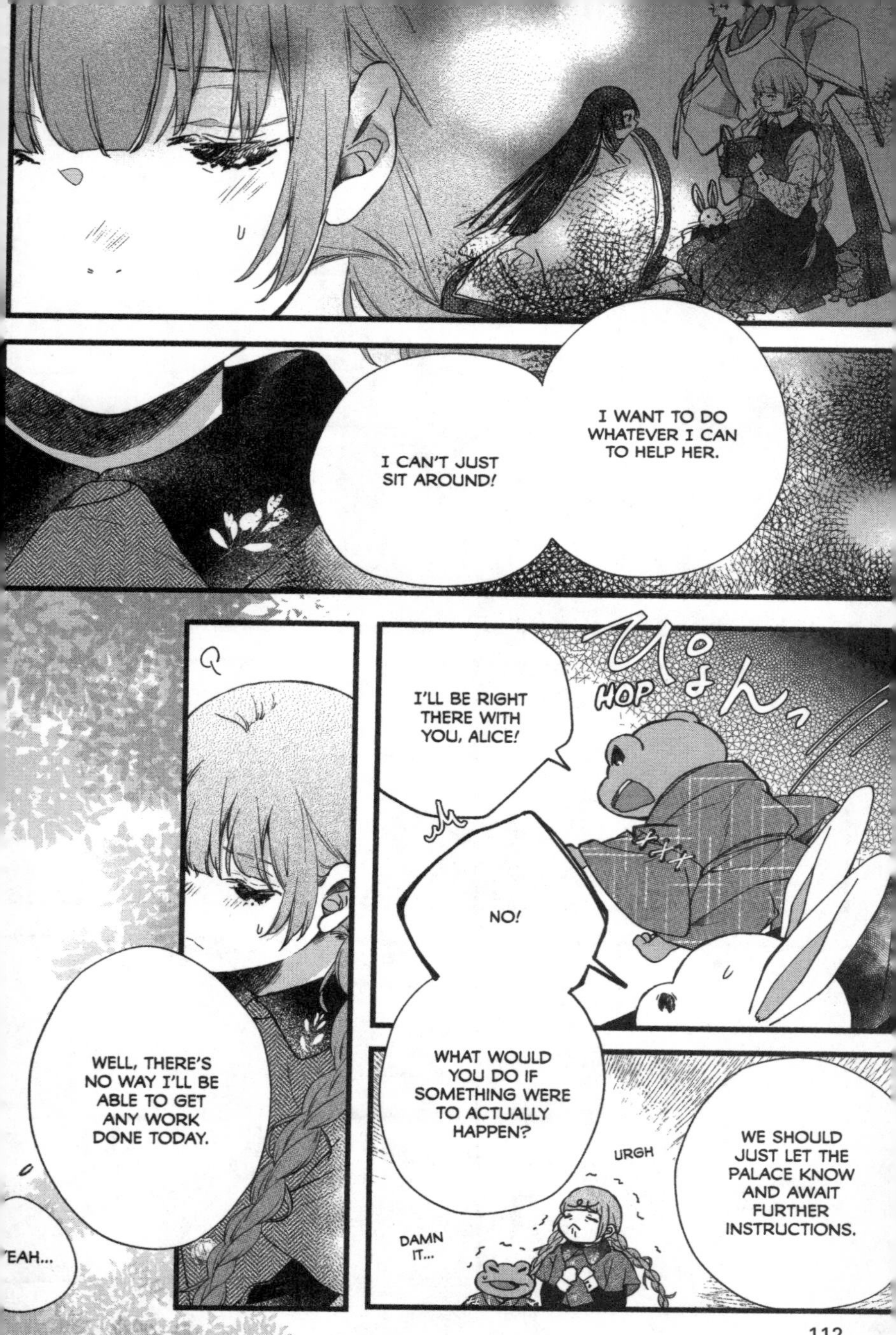
I WANT TO DO WHATEVER I CAN TO HELP HER.
I CAN'T JUST SIT AROUND!
ぴょん
HOP
I'LL BE RIGHT THERE WITH YOU, ALICE!
NO!
WHAT WOULD YOU DO IF SOMETHING WERE TO ACTUALLY HAPPEN?
WE SHOULD JUST LET THE PALACE KNOW AND AWAIT FURTHER INSTRUCTIONS.
URGH
DAMN IT...
WELL, THERE'S NO WAY I'LL BE ABLE TO GET ANY WORK DONE TODAY.
EAH...

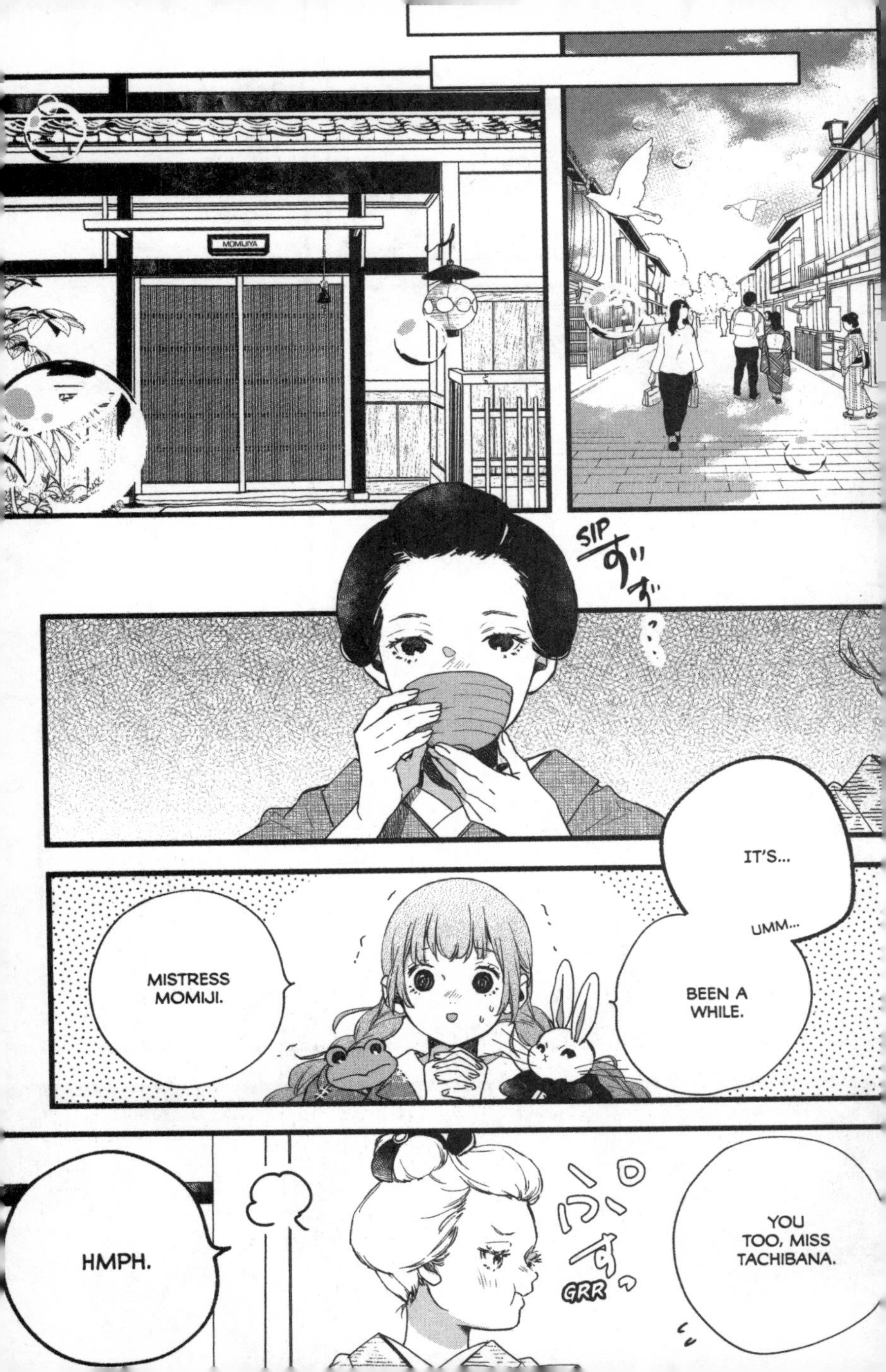
MOMIJIYA
SIP
ずず…
IT'S... UMM... BEEN A WHILE.
MISTRESS MOMIJI.
YOU TOO, MISS TACHIBANA.
GRR
HMPH.

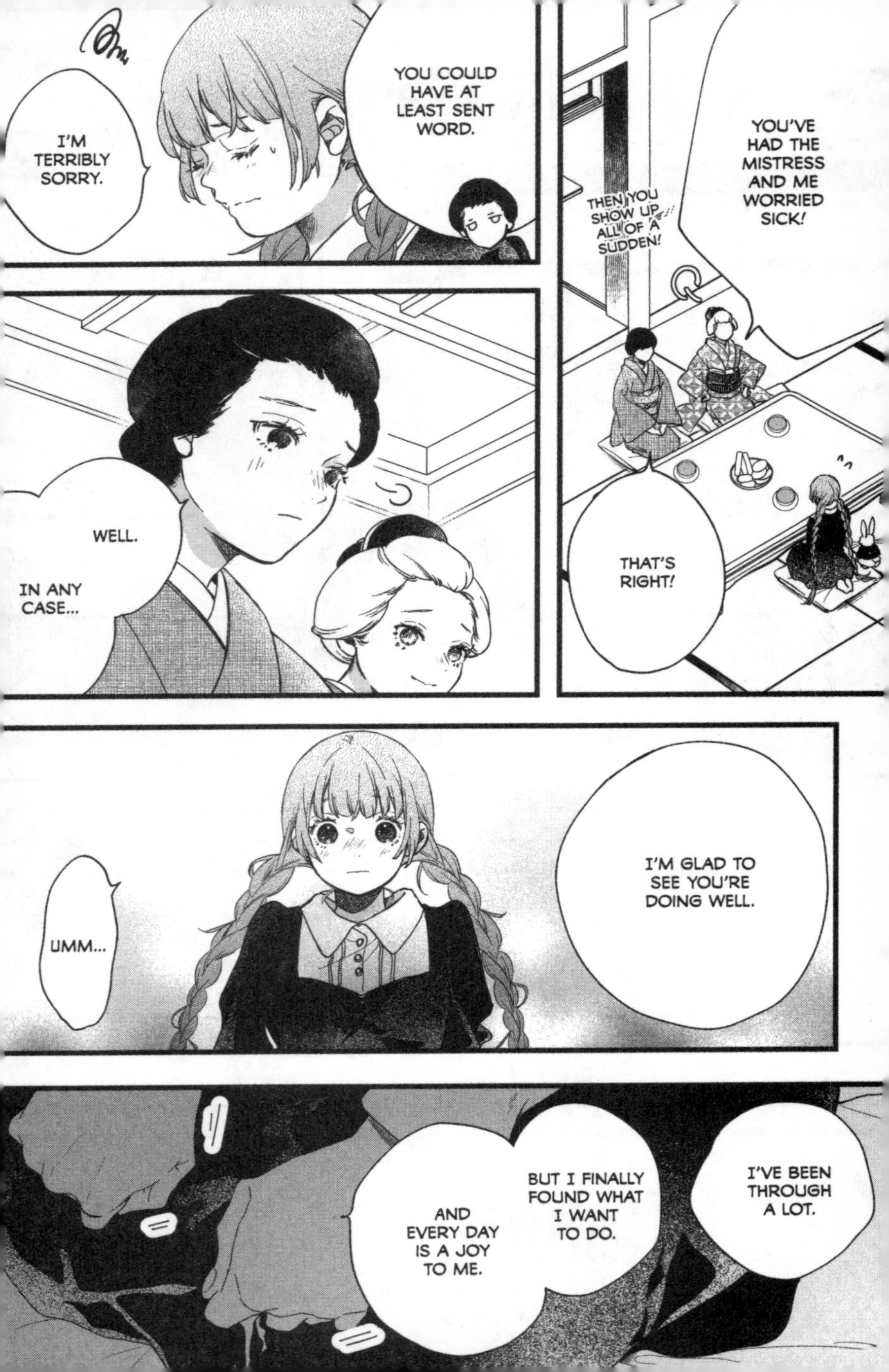
YOU'VE HAD THE MISTRESS AND ME WORRIED SICK!
THEN YOU SHOW UP ALL OF A SUDDEN!
THAT'S RIGHT!
YOU COULD HAVE AT LEAST SENT WORD.
I'M TERRIBLY SORRY.
WELL.
IN ANY CASE...
I'M GLAD TO SEE YOU'RE DOING WELL.
UMM...
I'VE BEEN THROUGH A LOT.
BUT I FINALLY FOUND WHAT I WANT TO DO.
AND EVERY DAY IS A JOY TO ME.

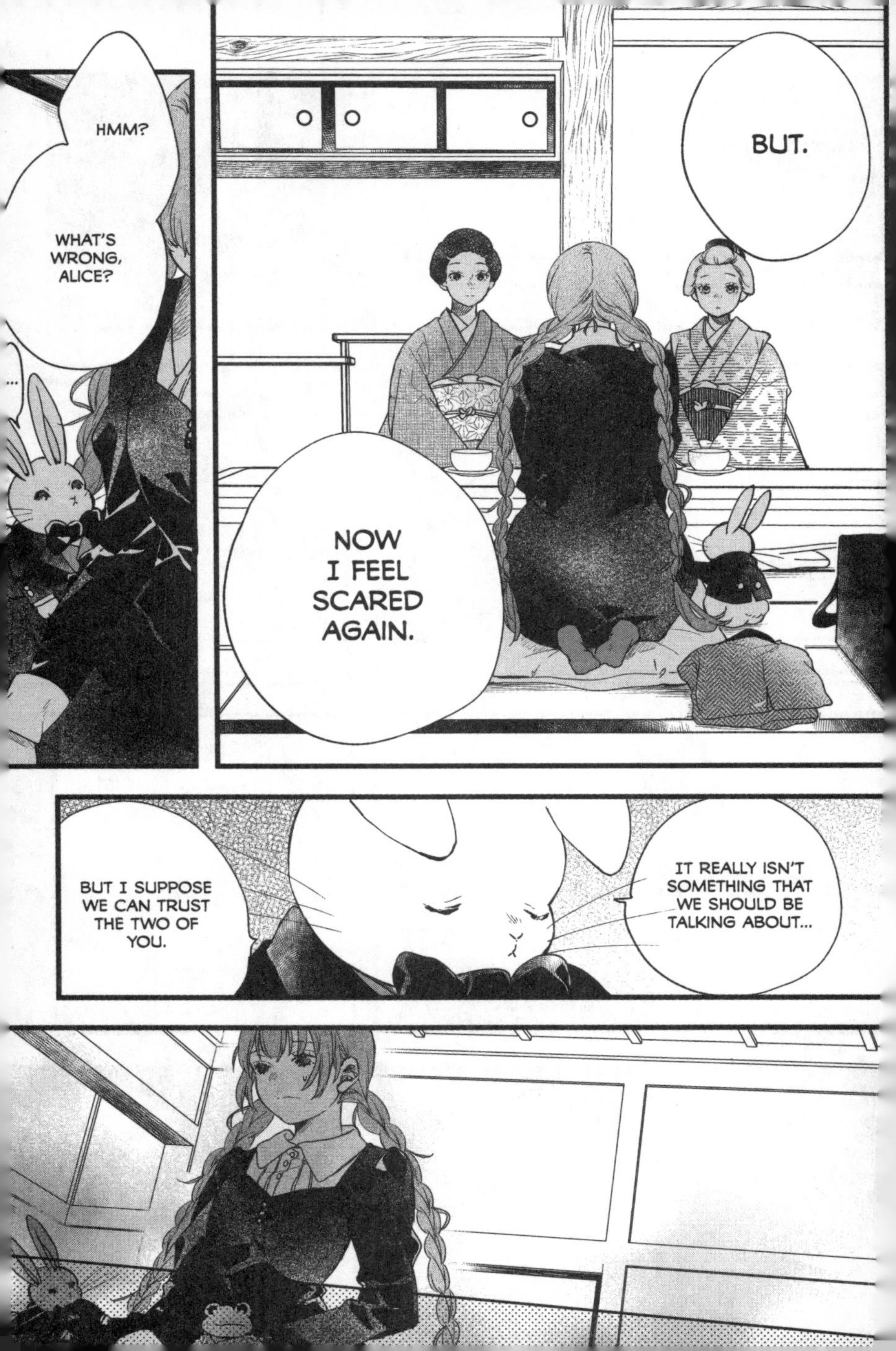
BUT.
NOW I FEEL SCARED AGAIN.
HMM? WHAT'S WRONG, ALICE?
...
IT REALLY ISN'T SOMETHING THAT WE SHOULD BE TALKING ABOUT...
BUT I SUPPOSE WE CAN TRUST THE TWO OF YOU.

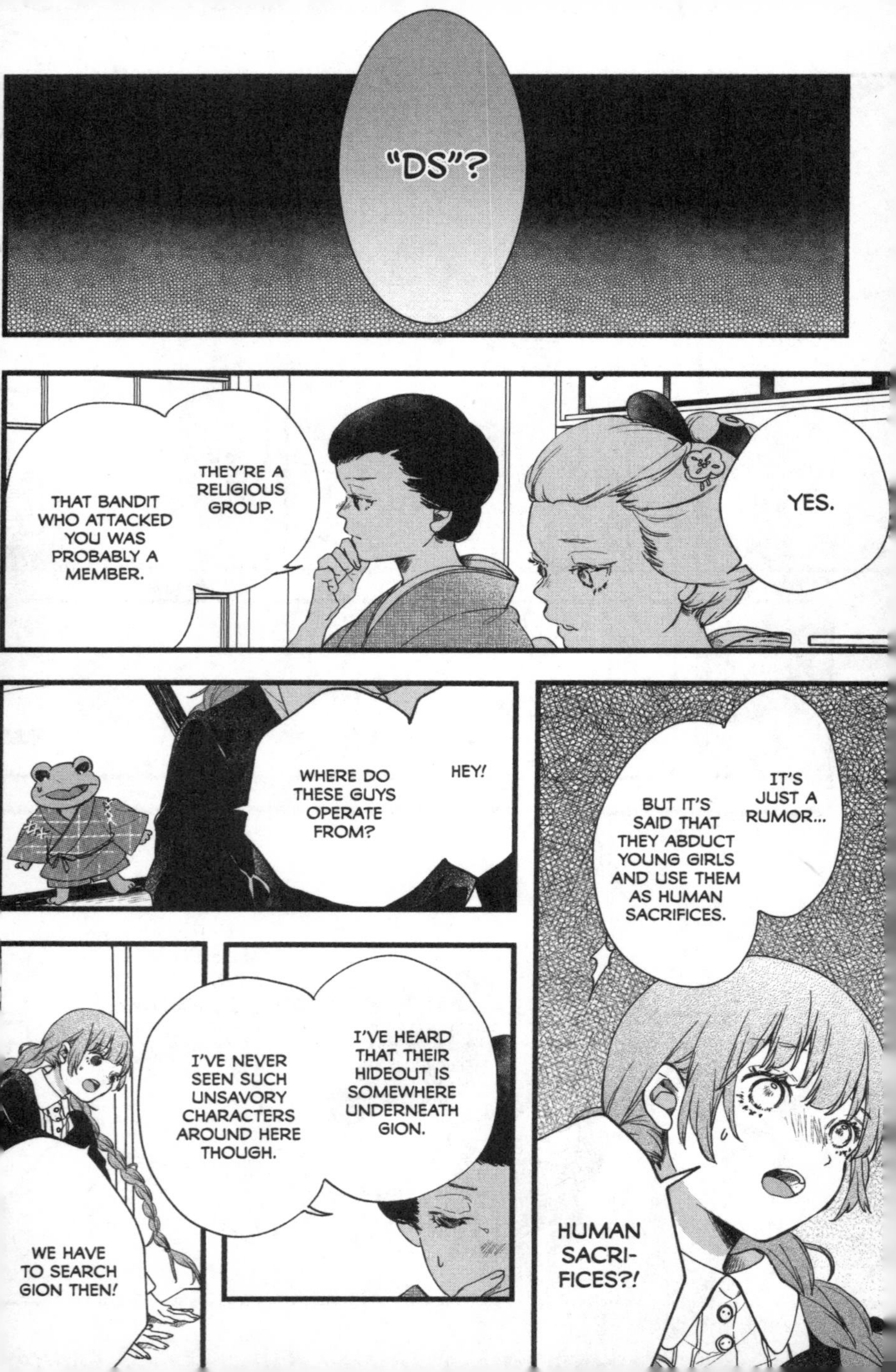
"DS"?
YES.
THEY'RE A RELIGIOUS GROUP.
THAT BANDIT WHO ATTACKED YOU WAS PROBABLY A MEMBER.
IT'S JUST A RUMOR...
BUT IT'S SAID THAT THEY ABDUCT YOUNG GIRLS AND USE THEM AS HUMAN SACRIFICES.
HUMAN SACRI-FICES?!
HEY!
WHERE DO THESE GUYS OPERATE FROM?
I'VE HEARD THAT THEIR HIDEOUT IS SOMEWHERE UNDERNEATH GION.
I'VE NEVER SEEN SUCH UNSAVORY CHARACTERS AROUND HERE THOUGH.
WE HAVE TO SEARCH GION THEN!

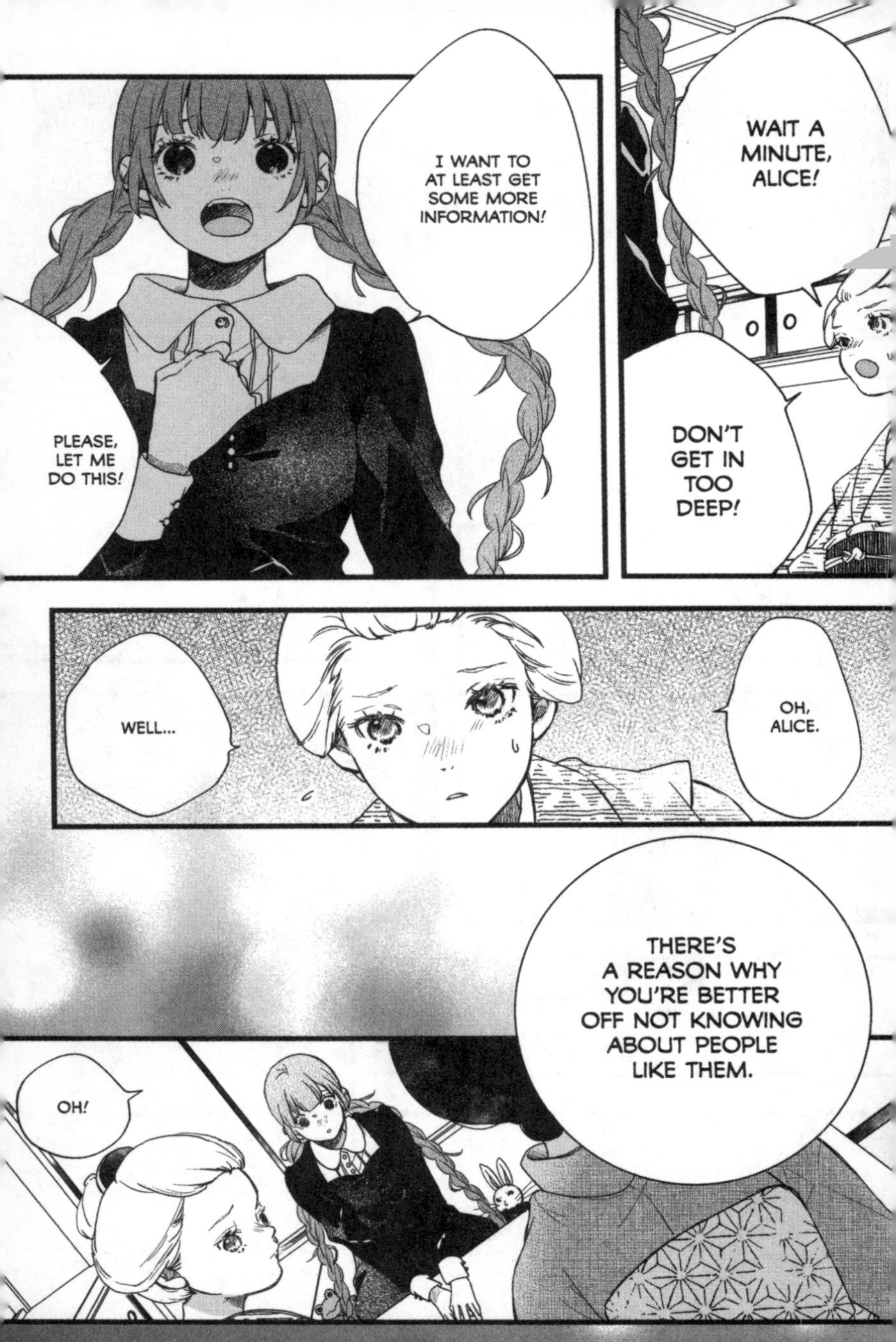
WAIT A MINUTE, ALICE!
DON'T GET IN TOO DEEP!
I WANT TO AT LEAST GET SOME MORE INFORMATION!
PLEASE, LET ME DO THIS!
OH, ALICE.
WELL...
THERE'S A REASON WHY YOU'RE BETTER OFF NOT KNOWING ABOUT PEOPLE LIKE THEM.
OH!

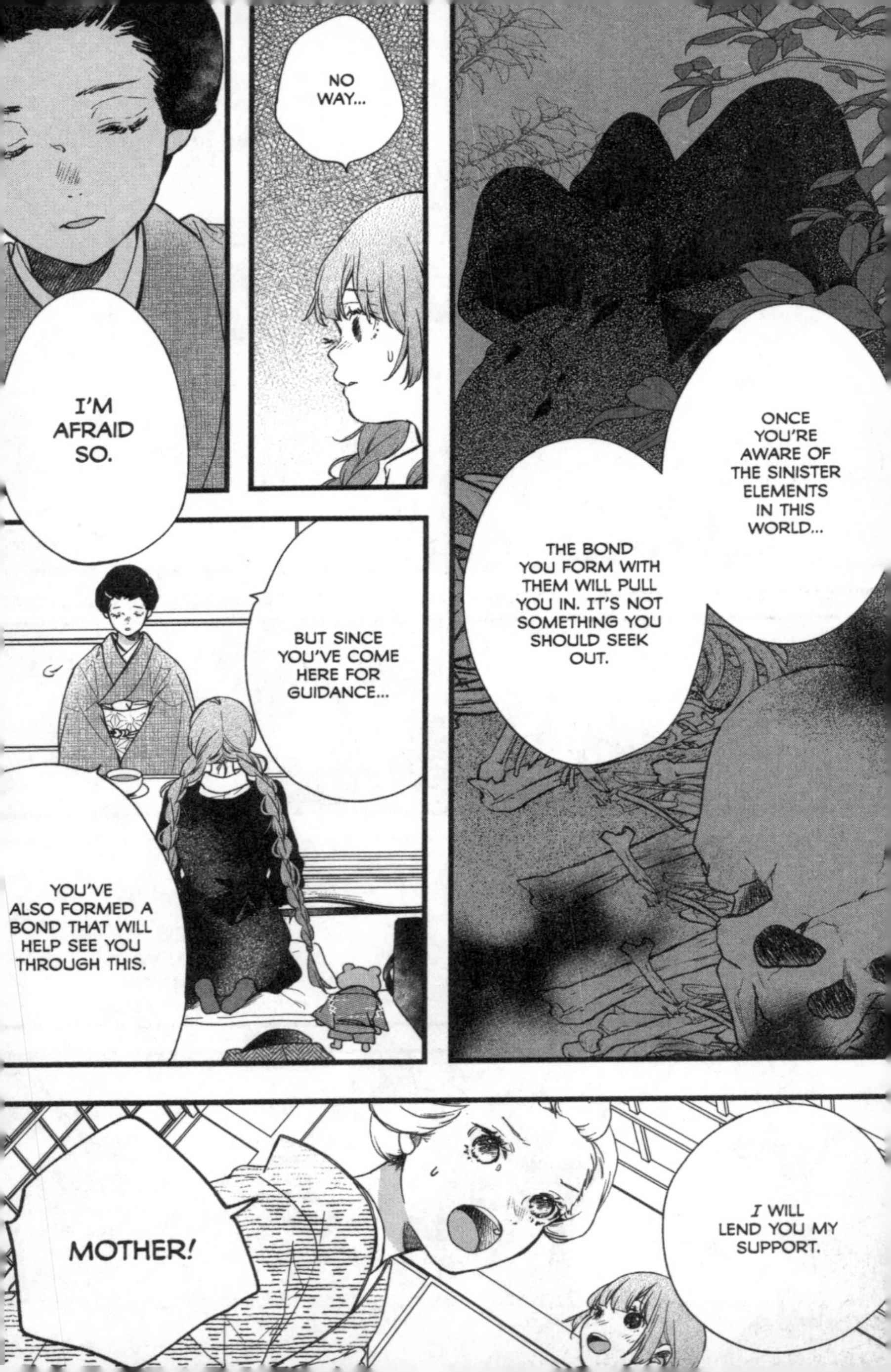
ONCE YOU'RE AWARE OF THE SINISTER ELEMENTS IN THIS WORLD...
THE BOND YOU FORM WITH THEM WILL PULL YOU IN. IT'S NOT SOMETHING YOU SHOULD SEEK OUT.
NO WAY...
I'M AFRAID SO.
BUT SINCE YOU'VE COME HERE FOR GUIDANCE...
YOU'VE ALSO FORMED A BOND THAT WILL HELP SEE YOU THROUGH THIS.
I WILL LEND YOU MY SUPPORT.
MOTHER!

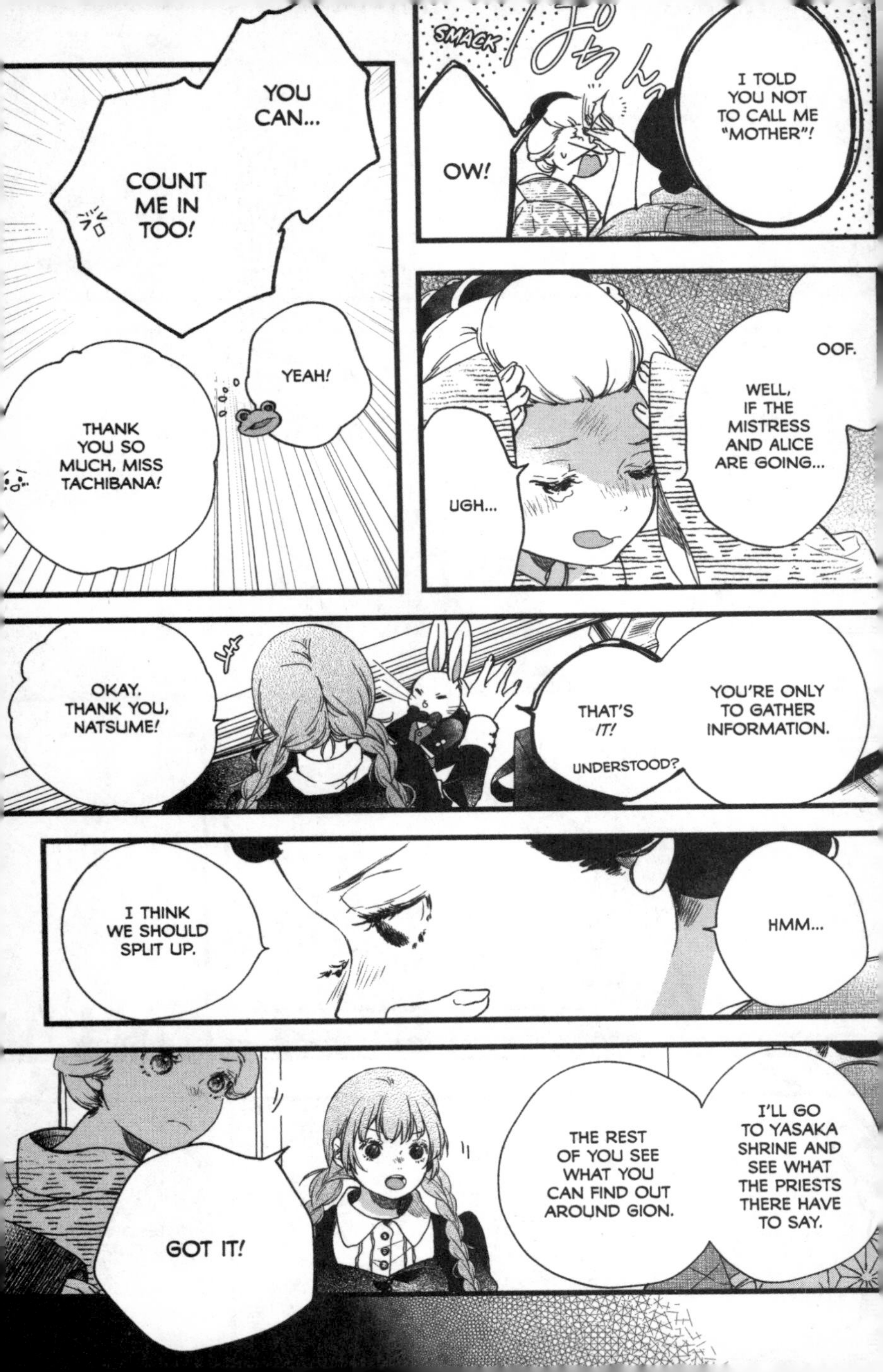
SMACK
I TOLD YOU NOT TO CALL ME "MOTHER"!
OW!
OOF.
WELL, IF THE MISTRESS AND ALICE ARE GOING...
UGH...
YOU CAN...
COUNT ME IN TOO!
YEAH!
THANK YOU SO MUCH, MISS TACHIBANA!
YOU'RE ONLY TO GATHER INFORMATION.
THAT'S IT!
UNDERSTOOD?
OKAY. THANK YOU, NATSUME!
HMM...
I THINK WE SHOULD SPLIT UP.
I'LL GO TO YASAKA SHRINE AND SEE WHAT THE PRIESTS THERE HAVE TO SAY.
THE REST OF YOU SEE WHAT YOU CAN FIND OUT AROUND GION.
GOT IT!

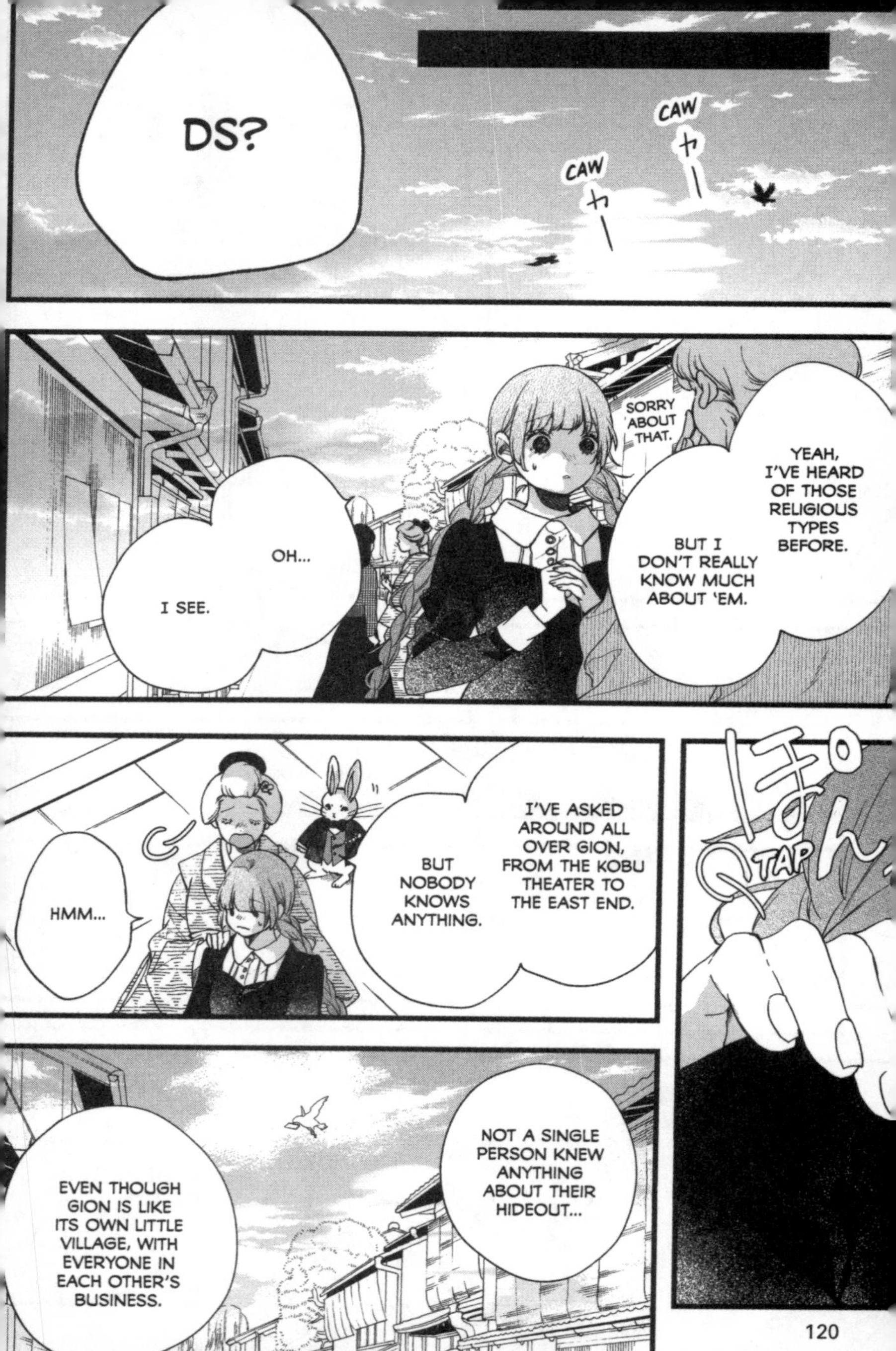
[redacted]
DS?
CAW
CAW
SORRY ABOUT THAT.
YEAH, I'VE HEARD OF THOSE RELIGIOUS TYPES BEFORE.
BUT I DON'T REALLY KNOW MUCH ABOUT 'EM.
OH...
I SEE.
TAP
I'VE ASKED AROUND ALL OVER GION, FROM THE KOBU THEATER TO THE EAST END.
BUT NOBODY KNOWS ANYTHING.
HMM...
NOT A SINGLE PERSON KNEW ANYTHING ABOUT THEIR HIDEOUT...
EVEN THOUGH GION IS LIKE ITS OWN LITTLE VILLAGE, WITH EVERYONE IN EACH OTHER'S BUSINESS.

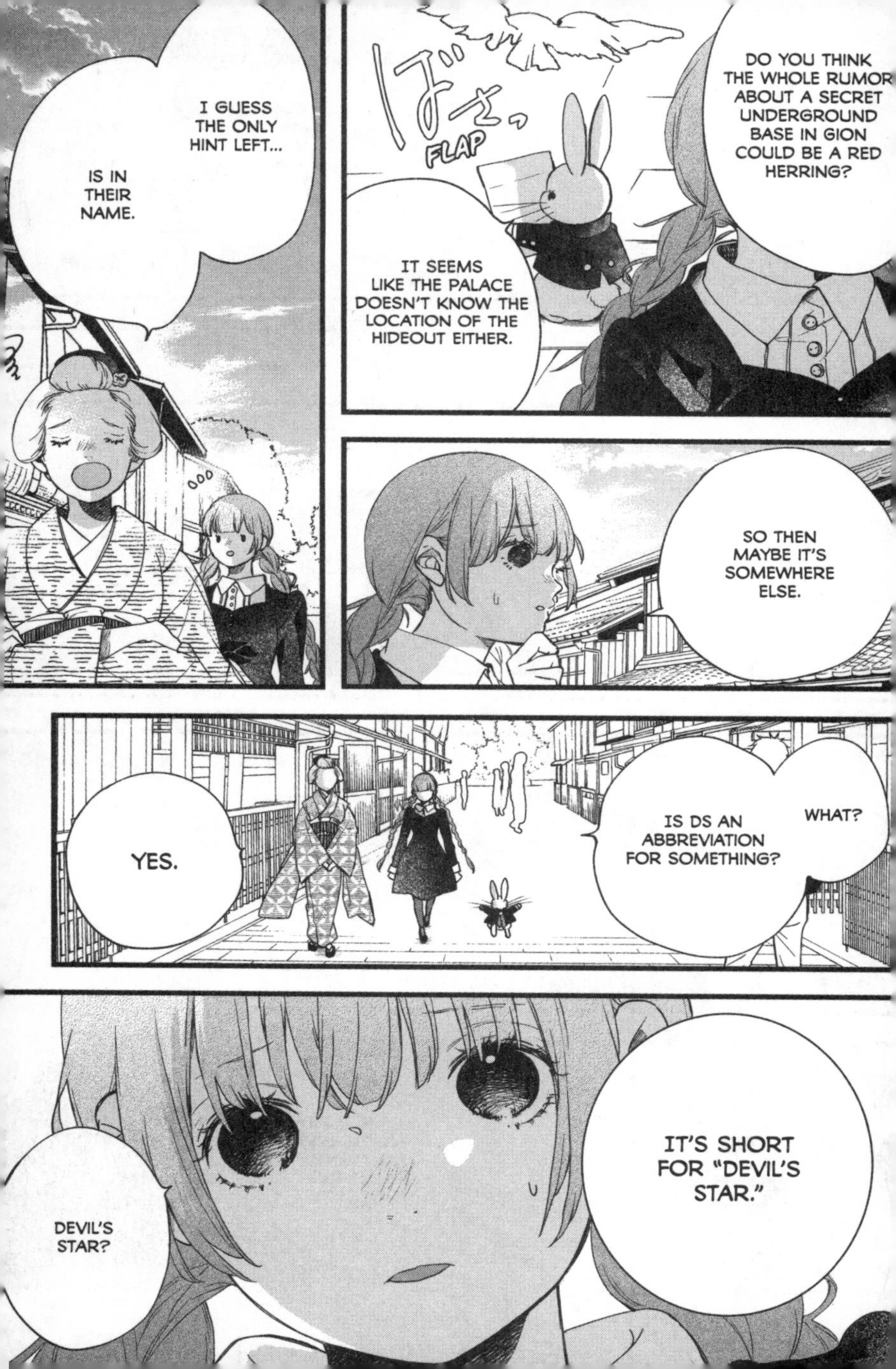

DO YOU THINK THE WHOLE RUMOR ABOUT A SECRET UNDERGROUND BASE IN GION COULD BE A RED HERRING?
ばさっ
FLAP
IT SEEMS LIKE THE PALACE DOESN'T KNOW THE LOCATION OF THE HIDEOUT EITHER.
SO THEN MAYBE IT'S SOMEWHERE ELSE.
I GUESS THE ONLY HINT LEFT...
IS IN THEIR NAME.
WHAT?
IS DS AN ABBREVIATION FOR SOMETHING?
YES.
IT'S SHORT FOR "DEVIL'S STAR."
DEVIL'S STAR?

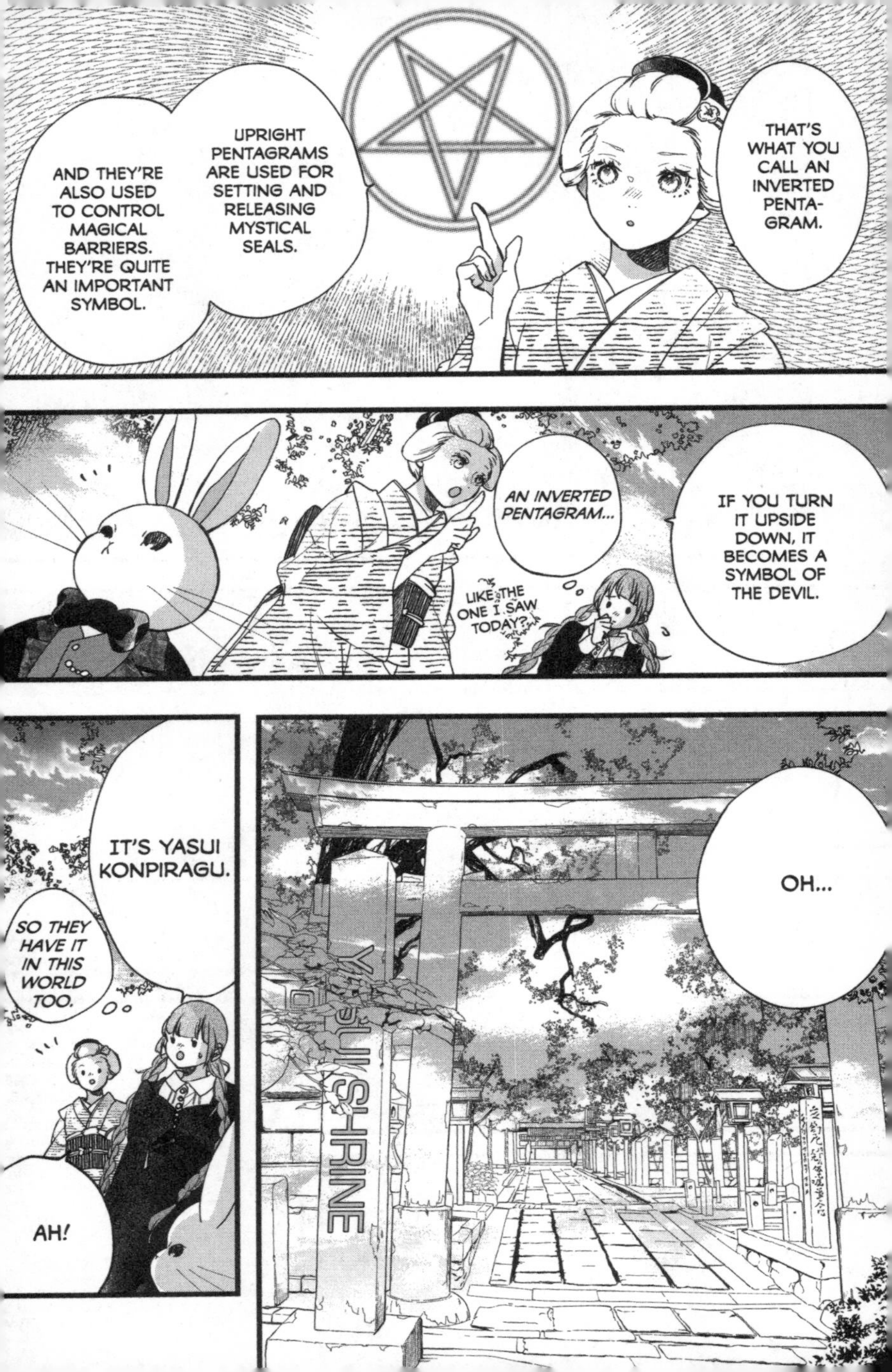
THAT'S WHAT YOU CALL AN INVERTED PENTA-GRAM.
UPRIGHT PENTAGRAMS ARE USED FOR SETTING AND RELEASING MYSTICAL SEALS.
AND THEY'RE ALSO USED TO CONTROL MAGICAL BARRIERS. THEY'RE QUITE AN IMPORTANT SYMBOL.
IF YOU TURN IT UPSIDE DOWN, IT BECOMES A SYMBOL OF THE DEVIL.
AN INVERTED PENTAGRAM...
LIKE THE ONE I SAW TODAY?
OH...
IT'S YASUI KONPIRAGU.
SO THEY HAVE IT IN THIS WORLD TOO.
AH!

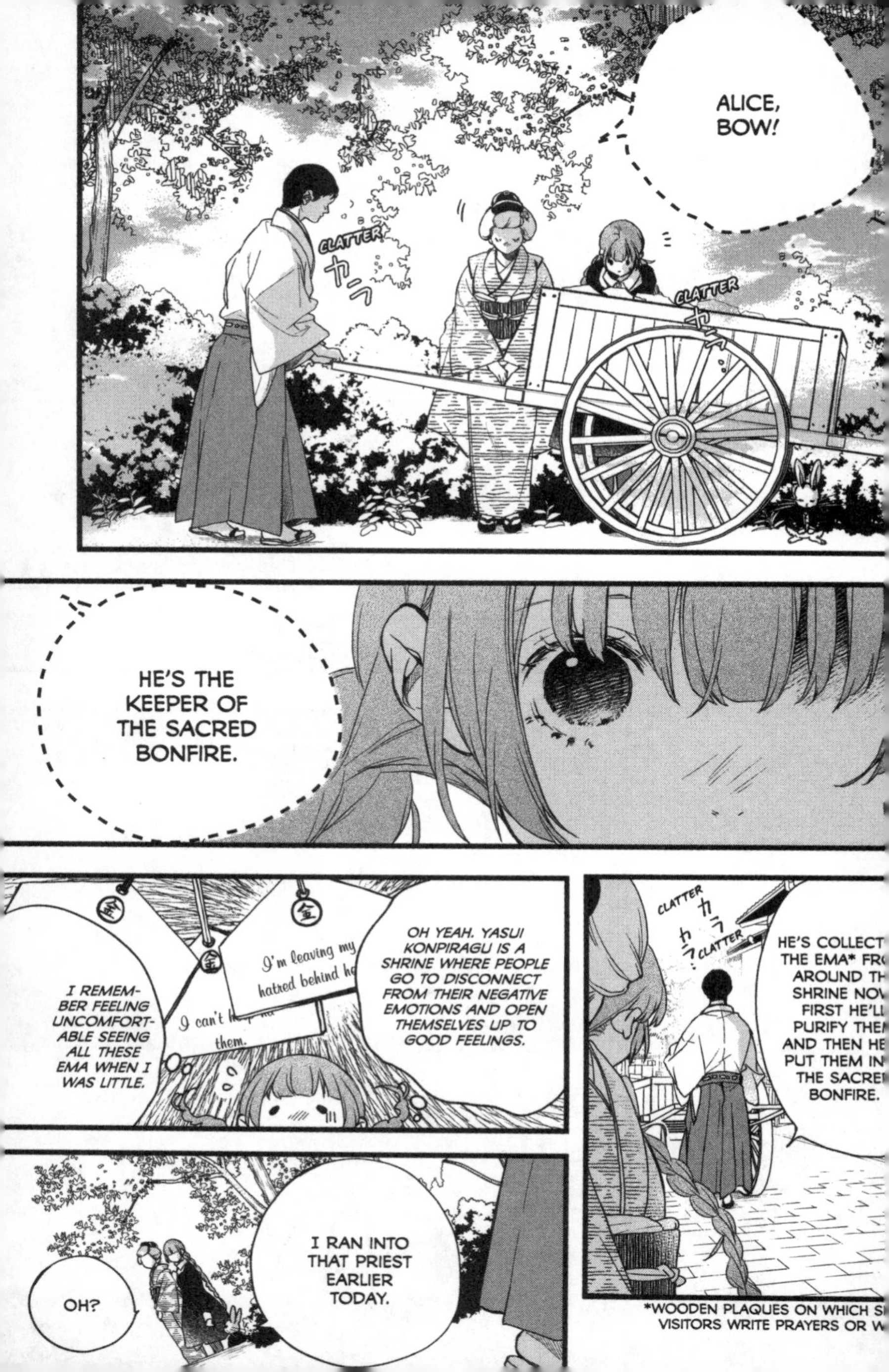

ALICE, BOW!
CLATTER
CLATTER
HE'S THE KEEPER OF THE SACRED BONFIRE.
CLATTER
CLATTER
HE'S COLLECT THE EMA* FR AROUND TH SHRINE NOV FIRST HE'LL PURIFY THEM AND THEN HE PUT THEM IN THE SACRE BONFIRE.
OH YEAH. YASUI KONPIRAGU IS A SHRINE WHERE PEOPLE GO TO DISCONNECT FROM THEIR NEGATIVE EMOTIONS AND OPEN THEMSELVES UP TO GOOD FEELINGS.
I'm leaving my hatred behind h
I can't h
them.
I REMEMBER FEELING UNCOMFORTABLE SEEING ALL THESE EMA WHEN I WAS LITTLE.
I RAN INTO THAT PRIEST EARLIER TODAY.
OH?

*WOODEN PLAQUES ON WHICH S VISITORS WRITE PRAYERS OR W

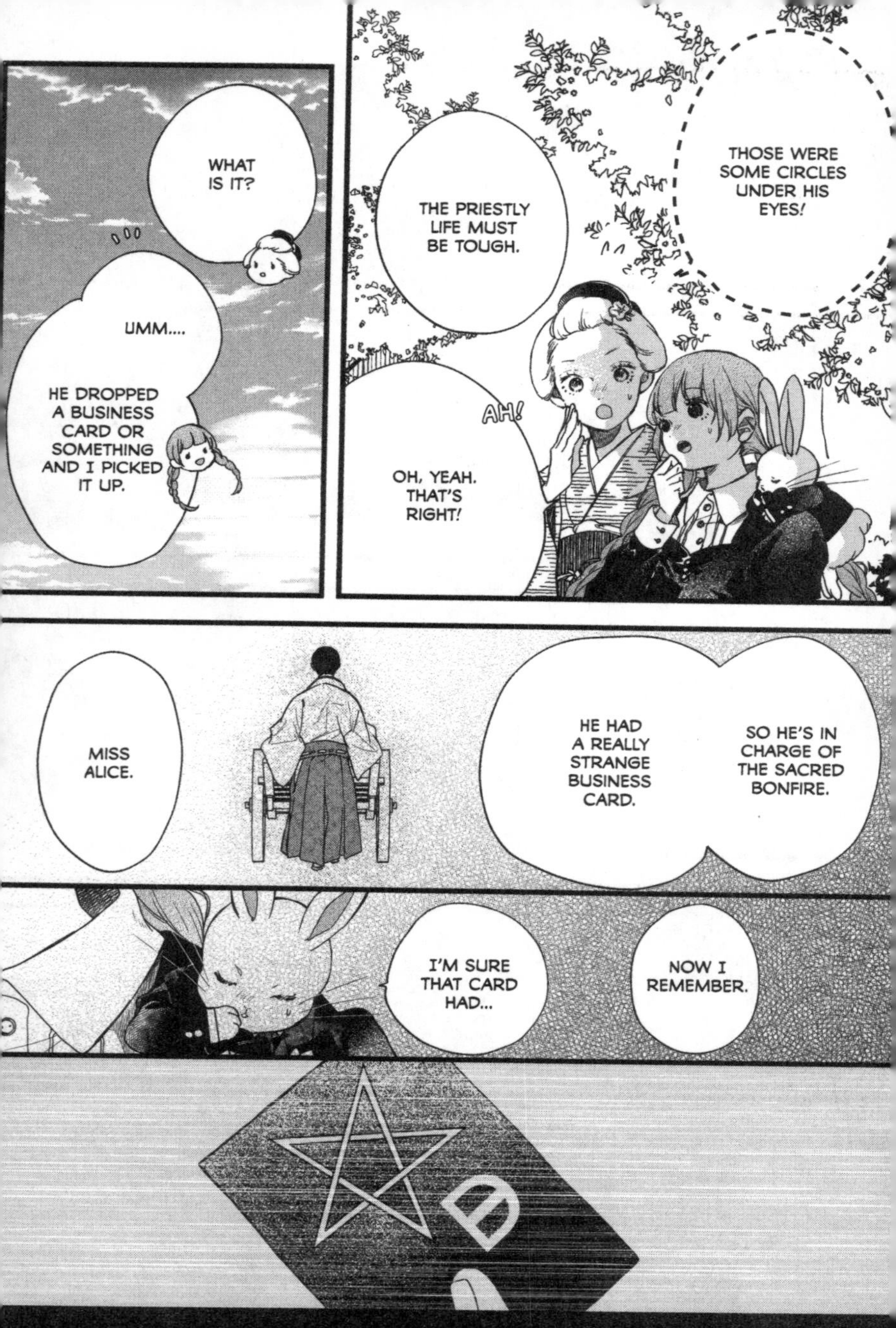
THOSE WERE SOME CIRCLES UNDER HIS EYES!
THE PRIESTLY LIFE MUST BE TOUGH.
AH!
OH, YEAH. THAT'S RIGHT!
WHAT IS IT?
UMM....
HE DROPPED A BUSINESS CARD OR SOMETHING AND I PICKED IT UP.
SO HE'S IN CHARGE OF THE SACRED BONFIRE.
HE HAD A REALLY STRANGE BUSINESS CARD.
MISS ALICE.
NOW I REMEMBER.
I'M SURE THAT CARD HAD...

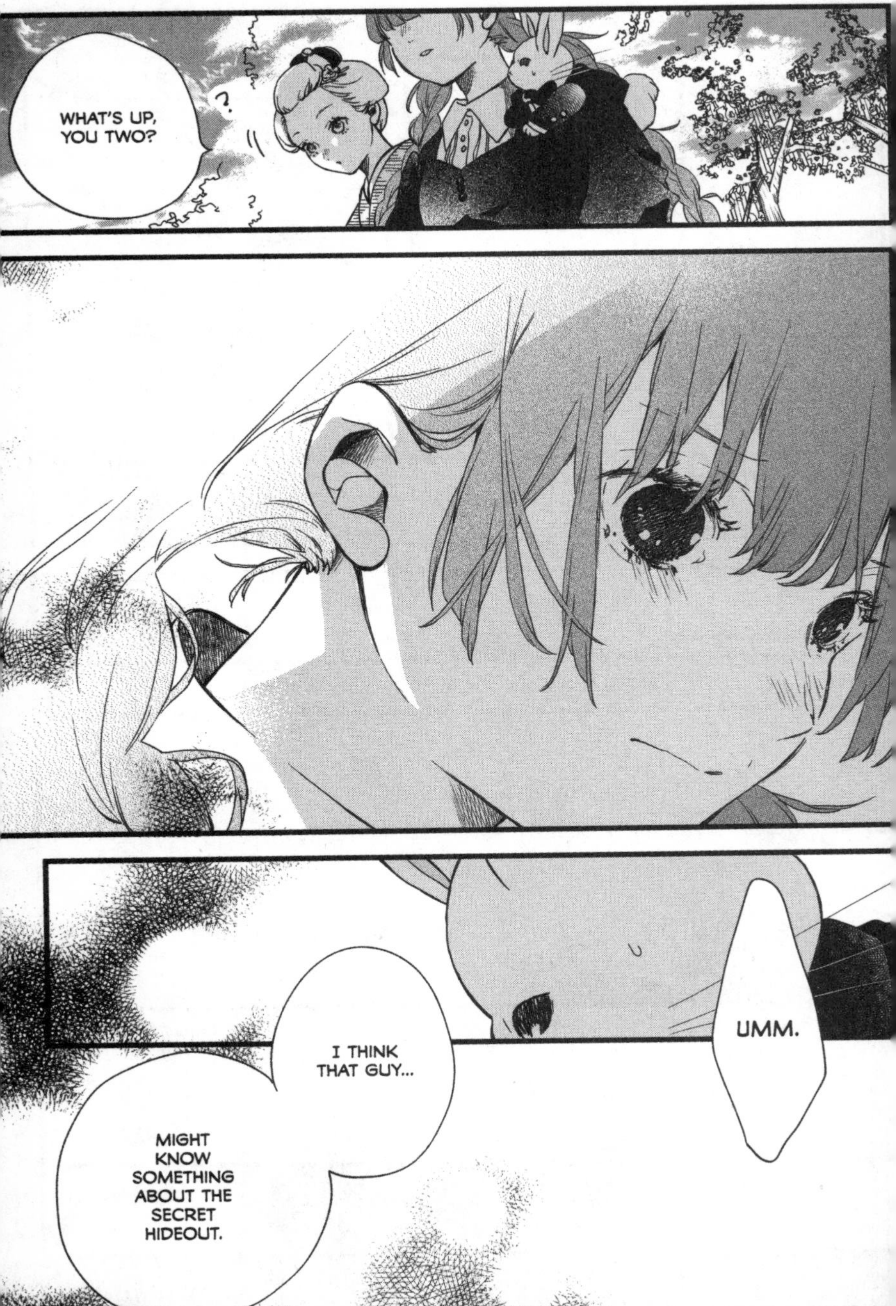
WHAT'S UP, YOU TWO?
UMM.
I THINK THAT GUY...
MIGHT KNOW SOMETHING ABOUT THE SECRET HIDEOUT.

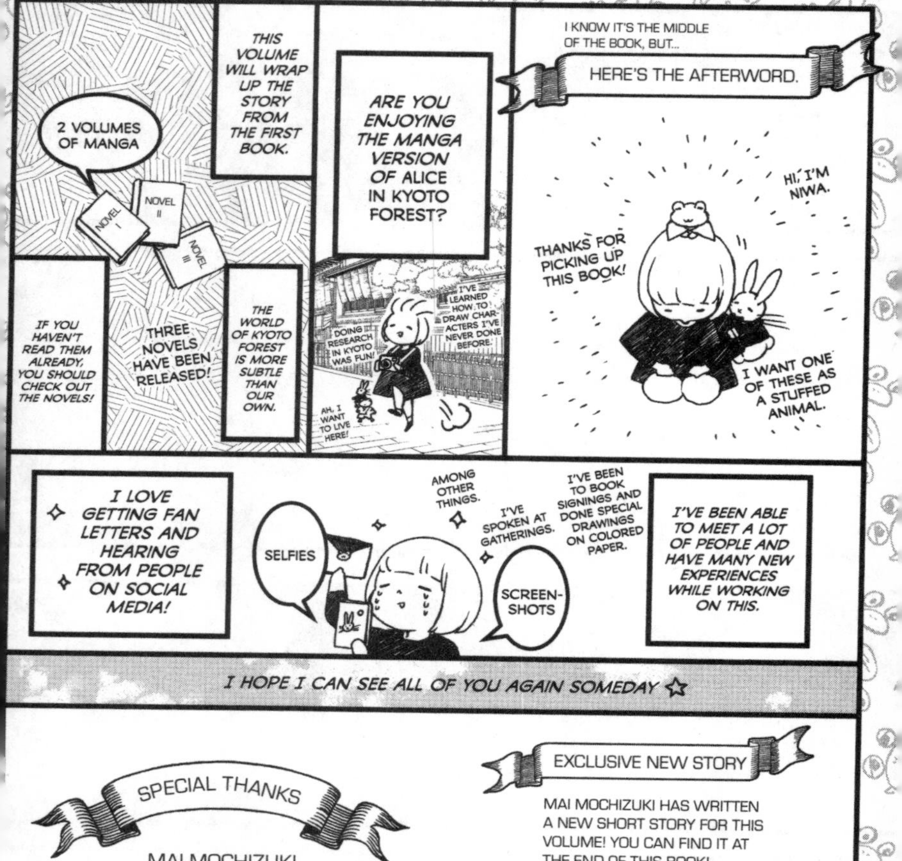
I KNOW IT'S THE MIDDLE OF THE BOOK, BUT...
HERE'S THE AFTERWORD.
HI, I'M NIWA.
THANKS FOR PICKING UP THIS BOOK!
I WANT ONE OF THESE AS A STUFFED ANIMAL.
ARE YOU ENJOYING THE MANGA VERSION OF ALICE IN KYOTO FOREST?
I'VE LEARNED HOW TO DRAW CHARACTERS I'VE NEVER DONE BEFORE.
DOING RESEARCH IN KYOTO WAS FUN!
AH, I WANT TO LIVE HERE!
THIS VOLUME WILL WRAP UP THE STORY FROM THE FIRST BOOK.
2 VOLUMES OF MANGA
NOVEL I
NOVEL II
NOVEL III
THE WORLD OF KYOTO FOREST IS MORE SUBTLE THAN OUR OWN.
THREE NOVELS HAVE BEEN RELEASED!
IF YOU HAVEN'T READ THEM ALREADY, YOU SHOULD CHECK OUT THE NOVELS!
I'VE BEEN ABLE TO MEET A LOT OF PEOPLE AND HAVE MANY NEW EXPERIENCES WHILE WORKING ON THIS.
I'VE BEEN TO BOOK SIGNINGS AND DONE SPECIAL DRAWINGS ON COLORED PAPER.
I'VE SPOKEN AT GATHERINGS.
AMONG OTHER THINGS.
SCREEN-SHOTS
SELFIES
I LOVE GETTING FAN LETTERS AND HEARING FROM PEOPLE ON SOCIAL MEDIA!
I HOPE I CAN SEE ALL OF YOU AGAIN SOMEDAY ☆

SPECIAL THANKS

MAI MOCHIZUKI

EVERYONE WHO HELPED MAKE THIS BOOK

EVERYONE WHO CHEERED US ON

EDITORS:
MIZUMOTO
YAMASHITA

BACKGROUND HELP:
TOBARI KOYU

She drew Hachisu and Natsume!

EXCLUSIVE NEW STORY

MAI MOCHIZUKI HAS WRITTEN A NEW SHORT STORY FOR THIS VOLUME! YOU CAN FIND IT AT THE END OF THIS BOOK!

BONUS MANGA

YOU CAN ALSO USE THIS QR CODE TO CHECK OUT A BONUS MANGA AVAILABLE IN JAPANESE. IT TAKES PLACE AFTER THE END OF THE STORY. YOU'LL GET TO SEE WHAT HAPPENS DURING THE PARTY AT THE IMPERIAL PALACE!▽

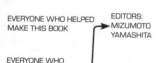

A NOTE FROM TOKYOPOP: SOME BONUS MATERIALS, INCLUDING THE DIGITAL BONUS MANGA, ARE ONLY AVAILABLE IN JAPANESE AS OF 2022. THANK YOU FOR SUPPORTING THE AUTHOR AND THE ENGLISH RELEASE OF THIS BOOK!

MORE INFO ON THE JAPANESE VERSION!

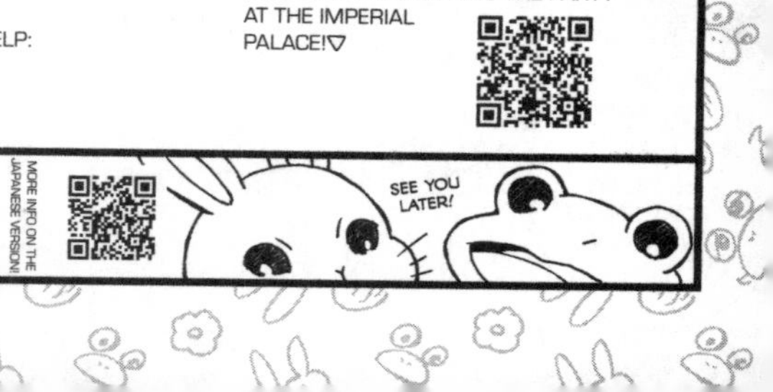
SEE YOU LATER!

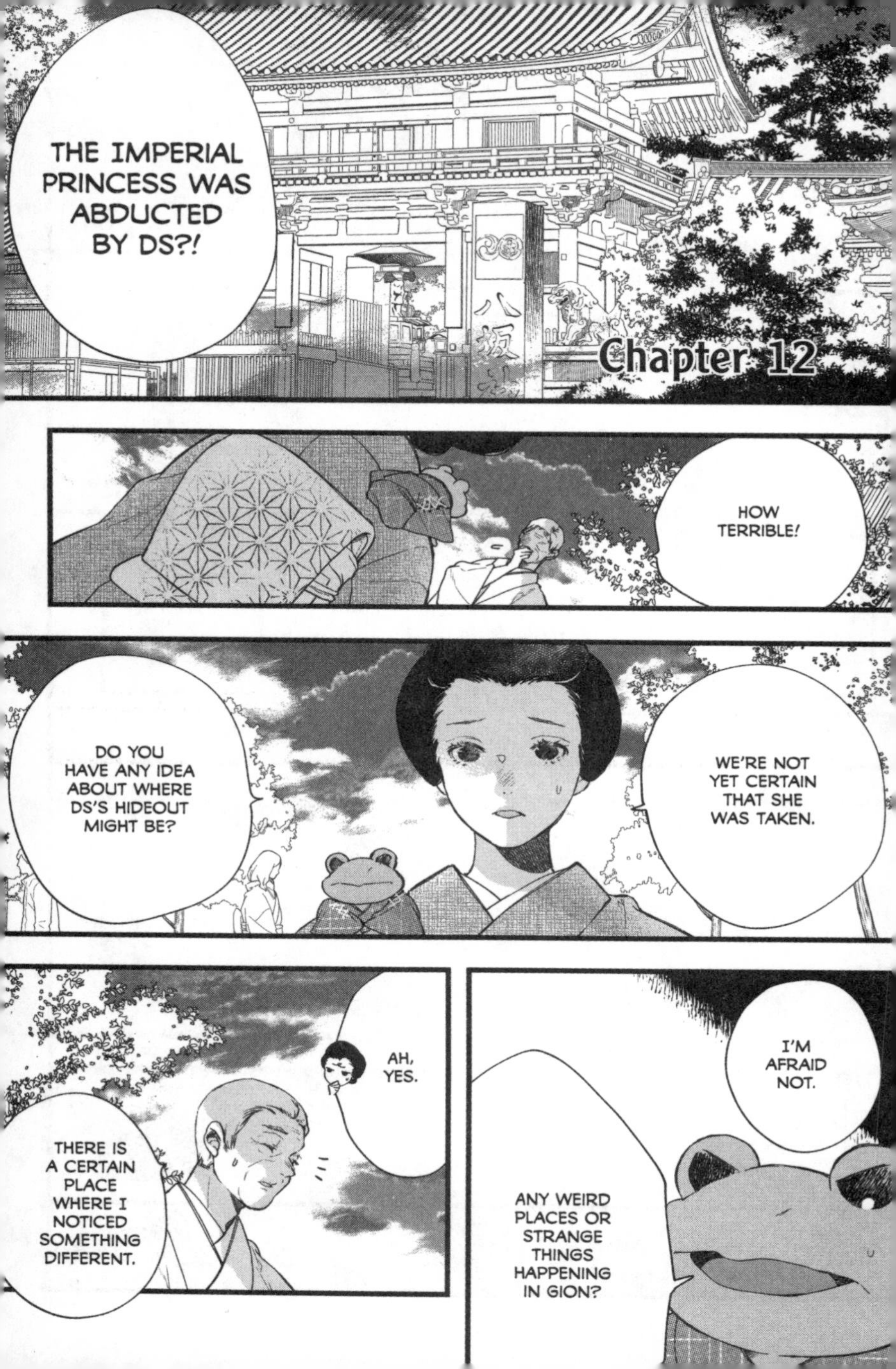
Chapter 12
THE IMPERIAL PRINCESS WAS ABDUCTED BY DS?!
HOW TERRIBLE!
WE'RE NOT YET CERTAIN THAT SHE WAS TAKEN.
DO YOU HAVE ANY IDEA ABOUT WHERE DS'S HIDEOUT MIGHT BE?
I'M AFRAID NOT.
ANY WEIRD PLACES OR STRANGE THINGS HAPPENING IN GION?
AH, YES.
THERE IS A CERTAIN PLACE WHERE I NOTICED SOMETHING DIFFERENT.

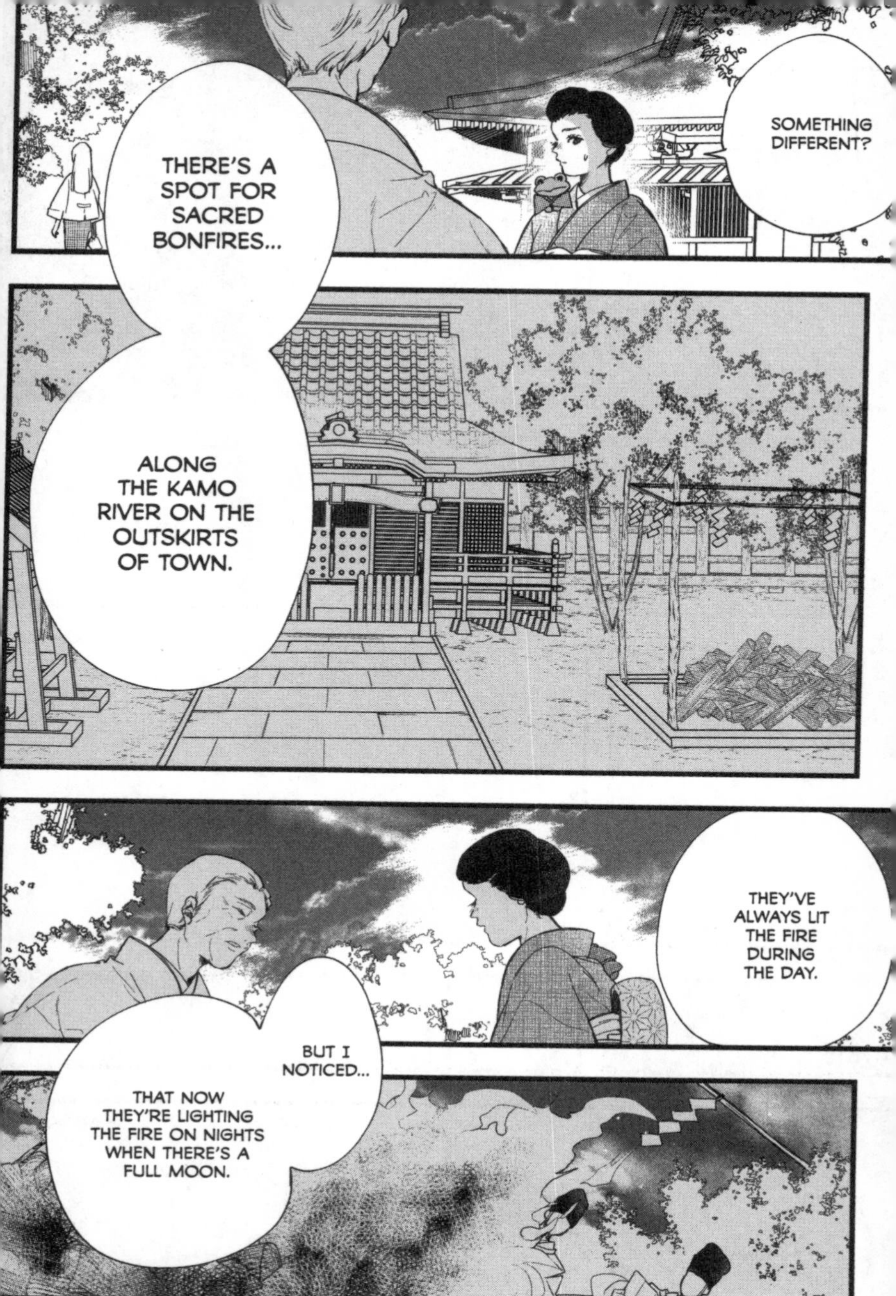
SOMETHING DIFFERENT?
THERE'S A SPOT FOR SACRED BONFIRES...
ALONG THE KAMO RIVER ON THE OUTSKIRTS OF TOWN.
THEY'VE ALWAYS LIT THE FIRE DURING THE DAY.
BUT I NOTICED...
THAT NOW THEY'RE LIGHTING THE FIRE ON NIGHTS WHEN THERE'S A FULL MOON.

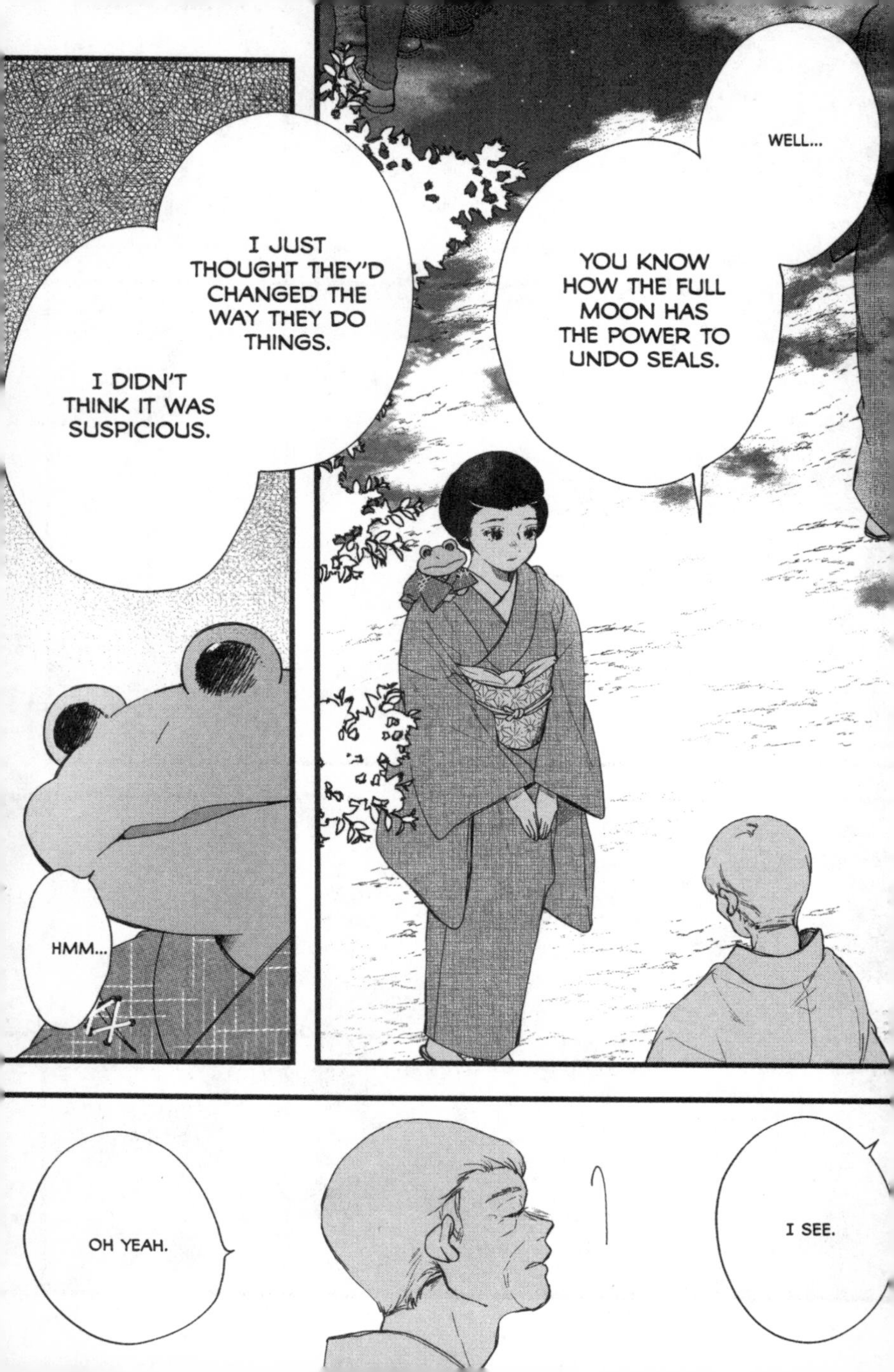
WELL...
YOU KNOW HOW THE FULL MOON HAS THE POWER TO UNDO SEALS.
I JUST THOUGHT THEY'D CHANGED THE WAY THEY DO THINGS.
I DIDN'T THINK IT WAS SUSPICIOUS.
HMM...
I SEE.
OH YEAH.

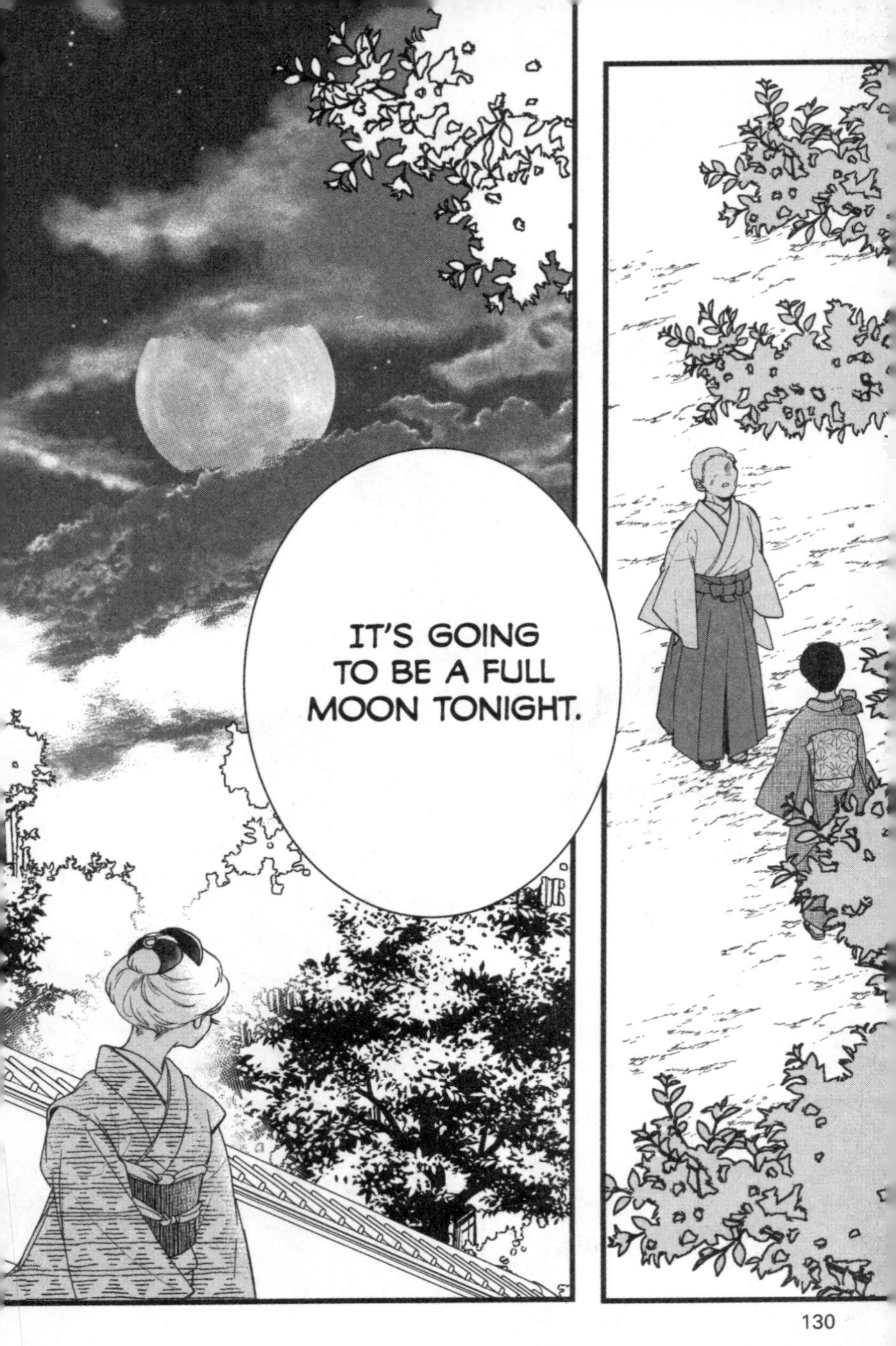
IT'S GOING TO BE A FULL MOON TONIGHT.

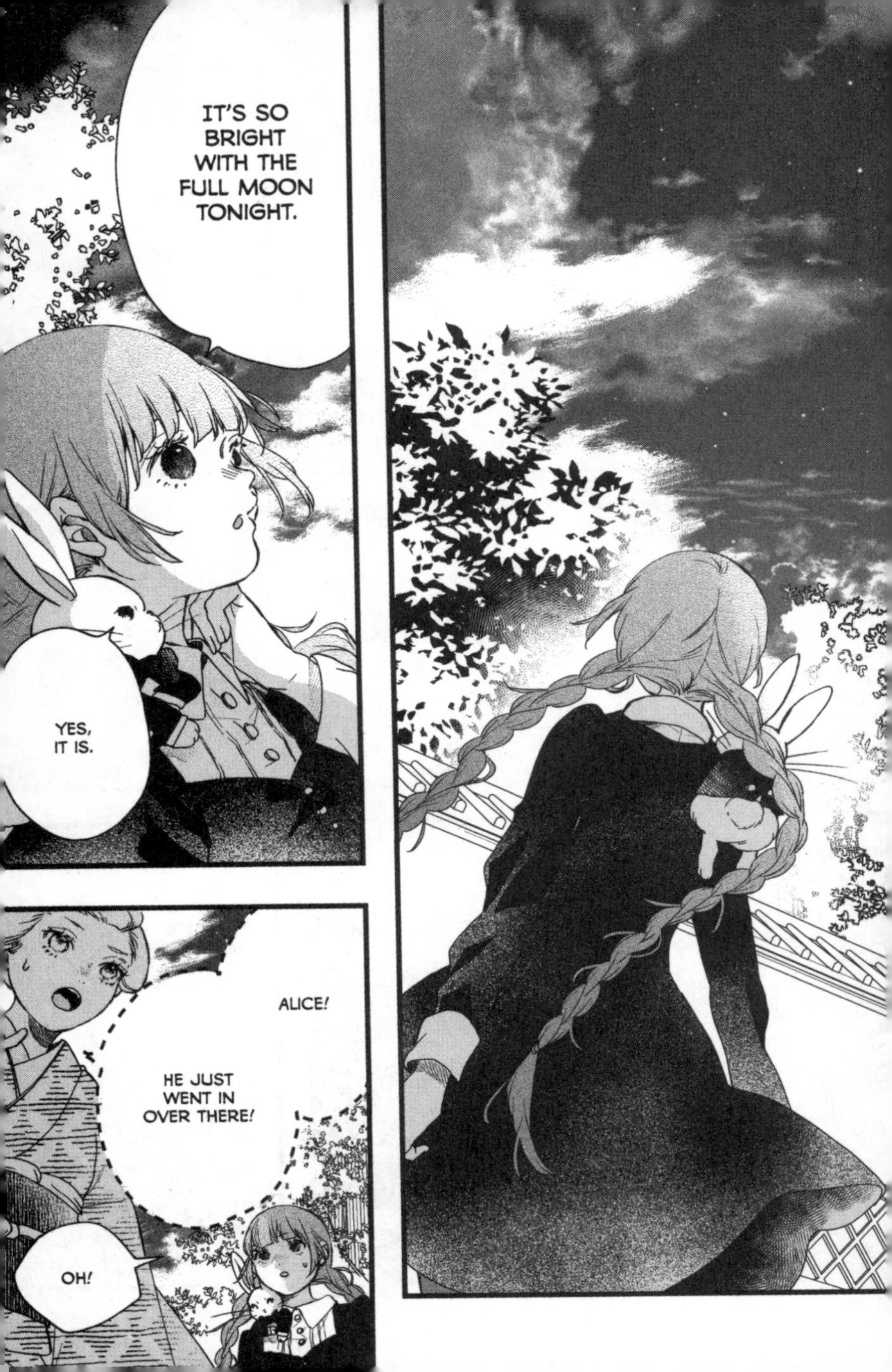
IT'S SO BRIGHT WITH THE FULL MOON TONIGHT.
YES, IT IS.
ALICE!
HE JUST WENT IN OVER THERE!
OH!

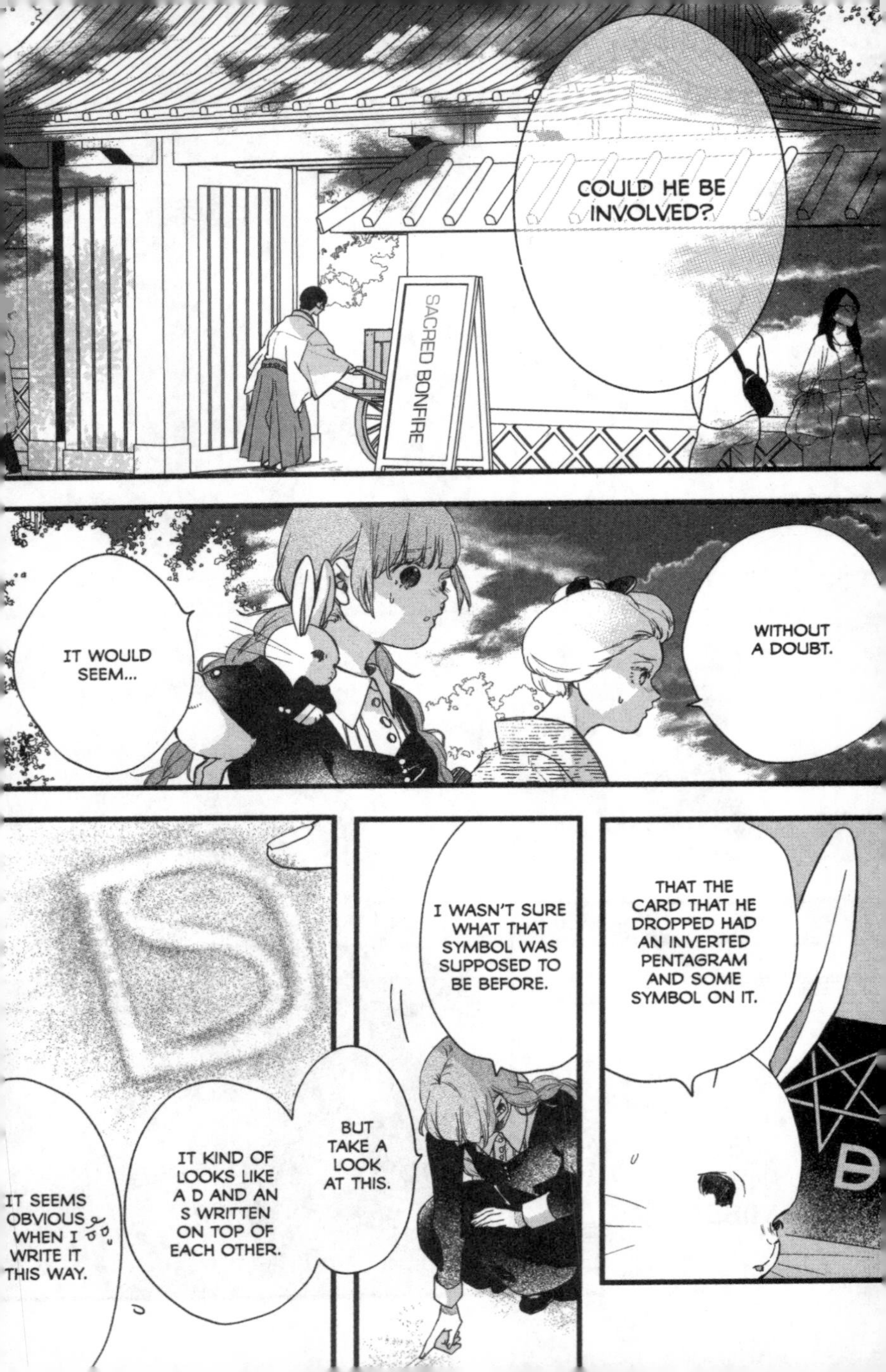
COULD HE BE INVOLVED?
SACRED BONFIRE
WITHOUT A DOUBT.
IT WOULD SEEM...
THAT THE CARD THAT HE DROPPED HAD AN INVERTED PENTAGRAM AND SOME SYMBOL ON IT.
I WASN'T SURE WHAT THAT SYMBOL WAS SUPPOSED TO BE BEFORE.
BUT TAKE A LOOK AT THIS.
IT KIND OF LOOKS LIKE A D AND AN S WRITTEN ON TOP OF EACH OTHER.
IT SEEMS OBVIOUS WHEN I WRITE IT THIS WAY.

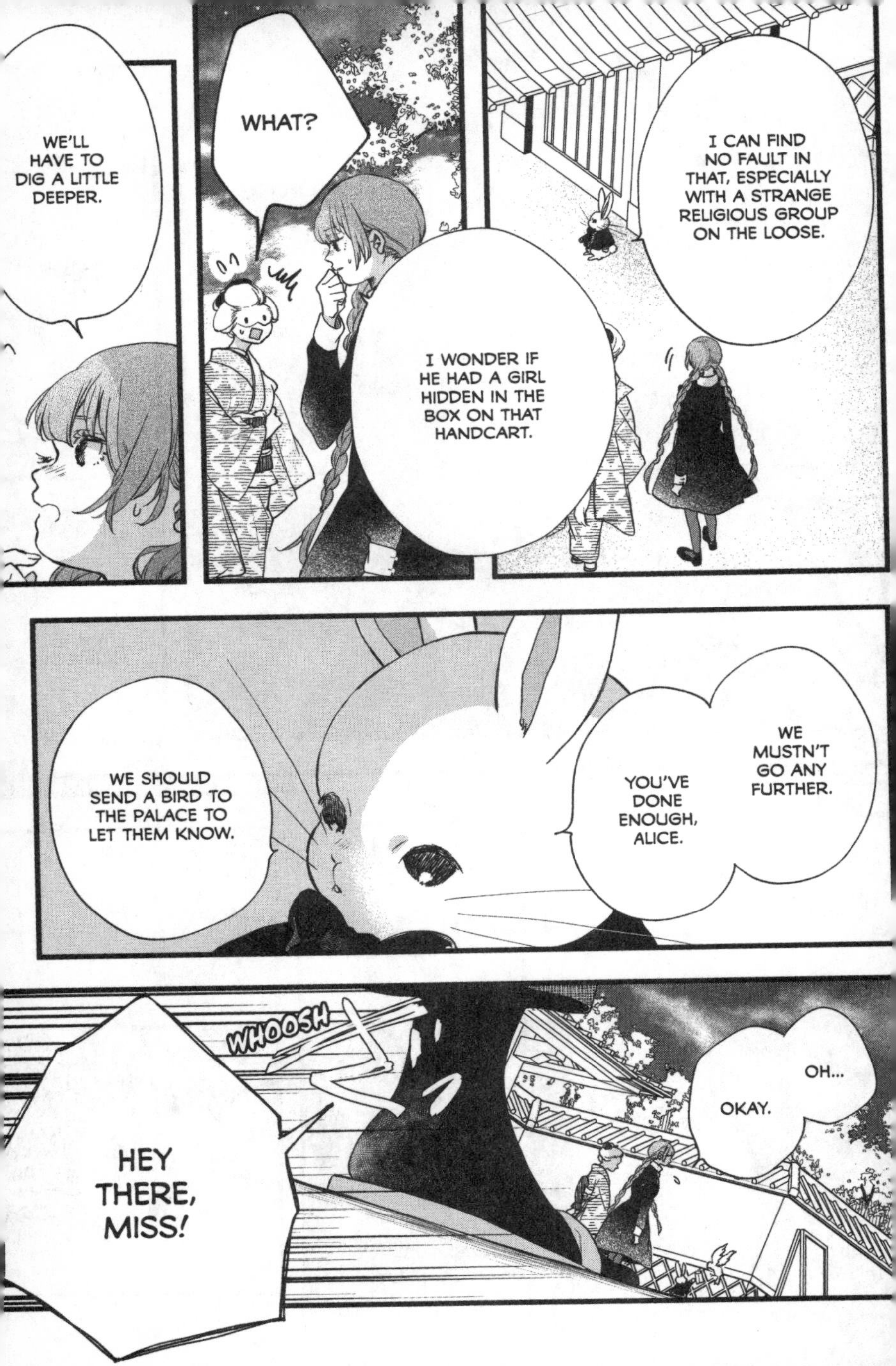

I CAN FIND NO FAULT IN THAT, ESPECIALLY WITH A STRANGE RELIGIOUS GROUP ON THE LOOSE.
WHAT?
I WONDER IF HE HAD A GIRL HIDDEN IN THE BOX ON THAT HANDCART.
WE'LL HAVE TO DIG A LITTLE DEEPER.
WE MUSTN'T GO ANY FURTHER.
YOU'VE DONE ENOUGH, ALICE.
WE SHOULD SEND A BIRD TO THE PALACE TO LET THEM KNOW.
OH...
OKAY.
WHOOSH
HEY THERE, MISS!

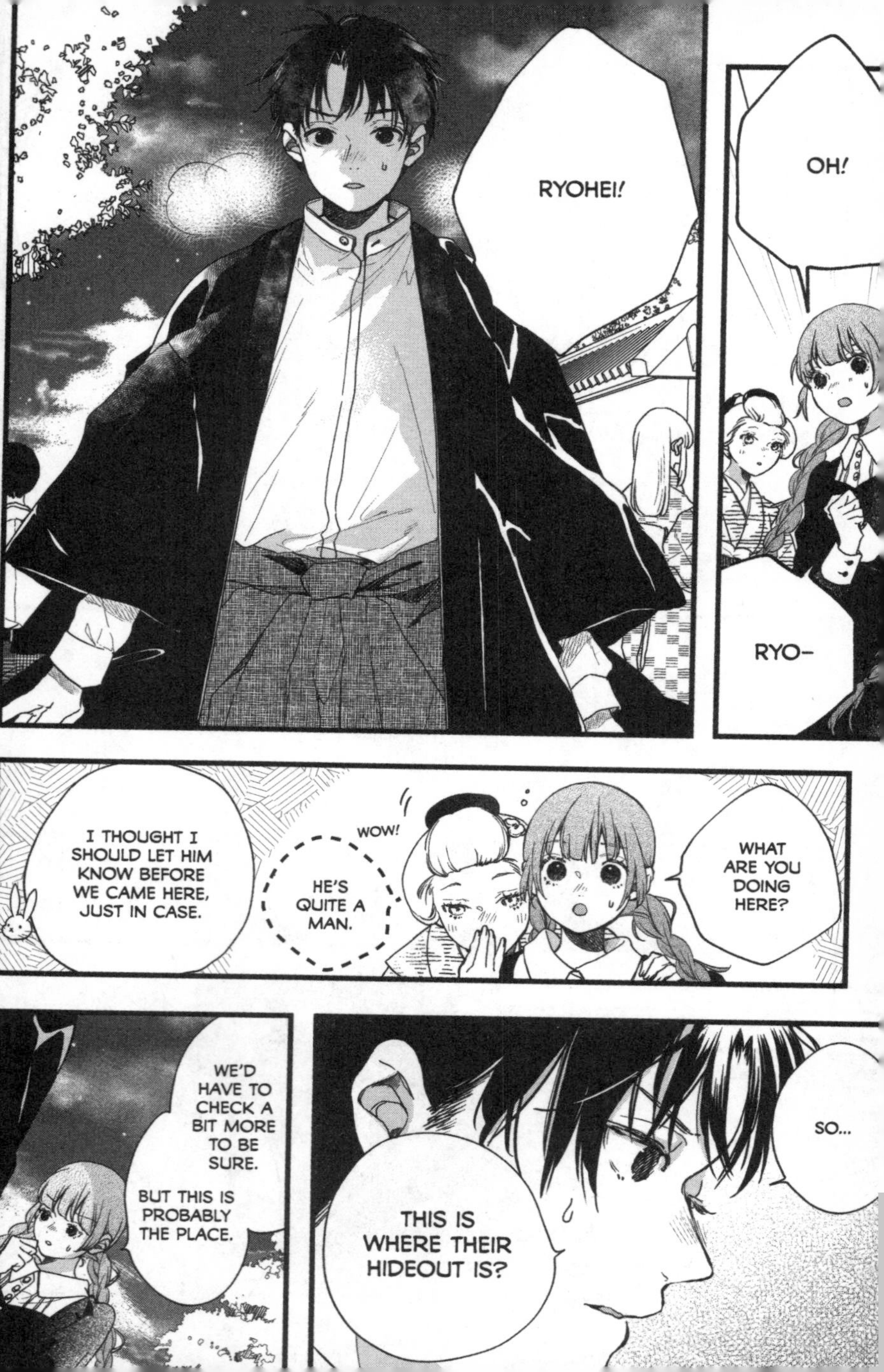
OH!
RYO-
RYOHEI!
WHAT ARE YOU DOING HERE?
WOW!
HE'S QUITE A MAN.
I THOUGHT I SHOULD LET HIM KNOW BEFORE WE CAME HERE, JUST IN CASE.
SO...
THIS IS WHERE THEIR HIDEOUT IS?
WE'D HAVE TO CHECK A BIT MORE TO BE SURE.
BUT THIS IS PROBABLY THE PLACE.

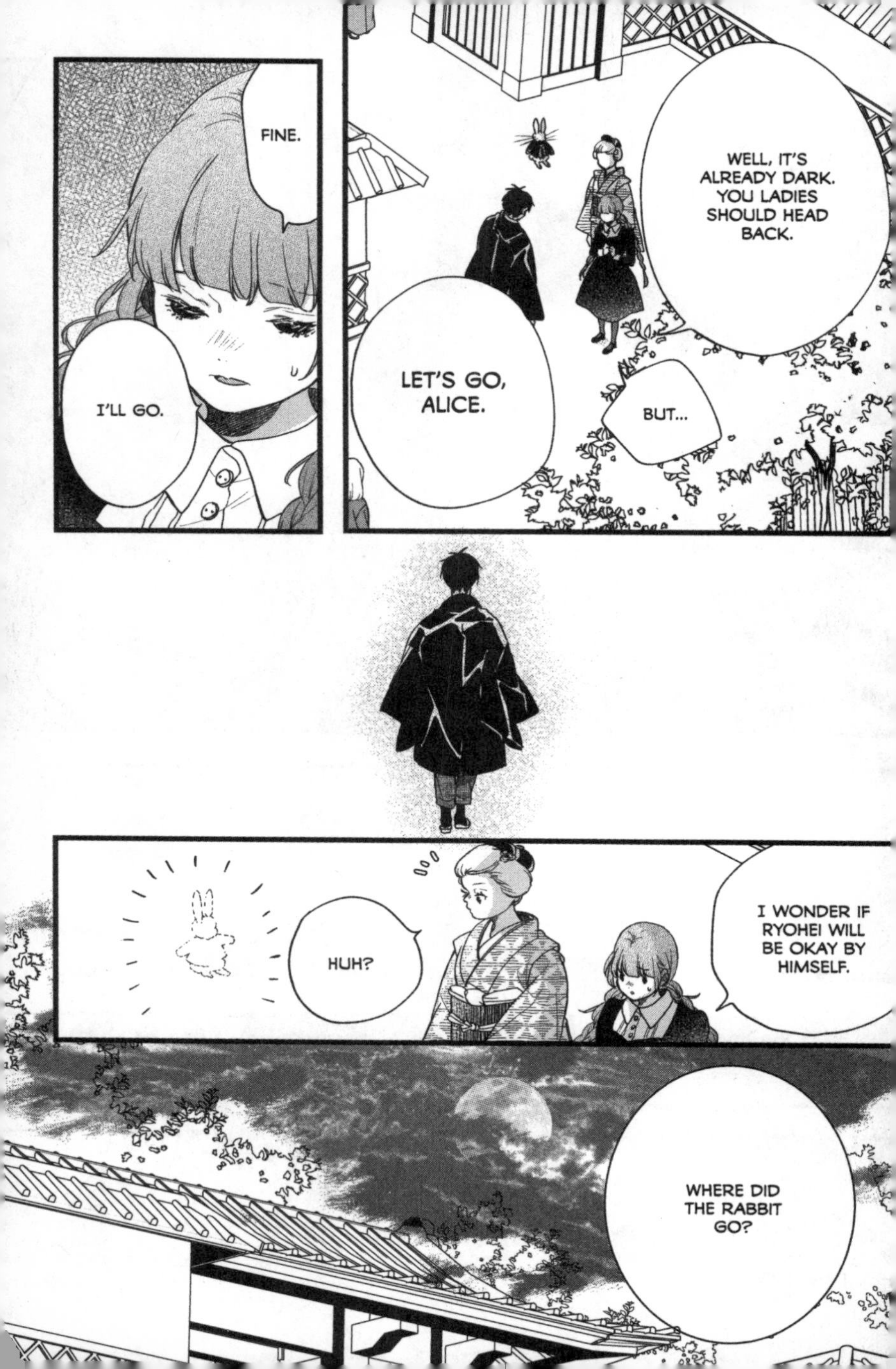
WELL, IT'S ALREADY DARK. YOU LADIES SHOULD HEAD BACK.
BUT...
LET'S GO, ALICE.
FINE.
I'LL GO.
I WONDER IF RYOHEI WILL BE OKAY BY HIMSELF.
HUH?
WHERE DID THE RABBIT GO?

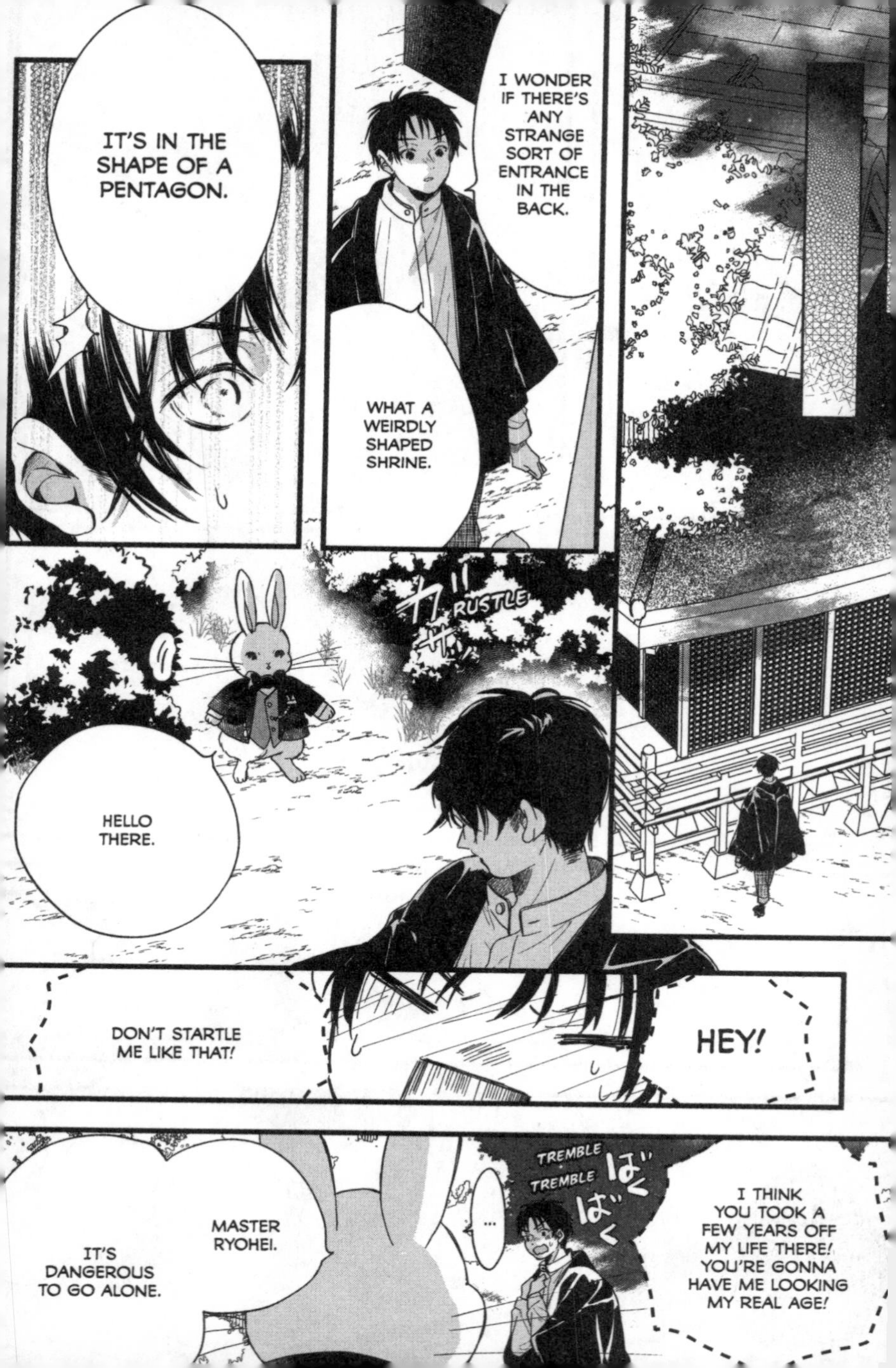
I WONDER IF THERE'S ANY STRANGE SORT OF ENTRANCE IN THE BACK.
WHAT A WEIRDLY SHAPED SHRINE.
IT'S IN THE SHAPE OF A PENTAGON.
RUSTLE
HELLO THERE.
HEY!
DON'T STARTLE ME LIKE THAT!
TREMBLE TREMBLE
ばくばく
I THINK YOU TOOK A FEW YEARS OFF MY LIFE THERE! YOU'RE GONNA HAVE ME LOOKING MY REAL AGE!
...
MASTER RYOHEI.
IT'S DANGEROUS TO GO ALONE.

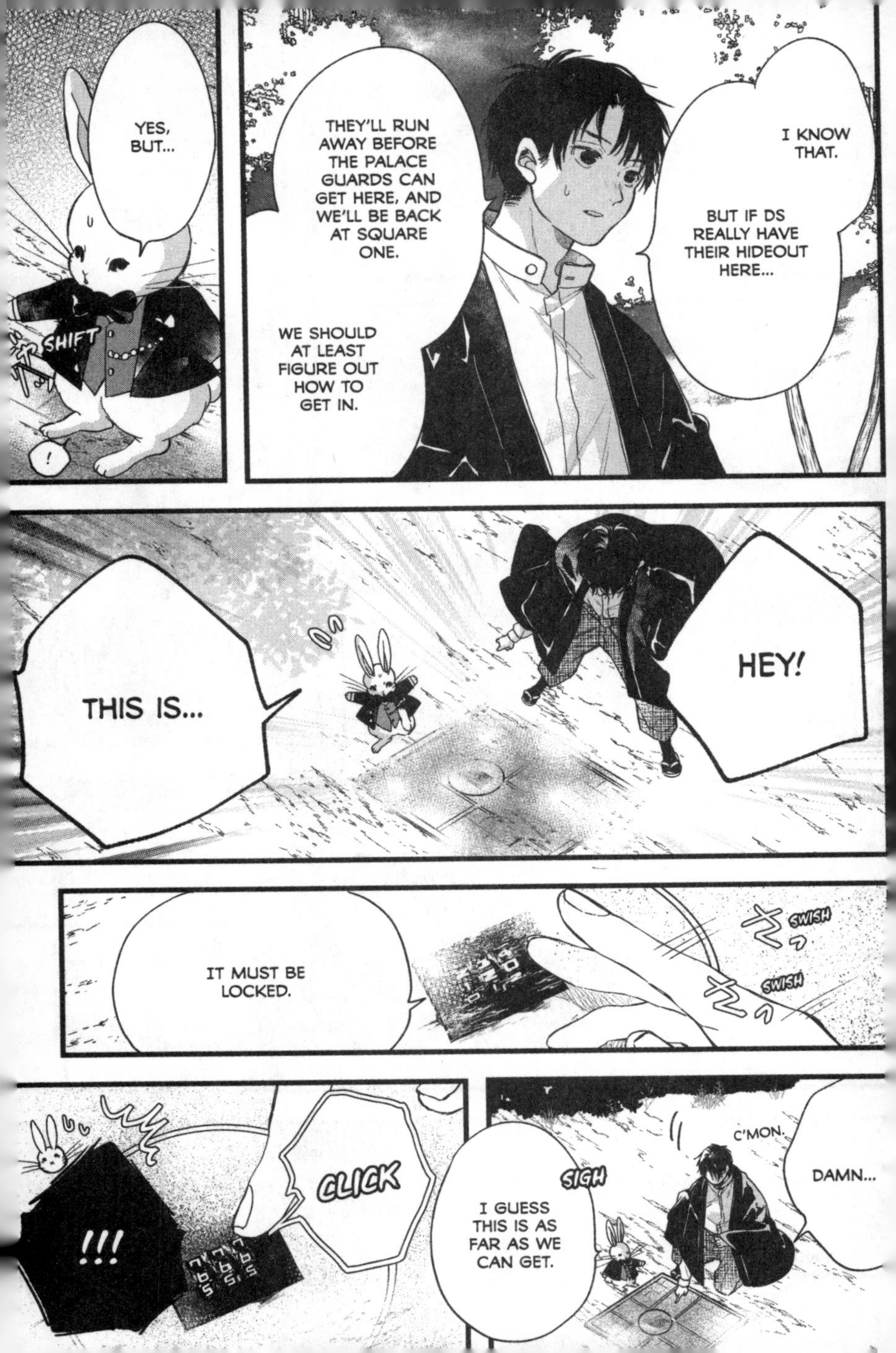
I KNOW THAT.
BUT IF DS REALLY HAVE THEIR HIDEOUT HERE...
THEY'LL RUN AWAY BEFORE THE PALACE GUARDS CAN GET HERE, AND WE'LL BE BACK AT SQUARE ONE.
WE SHOULD AT LEAST FIGURE OUT HOW TO GET IN.
YES, BUT...
SHIFT
!
HEY!
THIS IS...
SWISH
SWISH
IT MUST BE LOCKED.
DAMN...
C'MON.
SIGH
I GUESS THIS IS AS FAR AS WE CAN GET.
CLICK
!!!

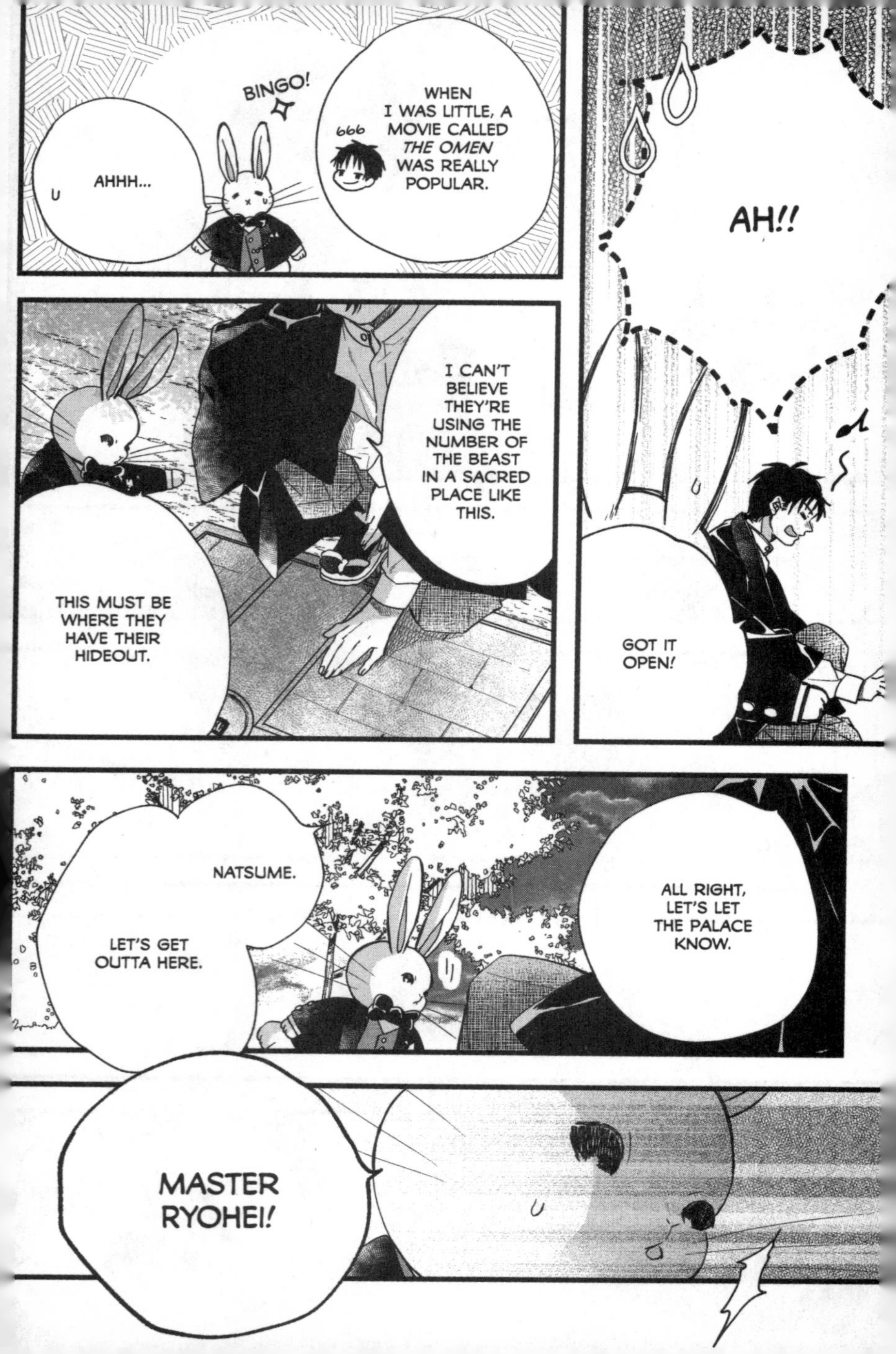

AH!!
GOT IT OPEN!
WHEN I WAS LITTLE, A MOVIE CALLED *THE OMEN* WAS REALLY POPULAR.
666
BINGO!
AHHH...
I CAN'T BELIEVE THEY'RE USING THE NUMBER OF THE BEAST IN A SACRED PLACE LIKE THIS.
THIS MUST BE WHERE THEY HAVE THEIR HIDEOUT.
ALL RIGHT, LET'S LET THE PALACE KNOW.
NATSUME.
LET'S GET OUTTA HERE.
MASTER RYOHEI!

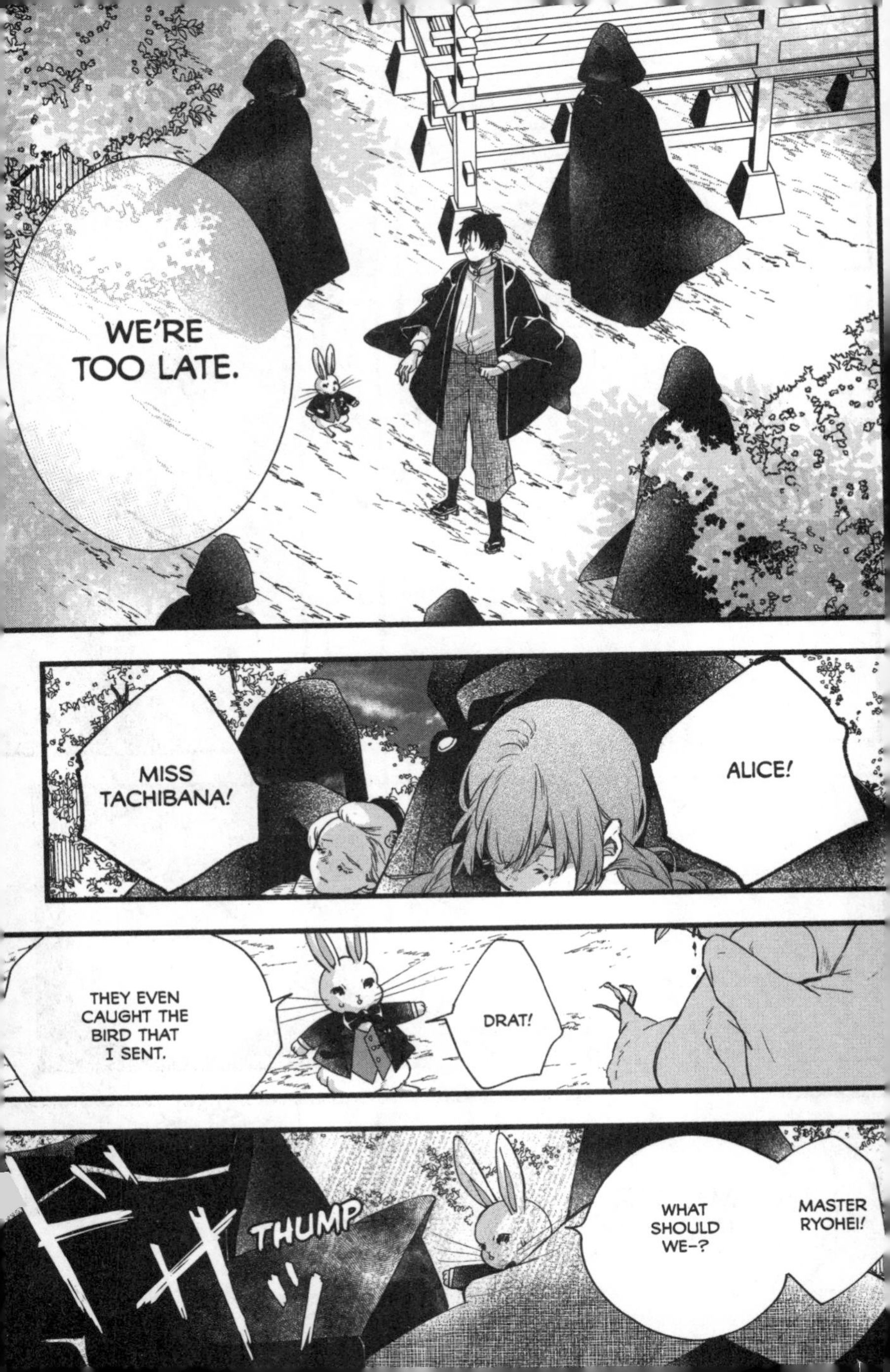
WE'RE TOO LATE.
ALICE!
MISS TACHIBANA!
DRAT!
THEY EVEN CAUGHT THE BIRD THAT I SENT.
MASTER RYOHEI!
WHAT SHOULD WE-?
THUMP

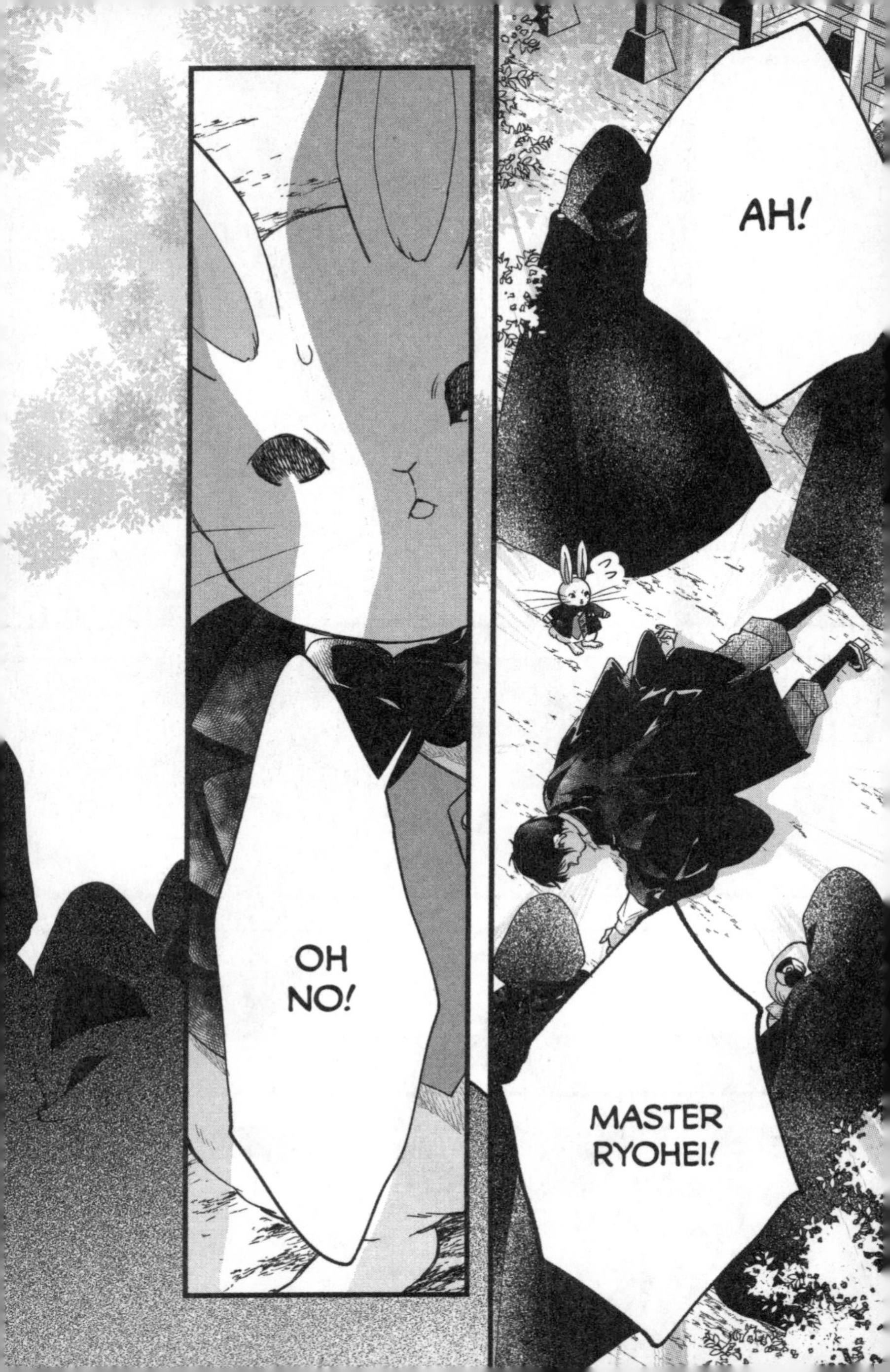
AH!
MASTER RYOHEI!
OH NO!

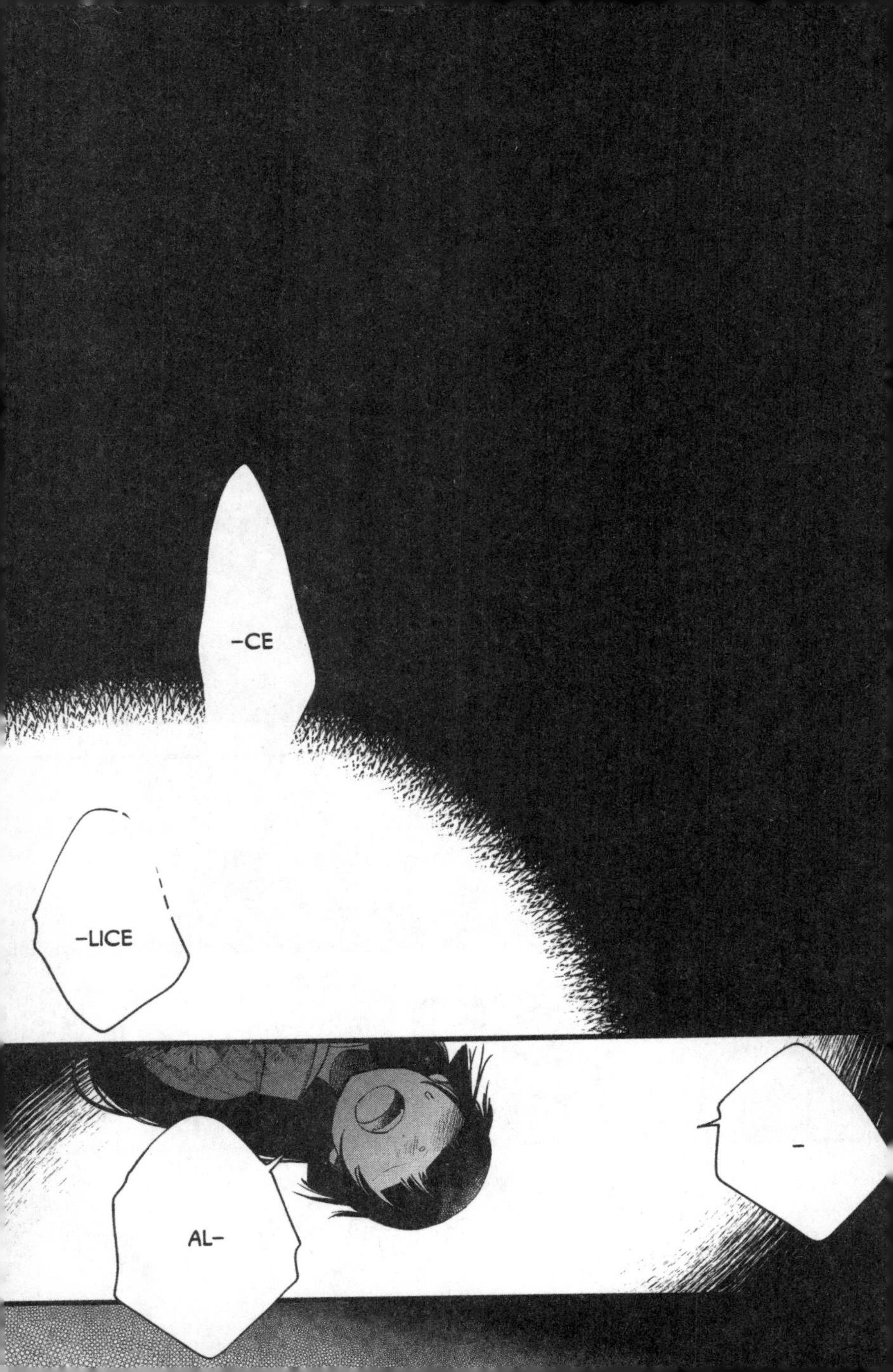
-CE
-LICE
-
AL-

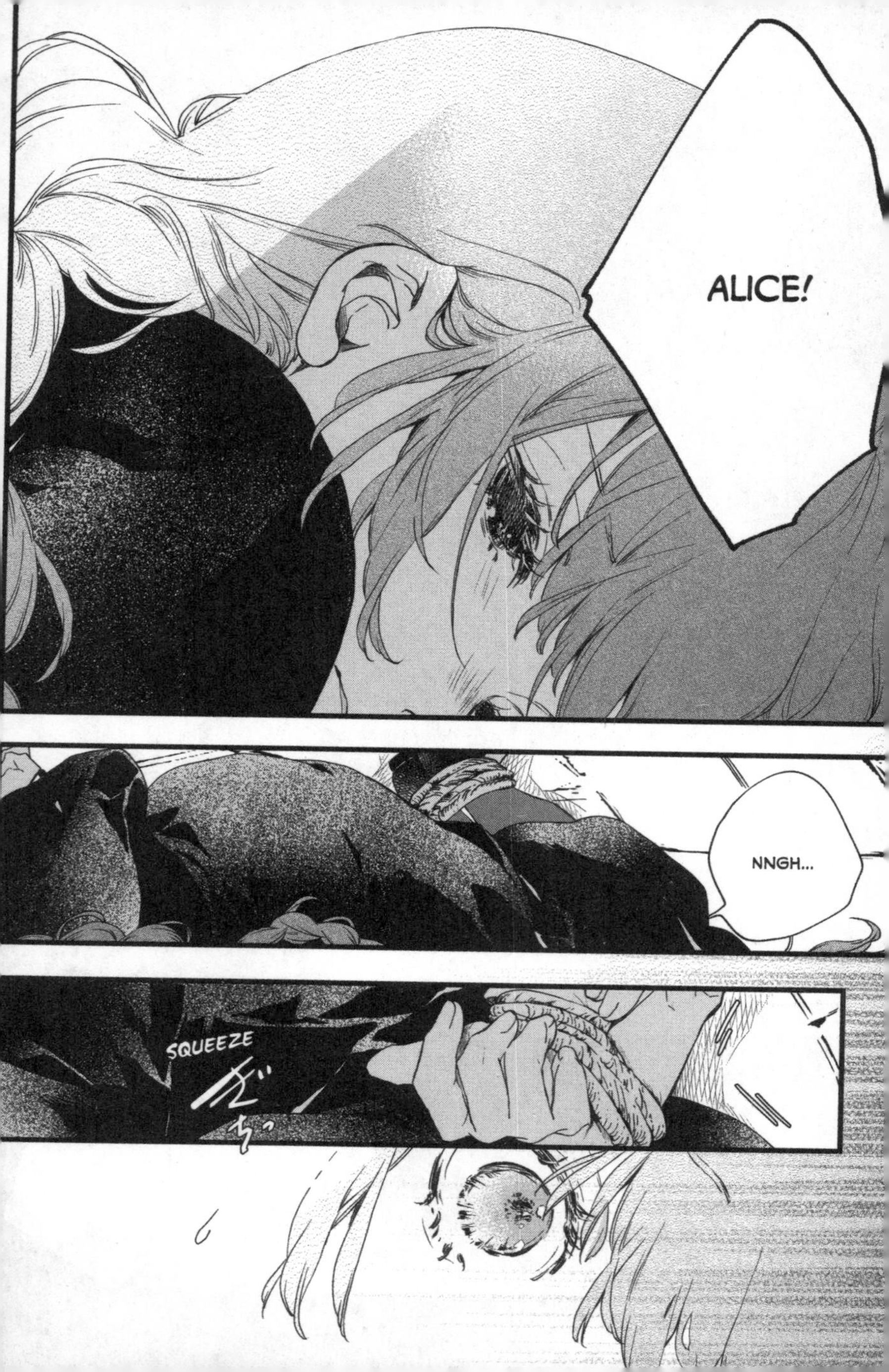
ALICE!
NNGH...
SQUEEZE

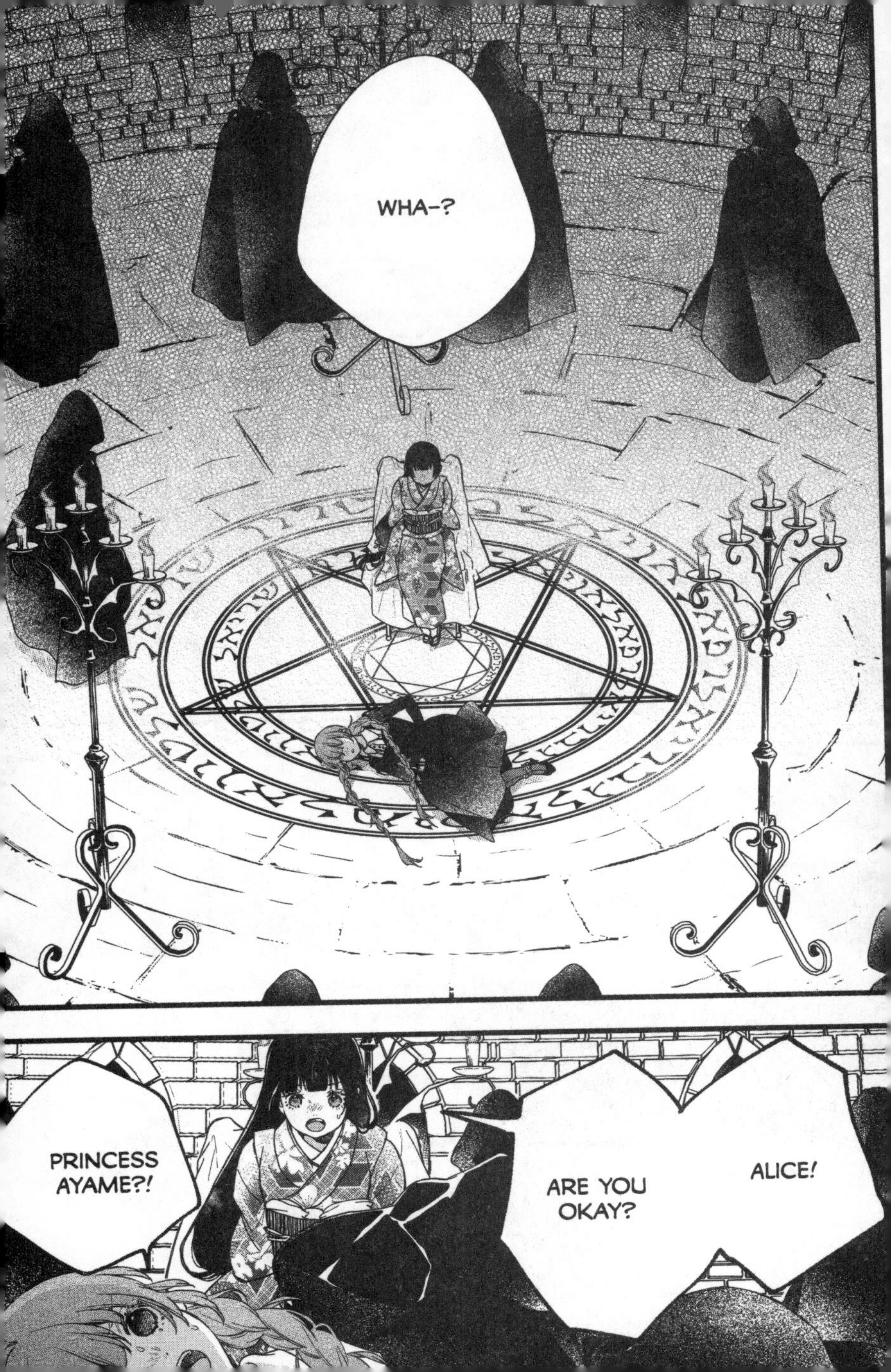
WHA-?
ALICE!
ARE YOU OKAY?
PRINCESS AYAME?!

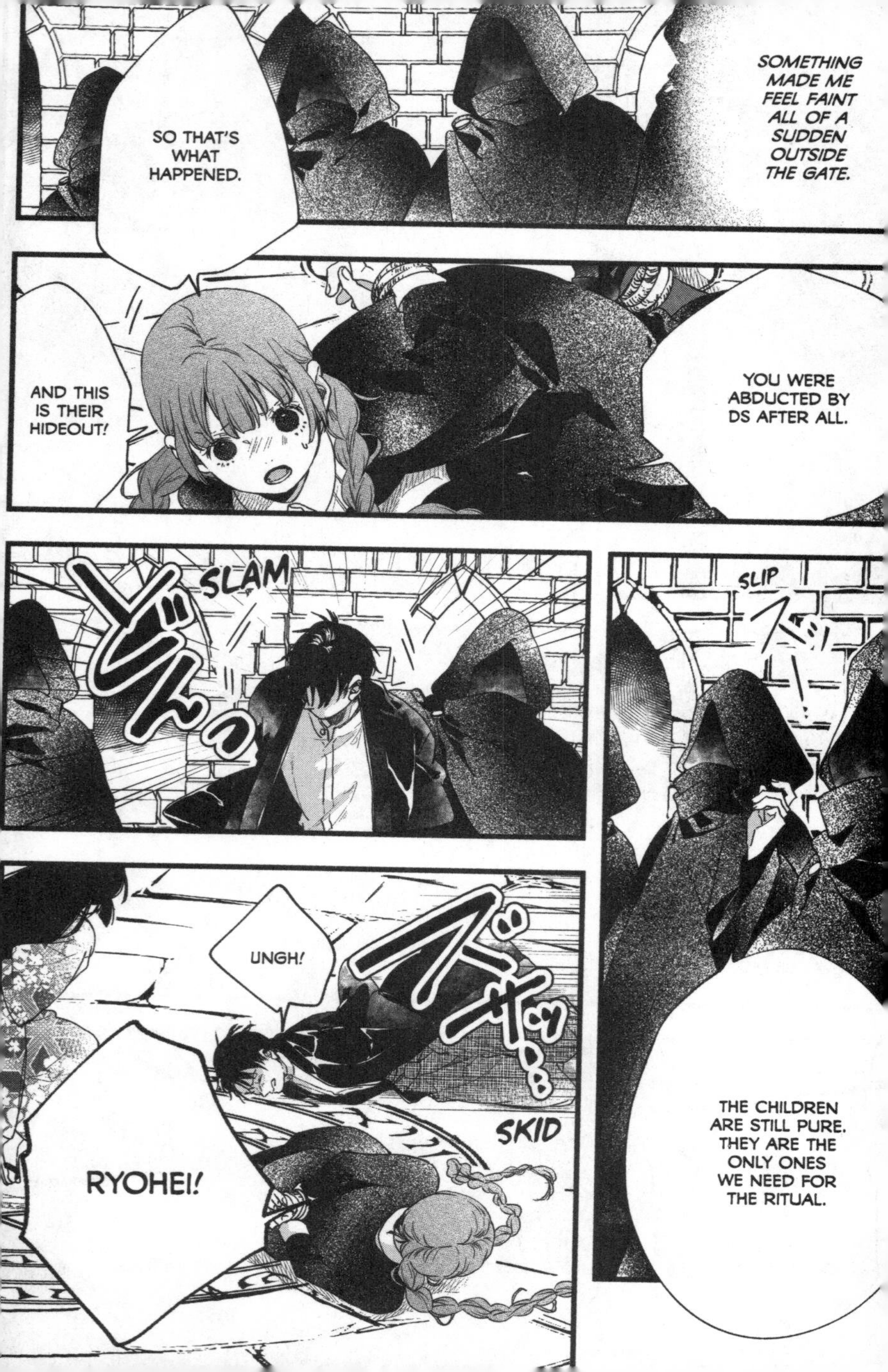
SOMETHING MADE ME FEEL FAINT ALL OF A SUDDEN OUTSIDE THE GATE.
SO THAT'S WHAT HAPPENED.
YOU WERE ABDUCTED BY DS AFTER ALL.
AND THIS IS THEIR HIDEOUT!
SLIP
ズッ
THE CHILDREN ARE STILL PURE. THEY ARE THE ONLY ONES WE NEED FOR THE RITUAL.
SLAM
ドンッ
UNGH!
ベザッ
SKID
RYOHEI!

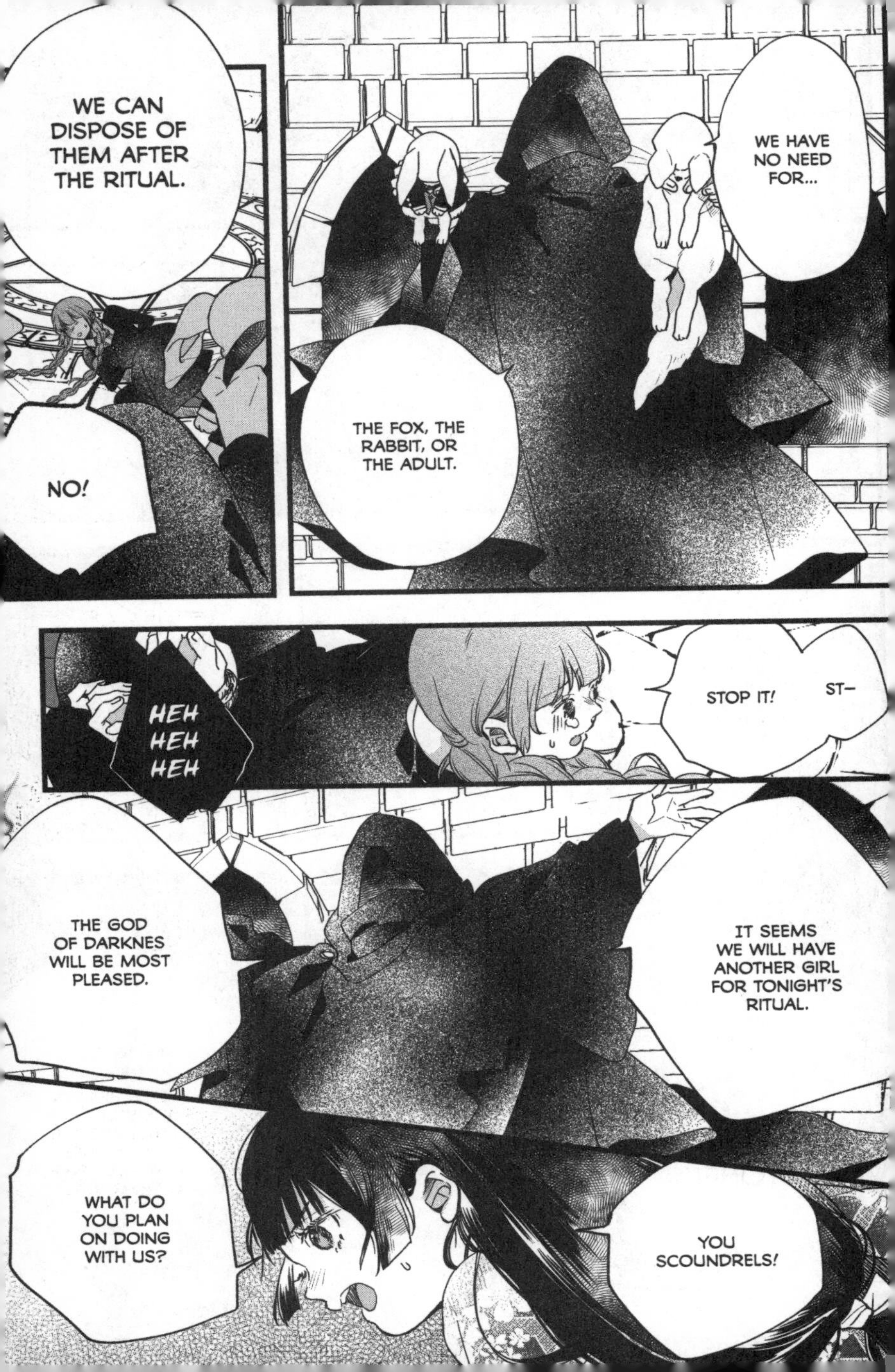
WE HAVE NO NEED FOR...
THE FOX, THE RABBIT, OR THE ADULT.
WE CAN DISPOSE OF THEM AFTER THE RITUAL.
NO!
STOP IT! ST–
HEH HEH HEH
IT SEEMS WE WILL HAVE ANOTHER GIRL FOR TONIGHT'S RITUAL.
THE GOD OF DARKNES WILL BE MOST PLEASED.
YOU SCOUNDRELS!
WHAT DO YOU PLAN ON DOING WITH US?

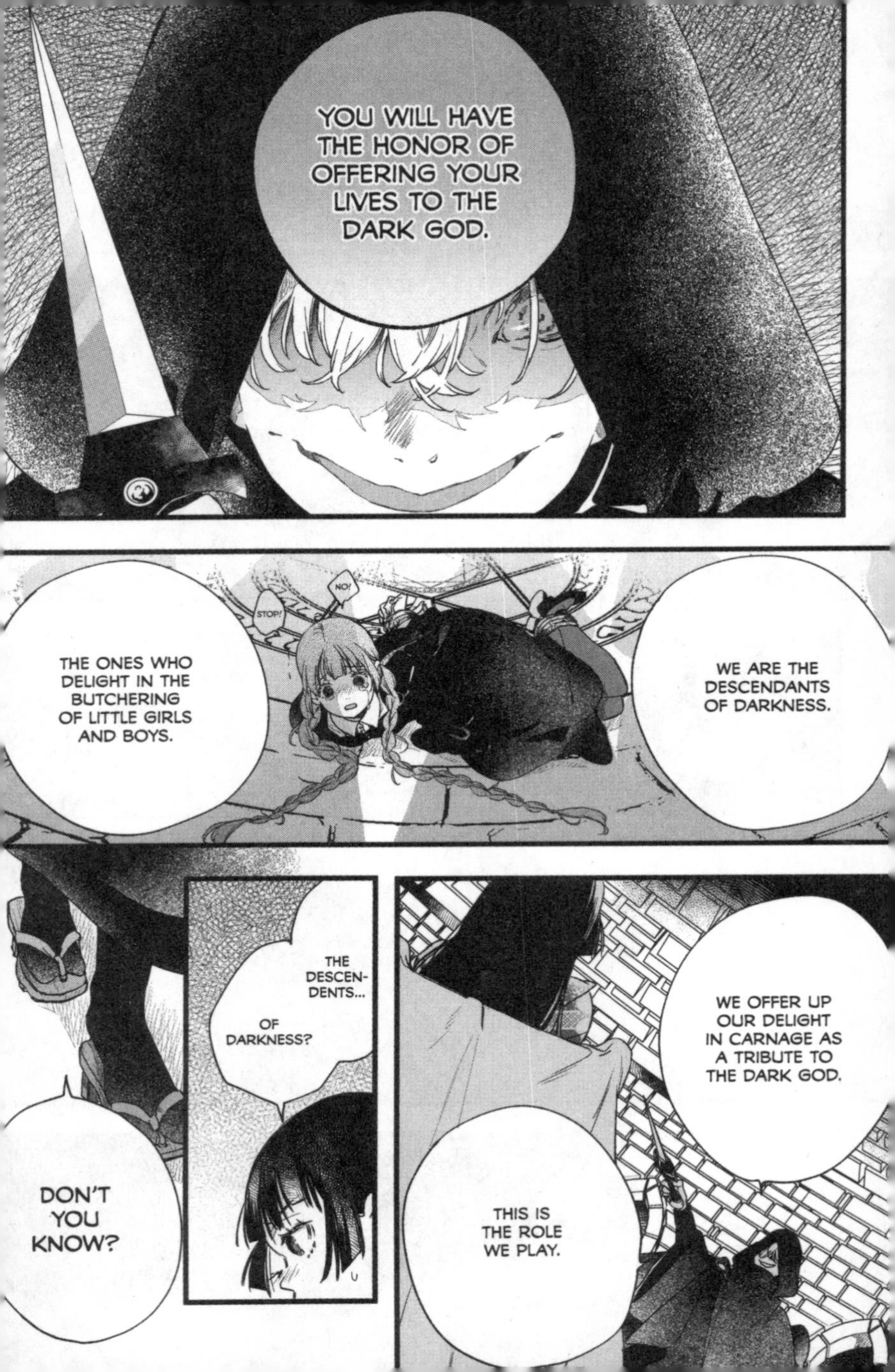
YOU WILL HAVE THE HONOR OF OFFERING YOUR LIVES TO THE DARK GOD.
WE ARE THE DESCENDANTS OF DARKNESS.
NO!
STOP!
THE ONES WHO DELIGHT IN THE BUTCHERING OF LITTLE GIRLS AND BOYS.
WE OFFER UP OUR DELIGHT IN CARNAGE AS A TRIBUTE TO THE DARK GOD.
THIS IS THE ROLE WE PLAY.
THE DESCENDENTS...
OF DARKNESS?
DON'T YOU KNOW?

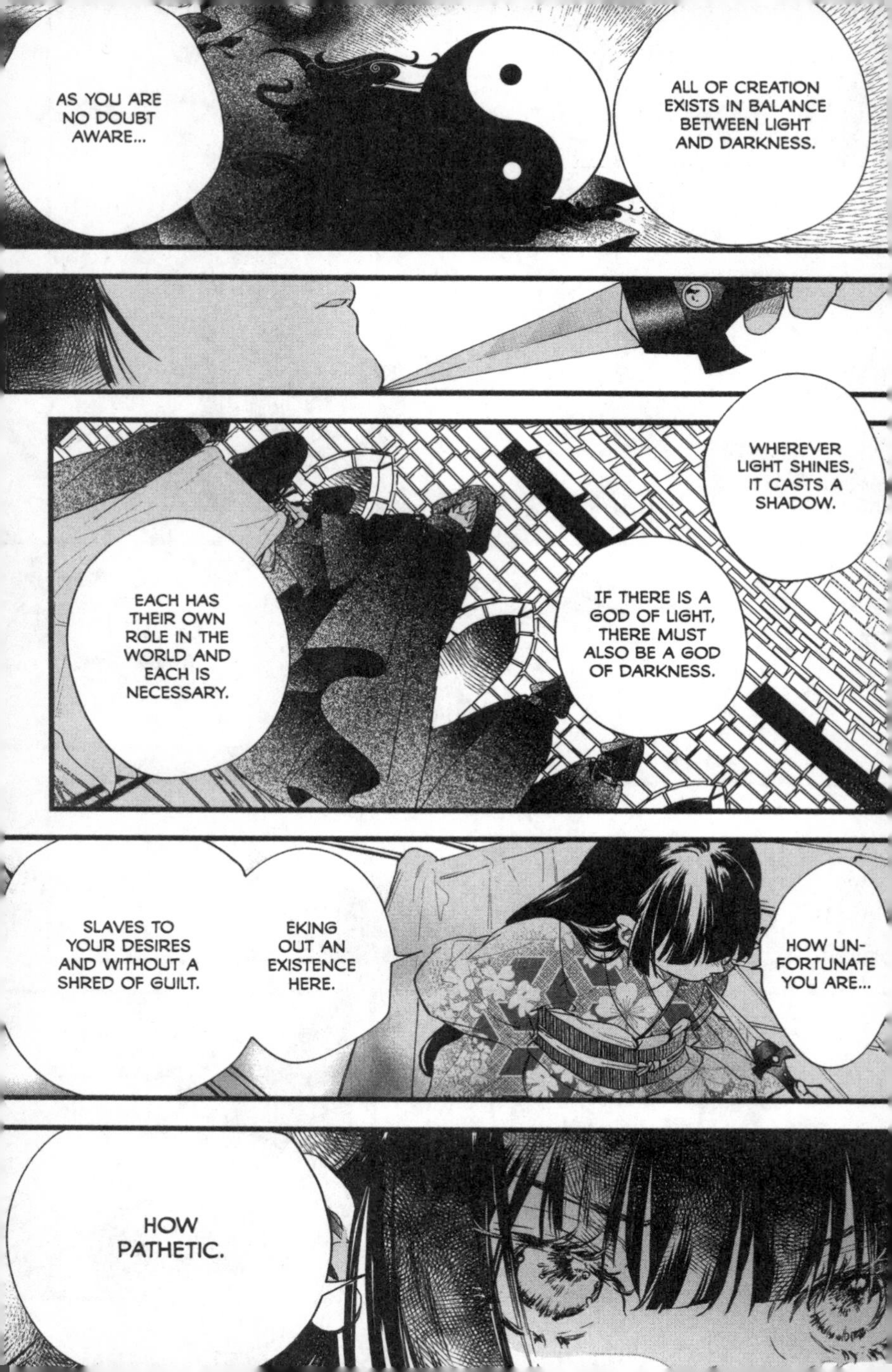
ALL OF CREATION EXISTS IN BALANCE BETWEEN LIGHT AND DARKNESS.
AS YOU ARE NO DOUBT AWARE...
WHEREVER LIGHT SHINES, IT CASTS A SHADOW.
IF THERE IS A GOD OF LIGHT, THERE MUST ALSO BE A GOD OF DARKNESS.
EACH HAS THEIR OWN ROLE IN THE WORLD AND EACH IS NECESSARY.
HOW UN-FORTUNATE YOU ARE...
EKING OUT AN EXISTENCE HERE.
SLAVES TO YOUR DESIRES AND WITHOUT A SHRED OF GUILT.
HOW PATHETIC.

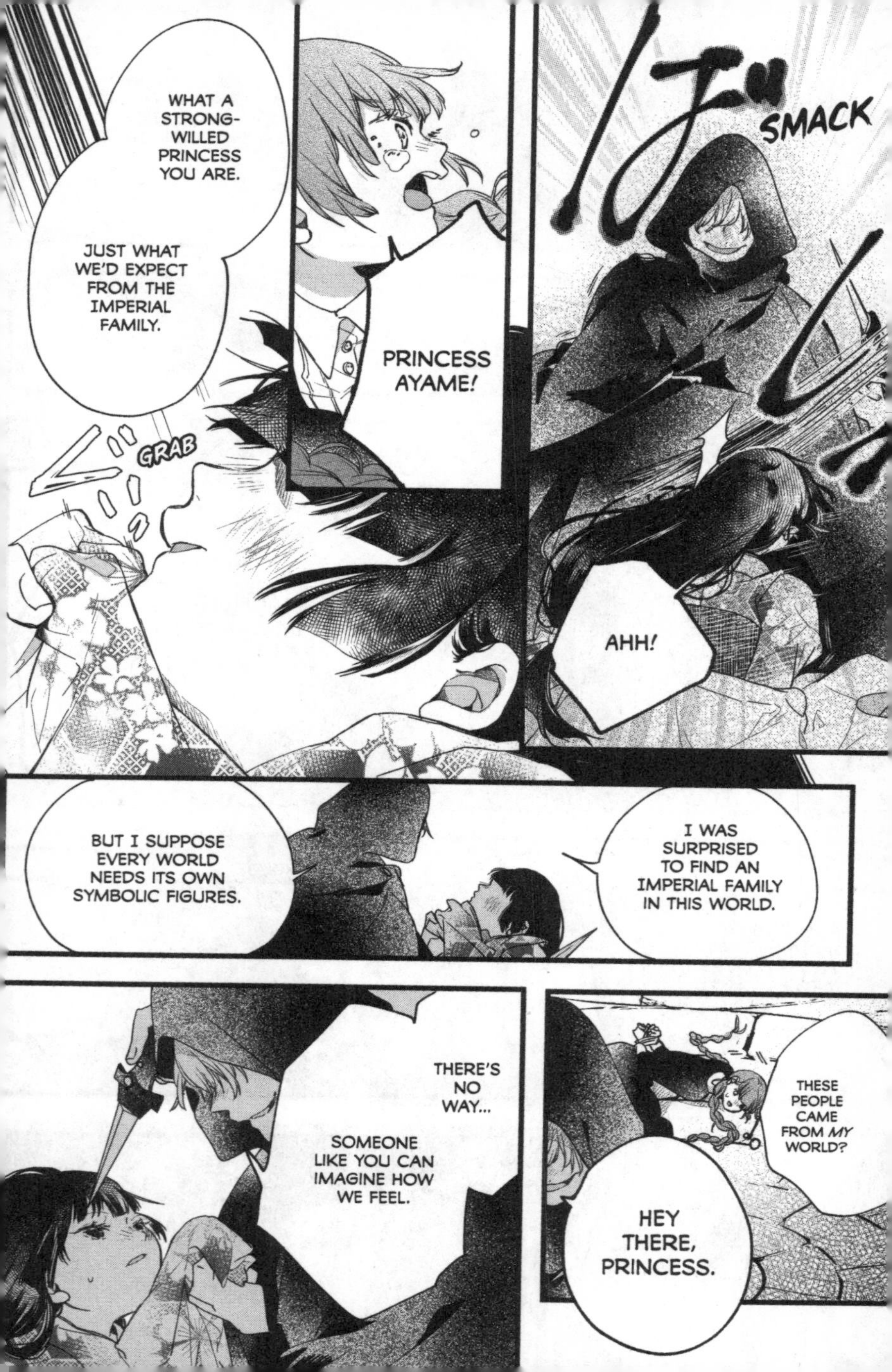
SMACK
AHH!
PRINCESS AYAME!
WHAT A STRONG-WILLED PRINCESS YOU ARE.
JUST WHAT WE'D EXPECT FROM THE IMPERIAL FAMILY.
GRAB
I WAS SURPRISED TO FIND AN IMPERIAL FAMILY IN THIS WORLD.
BUT I SUPPOSE EVERY WORLD NEEDS ITS OWN SYMBOLIC FIGURES.
THESE PEOPLE CAME FROM *MY* WORLD?
HEY THERE, PRINCESS.
THERE'S NO WAY...
SOMEONE LIKE YOU CAN IMAGINE HOW WE FEEL.

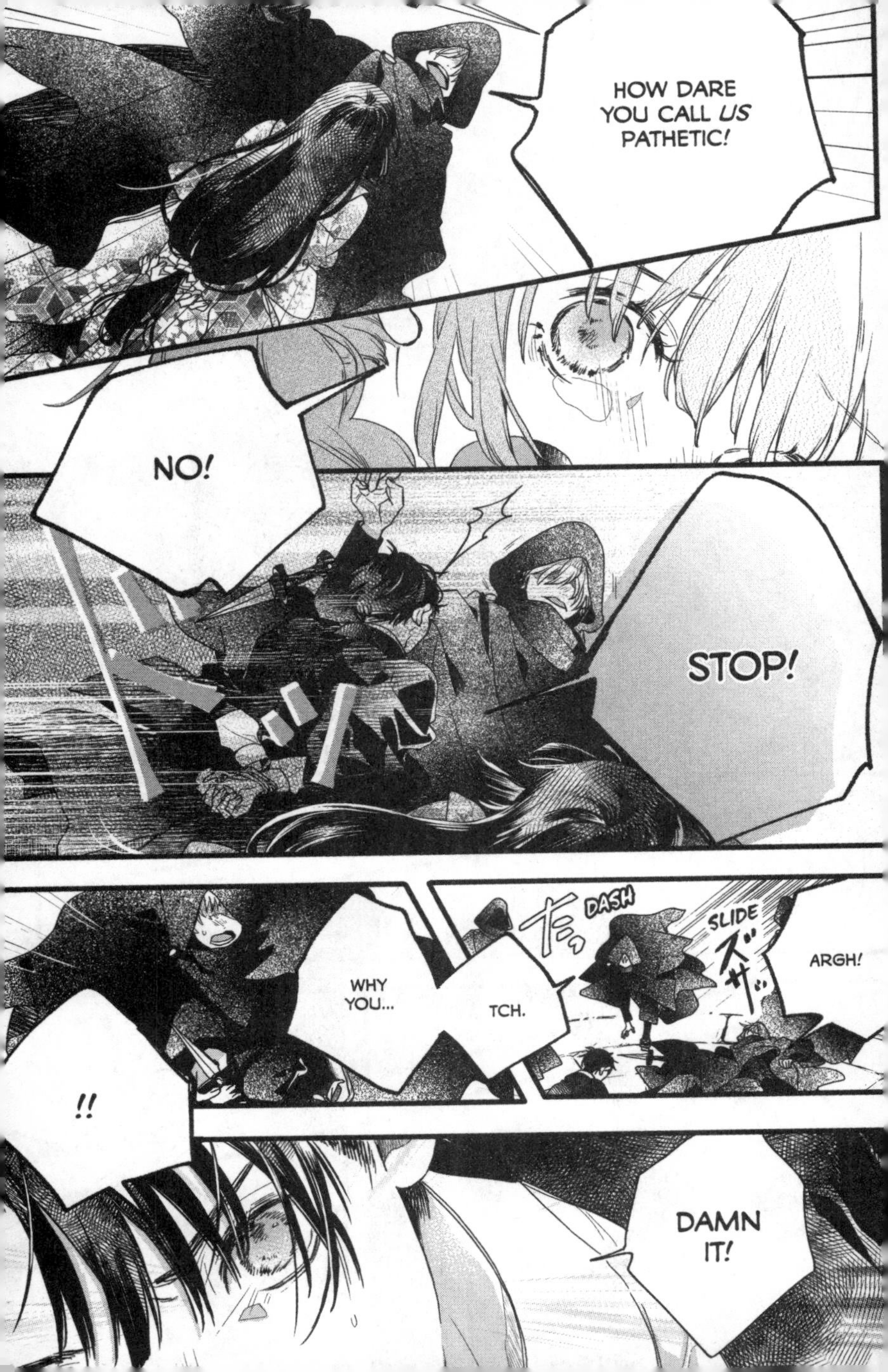
HOW DARE YOU CALL *US* PATHETIC!
NO!
STOP!
DASH
SLIDE
ARGH!
TCH.
WHY YOU...
DAMN IT!
!!

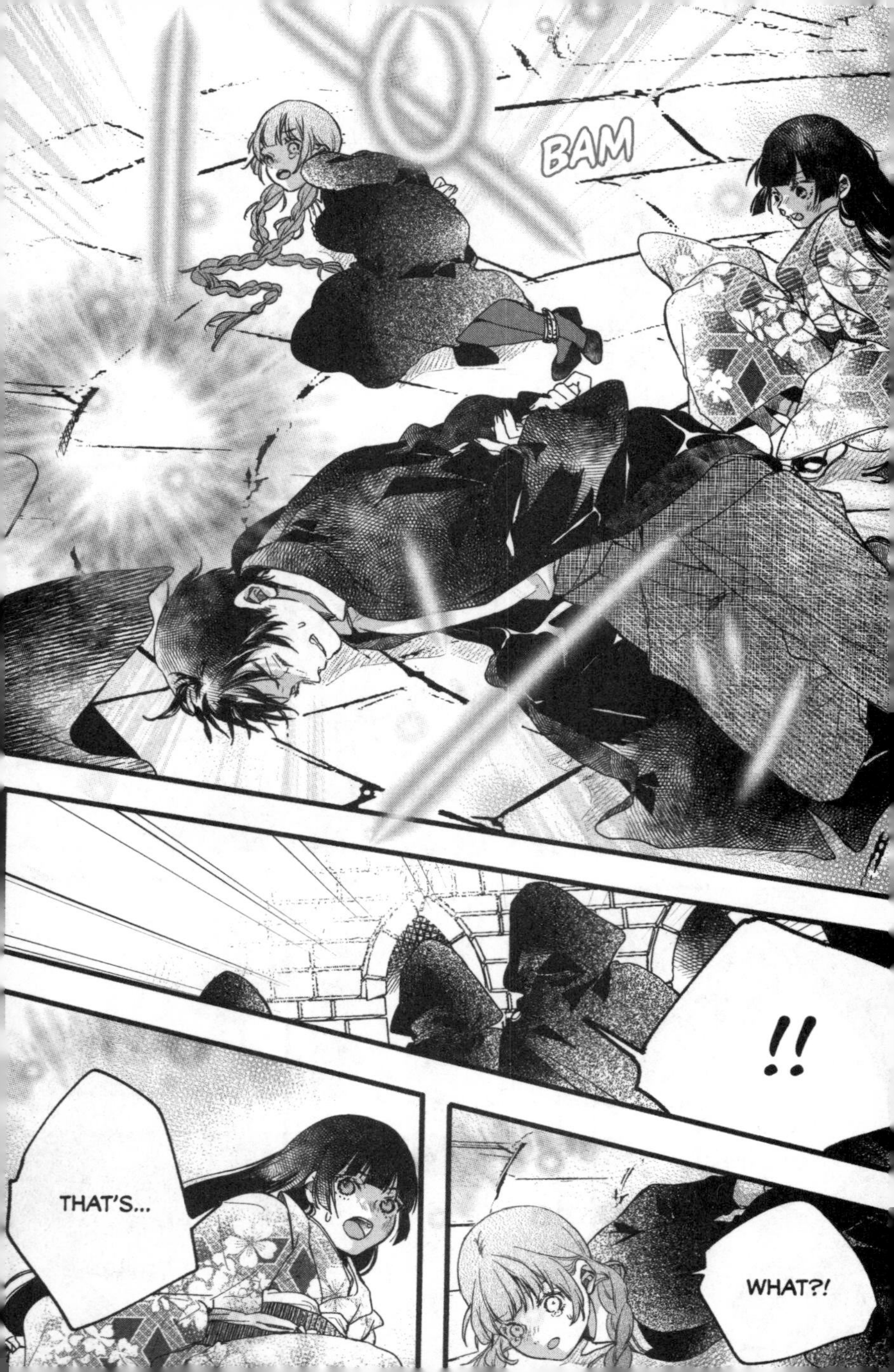
BAM
!!
WHAT?!
THAT'S...

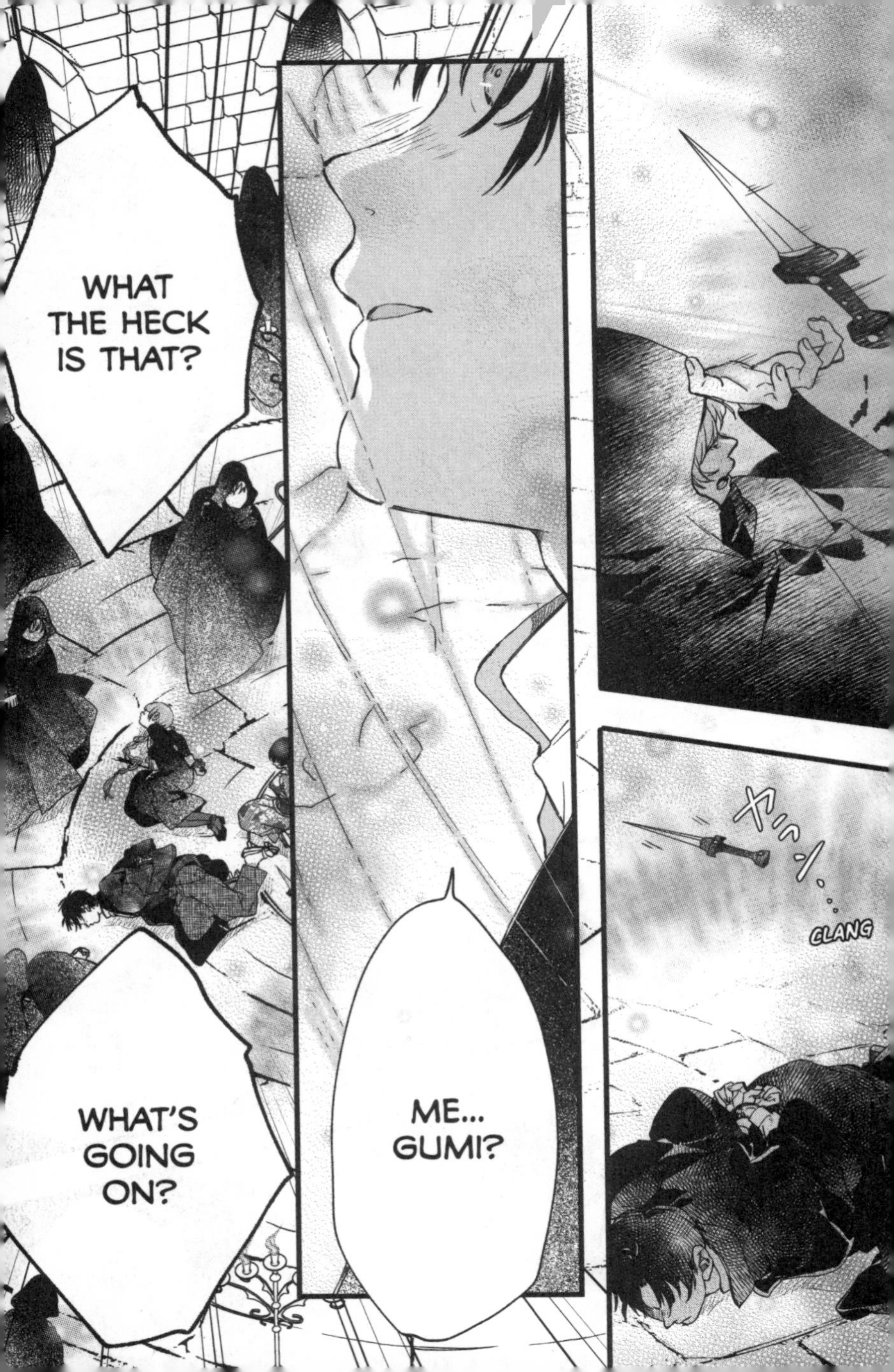
CLANG
ME... GUMI?
WHAT THE HECK IS THAT?
WHAT'S GOING ON?

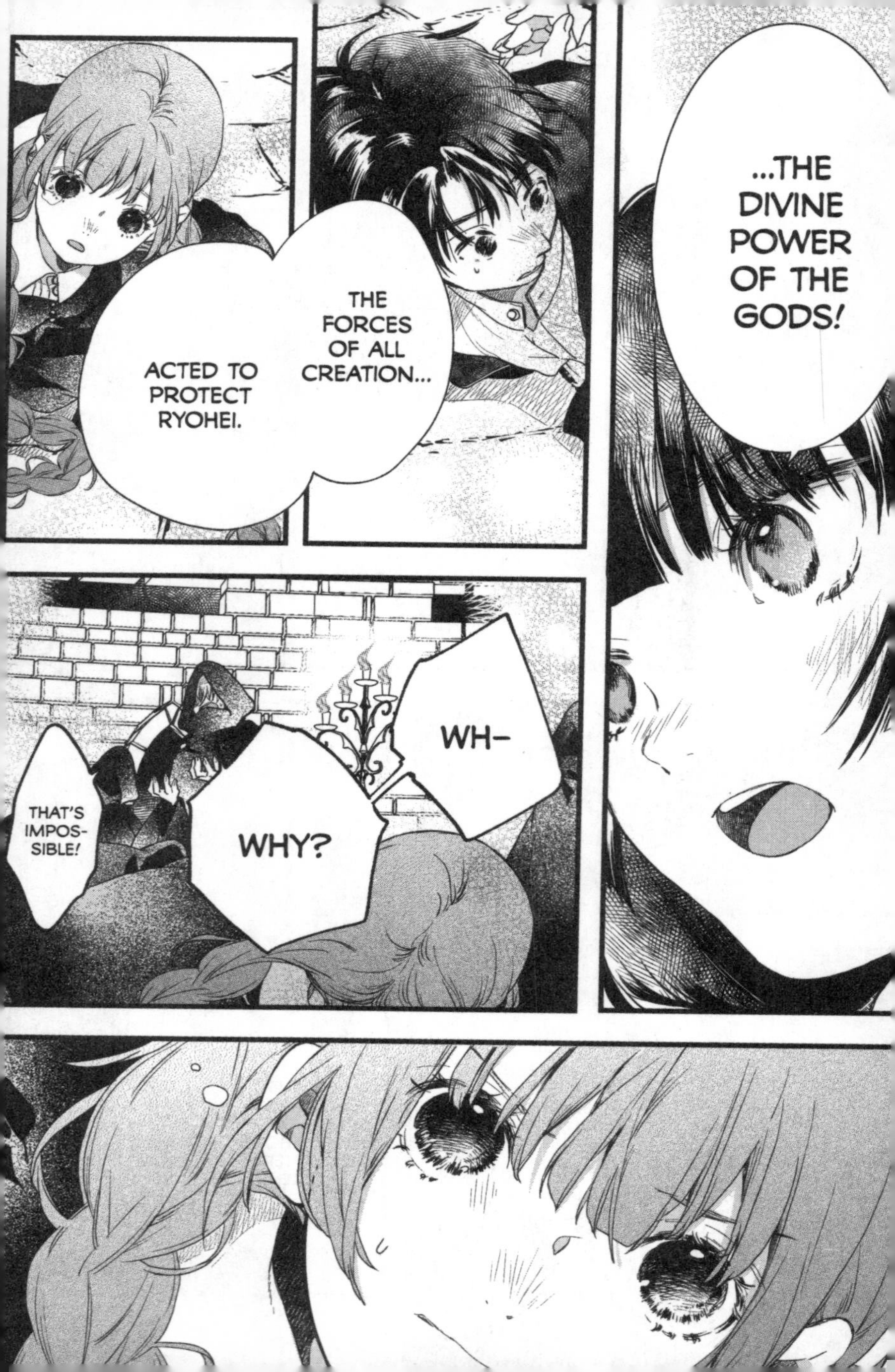
...THE DIVINE POWER OF THE GODS!
THE FORCES OF ALL CREATION...
ACTED TO PROTECT RYOHEI.
WH-
WHY?
THAT'S IMPOS-SIBLE!

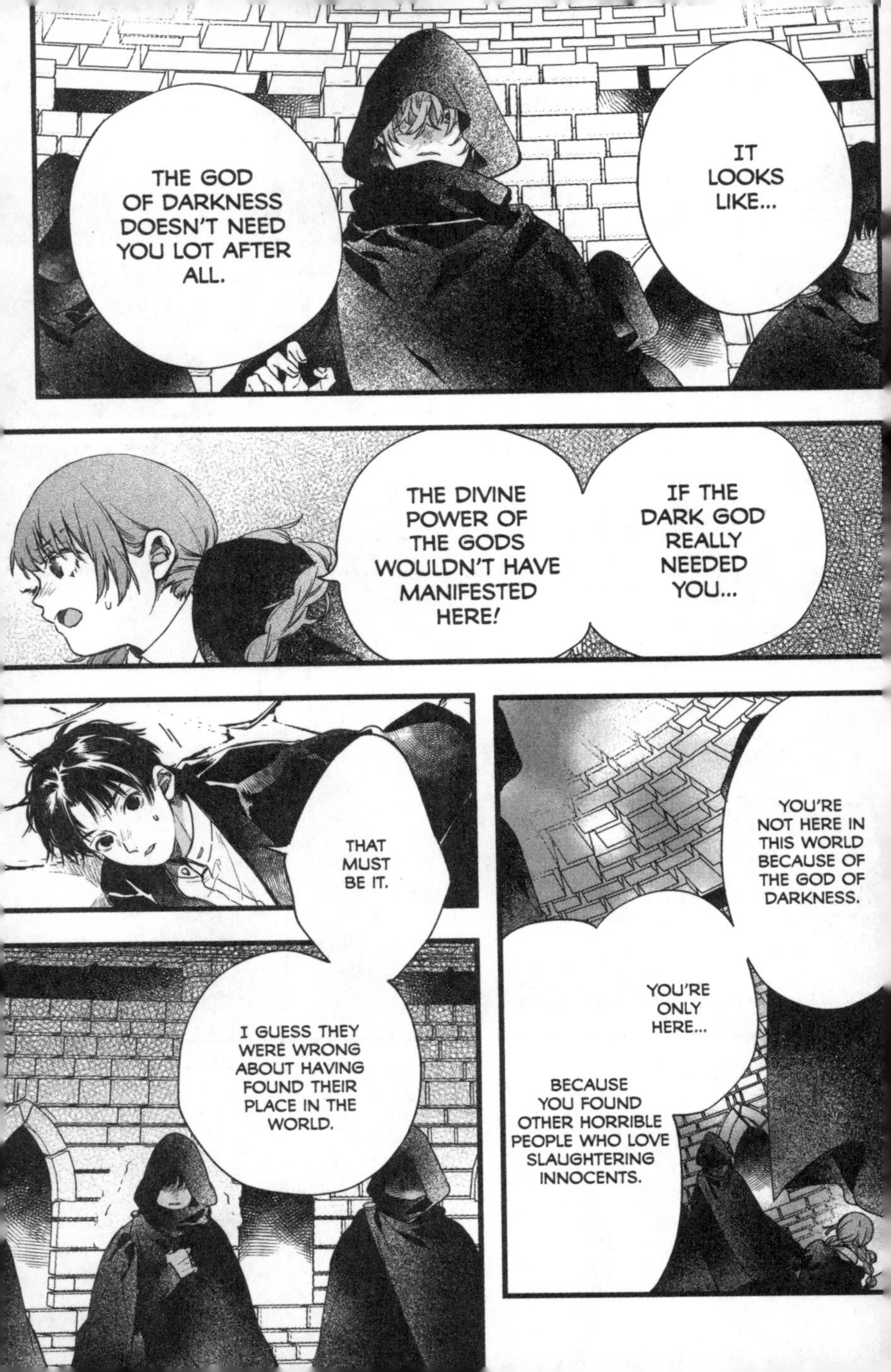
IT LOOKS LIKE...
THE GOD OF DARKNESS DOESN'T NEED YOU LOT AFTER ALL.
IF THE DARK GOD REALLY NEEDED YOU...
THE DIVINE POWER OF THE GODS WOULDN'T HAVE MANIFESTED HERE!
YOU'RE NOT HERE IN THIS WORLD BECAUSE OF THE GOD OF DARKNESS.
YOU'RE ONLY HERE...
BECAUSE YOU FOUND OTHER HORRIBLE PEOPLE WHO LOVE SLAUGHTERING INNOCENTS.
THAT MUST BE IT.
I GUESS THEY WERE WRONG ABOUT HAVING FOUND THEIR PLACE IN THE WORLD.

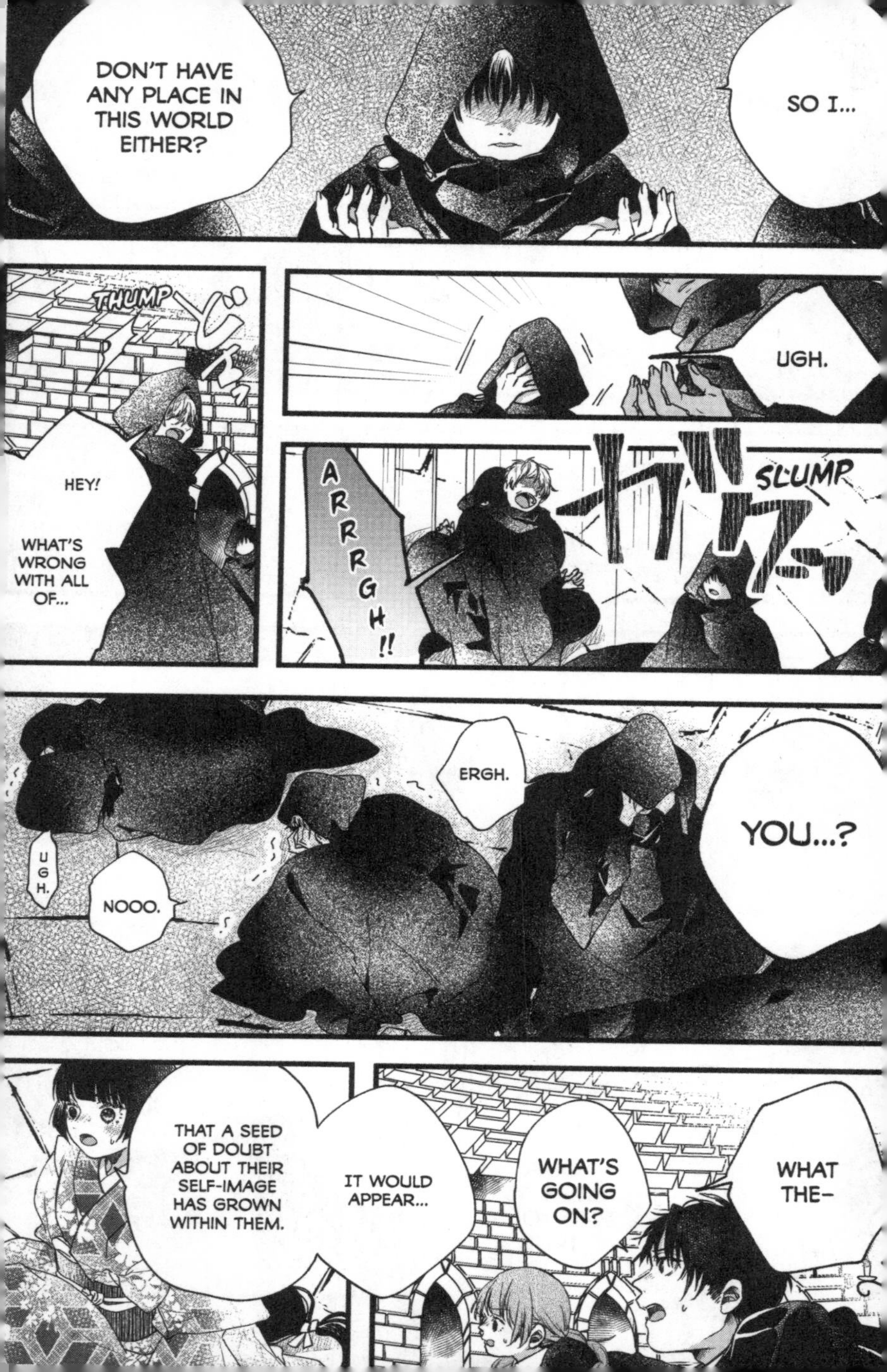
SO I...
DON'T HAVE ANY PLACE IN THIS WORLD EITHER?
UGH.
SLUMP
ARRRGH!!
THUMP
HEY!
WHAT'S WRONG WITH ALL OF...
YOU...?
ERGH.
NOOO.
UGH.
WHAT THE–
WHAT'S GOING ON?
IT WOULD APPEAR...
THAT A SEED OF DOUBT ABOUT THEIR SELF-IMAGE HAS GROWN WITHIN THEM.

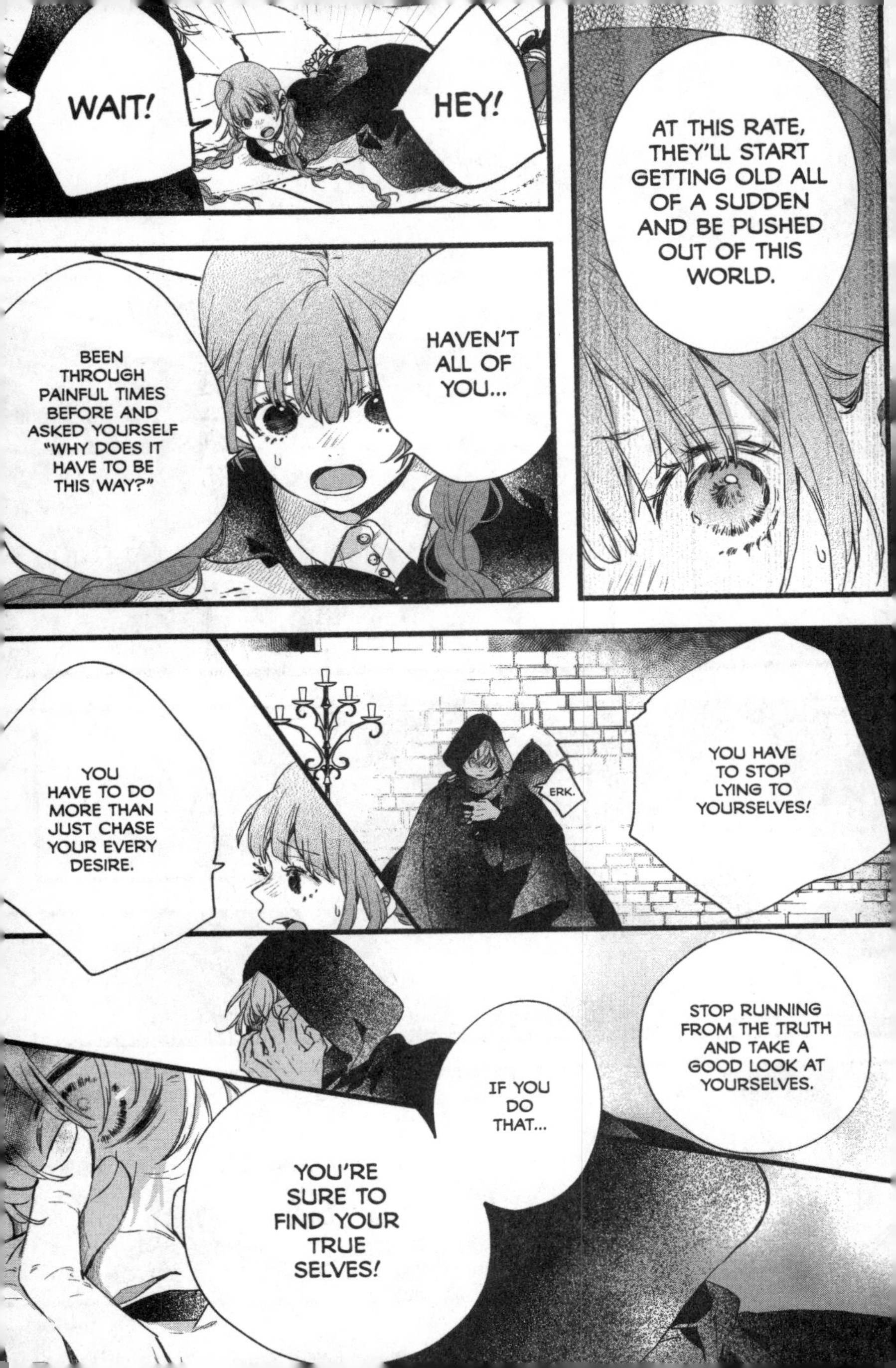
AT THIS RATE, THEY'LL START GETTING OLD ALL OF A SUDDEN AND BE PUSHED OUT OF THIS WORLD.
HEY!
WAIT!
HAVEN'T ALL OF YOU...
BEEN THROUGH PAINFUL TIMES BEFORE AND ASKED YOURSELF "WHY DOES IT HAVE TO BE THIS WAY?"
YOU HAVE TO STOP LYING TO YOURSELVES!
ERK.
YOU HAVE TO DO MORE THAN JUST CHASE YOUR EVERY DESIRE.
STOP RUNNING FROM THE TRUTH AND TAKE A GOOD LOOK AT YOURSELVES.
IF YOU DO THAT...
YOU'RE SURE TO FIND YOUR TRUE SELVES!

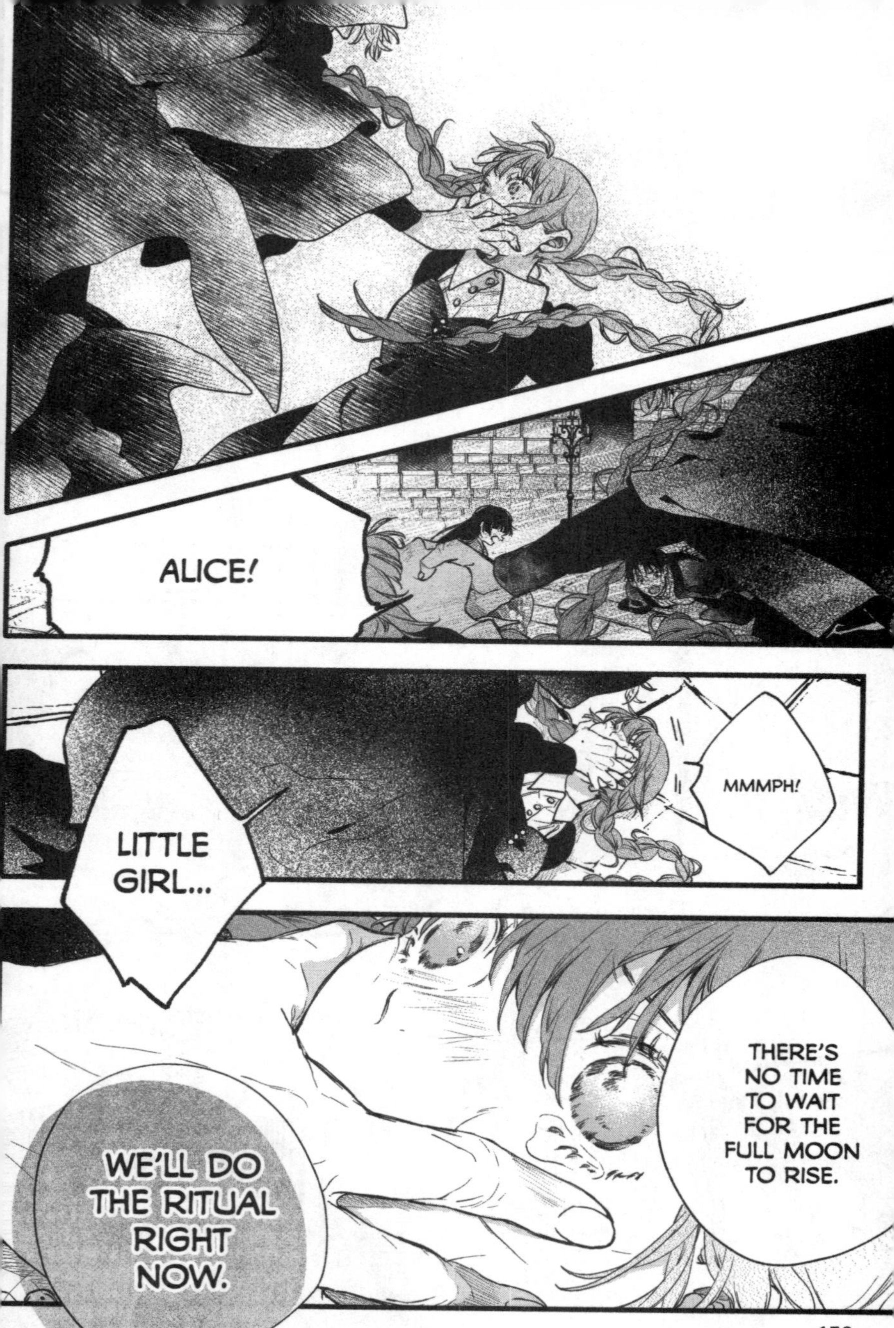
ALICE!
MMMPH!
LITTLE GIRL...
THERE'S NO TIME TO WAIT FOR THE FULL MOON TO RISE.
WE'LL DO THE RITUAL RIGHT NOW.

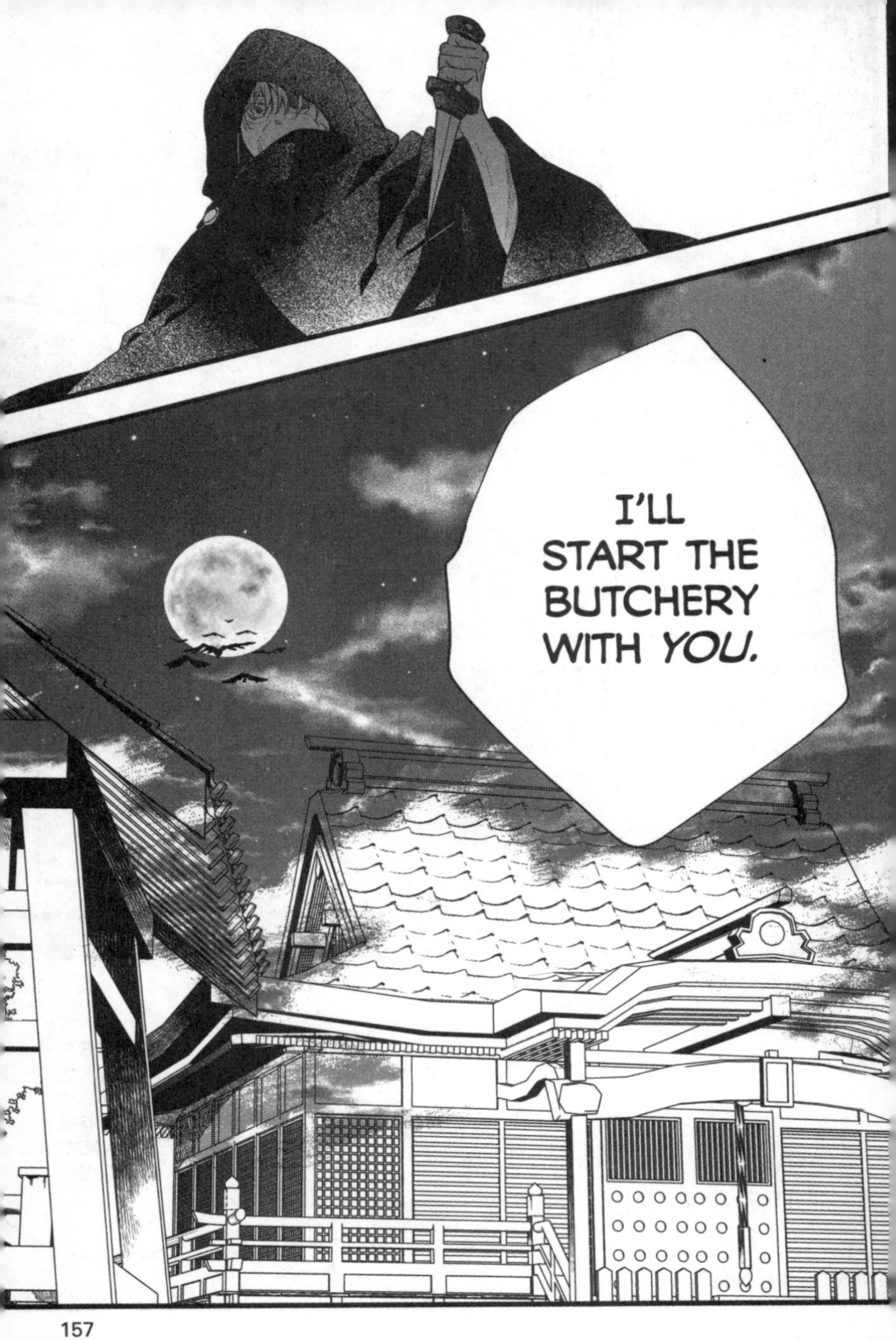
I'LL START THE BUTCHERY WITH *YOU.*

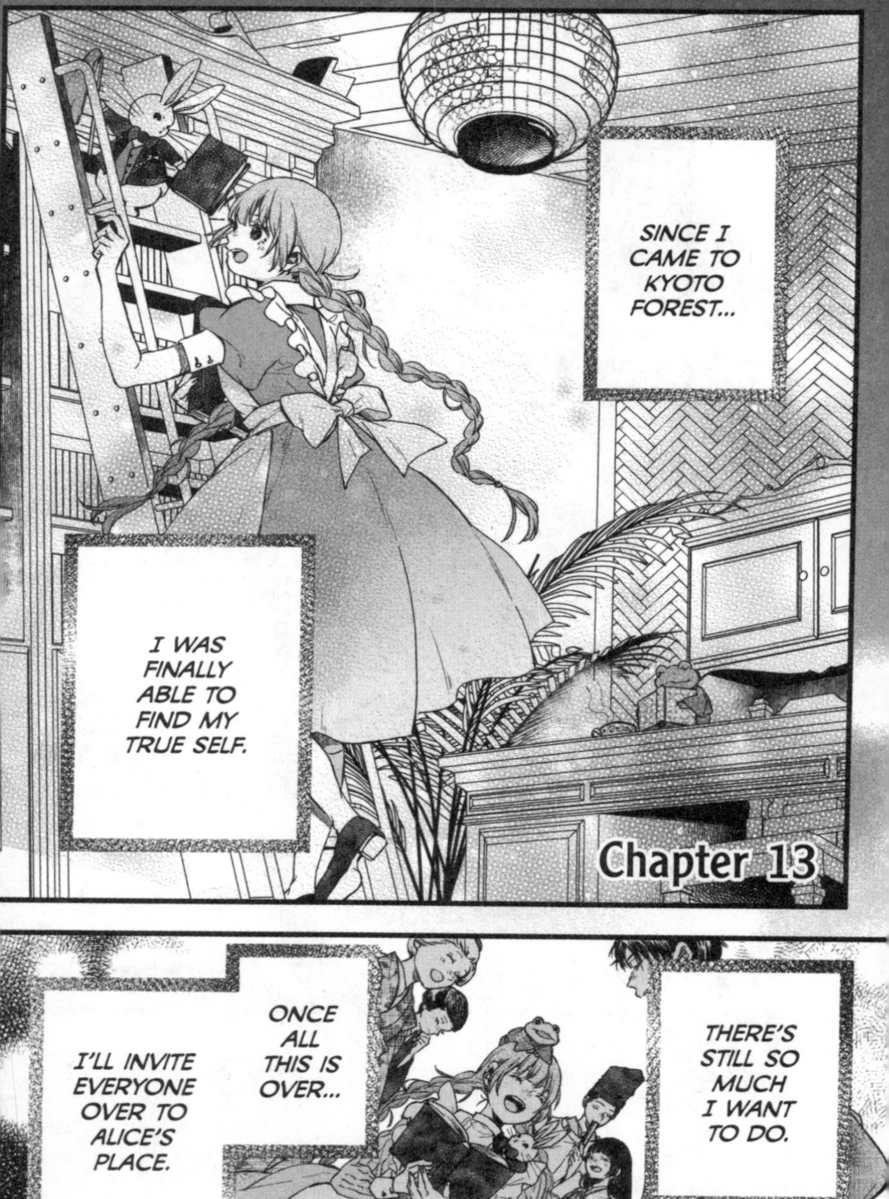
SINCE I CAME TO KYOTO FOREST...
I WAS FINALLY ABLE TO FIND MY TRUE SELF.
Chapter 13
THERE'S STILL SO MUCH I WANT TO DO.
ONCE ALL THIS IS OVER...
I'LL INVITE EVERYONE OVER TO ALICE'S PLACE.

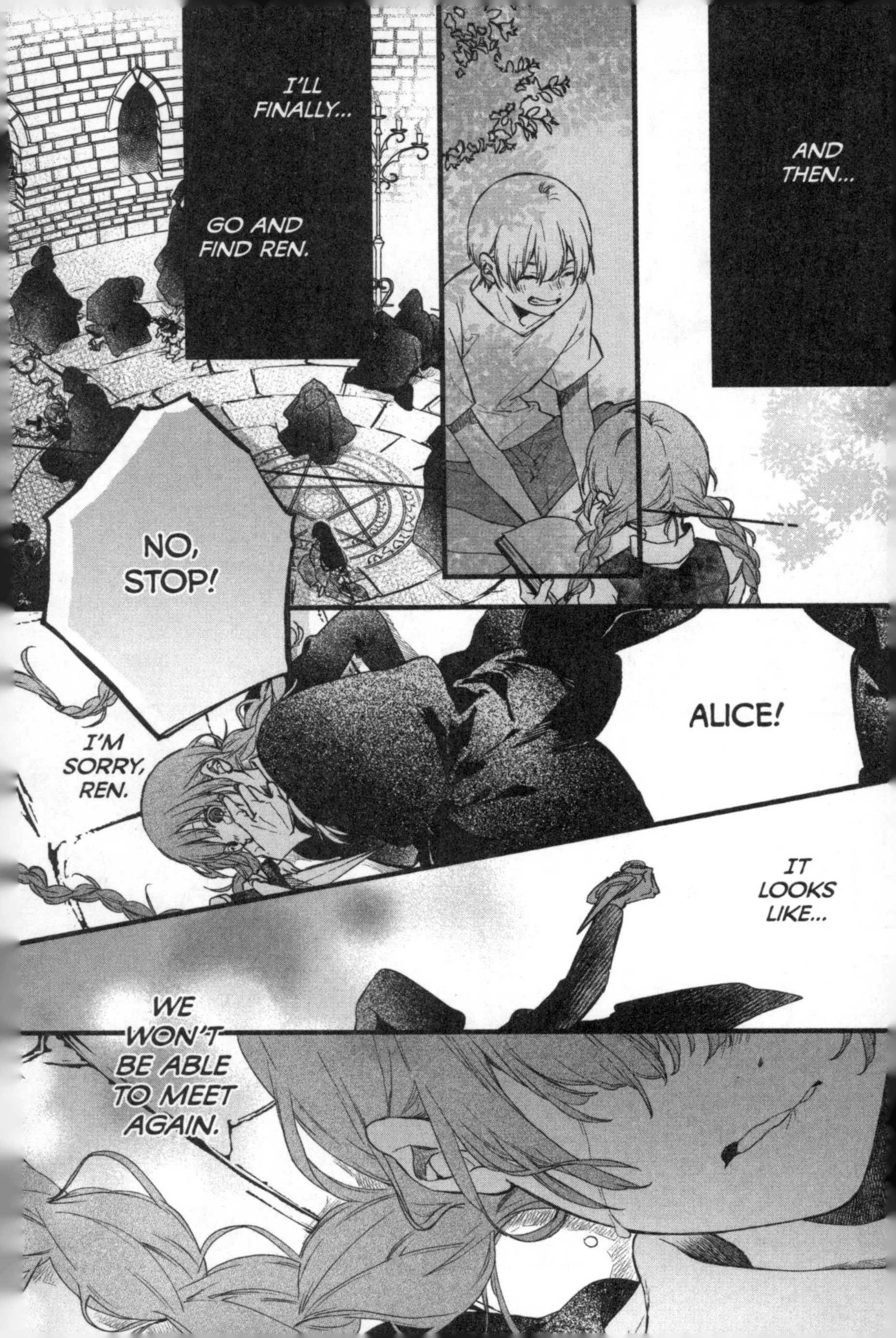
AND THEN...
I'LL FINALLY...
GO AND FIND REN.
NO, STOP!
ALICE!
I'M SORRY, REN.
IT LOOKS LIKE...
WE WON'T BE ABLE TO MEET AGAIN.

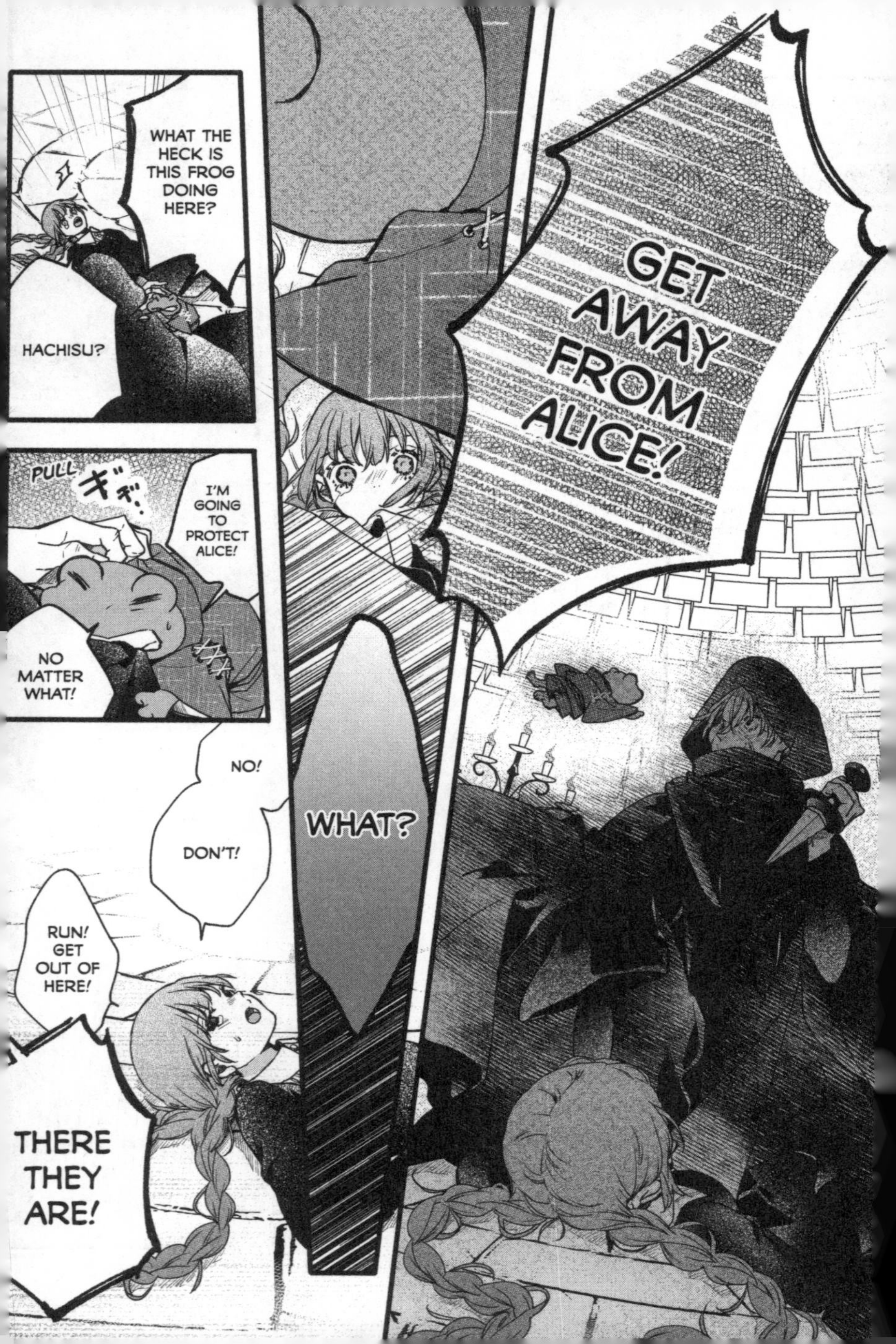
GET AWAY FROM ALICE!
WHAT?
WHAT THE HECK IS THIS FROG DOING HERE?
HACHISU?
I'M GOING TO PROTECT ALICE!
PULL
ギギ…
NO MATTER WHAT!
NO! DON'T!
RUN! GET OUT OF HERE!
THERE THEY ARE!

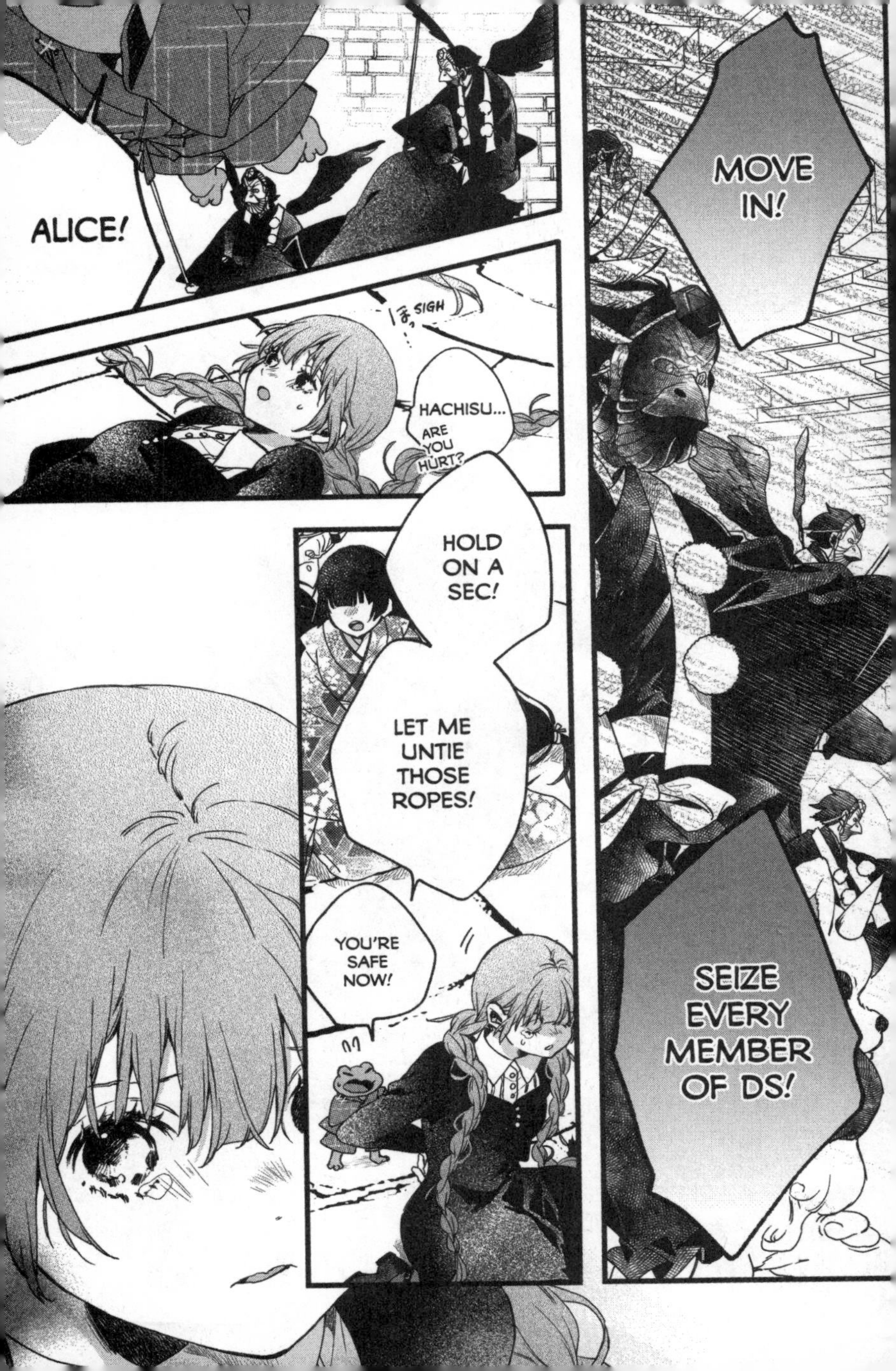

MOVE IN!
SEIZE EVERY MEMBER OF DS!
ALICE!
ほっ SIGH
HACHISU...
ARE YOU HURT?
HOLD ON A SEC!
LET ME UNTIE THOSE ROPES!
YOU'RE SAFE NOW!

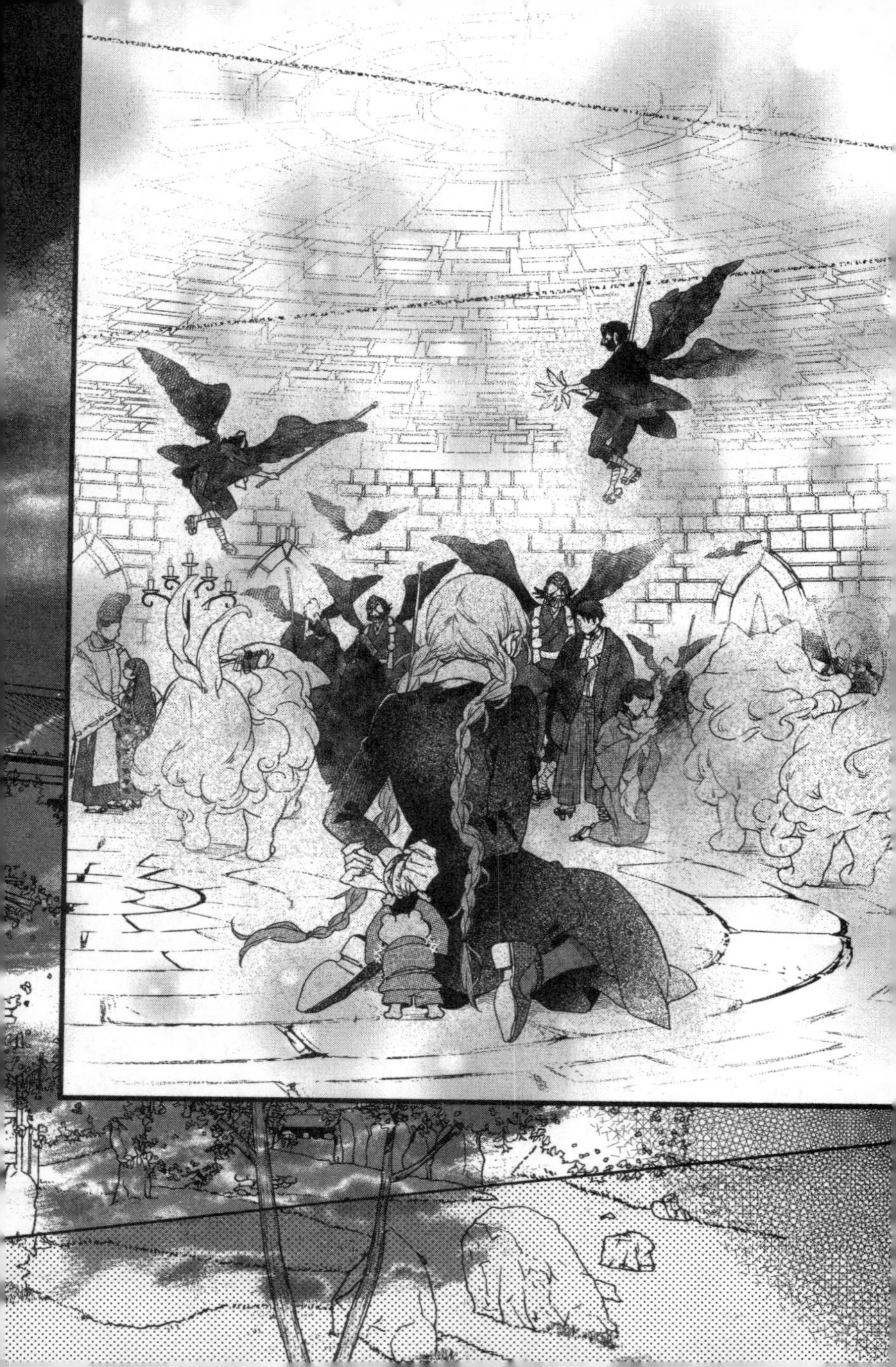

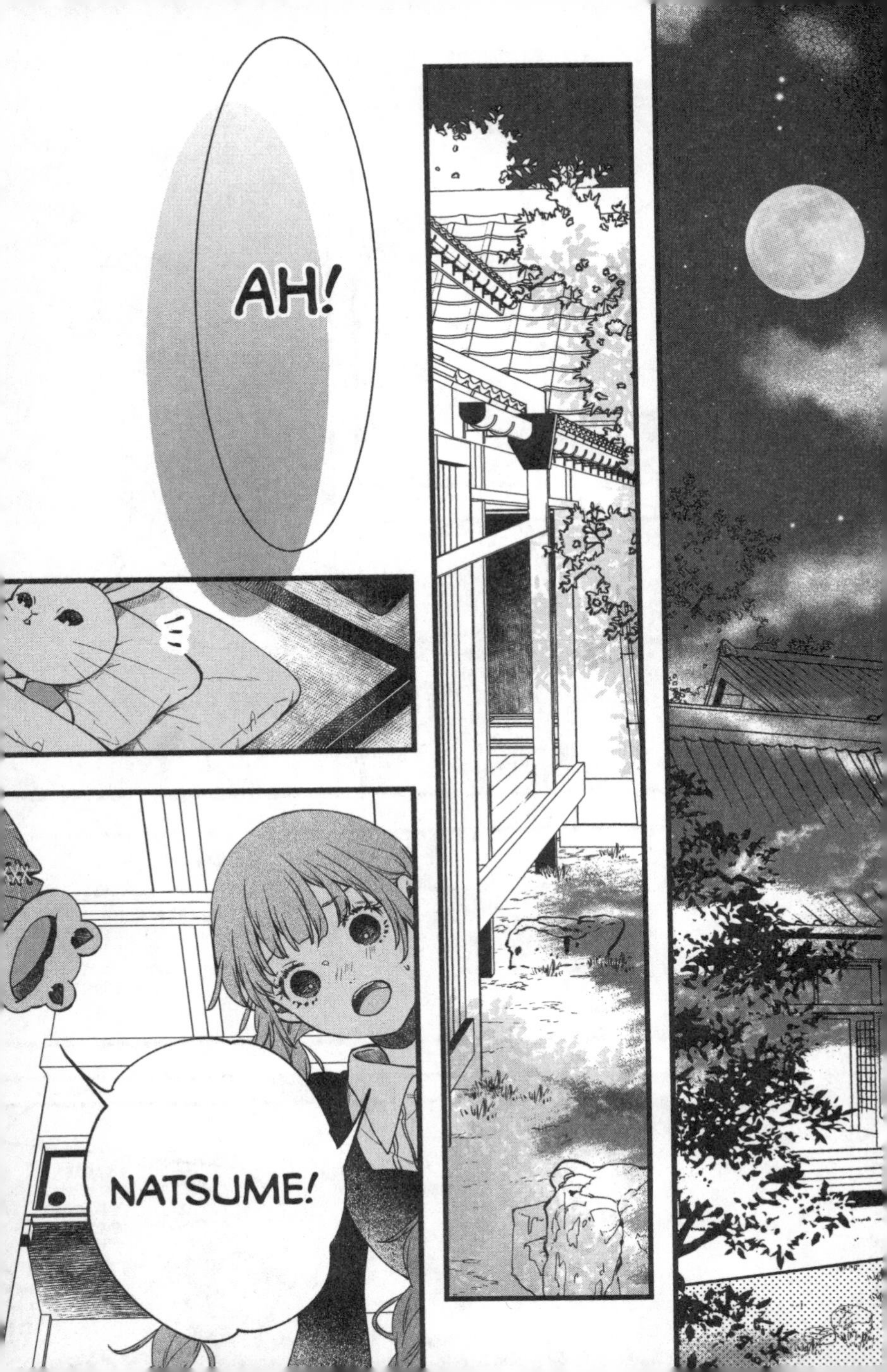
AH!
NATSUME!

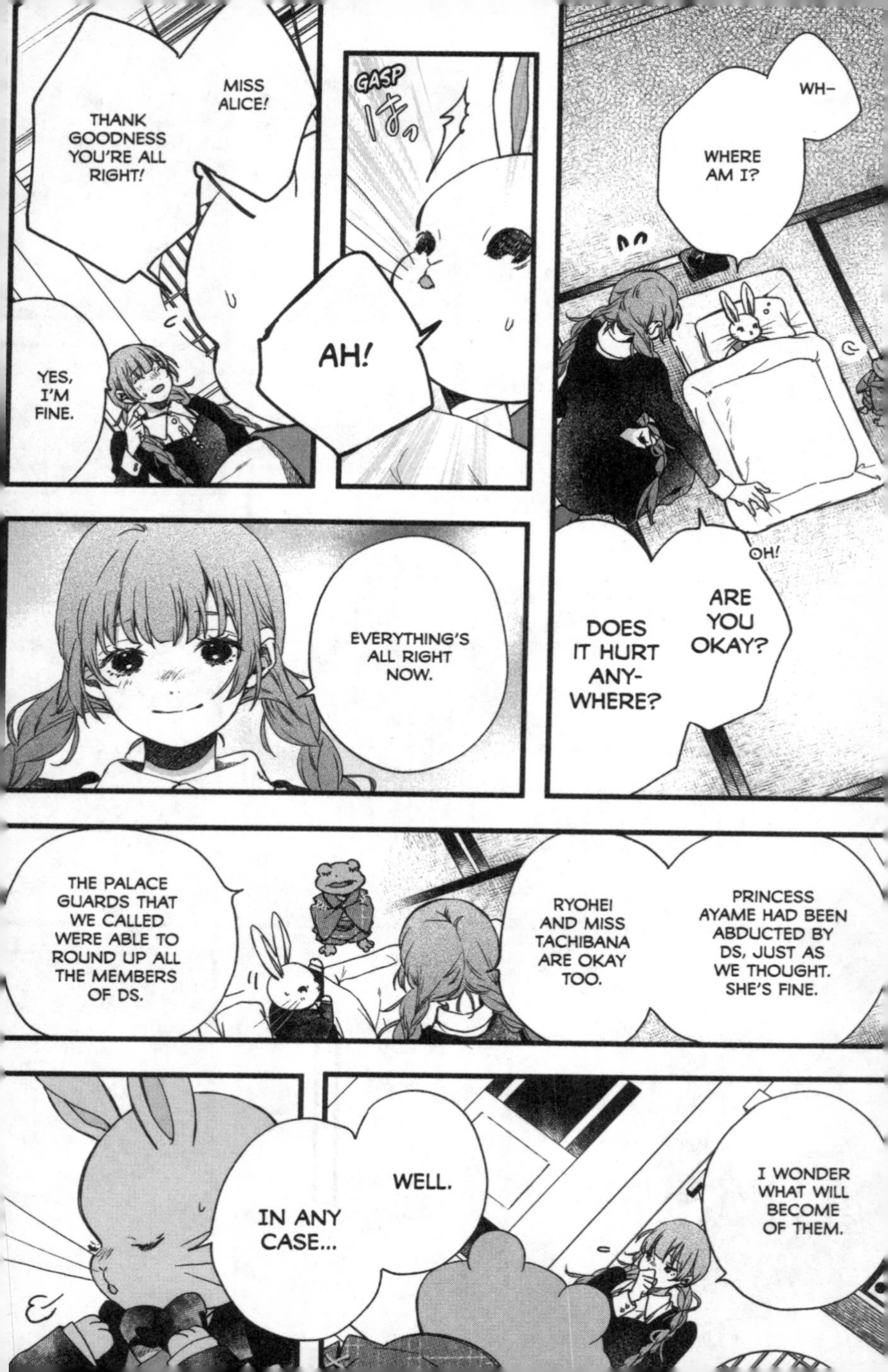
WH–
WHERE AM I?
GASP
はっ
AH!
MISS ALICE!
THANK GOODNESS YOU'RE ALL RIGHT!
YES, I'M FINE.
OH!
ARE YOU OKAY?
DOES IT HURT ANY-WHERE?
EVERYTHING'S ALL RIGHT NOW.
PRINCESS AYAME HAD BEEN ABDUCTED BY DS, JUST AS WE THOUGHT. SHE'S FINE.
RYOHEI AND MISS TACHIBANA ARE OKAY TOO.
THE PALACE GUARDS THAT WE CALLED WERE ABLE TO ROUND UP ALL THE MEMBERS OF DS.
I WONDER WHAT WILL BECOME OF THEM.
WELL.
IN ANY CASE...

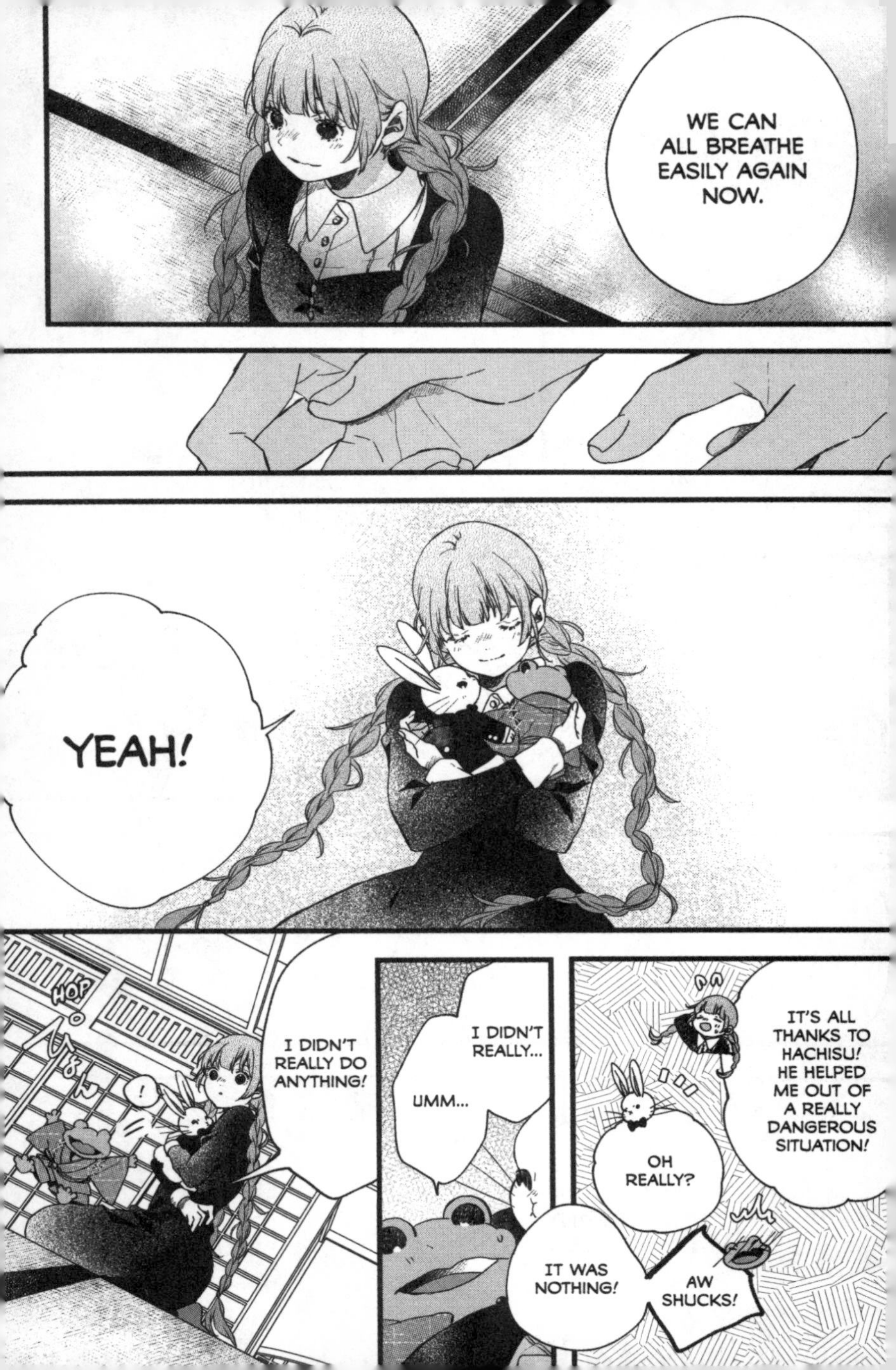
WE CAN ALL BREATHE EASILY AGAIN NOW.
YEAH!
IT'S ALL THANKS TO HACHISU! HE HELPED ME OUT OF A REALLY DANGEROUS SITUATION!
OH REALLY?
AW SHUCKS!
I DIDN'T REALLY...
UMM...
IT WAS NOTHING!
I DIDN'T REALLY DO ANYTHING!
HOP
!

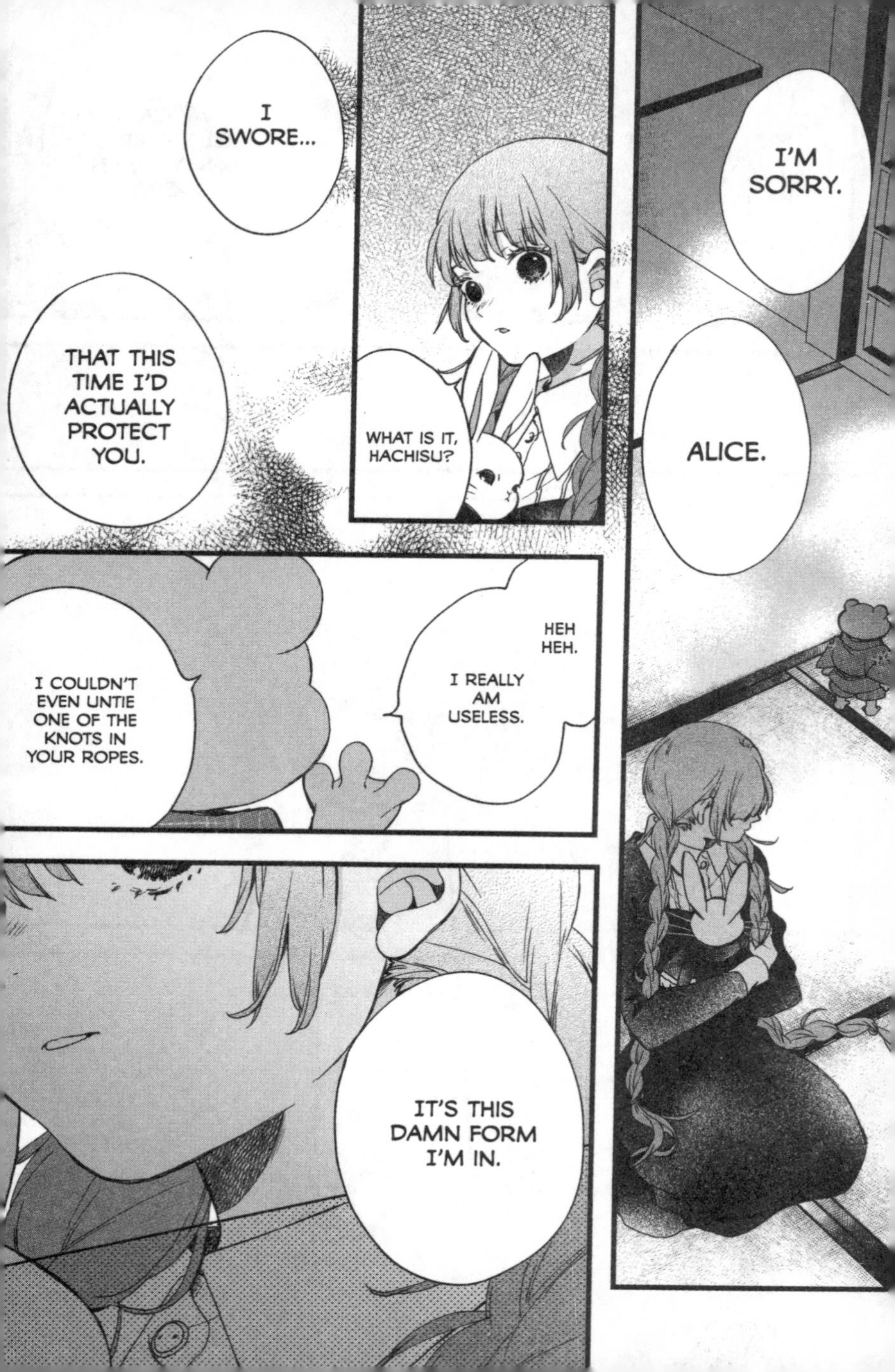
I'M SORRY.
ALICE.
WHAT IS IT, HACHISU?
I SWORE...
THAT THIS TIME I'D ACTUALLY PROTECT YOU.
HEH HEH.
I REALLY AM USELESS.
I COULDN'T EVEN UNTIE ONE OF THE KNOTS IN YOUR ROPES.
IT'S THIS DAMN FORM I'M IN.

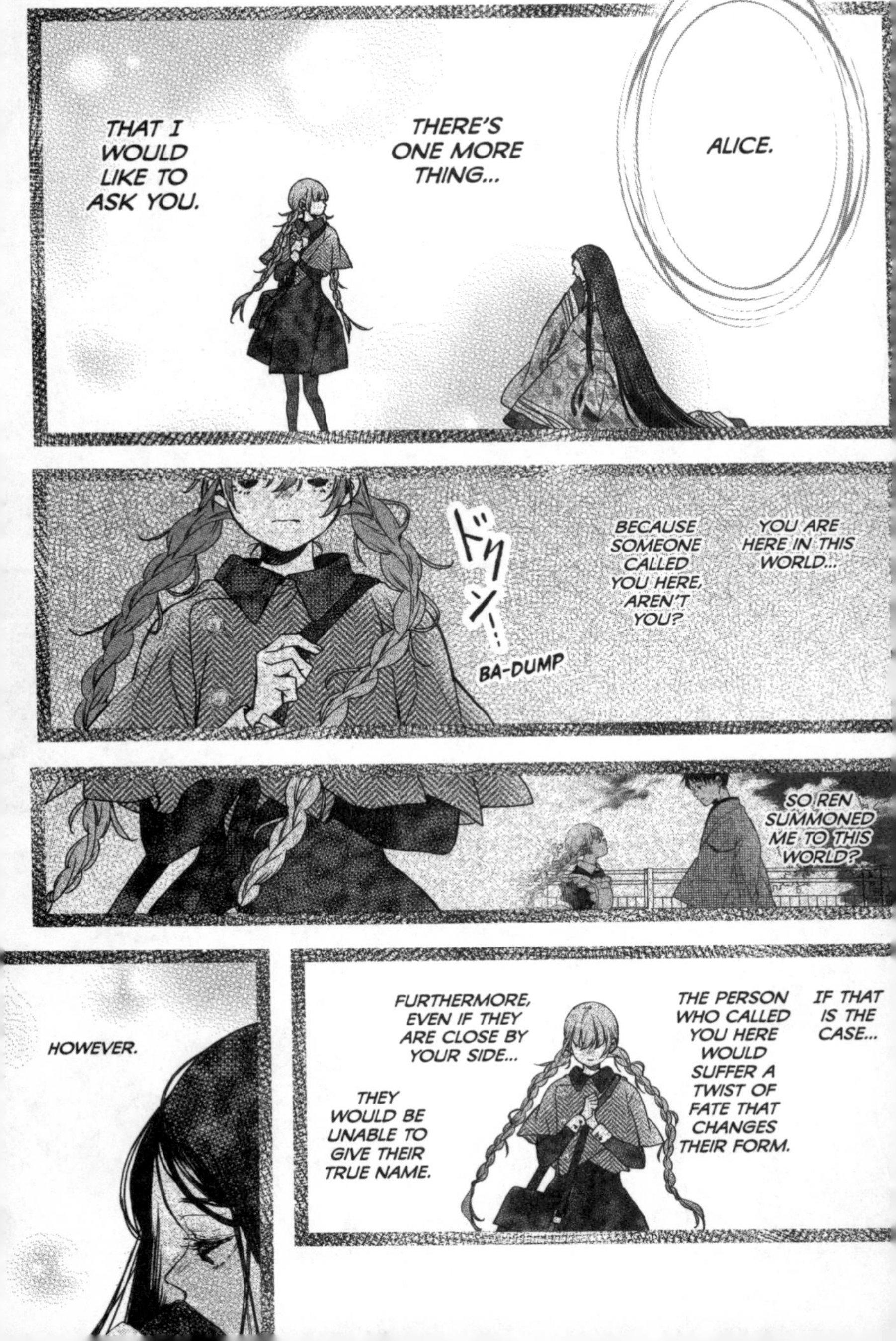
ALICE.
THERE'S ONE MORE THING...
THAT I WOULD LIKE TO ASK YOU.
YOU ARE HERE IN THIS WORLD...
BECAUSE SOMEONE CALLED YOU HERE, AREN'T YOU?
BA-DUMP
SO REN SUMMONED ME TO THIS WORLD?
IF THAT IS THE CASE...
THE PERSON WHO CALLED YOU HERE WOULD SUFFER A TWIST OF FATE THAT CHANGES THEIR FORM.
FURTHERMORE, EVEN IF THEY ARE CLOSE BY YOUR SIDE...
THEY WOULD BE UNABLE TO GIVE THEIR TRUE NAME.
HOWEVER.

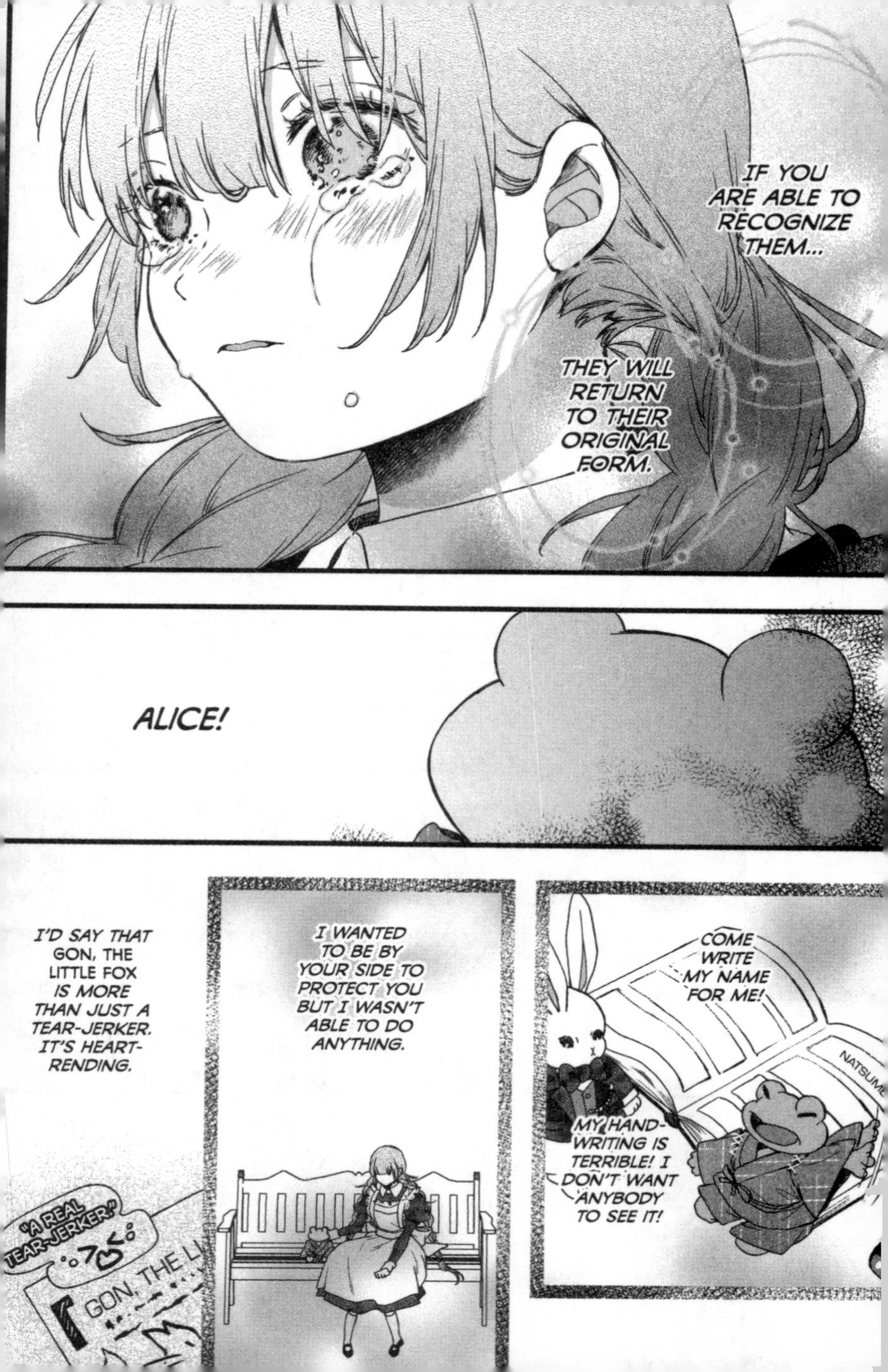
IF YOU ARE ABLE TO RECOGNIZE THEM...
THEY WILL RETURN TO THEIR ORIGINAL FORM.
ALICE!
COME WRITE MY NAME FOR ME!
NATSUME
MY HAND-WRITING IS TERRIBLE! I DON'T WANT ANYBODY TO SEE IT!
I WANTED TO BE BY YOUR SIDE TO PROTECT YOU BUT I WASN'T ABLE TO DO ANYTHING.
I'D SAY THAT GON, THE LITTLE FOX IS MORE THAN JUST A TEAR-JERKER. IT'S HEART-RENDING.
"A REAL TEAR-JERKER!"

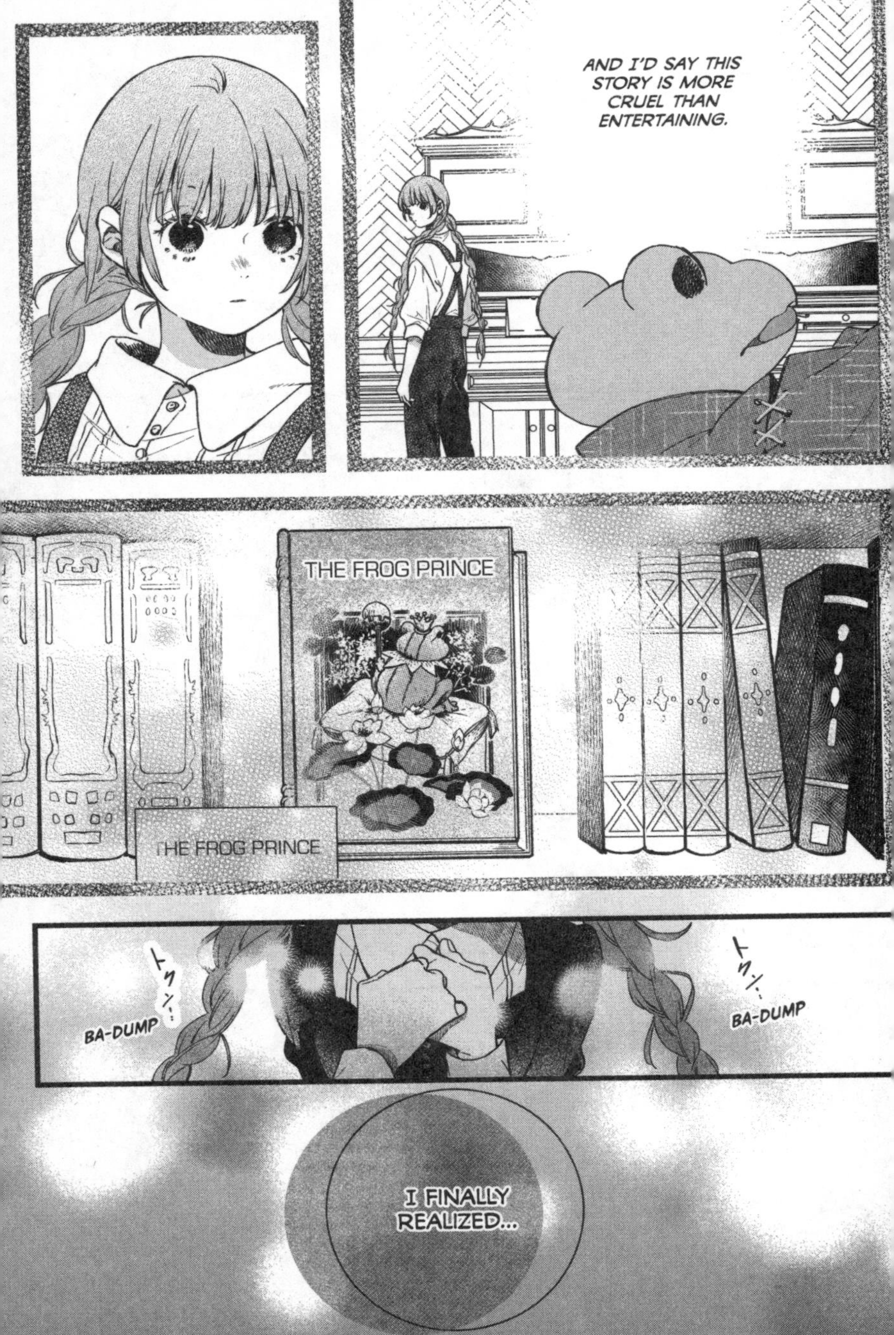
AND I'D SAY THIS STORY IS MORE CRUEL THAN ENTERTAINING.
THE FROG PRINCE
THE FROG PRINCE
BA-DUMP
BA-DUMP
I FINALLY REALIZED...

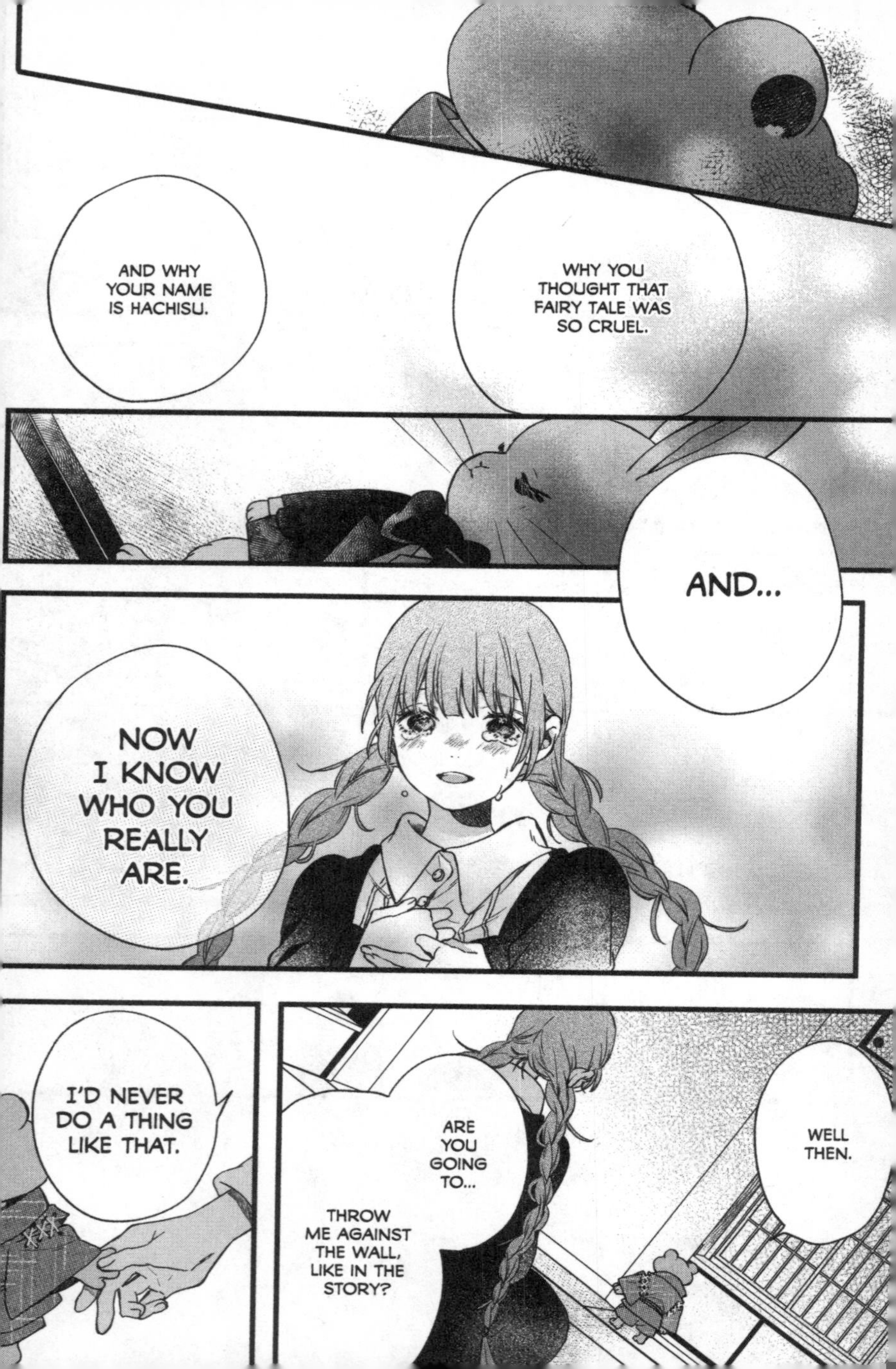
WHY YOU THOUGHT THAT FAIRY TALE WAS SO CRUEL.
AND WHY YOUR NAME IS HACHISU.
AND...
NOW I KNOW WHO YOU REALLY ARE.
WELL THEN.
ARE YOU GOING TO...
THROW ME AGAINST THE WALL, LIKE IN THE STORY?
I'D NEVER DO A THING LIKE THAT.

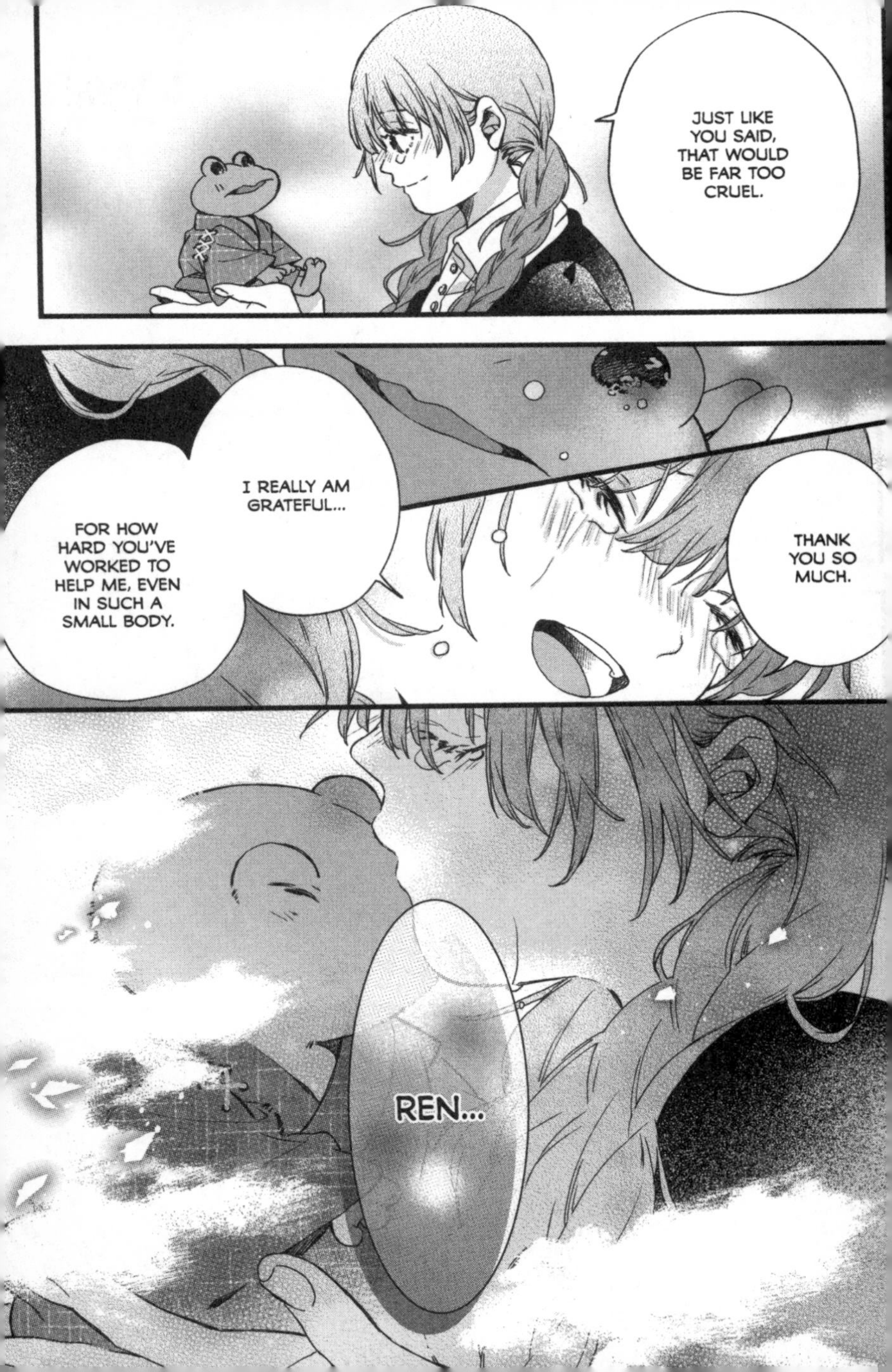
JUST LIKE YOU SAID, THAT WOULD BE FAR TOO CRUEL.
I REALLY AM GRATEFUL...
FOR HOW HARD YOU'VE WORKED TO HELP ME, EVEN IN SUCH A SMALL BODY.
THANK YOU SO MUCH.
REN...

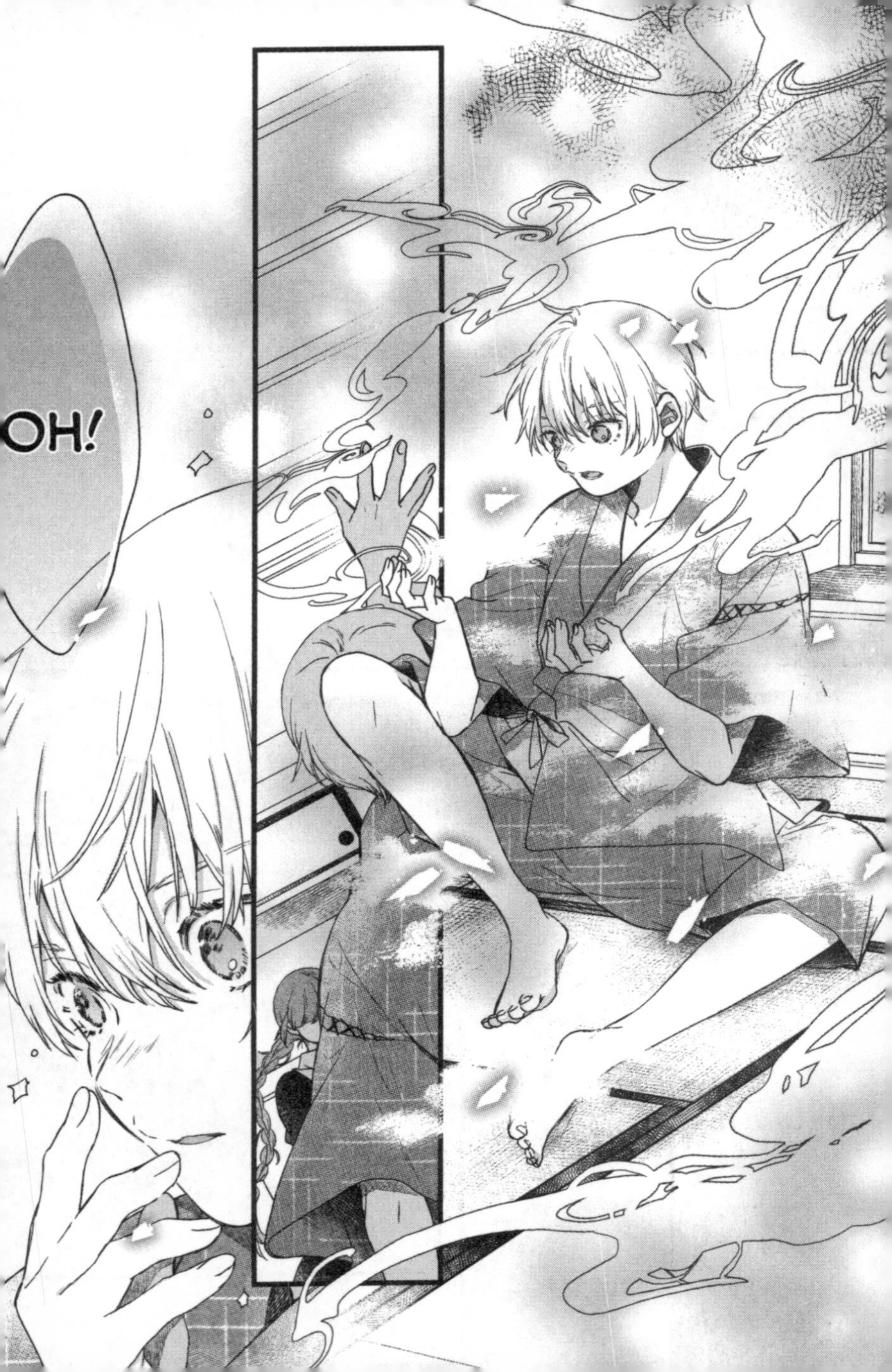
OH!

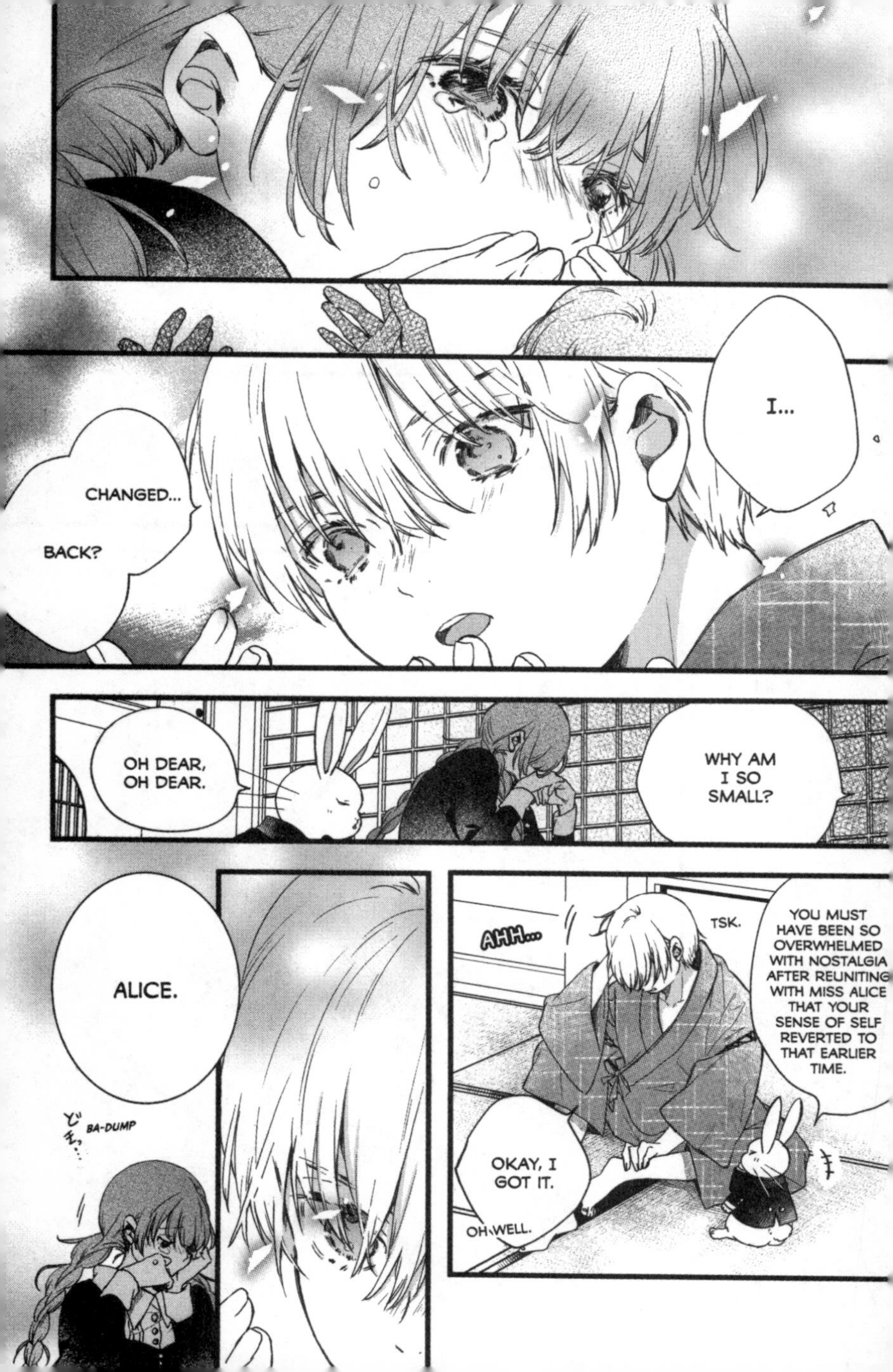
I...
CHANGED... BACK?
WHY AM I SO SMALL?
OH DEAR, OH DEAR.
YOU MUST HAVE BEEN SO OVERWHELMED WITH NOSTALGIA AFTER REUNITING WITH MISS ALICE THAT YOUR SENSE OF SELF REVERTED TO THAT EARLIER TIME.
TSK.
AHH...
OKAY, I GOT IT.
OH, WELL.
ALICE.
BA-DUMP

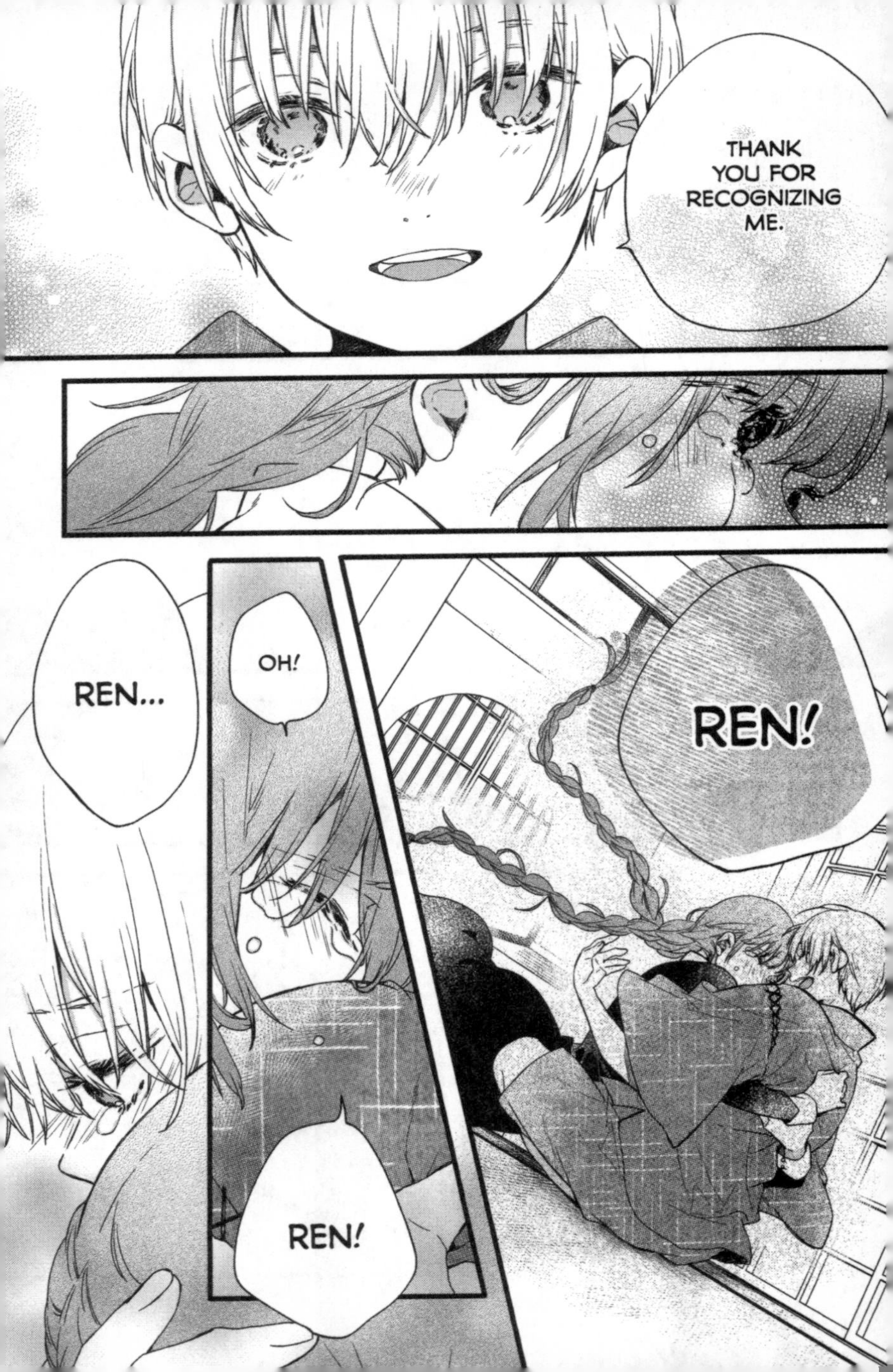
THANK YOU FOR RECOGNIZING ME.
REN!
OH!
REN!
REN...

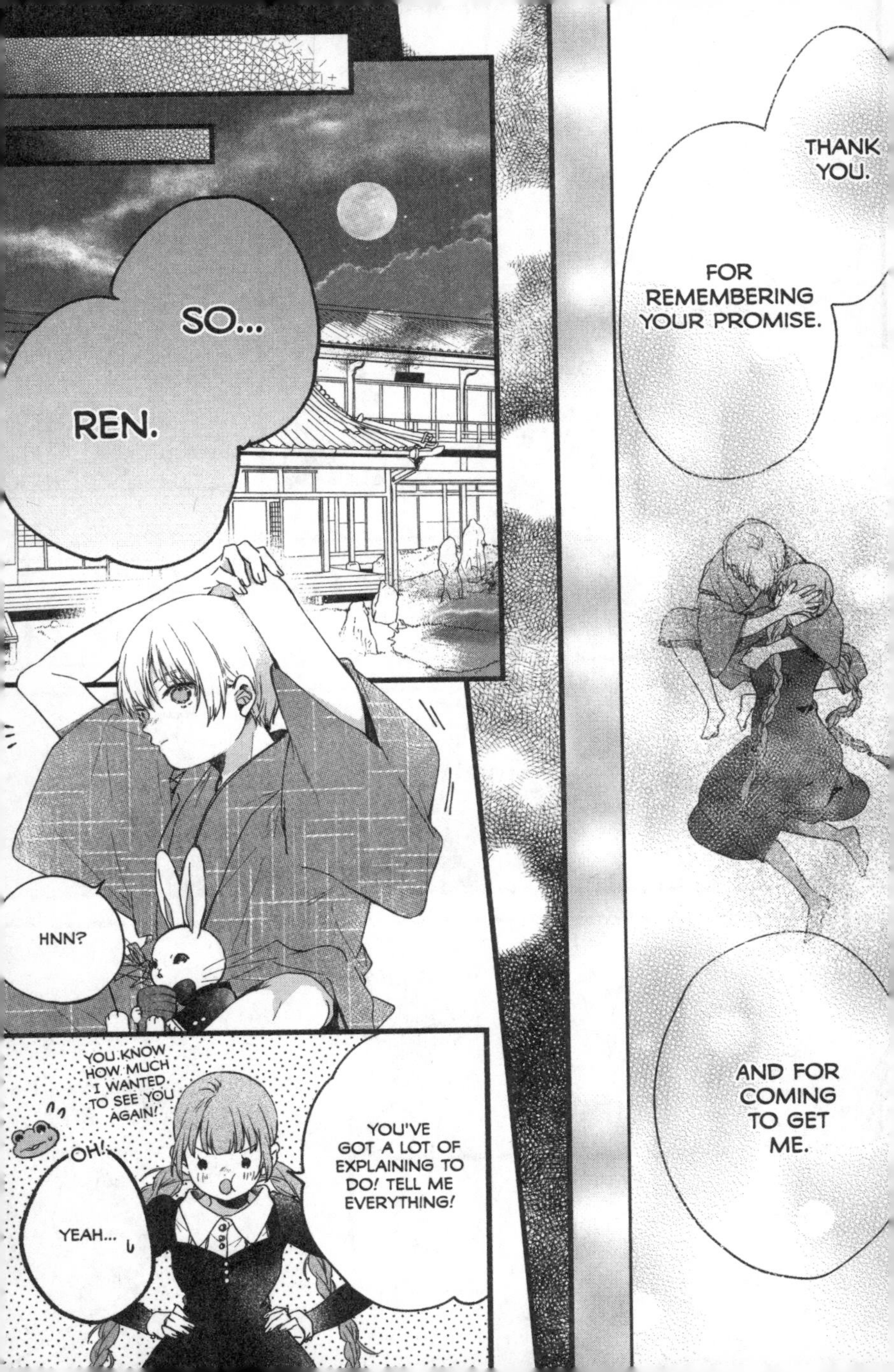
THANK YOU.
FOR REMEMBERING YOUR PROMISE.
AND FOR COMING TO GET ME.
SO...
REN.
HNN?
YOU'VE GOT A LOT OF EXPLAINING TO DO! TELL ME EVERYTHING!
YOU KNOW HOW MUCH I WANTED TO SEE YOU AGAIN!
OH!
YEAH...

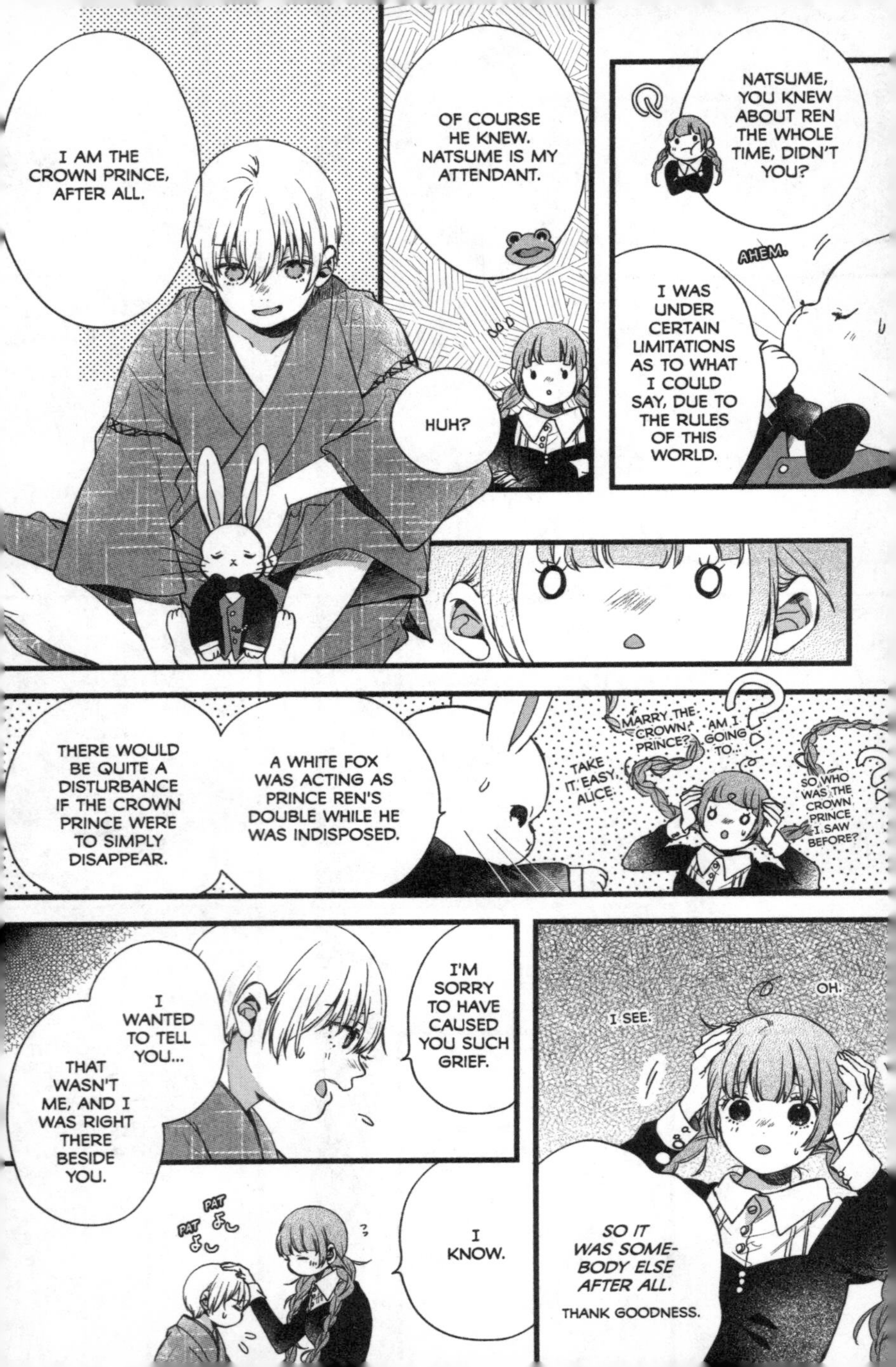
NATSUME, YOU KNEW ABOUT REN THE WHOLE TIME, DIDN'T YOU?
AHEM.
I WAS UNDER CERTAIN LIMITATIONS AS TO WHAT I COULD SAY, DUE TO THE RULES OF THIS WORLD.
OF COURSE HE KNEW. NATSUME IS MY ATTENDANT.
HUH?
I AM THE CROWN PRINCE, AFTER ALL.
SO WHO WAS THE CROWN PRINCE I SAW BEFORE?
AM I GOING TO...
MARRY THE CROWN PRINCE?
TAKE IT EASY, ALICE.
A WHITE FOX WAS ACTING AS PRINCE REN'S DOUBLE WHILE HE WAS INDISPOSED.
THERE WOULD BE QUITE A DISTURBANCE IF THE CROWN PRINCE WERE TO SIMPLY DISAPPEAR.
OH.
I SEE.
SO IT WAS SOME-BODY ELSE AFTER ALL.
THANK GOODNESS.
I'M SORRY TO HAVE CAUSED YOU SUCH GRIEF.
I WANTED TO TELL YOU...
THAT WASN'T ME, AND I WAS RIGHT THERE BESIDE YOU.
I KNOW.
PAT
PAT

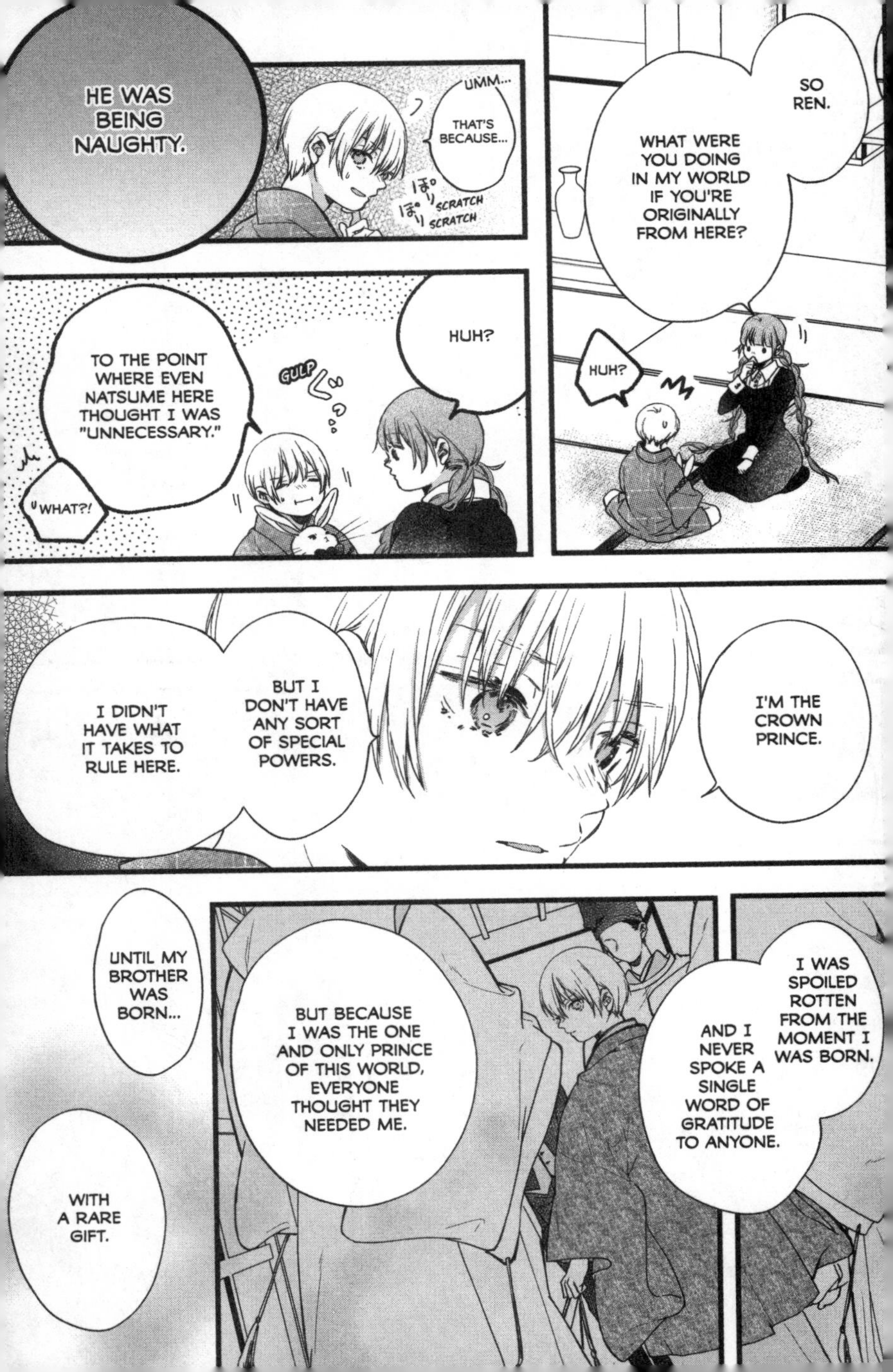

SO REN.
WHAT WERE YOU DOING IN MY WORLD IF YOU'RE ORIGINALLY FROM HERE?
HUH?
UMM... THAT'S BECAUSE...
SCRATCH SCRATCH
HE WAS BEING NAUGHTY.
HUH?
GULP
TO THE POINT WHERE EVEN NATSUME HERE THOUGHT I WAS "UNNECESSARY."
WHAT?!
I'M THE CROWN PRINCE.
BUT I DON'T HAVE ANY SORT OF SPECIAL POWERS.
I DIDN'T HAVE WHAT IT TAKES TO RULE HERE.
I WAS SPOILED ROTTEN FROM THE MOMENT I WAS BORN.
AND I NEVER SPOKE A SINGLE WORD OF GRATITUDE TO ANYONE.
BUT BECAUSE I WAS THE ONE AND ONLY PRINCE OF THIS WORLD, EVERYONE THOUGHT THEY NEEDED ME.
UNTIL MY BROTHER WAS BORN...
WITH A RARE GIFT.

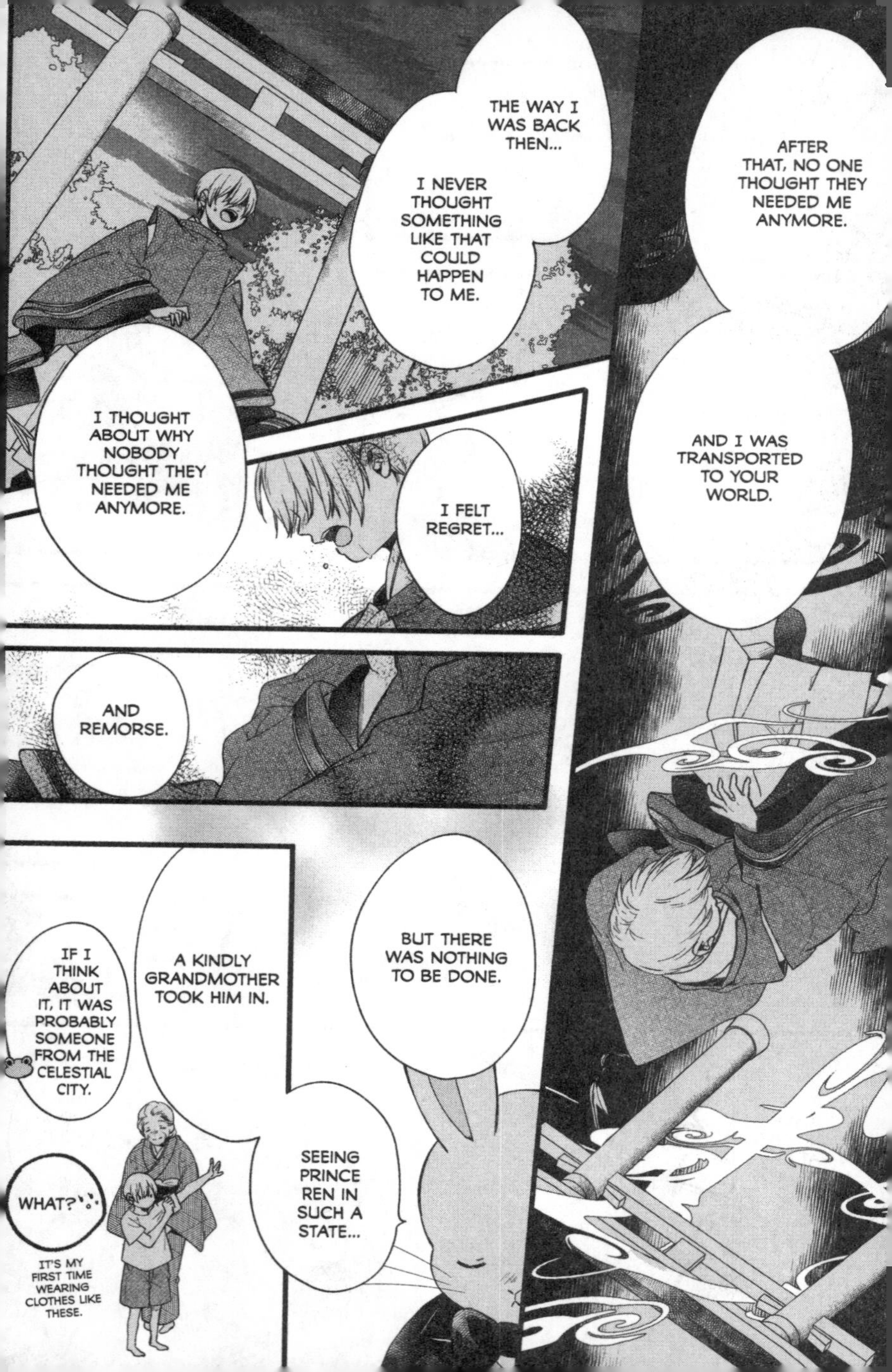
AFTER THAT, NO ONE THOUGHT THEY NEEDED ME ANYMORE.
AND I WAS TRANSPORTED TO YOUR WORLD.
THE WAY I WAS BACK THEN...
I NEVER THOUGHT SOMETHING LIKE THAT COULD HAPPEN TO ME.
I FELT REGRET...
I THOUGHT ABOUT WHY NOBODY THOUGHT THEY NEEDED ME ANYMORE.
AND REMORSE.
BUT THERE WAS NOTHING TO BE DONE.
SEEING PRINCE REN IN SUCH A STATE...
A KINDLY GRANDMOTHER TOOK HIM IN.
IF I THINK ABOUT IT, IT WAS PROBABLY SOMEONE FROM THE CELESTIAL CITY.
WHAT?
IT'S MY FIRST TIME WEARING CLOTHES LIKE THESE.

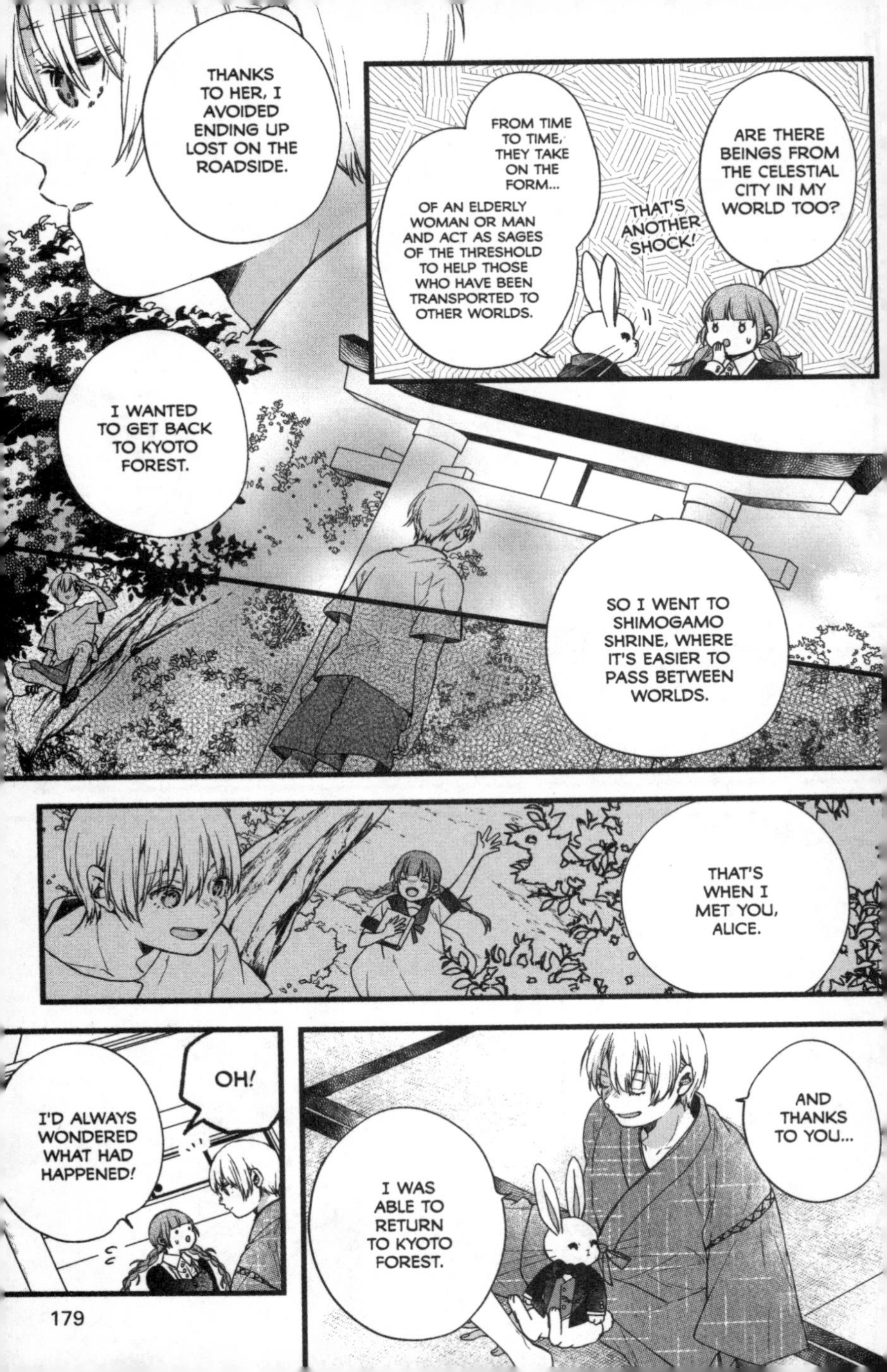
ARE THERE BEINGS FROM THE CELESTIAL CITY IN MY WORLD TOO?
THAT'S ANOTHER SHOCK!
FROM TIME TO TIME, THEY TAKE ON THE FORM...
OF AN ELDERLY WOMAN OR MAN AND ACT AS SAGES OF THE THRESHOLD TO HELP THOSE WHO HAVE BEEN TRANSPORTED TO OTHER WORLDS.
THANKS TO HER, I AVOIDED ENDING UP LOST ON THE ROADSIDE.
I WANTED TO GET BACK TO KYOTO FOREST.
SO I WENT TO SHIMOGAMO SHRINE, WHERE IT'S EASIER TO PASS BETWEEN WORLDS.
THAT'S WHEN I MET YOU, ALICE.
AND THANKS TO YOU...
I WAS ABLE TO RETURN TO KYOTO FOREST.
OH!
I'D ALWAYS WONDERED WHAT HAD HAPPENED!

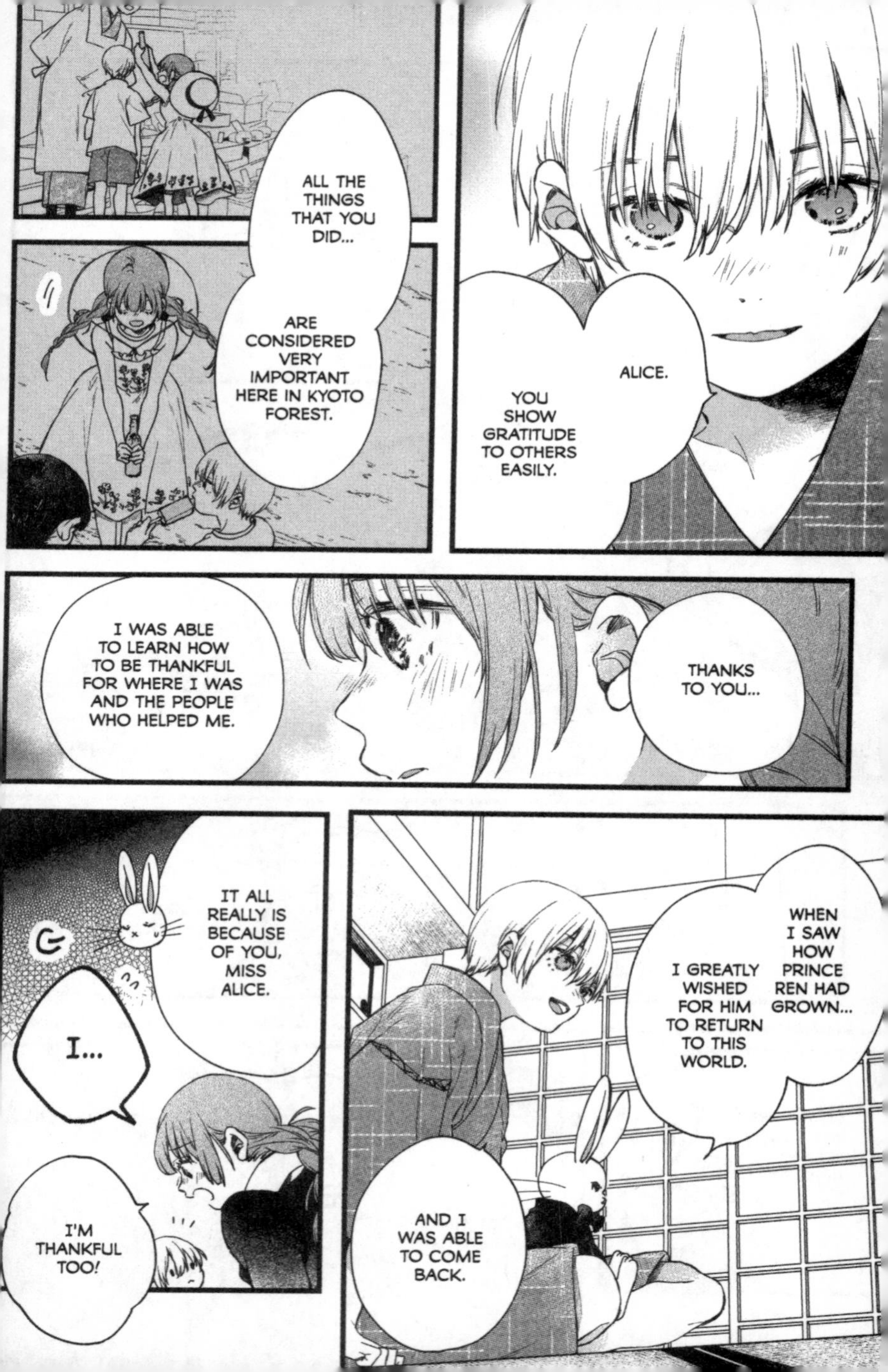

ALICE.
YOU SHOW GRATITUDE TO OTHERS EASILY.
ALL THE THINGS THAT YOU DID...
ARE CONSIDERED VERY IMPORTANT HERE IN KYOTO FOREST.
THANKS TO YOU...
I WAS ABLE TO LEARN HOW TO BE THANKFUL FOR WHERE I WAS AND THE PEOPLE WHO HELPED ME.
WHEN I SAW HOW PRINCE REN HAD GROWN...
I GREATLY WISHED FOR HIM TO RETURN TO THIS WORLD.
AND I WAS ABLE TO COME BACK.
IT ALL REALLY IS BECAUSE OF YOU, MISS ALICE.
I...
I'M THANKFUL TOO!

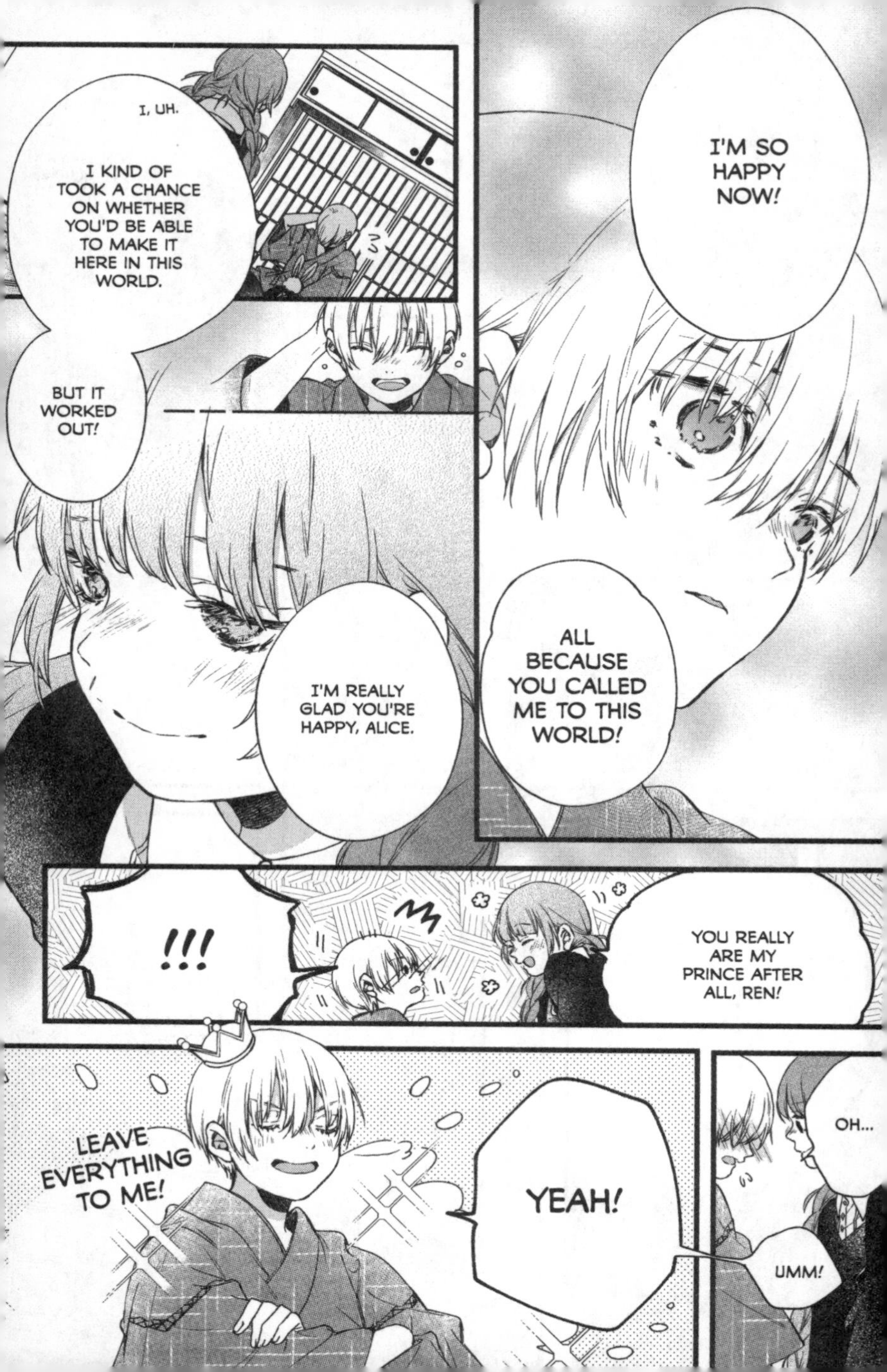
I'M SO HAPPY NOW!
ALL BECAUSE YOU CALLED ME TO THIS WORLD!
I, UH.
I KIND OF TOOK A CHANCE ON WHETHER YOU'D BE ABLE TO MAKE IT HERE IN THIS WORLD.
BUT IT WORKED OUT!
I'M REALLY GLAD YOU'RE HAPPY, ALICE.
YOU REALLY ARE MY PRINCE AFTER ALL, REN!
!!!
OH...
UMM!
YEAH!
LEAVE EVERYTHING TO ME!

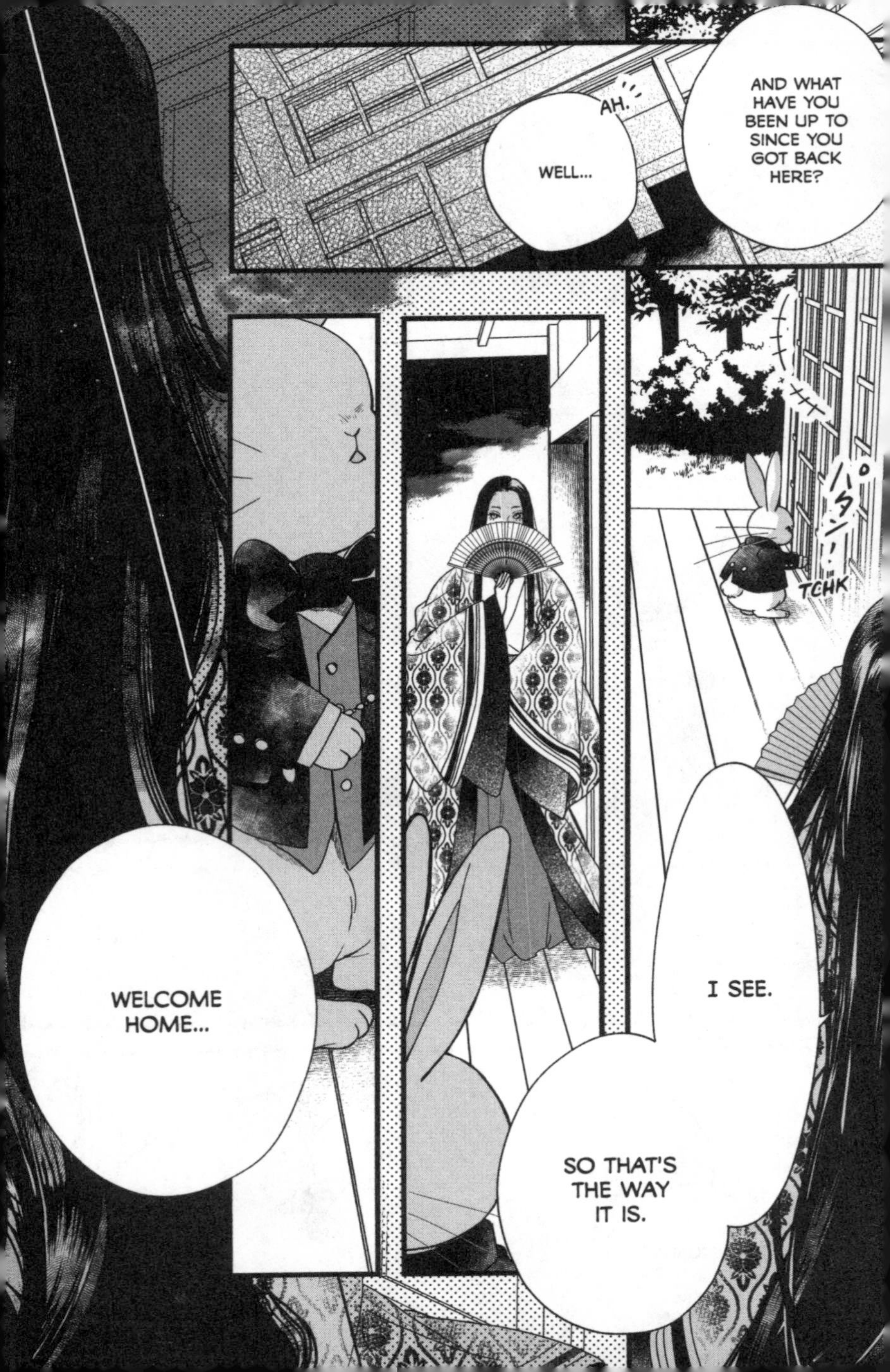
AND WHAT HAVE YOU BEEN UP TO SINCE YOU GOT BACK HERE?
AH.
WELL...
パタン!
TCHK
I SEE.
SO THAT'S THE WAY IT IS.
WELCOME HOME...

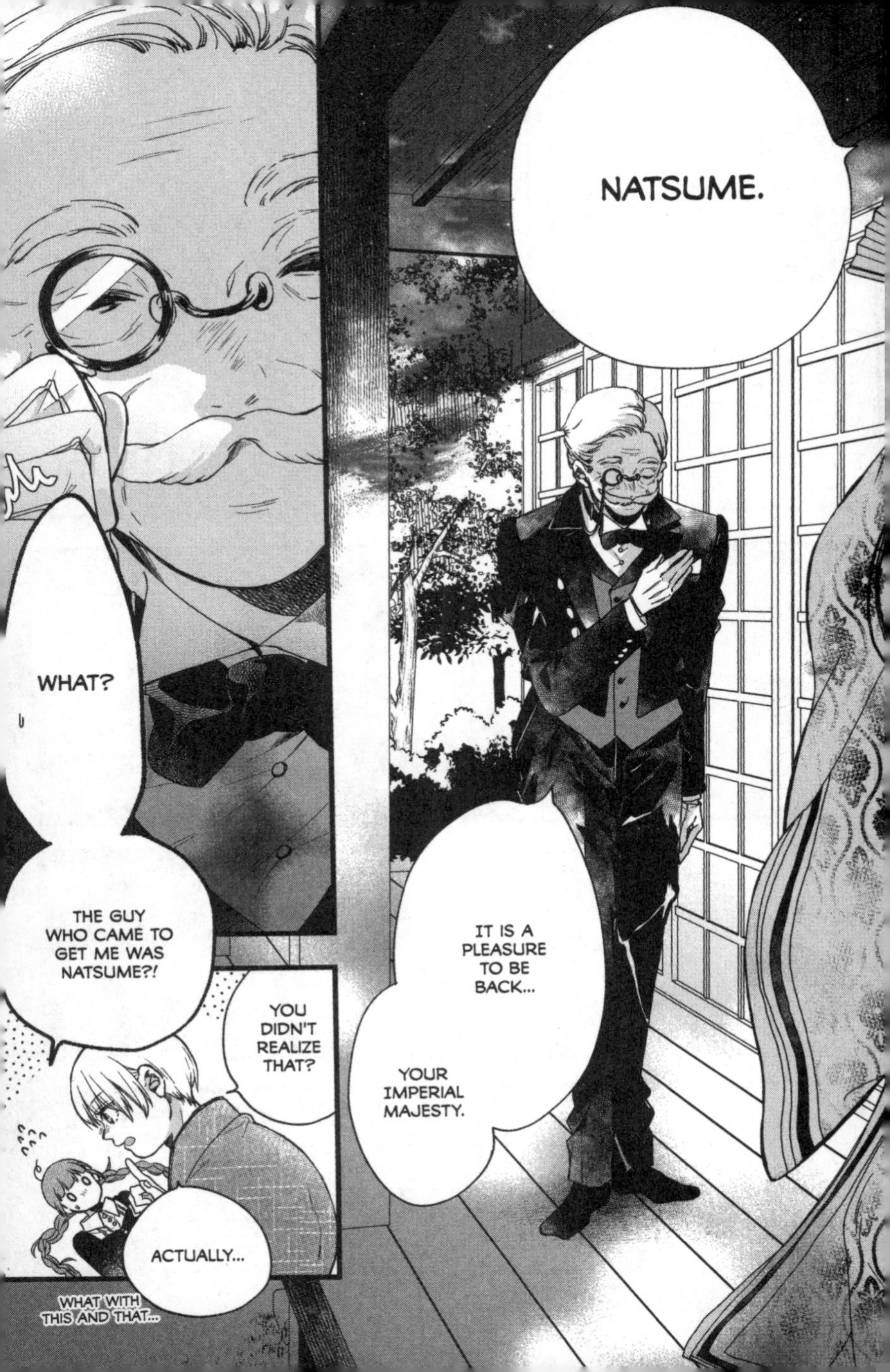
NATSUME.
IT IS A PLEASURE TO BE BACK...
YOUR IMPERIAL MAJESTY.
WHAT?
THE GUY WHO CAME TO GET ME WAS NATSUME?!
YOU DIDN'T REALIZE THAT?
ACTUALLY...
WHAT WITH THIS AND THAT...

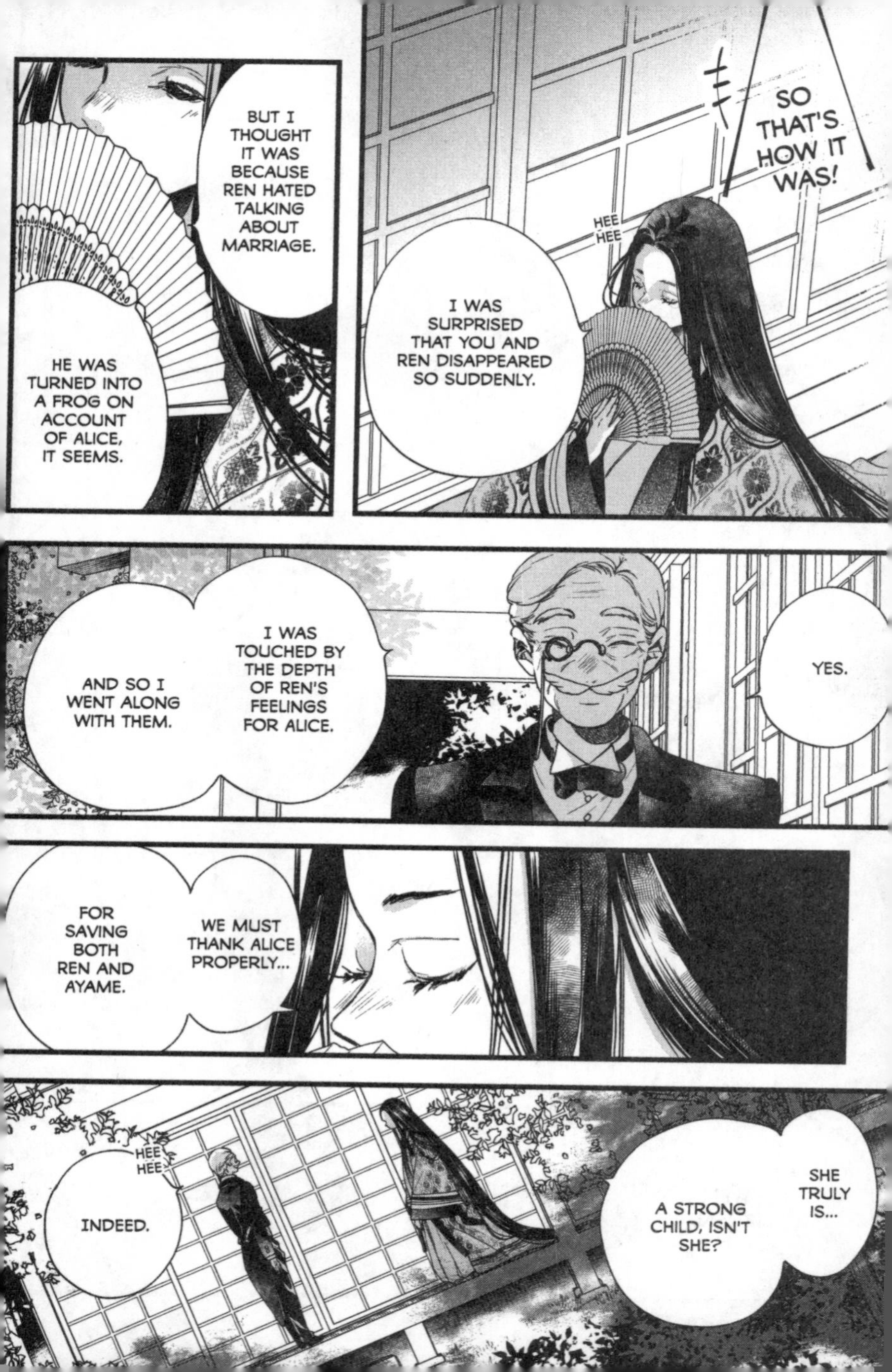

SO THAT'S HOW IT WAS!
HEE HEE
I WAS SURPRISED THAT YOU AND REN DISAPPEARED SO SUDDENLY.
BUT I THOUGHT IT WAS BECAUSE REN HATED TALKING ABOUT MARRIAGE.
HE WAS TURNED INTO A FROG ON ACCOUNT OF ALICE, IT SEEMS.
YES.
I WAS TOUCHED BY THE DEPTH OF REN'S FEELINGS FOR ALICE.
AND SO I WENT ALONG WITH THEM.
WE MUST THANK ALICE PROPERLY...
FOR SAVING BOTH REN AND AYAME.
SHE TRULY IS...
A STRONG CHILD, ISN'T SHE?
HEE HEE
INDEED.

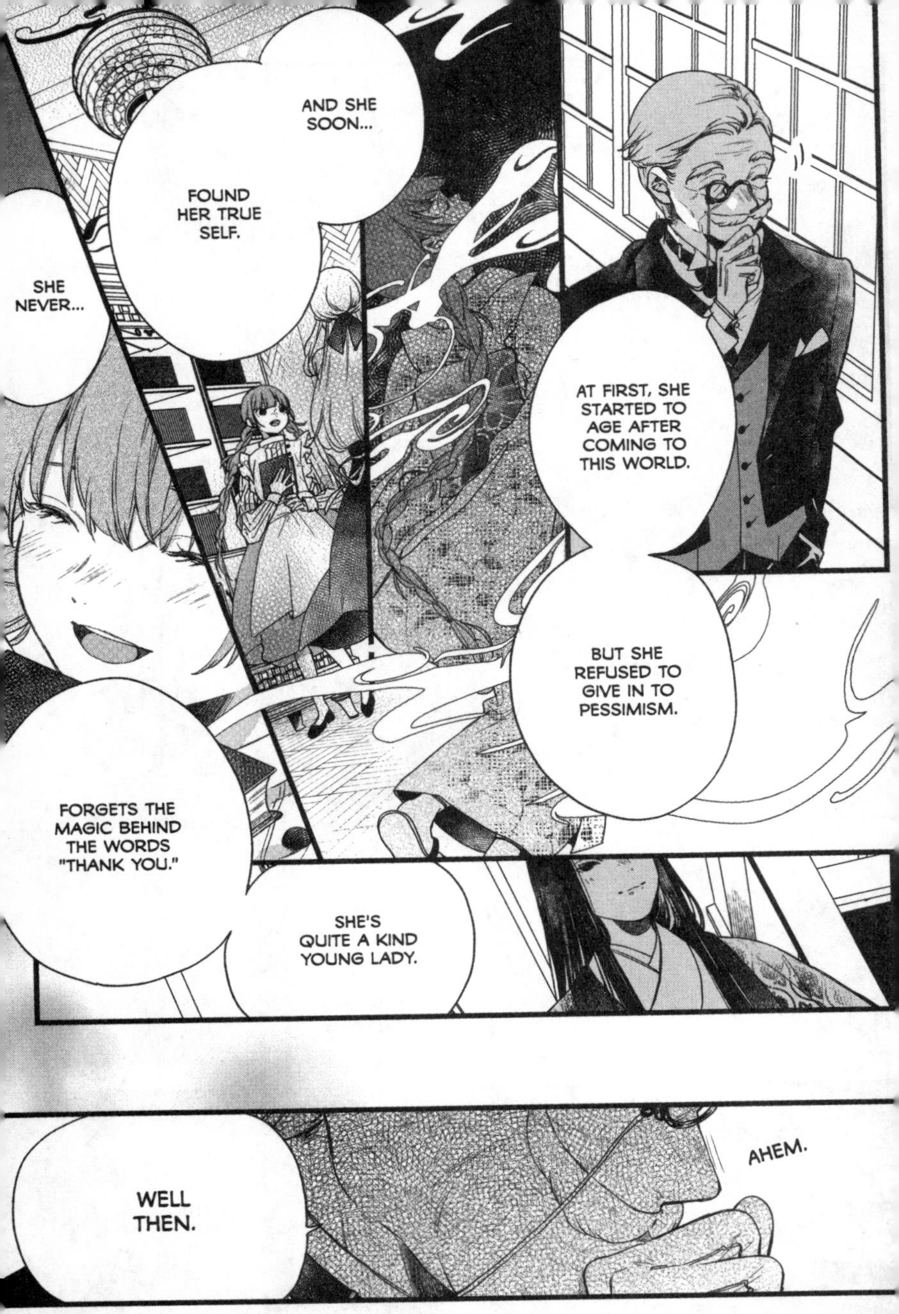
AT FIRST, SHE STARTED TO AGE AFTER COMING TO THIS WORLD.
BUT SHE REFUSED TO GIVE IN TO PESSIMISM.
AND SHE SOON...
FOUND HER TRUE SELF.
SHE NEVER...
FORGETS THE MAGIC BEHIND THE WORDS "THANK YOU."
SHE'S QUITE A KIND YOUNG LADY.
AHEM.
WELL THEN.

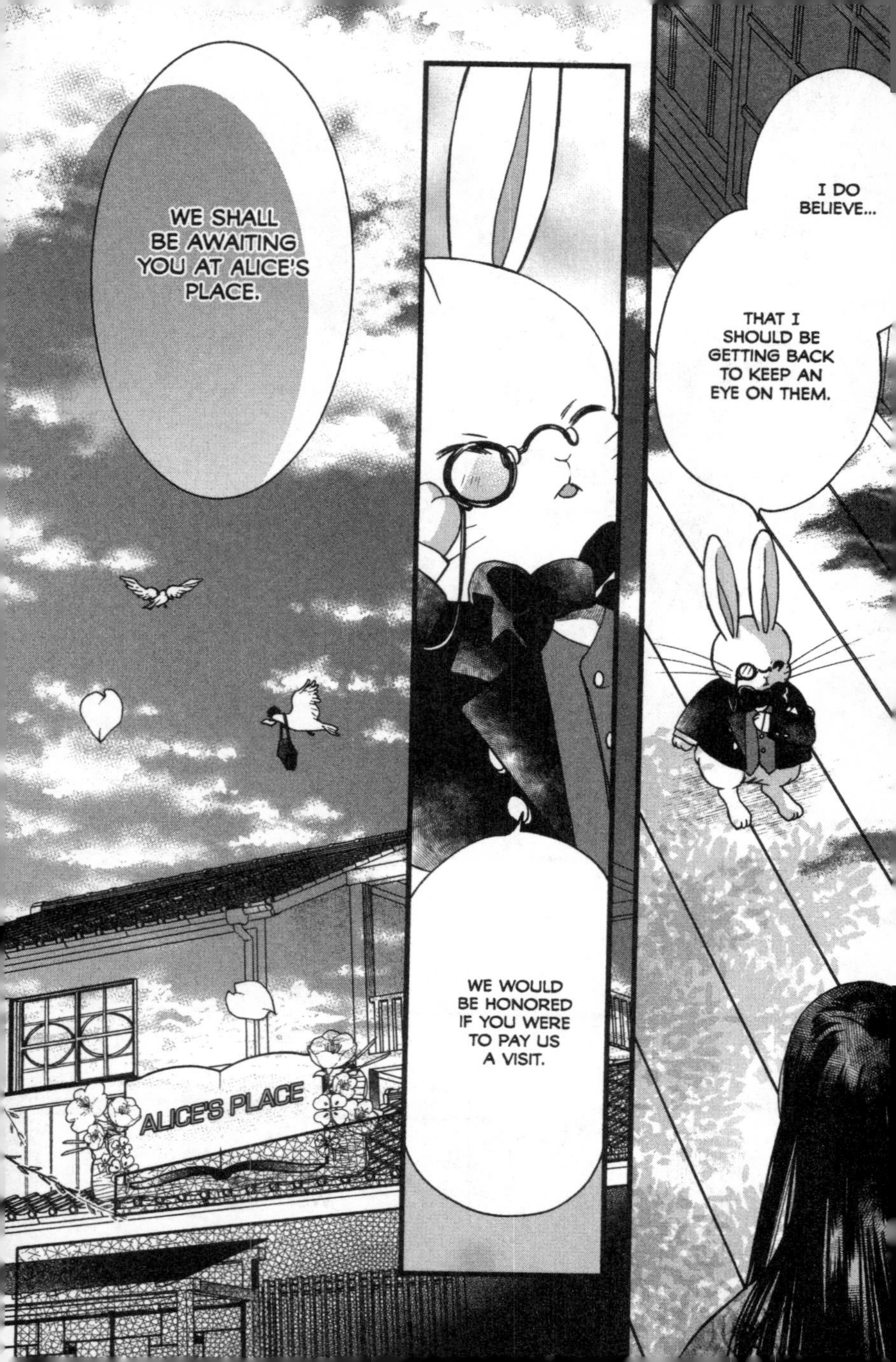
I DO BELIEVE...
THAT I SHOULD BE GETTING BACK TO KEEP AN EYE ON THEM.
WE WOULD BE HONORED IF YOU WERE TO PAY US A VISIT.
WE SHALL BE AWAITING YOU AT ALICE'S PLACE.
ALICE'S PLACE

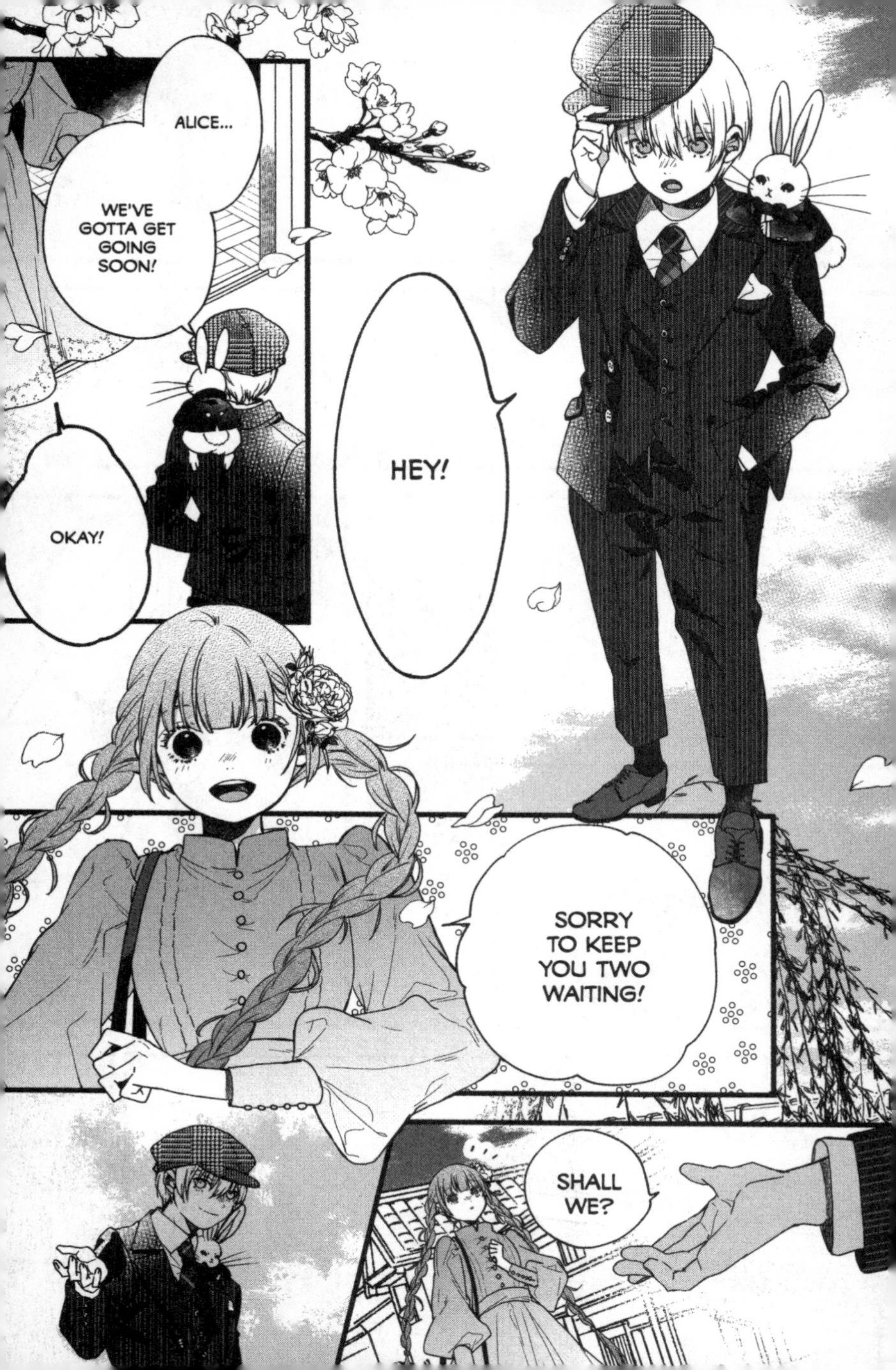
HEY!
ALICE...
WE'VE GOTTA GET GOING SOON!
OKAY!
SORRY TO KEEP YOU TWO WAITING!
SHALL WE?

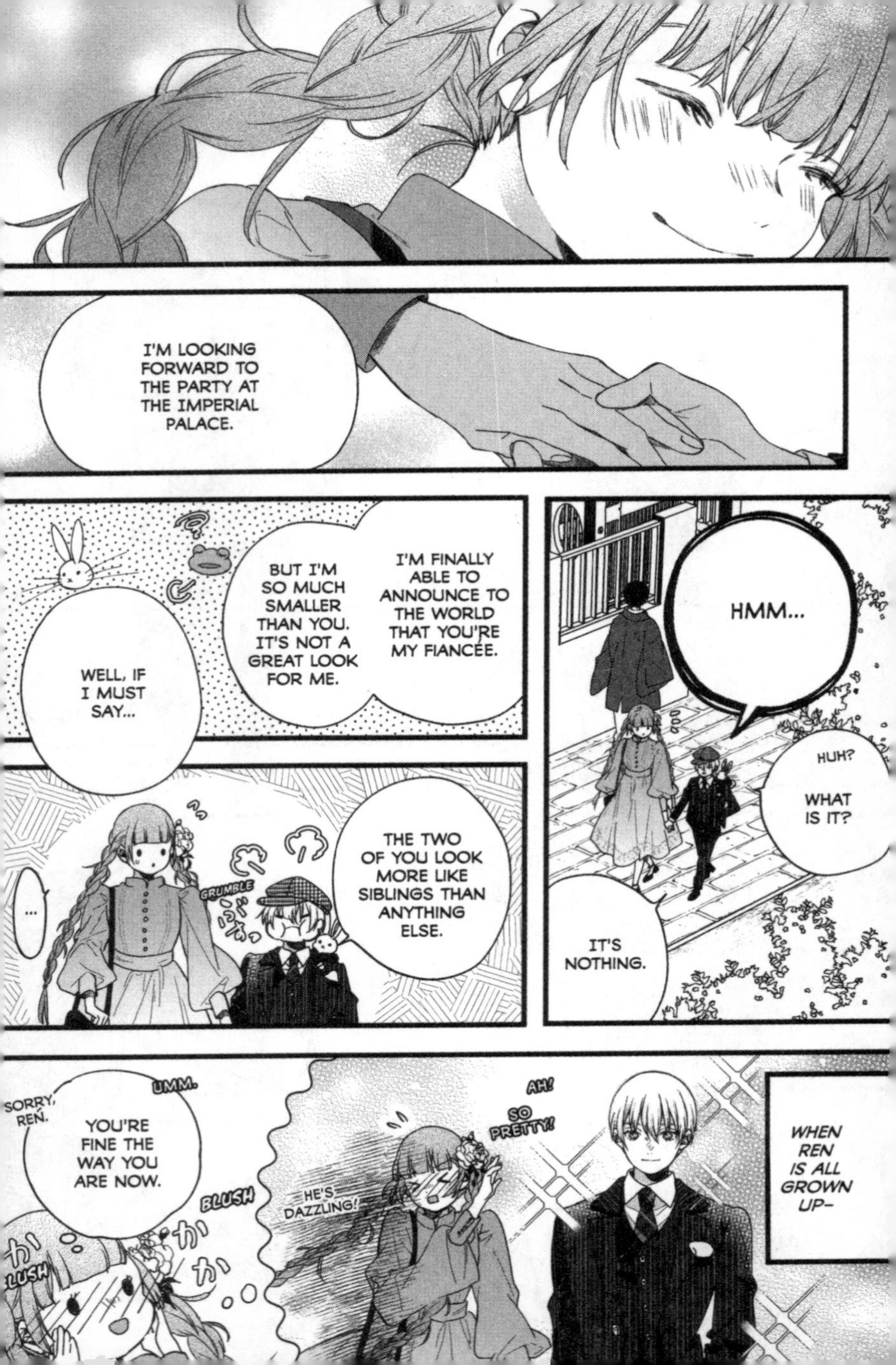
I'M LOOKING FORWARD TO THE PARTY AT THE IMPERIAL PALACE.
HMM...
HUH?
WHAT IS IT?
IT'S NOTHING.
I'M FINALLY ABLE TO ANNOUNCE TO THE WORLD THAT YOU'RE MY FIANCÉE.
BUT I'M SO MUCH SMALLER THAN YOU. IT'S NOT A GREAT LOOK FOR ME.
WELL, IF I MUST SAY...
THE TWO OF YOU LOOK MORE LIKE SIBLINGS THAN ANYTHING ELSE.
GRUMBLE
...
WHEN REN IS ALL GROWN UP–
AH!
SO PRETTY!
HE'S DAZZLING!
UMM.
SORRY, REN.
YOU'RE FINE THE WAY YOU ARE NOW.
BLUSH
BLUSH

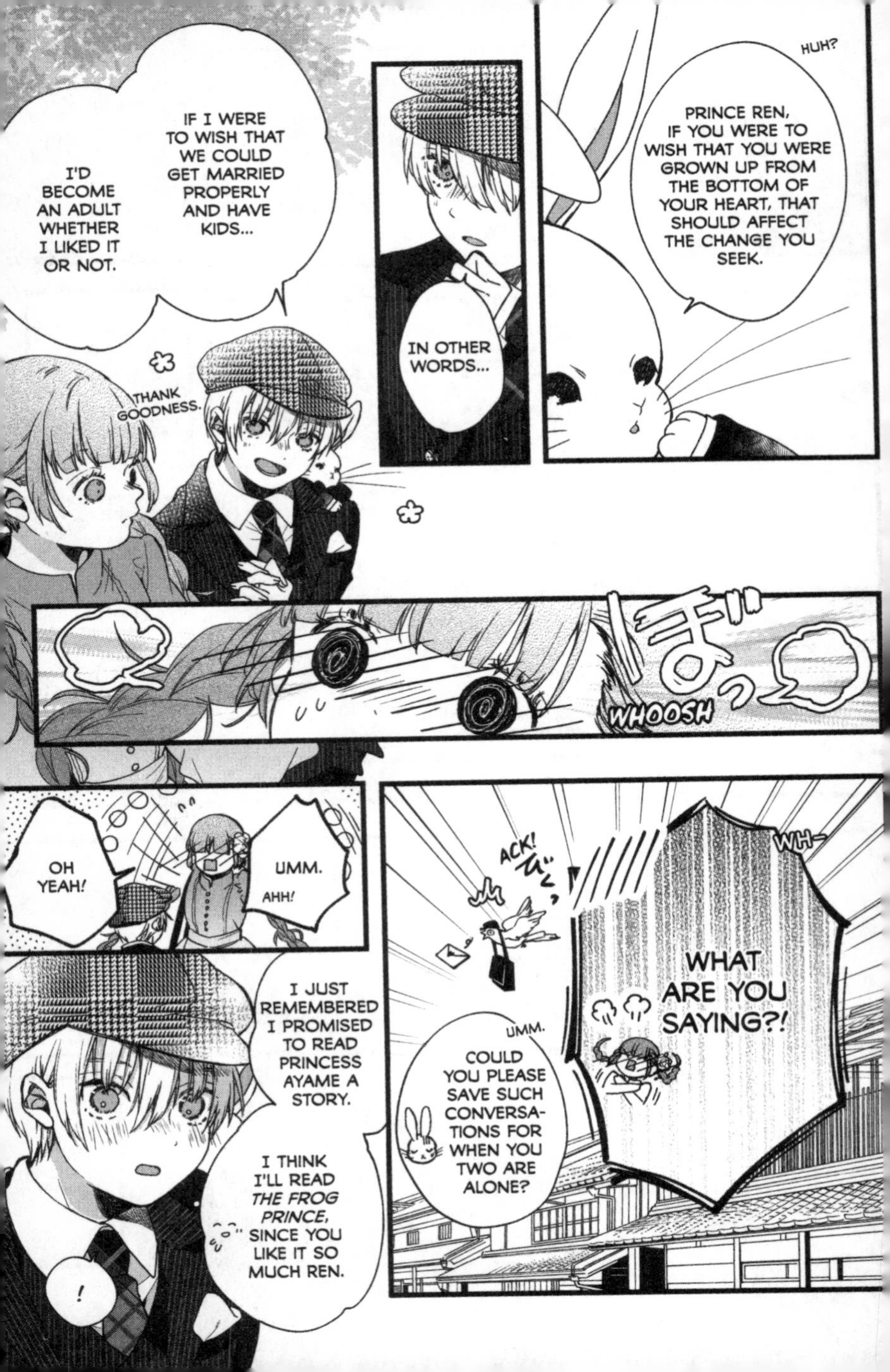
HUH?
PRINCE REN, IF YOU WERE TO WISH THAT YOU WERE GROWN UP FROM THE BOTTOM OF YOUR HEART, THAT SHOULD AFFECT THE CHANGE YOU SEEK.
IN OTHER WORDS...
IF I WERE TO WISH THAT WE COULD GET MARRIED PROPERLY AND HAVE KIDS...
I'D BECOME AN ADULT WHETHER I LIKED IT OR NOT.
THANK GOODNESS.
ぼっ
WHOOSH
WH-
WHAT ARE YOU SAYING?!
ACK!
びくっ
UMM.
COULD YOU PLEASE SAVE SUCH CONVERSA-TIONS FOR WHEN YOU TWO ARE ALONE?
UMM.
AHH!
OH YEAH!
I JUST REMEMBERED I PROMISED TO READ PRINCESS AYAME A STORY.
I THINK I'LL READ *THE FROG PRINCE*, SINCE YOU LIKE IT SO MUCH REN.
!

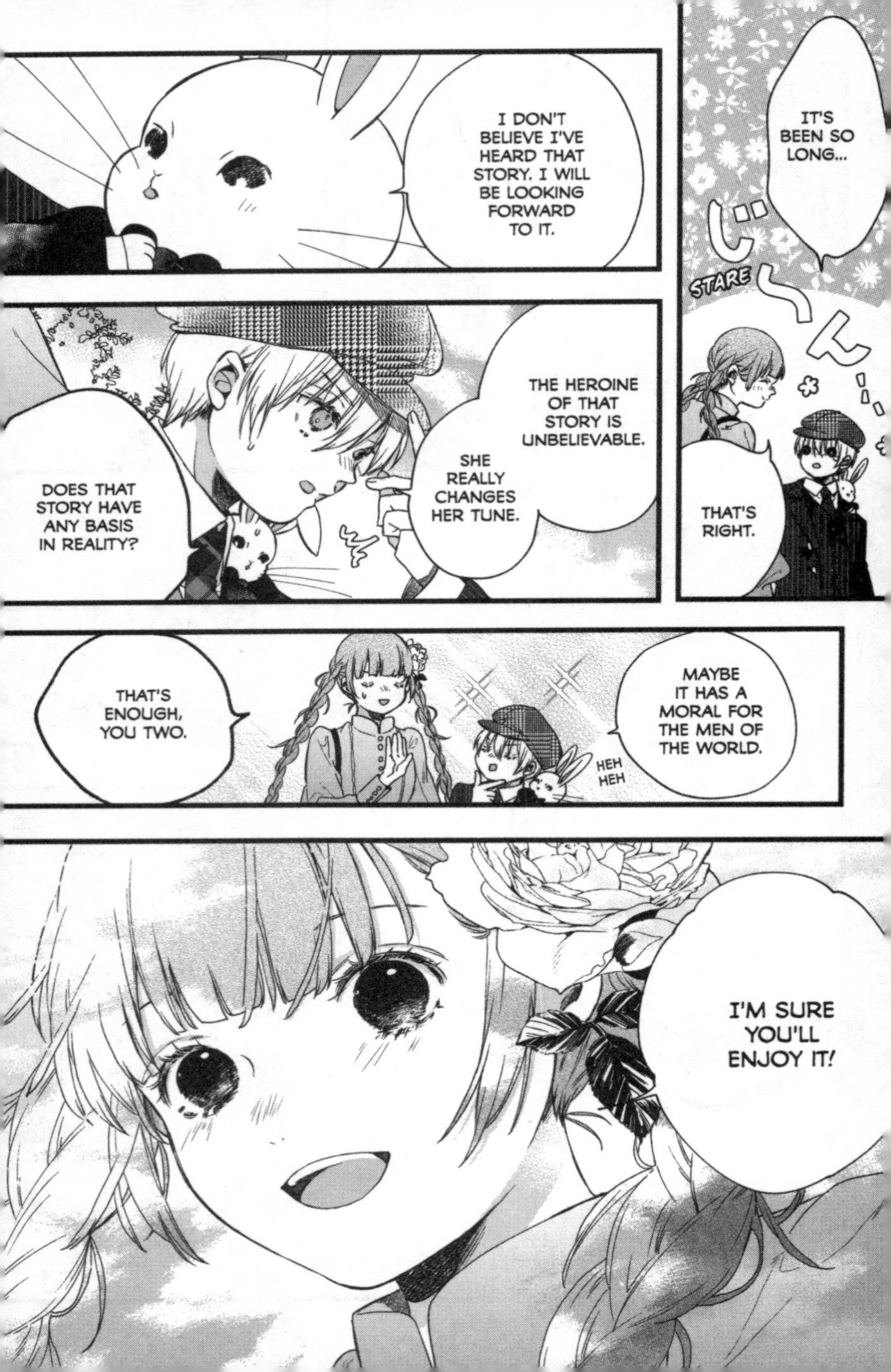
IT'S BEEN SO LONG...
STARE
THAT'S RIGHT.
I DON'T BELIEVE I'VE HEARD THAT STORY. I WILL BE LOOKING FORWARD TO IT.
THE HEROINE OF THAT STORY IS UNBELIEVABLE.
SHE REALLY CHANGES HER TUNE.
DOES THAT STORY HAVE ANY BASIS IN REALITY?
MAYBE IT HAS A MORAL FOR THE MEN OF THE WORLD.
HEH HEH
THAT'S ENOUGH, YOU TWO.
I'M SURE YOU'LL ENJOY IT!

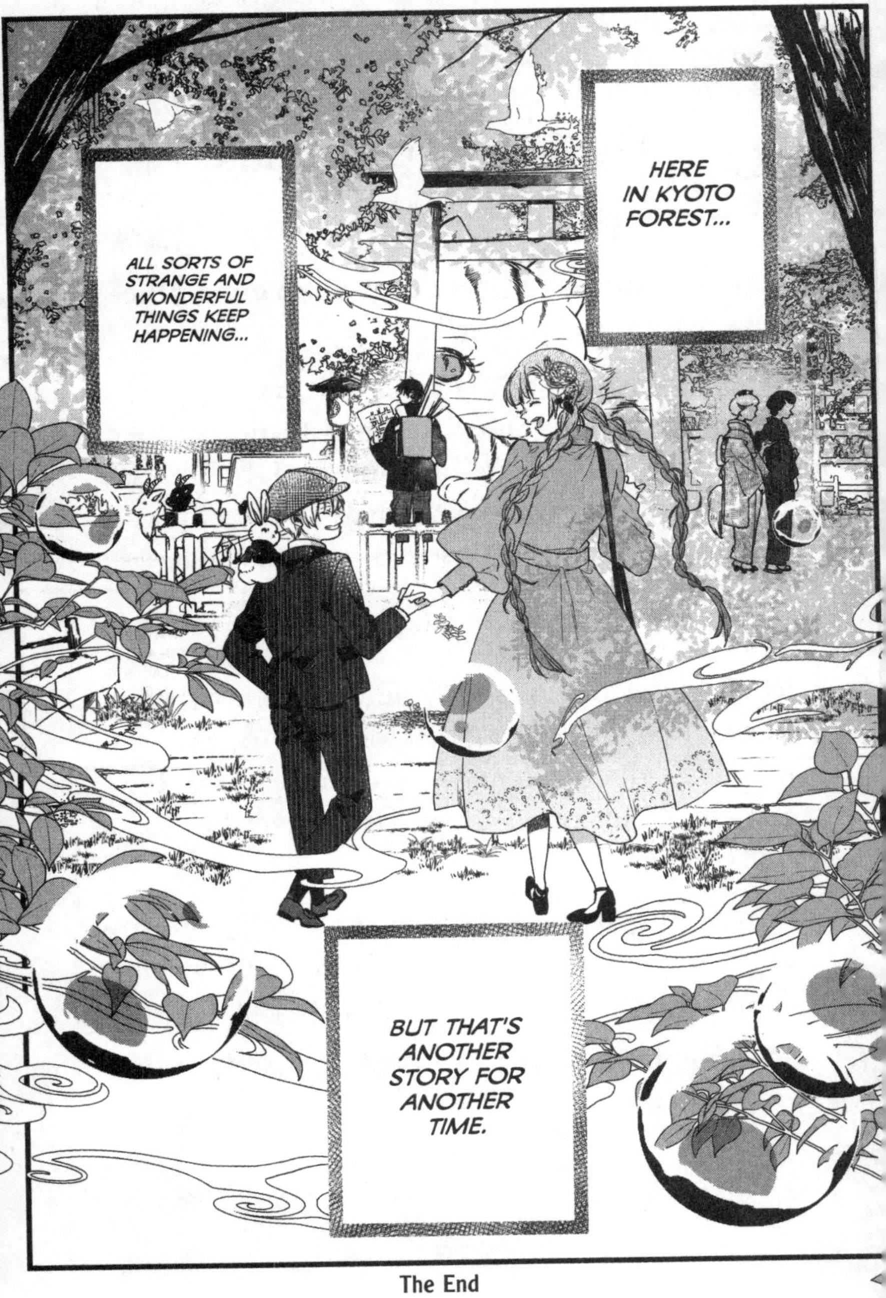
HERE IN KYOTO FOREST...
ALL SORTS OF STRANGE AND WONDERFUL THINGS KEEP HAPPENING...
BUT THAT'S ANOTHER STORY FOR ANOTHER TIME.

The End

Bonus Story!

The Story's Beginning
By Mai Mochizuki

"Wow, what's going on here? So many of these have arrived today, too!"

Ren looked at his desk and let loose an exasperated sigh. Since Ren had turned sixteen, piles of photographs of potential brides had continued to arrive, day after day. So many were the daughters of head priests or headmasters of schools.

"Her Imperial Majesty was thinking that things would calm down a bit once you are married, Prince Ren," laughed Natsume as he poured the tea. The older gentleman served not only as Ren's attendant but as the Imperial Palace's butler as well.

"I wish they'd leave me be. I've already got my heart set on someone," grumbled Ren, ignoring the photographs as he jumped onto the bed.

"No one believes that you will be marrying that girl, I'm afraid."

When Ren was transported to the Realm of Humans, he had met a girl named Alice who taught him about gratitude, which allowed Ren to return to his own world. Ren was adamant about keeping his promise to marry her.

However, no one around him took his declarations seriously. Even if Ren's feelings were true, surely that girl had forgotten him by now. Even Ren was not very hopeful about his prospects. With her living happily with her parents in the Realm of Humans, Ren was anxious about calling her to this world.

"Natsume, is there any way of knowing how Alice is doing from this world?" asked Ren, his face pressed into his pillow.

"Hmm. Birds are able to travel freely between the worlds, so let us send one on such an errand." Natsume stepped out onto the balcony and transformed into a rabbit. Natsume had suffered such a curse when he had brought Ren back to this world. By this time, however, changing his form was merely a pleasant parlor trick for Natsume. Natsume spotted a black kite that he was on friendly terms with and asked it to go look in on Alice.

"I'm sure she's still as cute and kind as ever. I'll bet she's living a happy life," grinned Ren, though his voice was touched with loneliness. Once Ren knew if she had forgotten all about him and was living a happy life, he would be able to set aside his devotion to her.

But the black kite's report was unexpectedly shocking. The visions that the bird had seen were reflected in a crystal, and Ren saw Alice's current situation. Alice had lost both of her parents and had been sent far away to live a rootless existence. He saw visions of her hiding in her closet or staying at the school library for hours because she didn't want to go home. He even saw her shut out of her house and left weeping outside.

Ren bounced to his feet, his voice trembling as he declared, "I have to call Alice here right away!"

"But Prince Ren, if you were to do so, you would lose your human form. If Miss Alice failed to recognize you, you would be unable to return to your current appearance," Natsume said in

reproach, thinking that Ren couldn't really mean what he said.

"I know that. And I don't care! Even if I'm never able to return to my human form again, it will be worth it if I can save Alice!" cried Ren, gripping his other hand into a fist.

"He really is quite single-minded. How admirable," Natsume mused to himself.

"Natsume, this is an order. Bring me to where Alice is!"

"As you wish," Natsume replied, putting his hand to his chest. He could not help but obey an order from one of the Imperial Line.

"I wonder what I'll be turned into," Ren wondered, worry creasing his brow. "Probably something like a wolf. I hope I don't frighten Alice." He could not know that the new form he would take when he went to meet his beloved would be far different from what he imagined.

And that is how the story began...

MAME COORDINATE, VOLUME 1

Sachi Miyabe

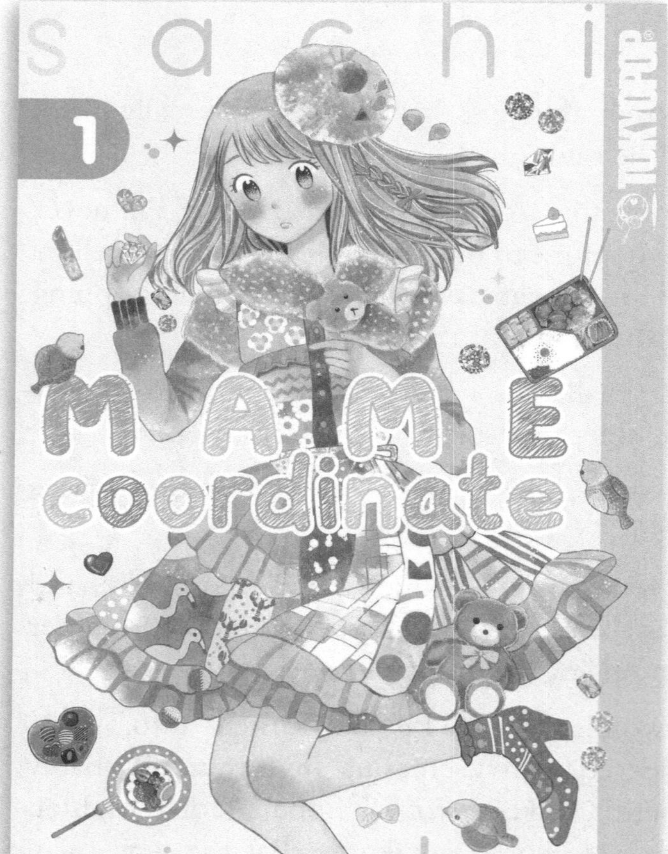
sachi
1
MAME
coordinate
miyabe
TOKYOPOP

FANTASY

She loves meat and fried foods, and eats only karaage bento. Wearing exclusively clothes with weird characters printed on them, her fashion sense is practically non-existent. No confidence in her own looks. Extreme social anxiety. She speaks with a country drawl, and even her name is unusual. But then Mame (born in Tottori prefecture) was discovered by an intimidating, bespectacled rookie manager, and now begins the arduous task of getting her ready for auditions! The road to Top Model looks awfully steep from here.

TOKYOPOP

MAME COORDINATE, VOLUME 2

Sachi Miyabe

SLICE OF LIFE

Audition day finally arrives, but standing next to the famed Noel, Mame's budding confidence nearly collapses!

At first, it seems like her modeling career really might end before it ever got started, but Uri campaigns for one last chance – for both of them. To make things work, they'll need to give it their all and then some, placing their bets for Mame's future on an indie brand and its young designer.

SUZUYUKI

Springtime by the Window

1

Suzuyuki

SPRINGTIME BY THE WINDOW, VOLUME 1

♀LOVE-x-LOVE♂

Cool and collected second-year Yamada is in love with his childhood friend, Seno. His classmates Akama and Toda are also starting to think about romance, though neither of them realizes yet that they might actually feel the same way about each other...High school love in the spring of adolescence blooms with earnest, messy emotions.

SPRINGTIME BY THE WINDOW, VOLUME 2

Suzuyuki

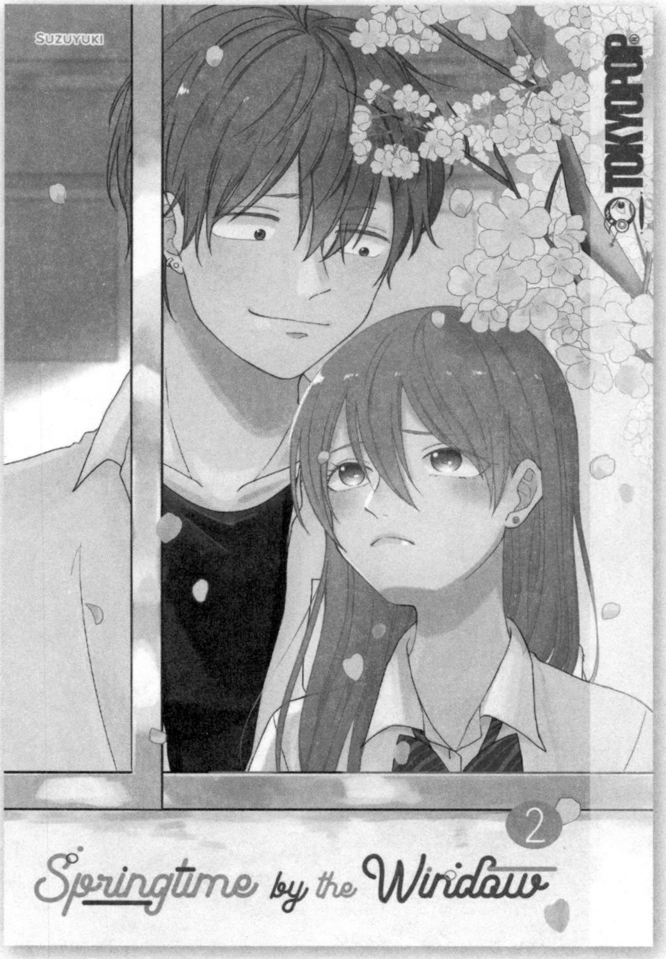

SUZUYUKI
TOKYOPOP
2
Springtime by the Window

LOVE-x-LOVE

TOKYOPOP

Yuki Yamada invites Kaede Seno to the summer festival, hoping that his feelings will finally reach his long-time crush. His friend, Akari Akane, also gathers the courage to ask Yousuke Toda to go with her, but receives a surprising response... What unexpected mishaps and sweet moments will summer bring to their adolescent hearts?

BIBI & MIYU, VOLUME 2

Hirara Natsume & Olivia Vieweg

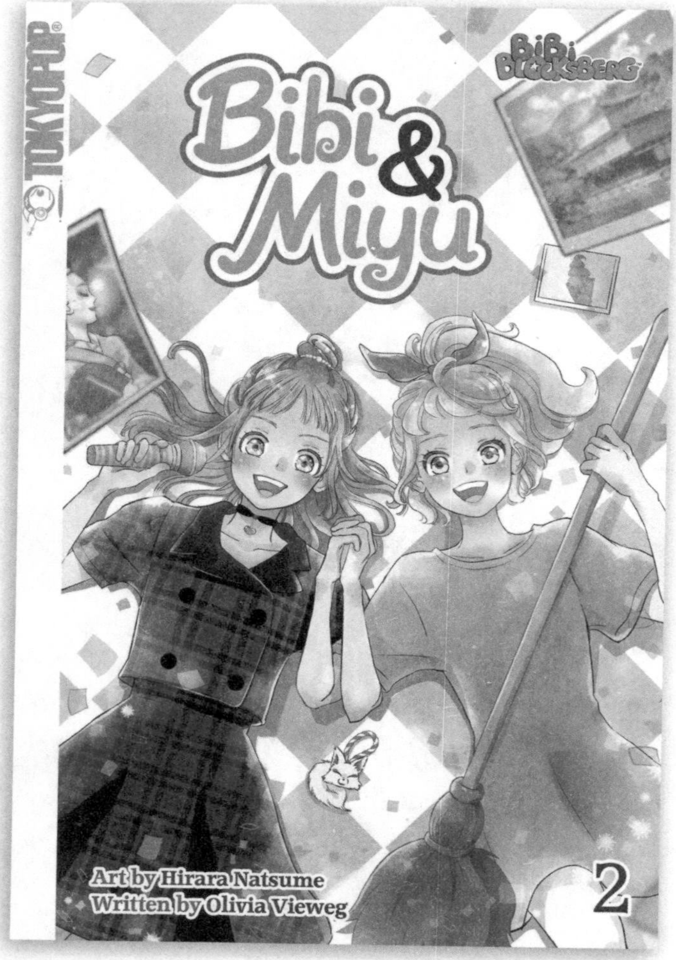
TOKYOPOP
Bibi Blocksberg
Bibi & Miyu
Art by Hirara Natsume
Written by Olivia Vieweg
2

FANTASY

Young witch Bibi Blocksberg was ecstatic when her new friend Miyu invited her to stay with her family in Japan for a cultural exchange trip. Unfortunately, ghost hunting keeps them too busy for any sight seeing, but a much-needed break for some karaoke fun leads Bibi to realize that Miyu is an amazing singer. With a big contest about to be held in Kyoto, the two magical girls must figure out how to keep the city safe from otherworldly spirits while preparing for the show.

THE FOX & LITTLE TANUKI, VOLUME 2

Mi Tagawa

FANTASY

Legends say that Senzou the Black Fox is one of the most vicious and powerful supernatural beasts to ever roam the land. At least, he used to be. Now, 300 years after he was imprisoned by the Sun Goddess for his bad behavior, Senzou is back — in the form of a small black fox with no powers! Tasked with protecting a young tanuki called Manpachi as he fulfills various tasks for the gods, Senzou must earn his powers back by learning how to be a good guardian to the energetic little pup. Though Senzou is a grumpy and reluctant companion at first, even a hard-hearted fox can be tamed by cuteness... and the little tanuki quickly learns there are some family ties that aren't decided by blood.

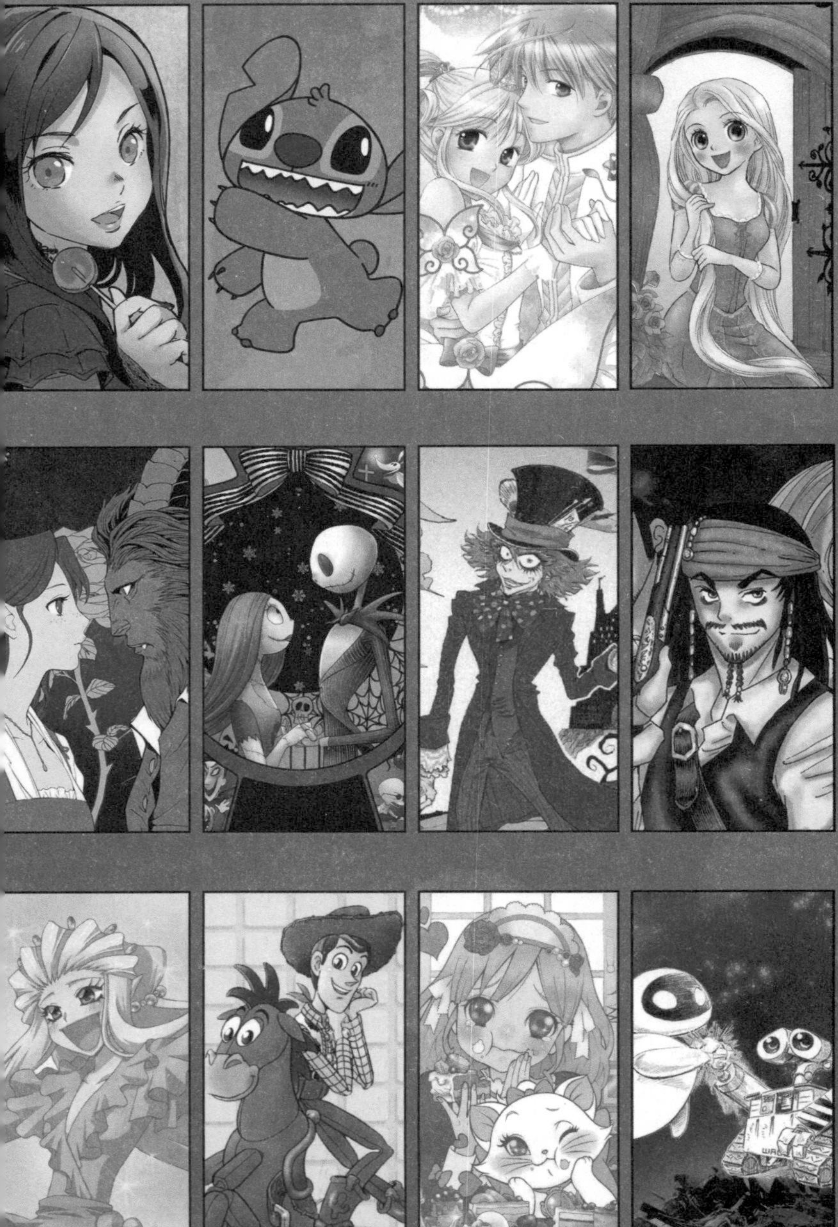

Check out a few sneak previews of these Disney Manga titles!

Disney MANGA 漫画

SHOJO

- ☐ DISNEY BEAUTY AND THE BEAST
- ☐ DISNEY KILALA PRINCESS SERIES

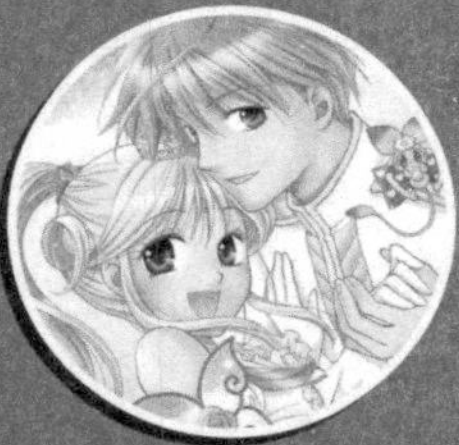

FANTASY

- ☐ DISNEY DESCENDANTS SERIES
- ☐ DISNEY TANGLED
- ☐ DISNEY PRINCESS AND THE FROG
- ☐ DISNEY FAIRIES SERIES
- ☐ DISNEY MARIE: MIRIYA AND MARIE

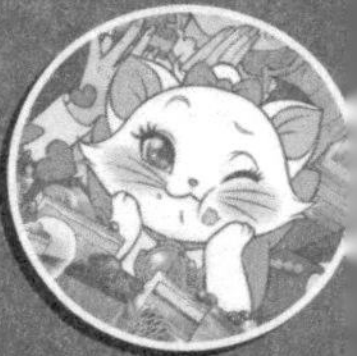

KAWAII

- ☐ DISNEY MAGICAL DANCE
- ☐ DISNEY STITCH! SERIES

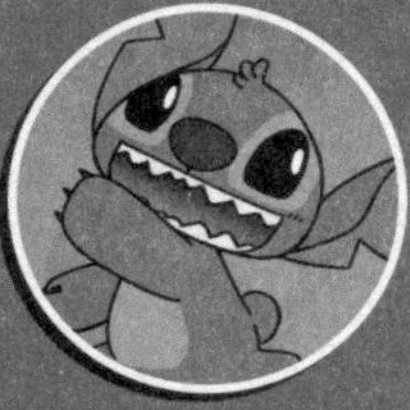

PIXAR

- ☐ DISNEY • PIXAR TOY STORY
- ☐ DISNEY • PIXAR MONSTERS, INC.
- ☐ DISNEY • PIXAR WALL • E
- ☐ DISNEY • PIXAR FINDING NEMO

ADVENTURE

- ☐ DISNEY TIM BURTON'S THE NIGHTMARE BEFORE CHRISTMAS
- ☐ DISNEY ALICE IN WONDERLAND
- ☐ DISNEY PIRATES OF THE CARIBBEAN SERIES

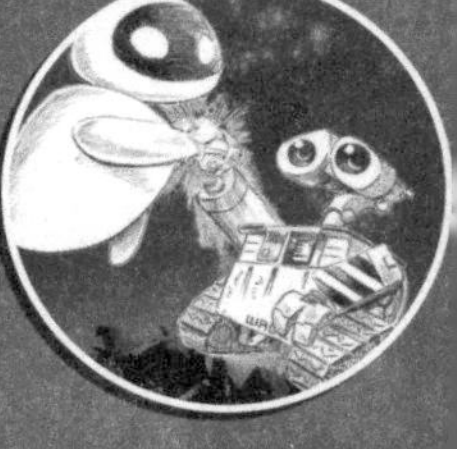

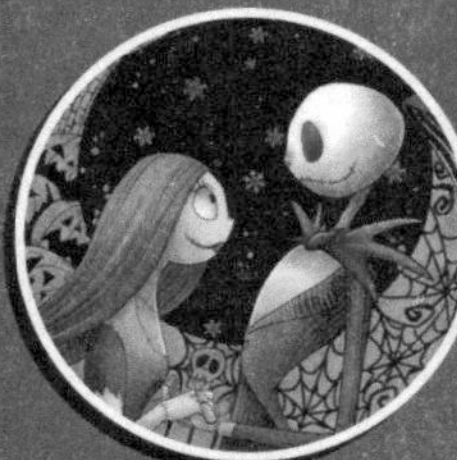

TOKYO POP

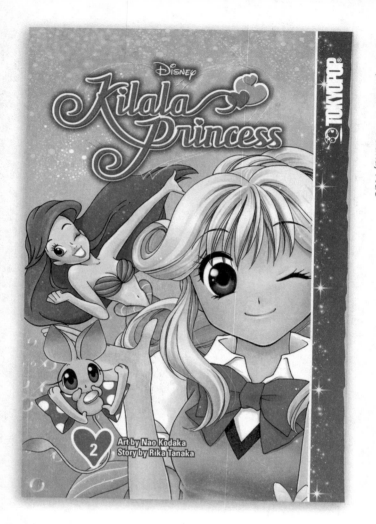

DISNEY MANGA: KILALA PRINCESS VOLUME 2

Tanaka, Rika & Kodaka, Nao

DISNEY MANGA

When a giant wave washes Kilala and Rei into the sea, they discover the magical world of *The Little Mermaid* under the sea. Kilala wishes she could enjoy singing and swimming with Ariel and the other mermaids, but she's worried—the sea is a vast place and Rei has suddenly disappeared. Join Kilala as she meets Ariel and her fishy friends!

DISNEY MANGA: STITCH AND THE SAMURAI, VOLUME 1
Hiroto Wada

DISNEY MANGA

While fleeing the Galactic Federation, Stitch's spaceship malfunctions and he makes an emergency landing... not in Hawaii, but in sengoku-era Japan! Discovered by the brutal warlord Lord Yamato and his clan, Stitch's incomparable cuteness is no match for the battle-weary samurai, who decides to bring the "blue tanuki" home with him. Will Stitch's love of chaos turn into a formidable advantage for the samurai's influence? Or will his cute and fluffy form disarm the noble lord's stern façade?

© Disney

Alice in Kyoto Forest, Volume 2
Art by Haruki Niwa
Story by Mai Mochiduki
"Alice in Kyoraku Forest" (BUNGEISHUNJU)

Editor - Lena Atanassova
Translator - David Bove
Copy Editor - Becca Grace
Logo & Cover Designer - Sol DeLeo
Editorial Associate - Janae Young
Marketing Associate - Kae Winters
Digital Marketing Assistant - Kitt Burgess
Retouching and Lettering - Vibrraant Publishing Studio
Licensing Specialist - Arika Yanaka
Editor-in-Chief & Publisher - Stu Levy

A TOKYOPOP® Manga

TOKYOPOP Inc.
4136 Del Rey Ave., Suite 502
Marina del Rey, CA 90292-5604

E-mail: info@TOKYOPOP.com
Come visit us online at www.TOKYOPOP.com

www.facebook.com/TOKYOPOP
www.twitter.com/TOKYOPOP
www.instagram.com/TOKYOPOP

First published in Japan in 2020 by MAG Garden Corporation.
English translation rights arranged with MAG Garden Corporation through Tuttle-Mori Agency, Inc, Tokyo.

ISBN: 978-1-4278-7122-0

First TOKYOPOP Printing: May 2022

Printed in CANADA

STOP

THIS IS THE BACK OF THE BOOK!

How do you read manga-style? It's simple! Let's practice -- just start in the top right panel and follow the numbers below!

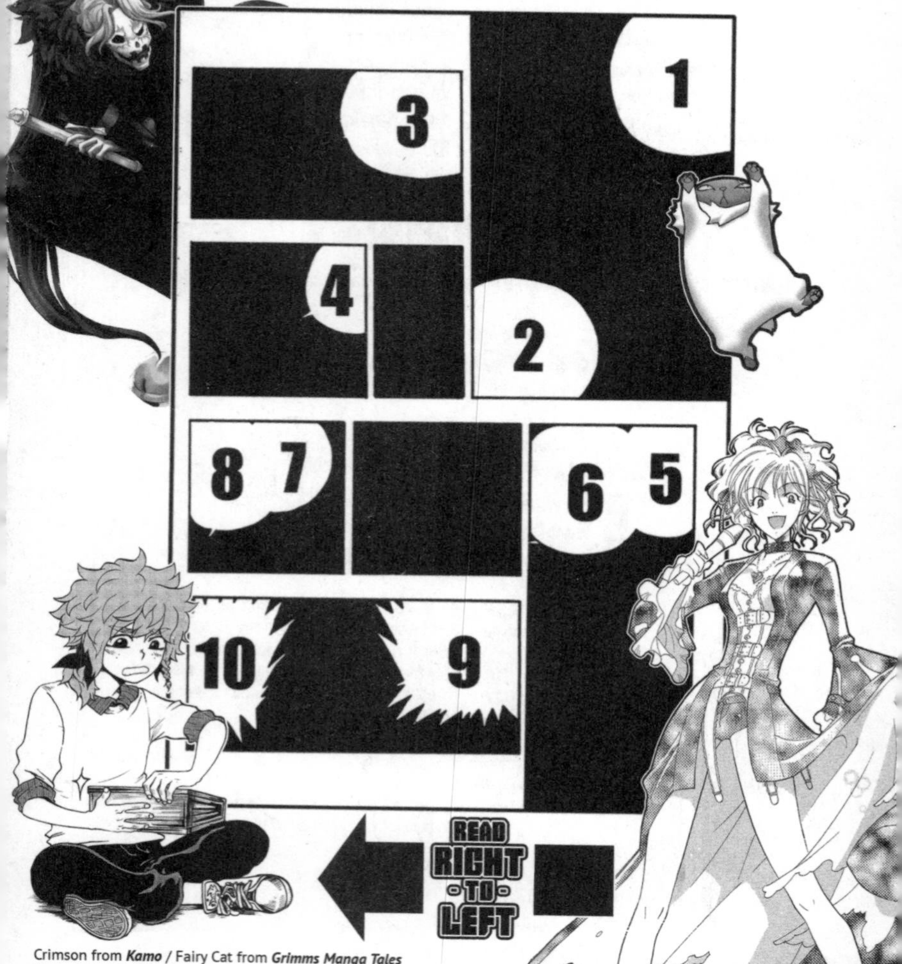

1
2
3
4
5
6
7
8
9
10
READ
RIGHT
-TO-
LEFT

Crimson from ***Kamo*** / Fairy Cat from ***Grimms Manga Tales***
Morrey from ***Goldfisch*** / Princess Ai from ***Princess Ai***